THE JEWS OF LITHUANIA

THE JEWS OF LITHUANIA

A Journey Through the Long Twentieth Century

NICK SAYERS

VALLENTINE MITCHELL
LONDON • CHICAGO

First published in 2024 by Vallentine Mitchell

Catalyst House,
720 Centennial Court,
Centennial Park, Elstree WD6 3SY, UK

814 N. Franklin Street,
Chicago, Illinois,
IL 60610 USA

www.vmbooks.com

Copyright © 2024 Nicholas Sayers

British Library Cataloguing in Publication Data:
An entry can be found on request

ISBN 978 1 80371 065 5 (Paper)
ISBN 978 1 80371 066 2 (Ebook)
ISBN 978 1 80371 067 9 (Kindle)

Library of Congress Cataloging in Publication Data:
An entry can be found on request

All rights reserved. No part of this publication may be reproduced in any form or by any means, electronic, mechanical, photocopying, reading or otherwise, without the prior permission of Vallentine Mitchell & Co. Ltd.

Contents

Acknowledgements vii
Glossary viii
Note on Place Names xi
Maps xiii

Introduction 1
1. Background 4
2. Jewish Life in Late Nineteenth Century Lithuania 18
3. Emigration 47
4. Lithuania 1896-1921 91
5. Inter-War Lithuania 124
6. To the Edge of the Abyss 137
7. An Outline of the Holocaust in Lithuania 148
8. A Survivor's Experience of the Holocaust in Lithuania 178
9. Trying to Explain the Holocaust in Lithuania 195
10. The End of the War 255
11. Post war 271

Conclusion 286

Bibliography 290
Index 299

Acknowledgements

I am immensely grateful to Shirli Gilbert for encouraging me to write this book, and for her support during the process. Tony Kushner offered invaluable insights and suggestions for further reading. My old university friend Sidney Myers read the text with great care and thoroughness, helping correct typographical and grammatical mistakes and suggesting removal of linguistic infelicities. Tim Aspden has made some very clear and useful maps. Beverley Winkler has compiled a user-friendly and comprehensive index. Yulik Gurvich of Jerulita guided me around sites of Jewish interest in Lithuania. The team at Vallentine Mitchell has been wonderfully supportive and I am particularly grateful to Toby Harris, Sue Garfield and Jenni Tinson. Many friends have read the text in various stages of its preparation and offered encouragement and helpful comment. I am hugely grateful to all of them. It goes without saying that I alone am responsible for any errors of fact or judgement that remain in the text.

I could not have written this book without the enduring patience, kindness and love of my wife Yvonne. This book is dedicated to her and to our four wonderful daughters.

Glossary

Agunah A woman whose husband has deserted her or has disappeared and who may not remarry until she gives proof of his death or obtains a bill of divorce.

Amidah A benediction recited while standing during the main section of the daily Jewish liturgy and at the additional service on Sabbaths and holy days.

Chazan A synagogue official who sings or chants liturgical music and leads the congregation in prayer.

Eretz Yisrael The Land of Israel.

Get A religious divorce by Jewish law.

Gymnazya A secondary school that prepares students for university.

Haganah The main Zionist paramilitary organisation that operated for the Yishuv in the British Mandate for Palestine. It was founded in 1920 and was disbanded in 1948.

Halacha The body of Jewish law supplementing the scriptural law and forming especially the legal part of the Talmud.

Hanukkah An 8-day Jewish holiday beginning on the 25th of the Jewish month of Kislev and commemorating the rededication of the Temple of Jerusalem after its defilement by Antiochus of Syria.

Haredi Ultra-Orthodox Jews who strictly observe Jewish religious law and separate themselves from Gentile society as well as from Jews who do not follow religious law as strictly as they do. Literally, Haredim are "those who tremble" in the presence of God (because they are God-fearing).

Haskalah An intellectual movement among Jews of eastern Europe in the 18th and 19th centuries that attempted to acquaint the Jewish masses with European and Hebrew languages and with secular education and culture to supplement Talmudic studies.

Heder An elementary Jewish school in which children are taught to read the Torah and other books in Hebrew.

Herem One of three forms of ecclesiastical excommunication pronounced by a rabbi or by the officials of a synagogue or community.

Kahal The local governing body of a former European Jewish community administering religious, legal, and communal affairs.

Kest The tradition of supplying a son-in-law with board and lodging.

Khaper Russian Jews employed by Kahals to kidnap Jewish boys so as to fulfill military service recruitment quotas imposed on Jewish communities in the Russian empire between 1827 and 1857.

Kiddush haShem A religious or moral act that causes others to reverence God.

Kiddush haChaim The religious or moral imperative to remain alive at a time when the Nazis and their collaborators sought the total destruction of the Jewish people.

Landsman A person who originates from the same region, town or shtetl as someone else, especially if one or both of them no longer live there.

Litvak A Lithuanian Jew.

Maskil A person versed in Hebrew or Yiddish literature; a follower or adherent of the Haskalah movement.

Matzo Unleavened bread eaten especially at Passover.

Mikveh A ritual bath or bathing place for purification in accordance with Jewish law.

Minyan The quorum required for Jewish communal worship, being, in the case of Orthodox Judaism, ten male adults.

Mitzvah A meritorious or charitable act.

Ninth of Av A day of mourning and fasting. The holiday commemorates various tragedies that have befallen the Jewish people, particularly the destruction of the temples in 586 BCE and in 70 CE.

Ostjuden Eastern European Jews; the term often has pejorative connotations.

Pale of Settlement This was a western region of the Russian empire, with borders which changed over time. It existed from 1791 to 1917. Permanent residency by Jews was permitted in this area but, beyond it, Jewish residency was mostly forbidden. It included all of modern Belarus and Moldova, much of Lithuania, Ukraine and east-central Poland and relatively small parts of Latvia and what is now the western Russian Federation. See map on Page XIV.

Palmach The Palmach was the elite fighting force of the Haganah, the underground army of the Yishuv during the period of the British Mandate for Palestine.

Passover A Jewish holiday beginning on the 14th day of the Jewish month of Nisan and commemorating the Hebrews' liberation from slavery in Egypt.

Purim A Jewish holiday celebrated on the 14th day of the Jewish month of Adar in commemoration of the deliverance of the Jews from the massacre plotted by Haman.

Sephardi Descendants of Jews who lived in Spain and Portugal until their persecution and mass expulsion in the last decades of the fifteenth century. The transplanted Sephardi Jews largely retained their native Judeo-Spanish language (Ladino), literature and customs.

Shammes The sexton of a synagogue.

Shavuot A holiday celebrated on the sixth day of the Jewish month of Sivan in commemoration of the revelation of the Ten Commandments at Mt. Sinai.

Shohet A person officially licensed by rabbinic authority as slaughterer of animals and poultry for use as food in accordance with Jewish laws.

Shtadlan A person appointed by a Jewish community to represent Jewish interests before a government or ruler.

Shtetl A small Jewish town or village found in Eastern Europe.

Sukkot A Jewish harvest festival beginning on the 15th of the Jewish month of Tishri and commemorating the temporary shelters used by Jews during the wandering in the wilderness.

Torah The five books of Moses constituting the Pentateuch.

Talmud The Talmud is the textual record of generations of rabbinic debate about law, philosophy and biblical interpretation, compiled between the 3rd and 8th centuries and structured as commentary on the Mishnah (a written collection of Jewish oral traditions) with interwoven stories.

Trefah A food, food product or utensil that is not ritually clean or prepared according to Jewish law and is thus prohibited as unfit for Jewish use.

Yeshiva An orthodox Jewish rabbinical seminary.

Yiddish A High German language written in Hebrew characters that is spoken by Jews and descendants of Jews of central and eastern European origin.

Yishuv The Jewish residents of Palestine before the establishment of the State of Israel in 1948.

YIVO Founded in Vilnius in 1925, but now based in New York, YIVO is a leading institution for scholarship in relation to Yiddish and the history and culture of East European Jews.

Yizkor In Hebrew Yizkor means 'remember'. It is an Askenazi Jewish memorial prayer service for the dead.

Note on Place Names

A particular difficulty in writing the history of Lithuania, as in writing the history of other parts of central and eastern Europe, is that many places have been known by different names at different times. Sometimes different communities have used different names to describe the same place at the same time. Moreover: political connotations can attach to the choice of name. An obvious example is the capital of modern Lithuania. It has been variously known as Wilno, Vilna and Vilnius. Wilno was the Polish name and until 1944 the majority of its population was Polish; Vilna was the Yiddish name and the name by which most Jewish people knew the city; Vilnius is the modern name of Lithuania's present-day capital. To use the name Vilnius when describing the City before 1944 is arguably anachronistic and might be said to carry political connotations.

What to do? There are no easy answers, but I have tried to adopt the following guidelines:

Where a place has a widely accepted English name I use that name. Examples include Warsaw, Kiev, Moscow, St Petersburg and Munich. Where a place has been known by different names at different times I use the name by which it is known by the current sovereign political power. Therefore, I refer to Wilno/Vilna/Vilnius as Vilnius. This is a blunt instrument but at least has the merit of simplicity and consistency.

The term 'Lithuania' requires special treatment. Jews have often used the term 'Lithuania' to refer to territory that is significantly larger than the borders of the independent Lithuanian republic of the interwar period (which did not include Vilnius), and significantly larger than the present Republic of Lithuania. This larger area was known in Yiddish as 'Lite' and, as well as today's Lithuania, comprised much of what is now northeastern Poland, northern and western Belarus, southern Latvia and northeastern Prussia. The map on page xv shows the boundaries of 'Lite'. This expansive definition of Lithuania corresponds roughly to the large territory under the jurisdiction of the Lithuanian Jewish Council which governed Jewish communal affairs from 1623–1764. Jews who came from this area were known as 'Litvaks'. I have had to use the term 'Lithuania' to describe different geographical areas, depending on the context. This is not ideal, but reference to the maps on pages xiii to xx should help to avoid confusion.

A map of the Baltic showing present day borders

A map of The Pale of Settlement. This was the part of the Russian empire that existed from 1791 until 1917 in which permanent residency by Jews was allowed and beyond which Jewish residency was mostly forbidden

A map showing the area known in Yiddish as 'Lite': the cultural and dialect borders of Jewish Lithuania

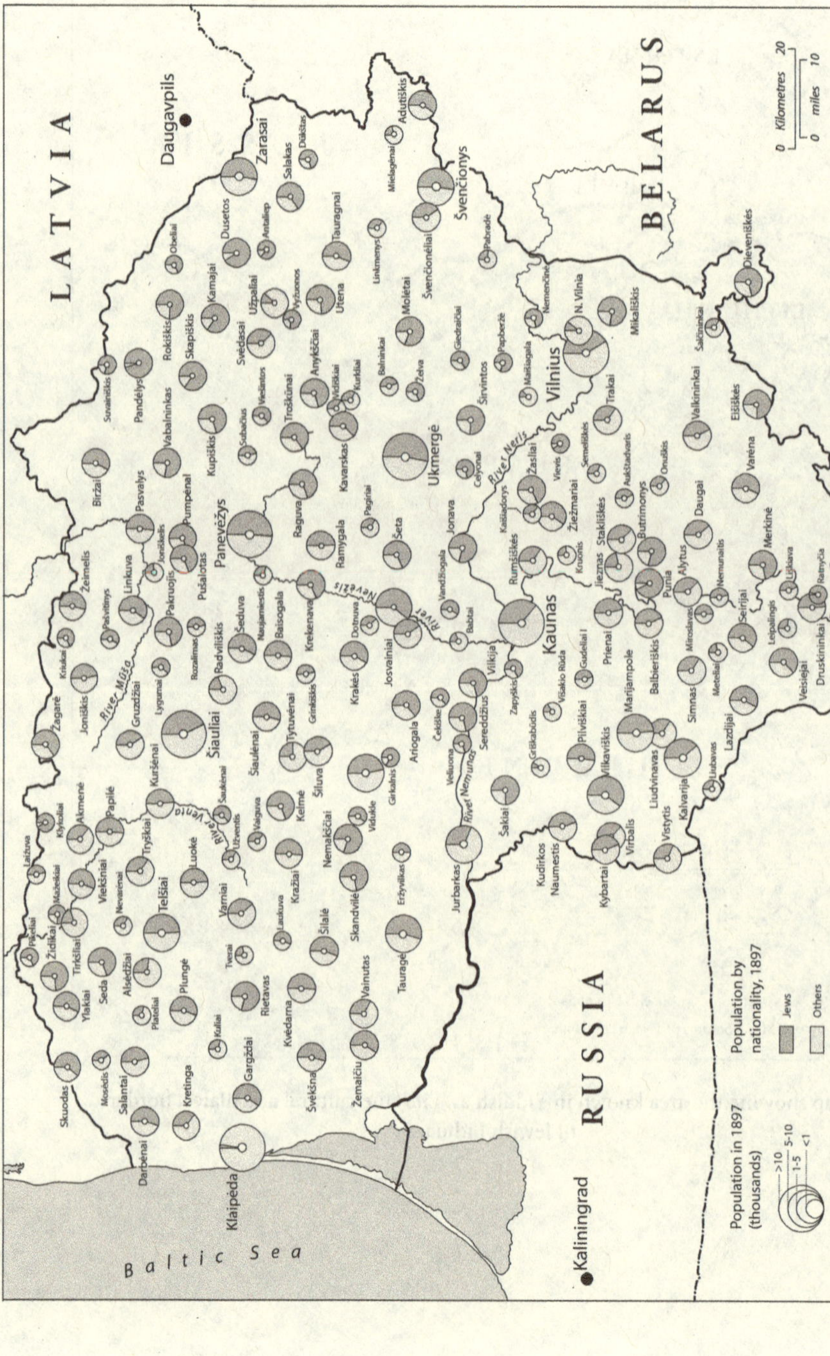

A map showing the proportion of Jews living in Lithuanian towns and villages, as shown by the census of 1897. The darker shading indicates the proportion of the residents of each settlement who were Jews

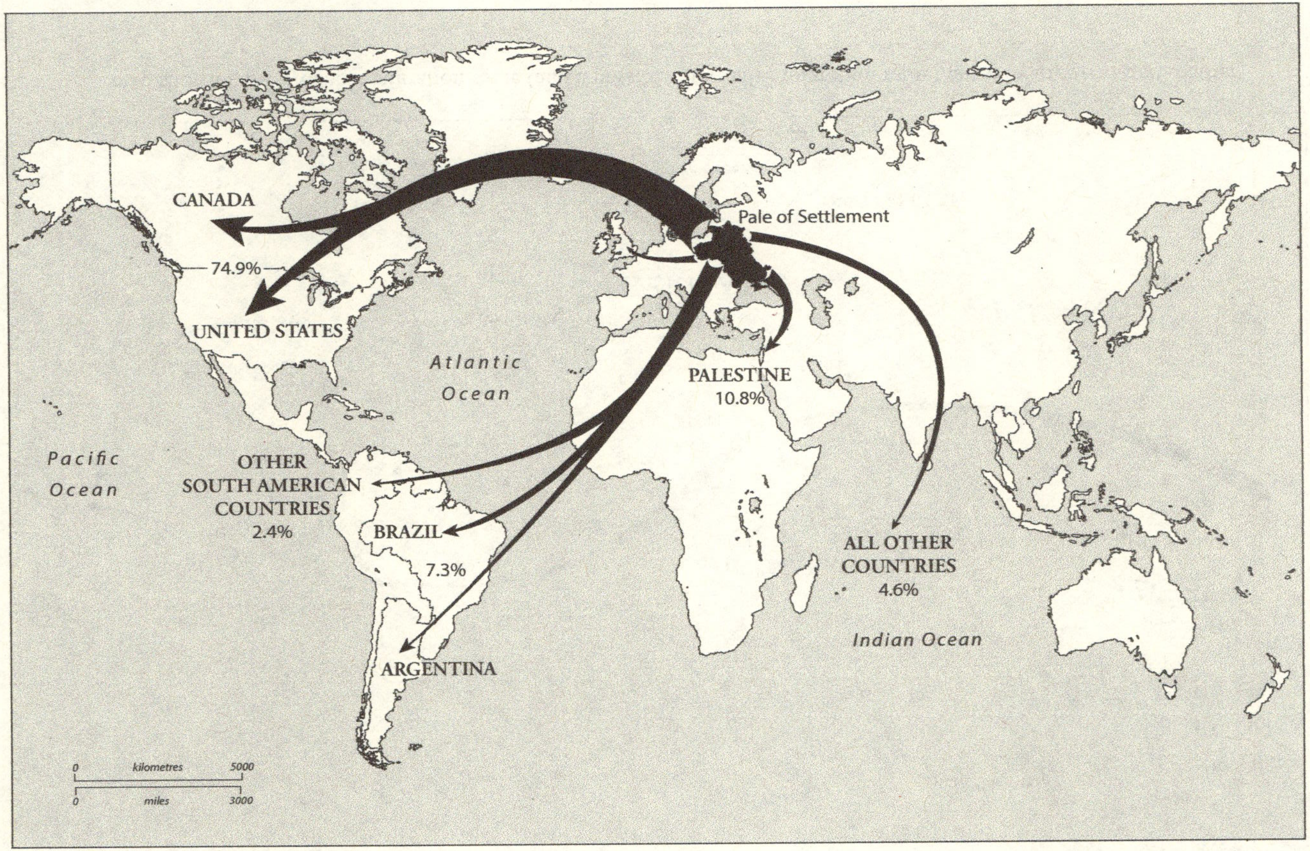

A map showing where Jews from the Pale of Settlement migrated to. N.B: these numbers relate to the period 1881-1914. They are estimates only. Great Britain is not included in the numbers because accurate figures for Jewish migration to Great Britain are not available, reflecting the fact that many emigrating Jews regarded their stay in Great Britain as temporary

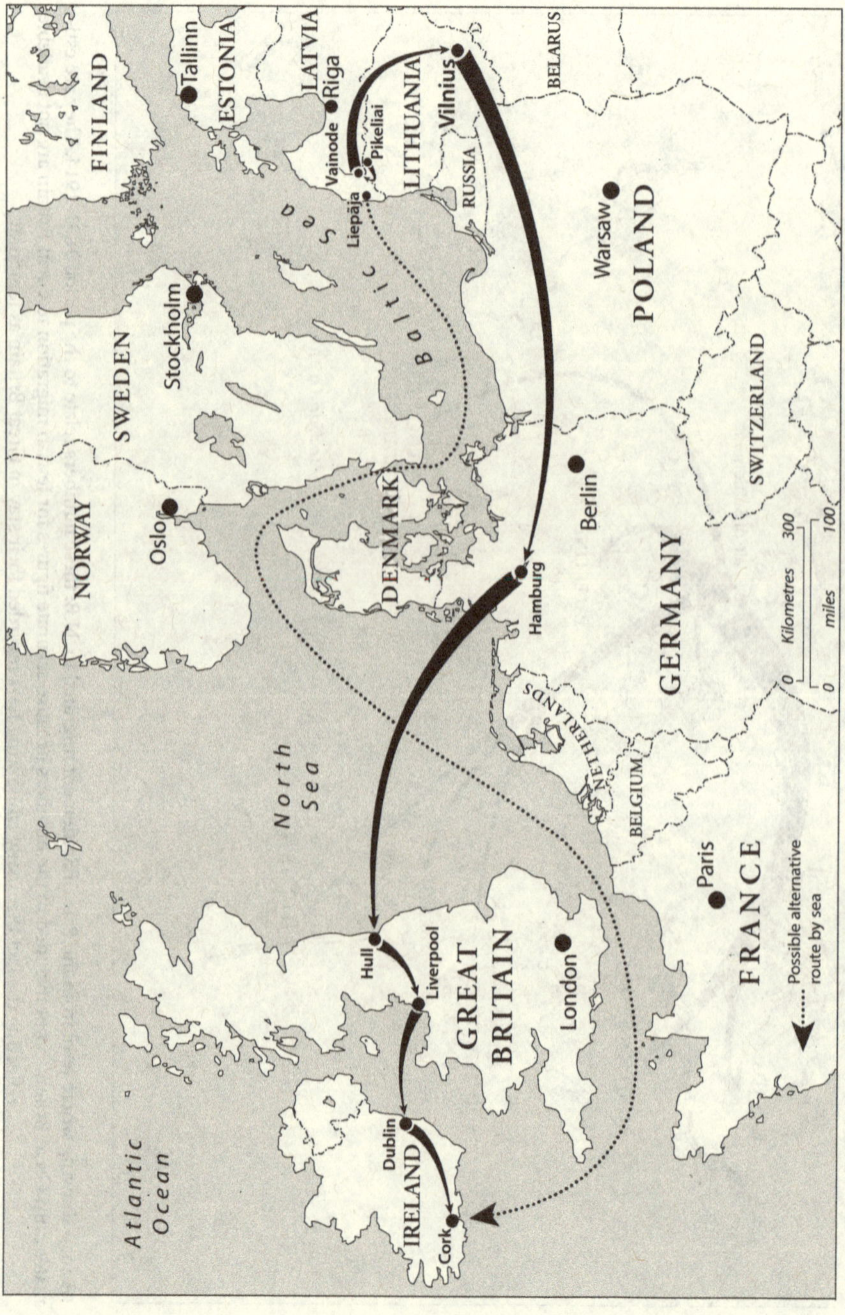

A map showing the probable migration route (and a possible alternative migration route) taken by my great-grandfather

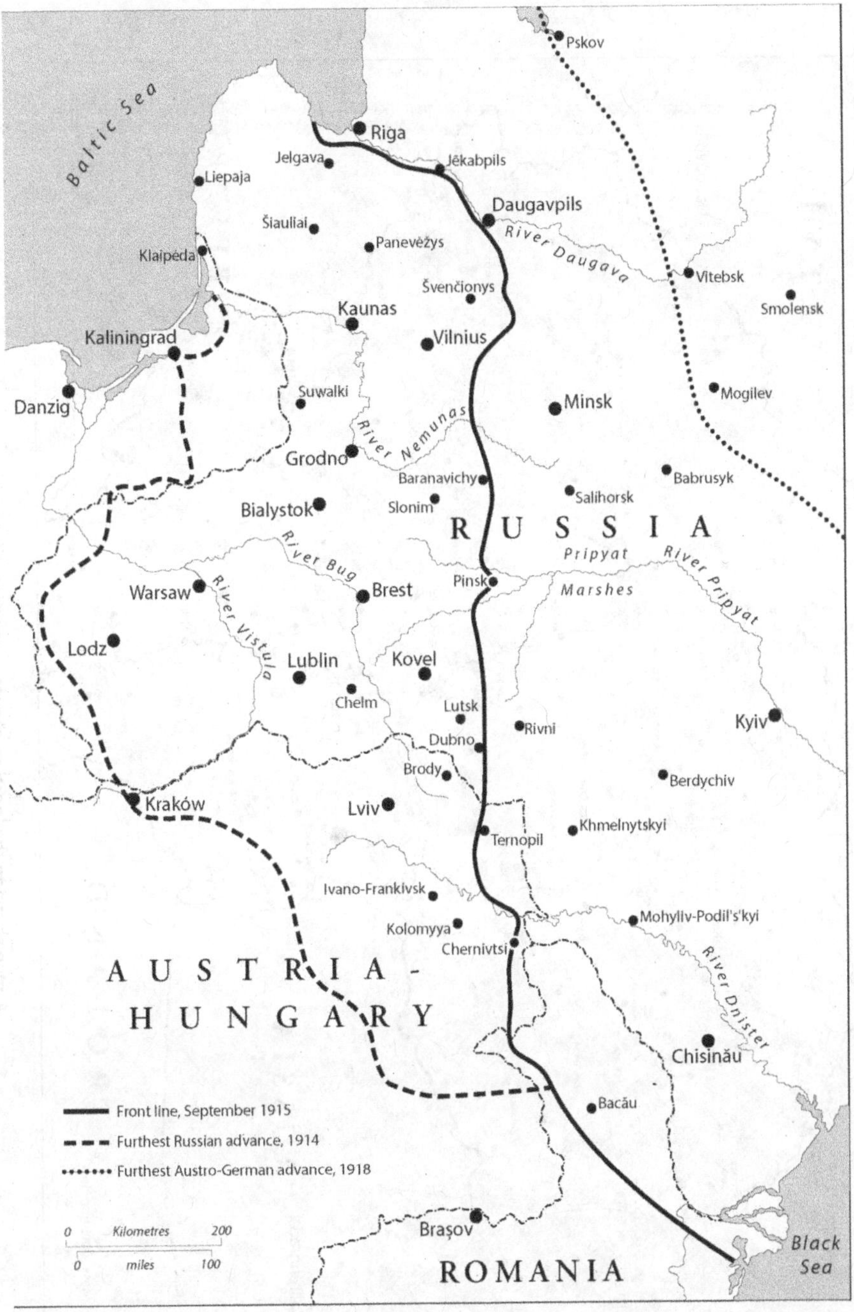

A map showing the position of the Eastern Front at different times in World War 1

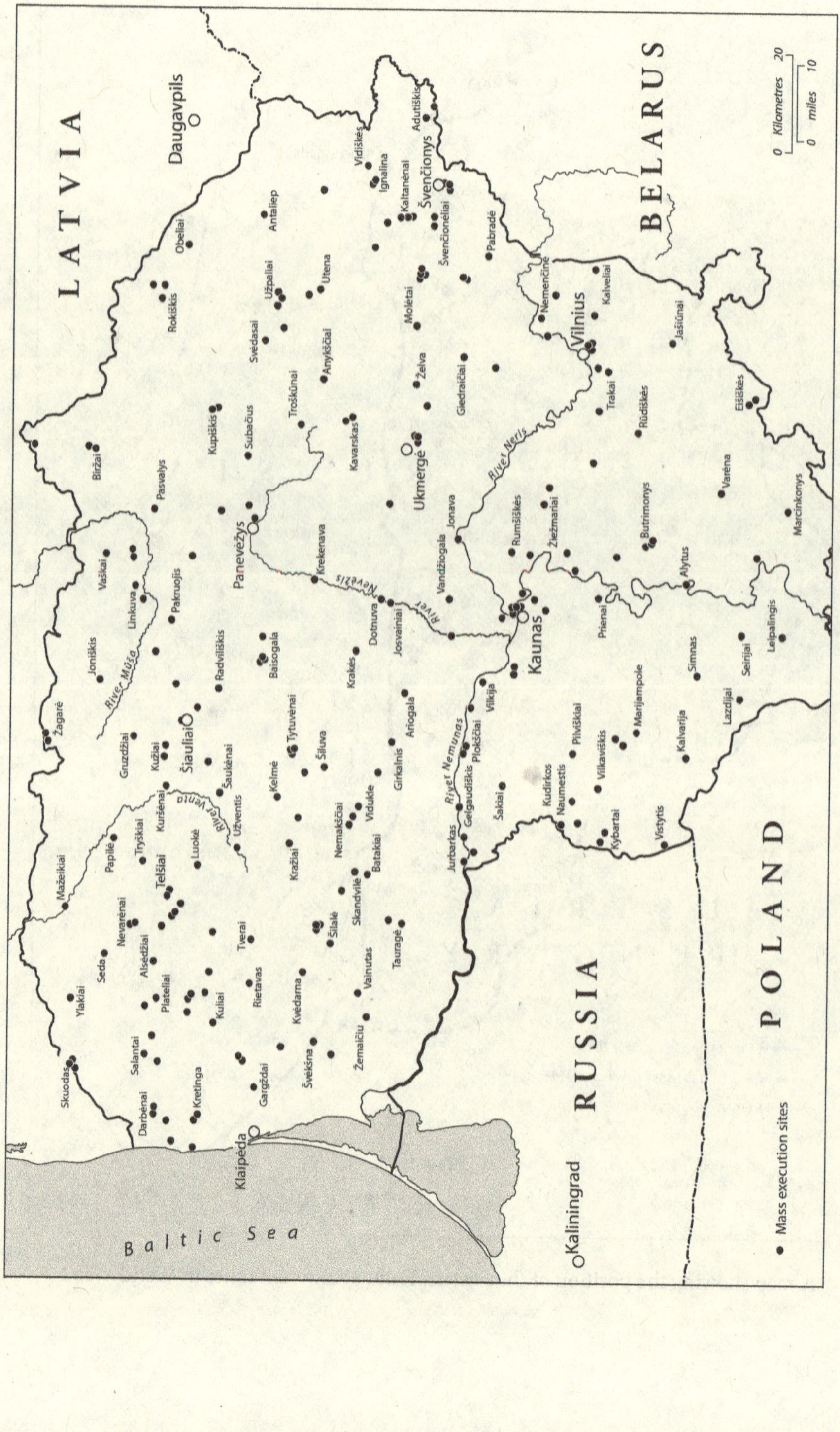

A map showing the location of mass execution sites in Lithuania

Introduction

This book was inspired by thinking about three generations in the patrilineal line of my family. My great-grandfather, Myer, was born and brought up in a small village, a *shtetl*, in what is now northern Lithuania about one kilometre south of the border with Latvia. It was a remote and poor place, and conditions for the Jewish inhabitants were difficult.

After working for a short time in a small town on the other side of the present Lithuanian/Latvian border Myer decided, in his late teens, and apparently quite suddenly, to emigrate to Cork in the south of Ireland. Cork was not, perhaps, an obvious choice as an emigration destination. However, Myer built a successful business, married his long-standing girlfriend from the Latvian port of Liepāja, and had a number of children including my grandfather Joseph, known as 'JD'.

In 1905 the family moved from Cork to Dublin, probably due to alarm at anti-Jewish disturbances in Limerick the previous year. JD was well-schooled and then trained as a doctor at the Royal College of Surgeons in Dublin, qualifying in 1923. Finding it difficult to obtain an opening in the medical profession in Ireland, he joined the Royal Navy as a ship's doctor and travelled widely in the Far East before settling in England and buying into a medical practice in New Cross on the edge of London's East End. JD and his wife May stayed in London during the Second World War which provided JD with a bird's eye view of the effect of enemy bombing on the poor of London's East End.

Their two sons had a peripatetic war-time existence as their parents repeatedly moved them to try to avoid the risk of their being bombed or being on the route of a possible invasion. The older of those two sons was called Michael. He was my father. In the immediate post-war years Michael won a scholarship to Winchester (the well-known English public school), read history at Oxford University, married into an acculturated Jewish family and became a successful lawyer in the City of London. This life was a far cry from a Lithuanian shtetl.

Such a family story is not uncommon in the Jewish world. And yet. Such a story seems to me both ordinary and extraordinary. It raises wider questions about modern Jewish history and it is those wider questions which this book seeks to address: Why were there substantial numbers of Jewish people in Lithuania in the late nineteenth century? How and why did their lives become more difficult at that time? Why did many of them emigrate and how did they choose where to go? Why did some choose to go to Ireland, of all somewhat unlikely places? What happened to their family and friends left behind in Lithuania, both during the First World War and in the inter-war period? How and why were Lithuania's Jews murdered in the Holocaust? How has the Lithuanian government and population come to terms with the Holocaust?

Books about the history of Jews in Lithuania tend to fall into one of two main categories. First, there are the academic works. These are in a number of different languages, including English, German and Lithuanian. Most are based on substantial original research, often in quite arcane areas. They are written by academics and with the expectation that they will mainly be read by an academic audience. A second and quite different kind of book is the family memoir. These are sometimes based on discussions with family members, and on genealogical research. They tend to concentrate on the Holocaust years and are sometimes intended, perhaps not explicitly, as an act of homage to murdered relations. The audience for such books is likely to be found mainly, but not exclusively, among descendants of the author.

This book does not fall into either of those two main categories, although it contains elements of both. Plainly, it is not a work written by an academic. My working life was spent as a lawyer, not in a university as an academic historian. Nor is this a family memoir, both because my Lithuanian Jewish family did not leave diaries, memoirs or letters on which such a memoir might be based, but also because that is not the kind of book I wanted to write.

Instead, I have tried to write about a number of the themes of the modern history of Jews in Lithuania by reference to the broad outline of the experience of the patrilineal line of my family. In other words, the family experience has been a way of choosing the wider themes about which to write. For example, as I know my great-grandfather was living in a shtetl in the late nineteenth century I discuss shtetl life, generally; as I know he emigrated from the Baltic in the 1880s I discuss the phenomenon of Jewish emigration from the Pale of Settlement; as I know that members of the family were killed in the Holocaust in Lithuania I attempt to understand how and why the Holocaust happened in Lithuania. It would be gratifying if this book were read by some academics and by some wider family members, but they are not the principal target audience. Instead, I aim for that elusive, and possibly mythical character, beloved of those who work in the book trade, the so-called 'intelligent general reader'. If that intelligent general reader is Jewish it may well be that some of their ancestors came from Lithuania and, if so, it is quite likely they know less than they would like to about their history, even if they are generally well-educated.

There are some good reasons why this is so. Jews who emigrated from Lithuania, and their descendants, tended to concentrate on making new lives in the countries to which they emigrated and did not want to look back; Jewish experiences in Lithuania during the First World War and during the Holocaust were so shattering that Lithuanian Jews in the west tended not to want to dwell on the past. During the period of Soviet occupation of Lithuania it became almost impossible for those based in the west to write about Jewish life in Lithuania and it was difficult to travel there. Only after establishment of Lithuanian independence in 1990 has it gradually become easier to write dispassionately about that fascinating but difficult story.

My hope in writing this book is that by exploring the historical context of the lives of my great-grandfather, grandfather and father I will enable others, both in and beyond the Jewish world, to understand more about the extraordinary modern history of Lithuanian Jews.

1

Background

My great-grandfather Myer Scher was born in a small village in what is now northern Lithuania, known in Lithuanian as Pikeliai, and in Yiddish as Pikeln. The name of the town is thought to have derived from the nearby Pikelhof estate, owned by local noble landlords. Precisely when Pikeliai was established as a village remains obscure, although it is clear it was already being referred to in the court books of the Grand Duchy of Lithuania as early as 1594. It seems to have grown modestly over the following two centuries to the point that in 1759 it received permission to maintain one weekly market and four fairs each year.[1] Pikeliai lies in an area that is rural and remote. It is surrounded by forests, and many of its buildings are constructed from wood. There are nearby rivers and lakes, and the Losha river is four miles away. There are few substantial towns in the area. It lies 278 kilometres from the Lithuanian capital Vilnius, and 256 kilometres from the second city, Kaunas. The nearest town of significance is the Baltic port of Liepāja, in present-day Latvia (known as Libau, in German). A feature of Pikeliai's location, which was to become highly consequential in the nineteenth century, is that it lies only about one kilometre from the present border between Lithuania and Latvia, and that Lithuania was inside the Pale of Settlement, while some parts of Latvia were outside it.

Lithuania lies on the eastern coast of the Baltic Sea. It is the largest of the three Baltic states but is nonetheless relatively small. It is approximately 65,000 square kilometres, and has a population of roughly 2,700,000. It is bordered by Latvia to the north, Belarus to the east, Poland to the south and East Prussia to the west (today a part of Russia). Lithuania is a small country surrounded by larger and more powerful neighbours.

Many Lithuanians descend from an Eastern Indo-European people. In earliest recorded times they were known as Samogitians or Aesti. Cornelius Tacitus (56-120 C.E.) briefly describes the Aesti in his 'Germania'. He remarks that they produce grain and other fruits of the earth and contrasts their assiduity in doing this with "the usual laziness of the Germans". He also records that the Aesti are the only people to gather amber, which they call 'glesum'. The export of amber became a substantial and thriving Baltic trade.[2]

The Lithuanian language is of considerable interest to philologists. It is thought to be one of the world's oldest living languages, closer to Sanskrit than any other. Written Lithuanian, however, has not been found from before the early sixteenth century; translations into Lithuanian of the Lord's Prayer, the Hail Mary and the Nicene Creed have been found from that time. Because the Lithuanian language is conservative in its grammar and phonology it retains archaic features otherwise found only in ancient languages, including Sanskrit. It is impossible to say exactly when Myer Scher's forebears first came to northern Lithuania, or why they came. But we do know something about the circumstances of early Jewish settlement in Lithuania.

Jews in small numbers seem first to have come to Lithuania in the twelfth century, fleeing hostility directed towards them in much of western Europe at the time of the Crusades; other Jews fled to Lithuania hoping to avoid plague. In the first half of the fourteenth century Grand Duke Gediminas encountered Jews while campaigning in Galicia and invited some Jewish merchants and craftsmen to settle in what was then known as the Zamut region of Lithuania, now known as Samogitia. Gediminas's grandson, Vytautas, actively welcomed Jewish settlement. It was during his rule that a Jewish community of some substance became established in Lithuania. By the time of his death in 1430 the number of Jews had probably grown to about 6,000, at a time when the total population in the Grand Duchy of Lithuania was approximately 2,500,000. Vytautas fought a series of wars against the Teutonic Knights, culminating in the Battle of Grunwald (Tannenberg) in 1410, which delivered a blow from which they did not recover. It effectively brought to an end the long effort of the Teutonic Knights to germanise the Baltic and impose their form of Christianity upon it.[3]

Vytautas also brought Karaite captives to Lithuania, following his campaigns in southern Russia and the Crimea, and defeat of the Tartars in 1392. The Karaites are a breakaway Jewish sect. They were founded in Babylonia in the eighth century CE. Karaites regarded scripture as the sole source of Jewish law, to the exclusion of rabbinical tradition. They developed a non-Biblical oral code of their own, known in English as the Yoke of Inheritance. Vytautas settled Karaites in Trakai, Lutsk and Halych and appears to have regarded them as being effectively Jewish, referring to them as "Jews of Trakai". The Karaites, for their part, saw themselves as being distinct from Jews. Nonetheless, Jews and Karaites lived side by side in Lithuania for centuries and shared some religious facilities such as the *shohet* (ritual slaughterer), certain religious books and *yeshivot* (Jewish educational institutions).

Vytautas transformed prospects for Jews in Lithuania by granting a charter to the Jews of Trakai and Brest in 1388 and to the Jews of Grodno in 1389. This charter was based on that granted to the Jews in Poland by King Boleslav the Pious in 1264. The provisions of Vytautas's charter were far-reaching: synagogues and Jewish cemeteries were exempted from taxation; Jews were granted the right to own property and live where they wished; Jews were permitted to trade in liquor and in commodities such as bread and corn; if a Christian killed a Jew he faced penalties including confiscation by the state of his property and possessions; and a Christian was liable to fines for throwing stones at Jewish-owned property.

Vytautas's charter made clear that Jews were to be afforded a measure of toleration in Lithuania and some Jews responded by migrating there. Importantly, a consequence of the charter was that Jews were placed under the protection of the King (grand duke) of Lithuania and, later, of the nobles and this afforded them a measure of protection in the centuries that followed. By 1500 approximately 6,000 Jews in Lithuania came under the direct jurisdiction of the royal government, represented by the Voivode in the cities and the Starosta in the provinces.

By the time of the Jews' expulsion from Spain in 1492, Lithuania was probably the only European state where Jews managed estates and practised a wide range of trades, crafts and skills in the economy of the villages and small towns.

It is striking that Lithuania was almost certainly the last European country to cease being pagan (broadly, during the late fourteenth century) and that in the succeeding decades it was exceptional in its tolerance of Jews and some other religious minorities, such as the Hussites.

The reasons for Vytautas's toleration, even friendliness, towards Jews seem inextricably connected to his own pagan upbringing. There is a description of Vytautas by a Flemish trader and diplomat called Guillebert de Lannoy. He describes Vytautas's laxity in religious matters, observing him dining with "Saracen infidels" and serving both meat and fish on Fridays. Lannoy also describes Vytautas's warm welcome of Hussites. Vytautas seems to have had no religious antagonism towards Jews and to have calculated that Jewish settlers would bring economic benefits.[4]

Despite this broadly tolerant atmosphere, there were sections of Lithuanian society that resented and were sometimes very hostile to Jewish presence. Burghers in larger towns (particularly Germans) and the guilds ("cechy") were periodically fearful of Jewish competition. In Vilnius, for example, the burghers repeatedly lobbied the King against the Jews, who in 1527 gave way and granted the burghers a privilege '*De Non Tolerandis Judaeis*', forbidding Jews from settling and trading in Vilnius. Later in the sixteenth century, Vilnius burghers made blood-libel accusations against the Jews and in 1564 a certain Berent Abramowicz, a Jewish trade official, was put to death. A number of other similar accusations by burghers only ended when the King issued a proclamation threatening with execution anyone bringing a false accusation against a Jew. The lower nobility was also sometimes hostile to Jews, probably motivated by the desire to take over leaseholds run by Jews. In 1559, for example, the nobles of the Samogitia region condemned the "deceit of the Jews" and demanded that their right to lease the royal customs be revoked. Clergy of the Orthodox and Catholic churches were also from time to time very hostile to Jews, perhaps inspired by an excess of religious enthusiasm; in 1533, for example, clerical pressure led to a ban on Lithuanian Jews employing Christian servants and maids.

Jewish life in Lithuania was seriously disrupted in the mid-seventeenth century by the Ukrainian Cossack and peasant rebellion, led by Bogdan Chmielnicki. Tens of thousands of Jews were massacred, and thousands more taken captive. Jewish refugees fled from the larger cities. In 1653, the Russian Tsar Alexei intervened, sending an army in support of Chmielnicki into Lithuania's eastern border region. Vilnius was sacked and some of its 3,000 Jewish inhabitants escaped; some managed to establish themselves in small towns and villages in Samogitia and Courland. The trauma of the mid-seventeenth century is vividly captured by Moises Rivkes, a member of the Lithuanian Jewish community, who eventually fled to Amsterdam:

> The whole of Lithuania is suffering from bands of Russians and Cossacks, who destroy cities and kill people. In Vilnius ... the murderers looted the houses before burning them. I left my beautiful house, abandoned my inheritance, my books, my goods...we went into exile, not knowing where to go, accompanied by the cries of terrified refugees...[5]

The Chmielnicki rebellion was a decisive turning point in Lithuanian Jewish history because it was from then that many of the smaller communities in villages and towns in central, northern and western Lithuania were established. By 1676, the Jewish population in the Grand Duchy had grown to 32,000, at a time when the total population of the

Grand Duchy was approximately 2,000,000. Life was difficult because of plague, heavy taxes and fines but the nobility needed Jewish skills as craftsmen, innkeepers, commercial agents, shopkeepers and pedlars. It has been estimated that more than 100 new Jewish settlements came into existence between the Cossack uprising of 1648 and Lithuania's annexation by Russia in 1795.

The Tsarist Russian empire conquered Lithuania in 1795 in what has become known as the Third Partition of Poland. This conquest was a major turning-point, one might even say a 'rupture', in the life of Lithuanian Jewry. Before the Third Partition of Poland, Jews had enjoyed considerable autonomy in administration of their affairs. The great Jewish historian Simon Dubnow was the first to draw wide attention to this. He was born in 1860, in Belarus, and studied Eastern European Jewish history, applying innovative sociological methods in doing so. He became active in politics, espousing 'autonomism', which challenged Zionism and Bundism in appeal to the Jewish masses of eastern Europe. His political philosophy grew directly from his reading of Jewish history. He made this point in his memoirs, by quoting Cicero: "Not to know what has been transacted in former times is to continue always as a child." Dubnow believed that Jews in Eastern Europe had, historically, enjoyed considerable control over their own affairs, a condition he characterised as 'autonomy'. They had

> A broad and well-ordered social organization with communities and associations of communities, and with a complex network of religious, social, and cultural institutions... The autonomy provided strength and unity to the outcast nation and, at the same time, gave it culture and laws and educated it in the spirit of discipline and self-rule. The Jew felt that he was a part of a living national body.[6]

Jewish autonomy was ultimately dependent on the fact that Jews had royal protection. This protection was legally embodied in the royal *privilegium*, first granted in the fourteenth century, amended over time, but still in effect in 1795. The *privilegium* conferred royal protection on Jews and set out how they were to pay tax. The Jewish community had responsibility for how tax was to be levied on its members, and how the tax was to be collected. The Jews helped the king maintain a mercenary army by paying their taxes directly to the various battalion commanders on receipt of instructions in writing from treasury officials.

At local level, leadership of Jewish communities was in the hands of the *kahal*. This was composed of members of a small number of families, prominent in the community. Membership of the *kahal* tended to depend on ownership of property, family lineage and religious scholarship. The *kahal* governed the local community; it enacted and enforced regulations in all walks of life, and its members periodically replaced one another either through rotation or secret elections. There was often a mutuality of interests between the leading Jewish families who ran the *kahal* and the local Polish noble families who owned surrounding land.

From 1561 a Jewish parliament – of sorts – came into existence. This was the Synod of the Four Lands. It was for the communities of Little Poland, Greater Poland, Belarus and Lithuania. Its work complemented that of the *kehillot.* In 1590 the Synod of the Four Lands split in two and a new Council of Lithuania (Hebrew: *Va'ad Lita*) also came into being, in addition to the Synod of the Four Lands. This council also functioned as a kind of legislative assembly on a Lithuania-wide basis. It had tax-raising powers and made regulations on matters such as business dealings, leasing of land and negotiations with the barons. To enforce its rulings the Council could invoke *herem* (excommunication), the effect of which was, in effect, to remove a person from participating in all aspects of Jewish community life. The Council of Lithuania met relatively infrequently – 37 times between 1623 and 1764. It was through studying the *pinkas* (official book of record) of the Council of Lithuania for the period 1623-1764 that Simon Dubnow came to develop his particular conception that Jews had enjoyed great autonomy in Lithuania before 1795. [7]

Contact between the Jewish community and the outside world was often in the hands of an agent, known as the *shtadlan.* His role is sometimes compared to that of a modern political lobbyist. A 1730 letter of appointment issued to the agent of the Council of the Four Lands charges:

> Wherever he is sent he will go and whatever he is commanded to do he will do ...he lies in wait at every corner to gain benefits and salvation for the general good both in the great councils [including meetings of the *Sejm*, the Polish parliament] and on the committees...[8]

In other words, the *shtadlan* was to be particularly involved in lobbying members of the national and regional parliaments of the Polish-Lithuanian commonwealth in matters of particular concern to the Jewish community. The reference in this letter of appointment to 'lying in wait at every corner' hints, perhaps, at the covert influence the *shtadlan* might deploy; and indeed his modus operandi might extend to making payments, exploiting family connections and providing financial services. There is no doubt that this approach to diplomacy could be effective. For example, Arieh Leib Meitess was thought by his interventions in 1784 to have resecured Jews' rights of domicile and economic privileges in Lithuania.[9] It is unsurprising that opponents of Jews were heavily critical of what they regarded as this unhealthy influence. In his memoirs R. Dov Ber of Bolechów described the hostility of the Jews' opponents:

> Under the constitution of Poland one member of the Diet could stop the business of the session by declaring: "I do not agree to this matter." The Polish nobles believed that the leading Jews bribed some of the deputies to bring the sessions of the Diets to an end by this means.[10]

In time, some early Zionist thinkers came to suspect that the *Shtadlan's* way of doing things was not in the best interests of Jews, and indeed that it was creating, or at least playing into, antisemitic tropes; they felt that the Jewish masses would be better off taking control of their own affairs, and emancipating themselves.[11]

Early modern Lithuanian society was highly stratified. Much of the land was owned by Polish landowning nobility. They were Catholic. There was also a large class of Lithuanian peasants, largely uneducated, who led a rather hand-to-mouth agricultural existence; they were mainly Catholic, although some were Orthodox. Between these groups were the Jews. Many Jews lived in towns and villages which were owned by the nobility. It has been estimated that two-thirds of the towns of the Polish-Lithuanian commonwealth in the eighteenth century were private towns owned by the nobility.[12] It was in these towns, and not in the other towns owned by the Crown and the Church, that Jews tended to live. Indeed, many Crown cities and almost all towns owned by the Church attempted to prevent Jews from residing in their jurisdictions. In many towns owned by nobles Jews made up a majority of the urban population. Jews tended to manage businesses that they leased from the nobility. In this respect, the economic life of Jews in Lithuania was different from that of Jews elsewhere in central Europe. There, a great deal of Jewish economic activity was connected, directly or indirectly, to moneylending but in Lithuania Jews were a part of the feudal economy, managing businesses they leased from the nobility. Many of these businesses were agricultural in nature or derived from agriculture. Jews processed and supplied agricultural products and were increasingly involved in the production of alcoholic beverages (beer, mead and vodka), and owned the taverns that supplied them. It is thought that in the villages about 80 per cent of Jews were engaged in occupations related to the liquor trade.[13]

British travellers to Poland and Lithuania in the eighteenth and early nineteenth centuries were often struck by the numbers of Jews they saw, and by their industry. John Thomas James (1786-1828) was a Church of England bishop and traveller. In 1816 he published a *Journal of a Tour in Germany, Sweden, Russia, and Poland, during 1813 and 1814*. He wrote:

> We now crossed the frontier of Poland...every house we saw was in the hands of Jews. They seemed, indeed, the only people who were in a state of activity, exercising almost all professions, and engaged in every branch of trade: millers, whitesmiths, saddlers, drivers, ostlers, innkeepers, and sometimes even as farmers. Their constant bustle makes them appear more abundant in number than they really are...[14]

William Coxe was an English historian and priest who served as a travelling companion and tutor to the nobility. He published his *Travels into Poland, Russia, Sweden and Denmark* in 1781. He observed:

> [t]he number of Jews is now prodigious, and they have in a manner engrossed all the commerce of the country; this flourishing state of affairs [can] be attributed to the industry of those extraordinary people, to the indolence of the country, and oppressed condition of the peasants[15]

It would appear that the nobles and the Jews had a kind of symbiotic relationship in pre-1795 Lithuania. The nobles needed the Jews to run their estates and to make a success of the towns and villages established on their land; the nobles valued the revenues the Jews produced; in return, the nobles gave Jews a measure of protection, and relative autonomy. If Jews felt unhappy with how they were being treated their main remedy was to leave their town or village and work elsewhere. It was clear that this symbiotic relationship had its limits. Although Jews were useful to them, the nobles do not appear to have liked Jews very much. An analysis of twenty-nine diaries of noblemen undertaken by the Polish historian Joanna Partyka found that these noble diarists shared a tendency to xenophobia and that they particularly disliked Jews.[16] There may have been economic inter-dependency, but in Polish-Lithuanian culture Jews were perceived as outsiders.

Life was not easy for Jews in eighteenth century Lithuania. There were a series of mini-pogroms, and the Royal Court which had jurisdiction over Jewish grievances was generally hostile to Jewish interests. The Jewish community was menaced by a great missionary campaign led by Father Turchinowitz, whose efforts were assisted by legislation providing that Jews who converted to Catholicism joined the lower nobility and automatically benefitted from their privileges. By his death in 1773 he had converted only a handful of Jewish men but about 500 young Jewish women, to widespread distress in the Jewish community. The eastern part of the Polish-Lithuanian commonwealth was menaced by the Ukrainian *Haidamack*, bands of serfs, peasants and outcasts who assaulted Jews in small towns and sometimes engaged in larger-scale massacres, as in attacks on Jews (and Poles) in the town of Umman, which were led by the *Haidamack* chieftain Gonta.[17] There was also the problem of foreign armies twice marching through Poland and Lithuania in the mid-eighteenth century; at the time of the Russo-Turkish war in 1735 and again in 1740-1763, during the Austrian Wars of Succession.

Historians have long thought that Jewish communal institutions were experiencing a kind of crisis in eighteenth century Lithuania.[18] Some writers have chosen to emphasise the pressures on communal institutions that flowed from persecution of Jews and their economic exploitation; others have pointed to 'interference' by noble landlords in Jewish communal affairs and others again (including Benzion Dinur) have suggested the main problem was "that the Jewish community establishment was being overrun by strongmen, habitués of the nobles' courts and those with access to political influence" and that these "new men" turned "Jewish self-government into a fiction, a caricature".[19]

For all the difficulties it faced, the Jewish community in eighteenth century Lithuania had, at least, enjoyed some considerable autonomy in the management of its affairs and had been provided a measure of protection by the nature of its relationship with Polish nobles. All of this was to change with the Third Partition of Poland in 1795.

In 1795 historic Lithuania came under Russian control. From 1795 until 1914 the counties of Kaunas, Grodno, Minsk, Moghilev and Vitebsk formed part of the 'Northwest Territory' of the Russian empire. Historically, Russia had been hostile to Jews - indeed it had not permitted Jews to live within its sovereign territory. Jews had been expelled from territories acquired by Russia as it expanded westwards during the eighteenth century. This had happened with conquests of 1727 and again in 1739 when Jews were driven from parts of Ukraine and Belarus. Russia was governed by Tsars, absolute monarchs who were strongly influenced by their orthodox Christian faith;

the Tsars were generally reactionary and hostile to minorities, especially towards Jews. After 1795 the fate of Lithuanian Jewry came to depend heavily on the character of the Tsar, on his whims and on the approach of who was advising him from time to time. This difficult situation was made worse by the weakened position of the Jews' traditional protectors, the Polish nobles.

The vulnerability of nineteenth century Lithuanian Jewry to Tsarist autocracy becomes clear by briefly considering policies towards Jews of Nicholas I (1825-1855) and of Alexander II (1855-1881).

Tsar Nicholas I was preoccupied with what he saw as Russia's Jewish problem. He recognised that many Jews were educated and clever and had economic value to the state; he thought Jews could be of most value to Russia if they could be 'cured' of their religion. His was a policy of forced and expedited assimilation. His first scheme was to issue a ukase of 1827 prescribing military conscription of all Jewish boys at the age of twelve for a period of twenty-five years. They were not ever to be eligible for promotion. Although no formal instructions were issued to this effect, it became generally understood in the army that Nicholas I's real purpose was that these young Jewish soldiers should be pressurised into baptism. This policy yielded slow results and so was supplemented by military schools in remote regions of southern Russia, devoted to the combined conversion and military training of very young boys. Each Jewish community, through its *kahal*, was given a quota of "Cantonists" it was to provide. Boys as young as eight or nine were kidnapped by professional "snatchers" (*khapers* in Yiddish), who the *kahal* employed to fill its quota. Members of the *kahal* often found ways to ensure that their own children were not made Cantonists, and so the burden fell disproportionately on the poor and unprotected. It is thought that about 50,000 young Jewish boys were taken from their families in this way. The Cantonists were coerced into baptism. Harold Frederic reported:

> Some of these lads used to resist baptism. Then it was the commandant's thoughtful custom to put them into solitary confinement and feed them on salt herrings, without water to drink, until they consented to accept the baptismal rite.[20]

Forced conscription of young boys into the Tsarist army visited a lasting trauma on the Jewish community of Lithuania. It was spoken of and written about for decades afterwards. Nicholas I also made efforts to coerce Jews into becoming agriculturalists by planting agricultural settlements for them in remote areas. No proper training in agriculture was provided; local officials stole most of the money allocated to the projects. Harold Frederic describes the report of a M. Stempel, Superintendent of the Ekaterinoslav settlements, which he made in 1847:

> the colonists arriv[ed] at the beginning of winter, to find a cluster of wretched huts, damp, half open, and too low for a man to stand upright in...the Jews begged to be allowed to reconstruct these shanties; permission was refused by officials. Stempel then suggested the Jews should be allowed to find shelter in neighbouring villages until spring. This also was refused. Those who had already sought refuge in the villages roundabout were driven back by Cossacks under circumstances of the greatest barbarism. Epidemics of scurvy and smallpox broke out shortly thereafter.[21]

In 1835 Nicholas 1 introduced a Statute for the Minorities codifying the extensive restrictions on Jews (and others) which had been introduced since 1804. And other efforts to force Jewish assimilation continued apace: Nicholas I's education minister Uvarov established a network of government schools in the Pale of Settlement, but these failed for a shortage of parents willing to send their children to schools they suspected of being designed to promote conversion, not education. The *kehillot* were disbanded and Jews placed under the jurisdiction of the police and municipal authorities. In 1851 Jewish men were forbidden to wear their traditional clothes and sidelocks and married Jewish women were ordered to stop shaving their heads.

In 1846 Sir Moses and Lady Montefiore journeyed through parts of the Russian empire, including Lithuania, to see for themselves the conditions in which Jews were living. Some of Sir Moses's impressions of Lithuanian Jewry at that time are recorded in his diary.[22] It makes for pitiful reading. It describes, for example, how

> we left Wilna for Wilkomir. The recent rains had left the roads very bad... After a ride of seventy-six and a half versts we reached Wilkomir, where a deputation from the Hebrew community brought us wine and cake. The account which they gave of their brethren was but sorrowful. Of five hundred families, they said, one-fourth died last year from destitution…

On return to England Sir Moses composed a letter to Count Kissileff, a close adviser to Tsar Nicholas 1, with the intention that Kissileff show this letter to the Tsar. Behind a façade of elaborate courtesy, Sir Moses explains that in reviewing the condition of Jews in lands controlled by the Tsar he feels: "there exist some obstacles which prevent the benign rays of His Majesty's mercy from imparting to His Hebrew subjects the full measure of comfort to which the wise and just general laws of the Russian government would entitle them". He goes on to itemise the extensive restrictions imposed on Jews by Russian law and to set out a number of specific areas where laws should be changed. He suggests that Jews should have greater freedom as to where they live in the Russia empire, that Jewish artisans should be free to employ who they wish, that the *kehillot* should be re-established, that Jews in the military should be eligible for promotion, and that taxes targeted specifically at Jews (including a tax on lighting sabbath candles) should be abolished. Sir Moses's description of the condition of Jews under Russian control and his proposals for legislative change were thorough and well-judged; but it was to no avail. Tsar Nicholas I was set in his ways and became even more obdurate after the Polish revolution of 1848. He was both very devout and very determined that Jews should be forcibly assimilated. Lithuanian Jews came to look back on his reign as a particularly dark period.

Nicholas was succeeded by his son, Tsar Alexander II. At the beginning of his reign, Alexander appeared relatively liberal, influenced by enlightened ideas from the West and by a hard-headed realisation that Russia needed to learn lessons from its defeat in the Crimean war. Some commentators came to regard the period 1857-1877 as a 'golden age' for Jews in Russia.[23] For example, Alexander ended the Cantonist system and reduced the term of military service from 25 to 16 years; education of Jewish young people improved as more parents were prepared to send their children to Russian public schools as fears these schools were being used to convert Jewish children receded. By 1864, 7,500 Jewish students had been enrolled. There was some relaxation as to where Jews could live. In 1858, Jews were permitted to move from one locality to another within the Pale. By a law of 1865 particular groups of Jews, notably 'artisans', were permitted to live outside the Pale, but on strict terms including that they did not buy property or take up residence. Also, increasing numbers of Jews moved beyond the Pale without permission to do so. It is thought that by the end of Alexander's reign as many as one million Jews were living in Russia outside the Pale of Settlement.

One should not get carried away by the idea of a 'golden age' for Jews under Alexander II. For one thing, his approach changed markedly after 1866, following an attempt to assassinate him by D. Karakazov, a leader of the

Narodniki party. He then turned his back on the liberal image he had sought to cultivate and surrounded himself by much more conservative advisers. Moreover, although his reign might be seen as a "golden age" for a few, the overwhelming majority of Jews continued to live in the Pale, and in grinding poverty. Even the Jews who moved beyond the Pale and achieved business success tended to experience considerable difficulty, encountering fierce resentment. Harold Frederic was particularly struck by this during travels in Russia and the Pale for research on his book, *The New Exodus* :

> The Russian tradesman dislikes exertion…His idea of commerce is to mark a fifty or sixty per cent. profit on his goods, and then sit down and drink tea and play draughts till God sends him a customer… the Jew, on the other hand, has a real delight in activity.

Russians who Harold Frederic met told him how much they resented Jews who got up earlier and worked harder than Russian businesspeople.[24]

For some time after 1795 relations between Lithuanian Jews and Polish nobles from whom they leased estates and who gave them some protection in a feudal economy continued unaffected; but, over time, the autonomy of the Polish nobility within Lithuanian society was itself undermined. The fundamental reason why the Polish nobility in Lithuania lost its autonomy was the failure of Polish rebellions against Russian rule: in 1830-31 and then again in 1863. Following the failure of the 1863 revolt the Russians eradicated almost all remnants of Polish autonomy within their empire.

After 1863 the Jews of Lithuania found themselves in the dangerous position of being dependent on the whims of highly autocratic and unsympathetic Russian Tsars, with the authority of the Polish nobles, their traditional protectors, all but destroyed.

On 13 March 1881 Tsar Alexander II was assassinated.

Notes

1 Yizkor Book Database: https://www.jewishgen.org/yizkor/database

2 Masha Greenbaum, *The Jews of Lithuania: A History of a Remarkable Community, 1316-1945* (Gefen,1995)

3 Dov Levin, *The Litvaks: A Short History of the Jews in Lithuania* (Berghahn Books, 2000).

4 Laimonas Briedis, *Vilnius City of Strangers* (Baltos Lankos, 2021)

5 Greenbaum, p. 33.

6 Israel Bartal, *The Jews of Eastern Europe, 1772-1881* (University of Pennsylvania Press, 2011), p. 20.

7 Greenbaum, p. 54.
8 Bartal, p. 22.
9 Greenbaum, p. 65.
10 Bartal, p. 26.
11 Arthur Hertzberg, *The Zionist Idea: A Historical Analysis and Reader* (Jewish Publication Society, 1997), p. 179.
12 Gershon David Hundert, *Jews in Poland-Lithuania in the Eighteenth Century: A Genealogy of Modernity* (University of California Press, 2004), p. 36.
13 Hundert, p. 53.
14 John Thomas James, *Journal of a Tour in Germany, Sweden, Russia, Poland, During the Years 1813 and 1814* (J. Murray, 1816), Vol 2, p. 367.
15 William Coxe, *Travels Into Poland, Russia, Sweden, and Denmark: Interspersed with Historical Relations and Political Inquiries* (S. Price, 1784), Vol 1: p. 193.
16 The work of Joanna Partyka is referred to in Hundert, p. 39.
17 Greenbaum, p. 61.
18 Isaac Levitats, *The Jewish Community in Russia, 1772-1844* (Columbia University Press, 1943).
19 Hundert, p. 99.
20 Harold Frederic, *The New Exodus: A Study of Israel in Russia* (W. Heinemann, 1892).
21 Frederic, Chapter 5.
22 Sir Moses Montefiore, *Diaries of Sir Moses and Lady Montefiore: Comprising Their Life and Work as Recorded in Their Diaries from 1812-1883 ...* (Belford-Clarke Company, 1890).
23 Frederic, Chapter 6.
24 Frederic, Chapter 6.

2

Jewish Life in Late Nineteenth Century Lithuania

My great-grandfather Myer was born and brought up in the shtetl of Pikeliai. The term 'shtetl' is Yiddish and, simply put, it means a small town. It describes a settlement where there was a relatively substantial Jewish population who lived alongside or near their gentile, mainly peasant, neighbours, but differed from them in religion, occupation, language and culture.[1] In contrast to many Jewish diaspora communities, the Jewish population of the shtetl was often in a majority and they spoke a language, Yiddish, which was different from that of their neighbours, and which reinforced their separateness. Jews in the shtetl were engaged in a wide variety of occupations, many of them linked to the fact that local Polish nobles owned estates and needed competent managers and entrepreneurs as well as regular markets and fairs on their estates. Yiddish distinguishes between a shtetl (a small town), a shtetele (a very small town), a shtot (a city), a dorf (a village) and a yishev (a tiny rural settlement). Steven Katz identifies the defining characteristics of the shtetl in this way:

> A shtetl was big enough to support the basic network of institutions that was essential to Jewish communal life – at least one synagogue, a *mikveh* [a ritual bath], a cemetery, schools, and a framework of voluntary associations that performed basic religious and communal functions. This was a key difference between the shtetl and even smaller villages … On the other hand, what made a shtetl different from a provincial city was that the shtetl was a face-to-face community. It was small enough for almost everyone to be known by name and nickname[2]

In trying to understand what life was like in late nineteenth century Pikeliai, and other small villages and towns in northern Lithuania, one is at once confronted by the difficulty that much of what we know, or think we know, about this subject derives from 'collective memory' and from the many and colourful works of literary fiction. But, do collective memory and literature give a true picture of what life in the shtetl was really like?

Collective memory is the image of a place and way of life handed down by word of mouth, communicated by folk-stories and ritual, and which becomes embedded in a community as received wisdom of how life was; the academic discipline of history, on the other hand, is more dispassionate; it is grounded in a study of how things actually were and is based on evidence. It seeks the truth, heedless of the consequences of finding it.

The audience for history is smaller, but perhaps more discerning. In many cultures the gap between collective memory and history is wide, but this gap may be particularly wide in Jewish culture. Yosef Hayim Yerushalmi has, as he put it, 'ruminated' on why this might be so, in his book *Zakhor.*[3] Traditional Judaism was full of injunctions to remember: "Remember the days of old, consider the years of ages past" (Deuteronomy 32;7); "Remember these things, O Jacob, for you, O Israel are my servant" (Isiah 44;21). Above all, remembrance was to be by ritual and recital, and it was to have the purpose of remembering God's interventions in history, and man's responses to them. This conception of the past is encapsulated in the Passover seder where, around the family table, ritual, liturgy and food are combined to transmit knowledge of the past from one generation to the next. The fundamental features of the past are: slavery – deliverance –and ultimate redemption. In Yerushalmi's understanding, this approach dominated Jewish attitudes to the past until the early nineteenth century when a small group of German Jews pioneered a very different approach, one based on *Wissenschaft* – science. A manifesto emerged from this group. It was published by Immanuel Wolf in 1822 and was entitled *On the concept of a Science of Judaism.* This academic and historical approach to the past is still quite new and confined to a minority. Writing in 1981, Yerushalmi said:

> As a professional Jewish historian I am a new creature in Jewish history. My lineage does not extend beyond the second decade of the nineteenth century, which makes me if not illegitimate, at least a parvenu within the long history of the Jews… I live within the ironic awareness that the very mode in which I delve into the Jewish past represents a decisive break with that past.[4]

Collective memory visualised shtetl life in nineteenth century Lithuania in two particular ways: the first was to see it as very traditional; the villages were small, the Jews very religiously observant, largely ignorant of secular culture and engaged in traditional craft and artisanal activity. They were poor. This is an image heavily indebted to the film *Fiddler on the Roof* and Topol's memorable depiction of the milkman Tevye, as well as from the striking pre-war photographs of Roman Vishniac. A second feature of collective memory is that the shtetl was a place of suffering and torment; it was a place where Jews were surrounded by antisemitism and where they felt unsafe. In collective memory life in Lithuania was a kind of enslavement, from which emigration to the new world offered hope of redemption.

In trying to understand what a shtetl was really like one is also faced by the fact that much of what we think we know comes from literary representations of the shtetl. Literature is always a difficult source for the historian. Thomas Hardy describes nineteenth century Dorset. Charles Dickens describes nineteenth century London. Their descriptions are vigorous and colourful, but the careful historian would hesitate to rely on them for an understanding of those societies, absent strong corroborating material. The substantial influence of literary descriptions in shaping our view of the shtetl is, in part, a reflection of the relative lack of other good sources, albeit there are some very interesting memoirs and travellers' accounts. But it also reflects the vibrancy and depth of the Yiddish literary tradition. This began about one hundred and fifty years ago with works by Sholem Y. Abramovitsh and Yitschok Yoel Linetski: *The Little Man, The Magic Ring, and Fishke the Lame.* It reached a golden age in the late nineteenth century with works by the mature Abramovitsh, Sholem Aleichem and Y.L. Peretz. In the early twentieth century there were great works by Dovid Bergelson and Der Nister and other works from talented writers such as Sholem Asch, Avrom Reyzn and Itshe Myer Vaysenterg. This literary tradition perhaps reached its peak with Isaac Bashevis Singer, who won the Nobel Prize for Literature in 1978.[5] Thereafter the tradition rapidly fell away. Not only was the world of the shtetl destroyed by the Holocaust but, with short delay, the literary tradition which described that world has also largely vanished: As Dan Miron puts it: "Isaac Bashevis [Singer] was the last great emissary of the kingdom of Yiddish to the world of Western culture in the second half of the twentieth century".[6]

Depictions of the shtetl in Yiddish literature are very vivid, affecting and often amusing. But they contain a considerable amount of mythology.

One way of illustrating the extent of this mythology is to compare and contrast the novelist Sholem Aleichem's literary depiction of the Ukrainian shtetl in which he was brought up (which was actually called Voronke but which, in his fiction, he called 'Kasrilevke') with the description of Voronke by his younger brother, Volf Rabinovitsh, who wrote a book of memoirs. The most striking difference is that the surrounding Christian world is largely absent from Sholem Aleichem's fictional descriptions but, in his memoirs, Volf remembers that the alley near the family home was called *dos kloyster gesl* (the church alley) and that rowdy groups of Jewish boys would throw dirt and stones into the charity box that was nailed up outside the church. In other words, the surrounding Christian world was ever-present, despite its absence from many literary depictions of the shtetl and from the imaginations of many of its inhabitants. [7]

Another way to demonstrate the extent to which the literary depictions of the shtetl can be misleading is by looking at the way Yiddish literature describes the geography of the shtetl, and comparing those descriptions with what we know from other sources. Typically, fiction writers describe the shtetl as being an all-Jewish environment, chaotically constructed, dirty and squalid. For example, Abramovitsh describes the fictional Kislon in this way:

> Kislon is an all-Jewish town in every detail. The builders' art is despised there, and its rules are never followed. Its houses do not stand upright…some of them tilt precariously and their roofs are buried in the ground…pigs come and wallow up to their ears in the mud and mire, for their benefit and pleasure, and make the place stink...[8]

It is possible to compare these descriptions to those in historical documents, city maps and memoirs. These suggest that the shtetl was usually constructed according to a careful town plan, and this did not segregate Jews from their Christian neighbours, indeed Christian religious establishments and Jewish public buildings stood side by side. Much of the fiction omits the Polish gentry almost entirely, tends to suggest that the towns were smaller than they were and banishes poor Lithuanians to the suburbs or to the surrounding villages: "The real geographic map gave way to an ahistorical map that was entirely Jewish - a densely populated shtetl, chaotic and disordered, surrounded by an alien and hostile population". [9]

Many works of Yiddish fiction employ the same plot devices in describing shtetl life. Often, there is a fire. In his short story "*Di nisrofim*" (Those who lost everything in a fire), Abramovitsh relates how the entire town of Kabtansk is reduced to ashes and in Mordkhe Spektor's *Reb Treytl* a detailed description of a shtetl fire occupies much of the first part of the novel. Of course, there were fires in the shtetlach, and not least because most of the buildings were constructed from wood. Sometimes these fires were terrifying and left an enduring impression on those who experienced them. For example, Hayim Bialik, the great Hebrew poet, described a fire he had experienced as a seven-year-old in his prose poem *Megilat ha-esh* (The Scroll of Fire). But fires were by no means as frequent as one might guess from reading the fiction. In truth, authors were putting the fire to metaphorical use. The fire was a metaphor for the vulnerability and proximity of disaster and, so Dan Miron suggests, "these fires are presented as reflections and duplications of the one great historical fire that lay at the very root of the Jewish concept and myth of *gålut* (exile): the fire that had destroyed both the First and Second temples of Jerusalem."[10]

Another favourite theme of novelists is of people departing from the shtetl; sometimes they depart singly or in couples, and at other times they depart in larger groups. For Abramovitsh, departing from the shtetl is a recurring plot device. He compares the people of Kabtansk to migratory birds. Once summer with its friendly weather and plentiful food is gone, they must leave their hometown. Scenes of exodus almost always appear in Sholem Aleichem's major works, including *Funem yarid* and *Blonzhende shtern*. Of course, people did leave the shtetlach regularly, but this hardly accounts for the way this subject dominates so much Yiddish fiction, or for the tone in which it is conveyed. Again, it seems there is something metaphorical going on. Departure seems to be a metaphor for alienation and uprootedness, a link in a chain of national disasters and "all of the links in that chain were understood as duplications, or at least approximations, of the original event the destruction of the temple and the fall of Jerusalem."[11]

Yiddish novelists also make great play with the unexpected visitor as a literary device. As Abramovitsh says in The *Brief Travels of Benjamin the Third,* when a stranger appears: "The townsfolk open their doors and windows to gawp and gape at the newcomer. Neighbours peering through open windows ask one another, "Ha! Now just who could that be? Now just where did he pop up from?" Visitors come in different guises: sometimes they are angels, and the visit is a kind of supernatural visitation; sometimes the visitor is an emissary from the Holy Land, perhaps a Sephardi, speaking a confusingly different kind of Hebrew and bearing dates as gifts; and sometimes the unexpected visitor was a Jew from western Europe, usually from Germany, who was emancipated. He was often treated with suspicion even if he turns out to be a prodigal son who had left the shtetl as a boy or young man, returning as an adult who had prospered in the West. The unexpected visitors also serve a metaphorical purpose. "They appear magically in the depressed, anxious shtetl and immediately hurry to the spot where their help is most urgently needed. They are, in fact, minor messiahs."[12] The metaphorical purpose of the unexpected visitor was to underline that the shtetl was in distress and unable to help itself; help was needed from the outside, be it from heaven, from the Land of Israel or from the enlightened West.

This leads to a rather difficult, quasi-philosophical point. The great Yiddish novelists described the world of the shtetl in a highly mythologised way; but, similarly, many Jews who lived in the shtetl also lived their lives in a highly mythologised way. Their lives cannot be summed up by what Dan Miron calls "the mere accumulation of metonymic physical, social, and behavioural truths". The point is made by looking at Abramovitsh's autobiographical novel *Shloyme Reb Khayims.* The autobiographical narrator discovers, aged eleven or twelve, that the trees he looks at in the Pale of Settlement are pines, birches and oaks, and not the fig trees, date trees, and olive trees of the bible. The shtetl housed Talmudic scholars and experts in bible studies, but also many who were uninterested in the Talmud and halachic studies. Some of the better streets in the town were actually owned by people who were not Jewish and who, as weavers, produced the fabric that the Jewish inhabitants marketed. Shloyme came to realise that "he had been living in a Judaic, pseudo biblical dreamworld of memory and legends, of texts and myths, of chimeras and monsters, a world that had usurped reality, sucking the very marrow out of actual existence." [13] In other words, many of the great Yiddish writers, influenced by Western education, had come to see that much of the mental world of the inhabitants of the shtetl was encumbered by layers of myth and, by describing that mental world, they were - in one way - conveying an essential truth.

For all this, many novels set in the shtetl did offer a mythologised, romanticised picture of everyday life which has coloured the perception of subsequent generations, and perhaps misled them. Why did the novelists do this?

The first part of the answer is that, for the most part, novelists wrote at a time when the shtetl was already in decline, and they wrote nostalgically. The shtetl enjoyed a kind of 'golden age' between the third partition of Poland in 1795 and about 1830.[14] The 'golden age' existed because the tsars of that time were relatively enlightened. Catherine the Great said:

> It goes without saying that Jewish communities dwelling in the towns and lands attached to the Russian Empire, will maintain all those freedoms which they now legally enjoy because her majesty's love of

> humanism makes it impossible to exclude them from the universal future commonwealth under her blessed rule ...[15]

Early nineteenth century Russian observers of the shtetl were impressed: Count Ivan Dolgorukov, touring newly acquired Russian lands with their teeming Jewish settlements, commented approvingly of one shtetl where you can find "anything you want" and praised the trading stalls of another where the Jews "trade in anything one can think of."[16]

The golden age of the shtetl also existed because relations between the Russian state and the Polish nobility, who owned many shtetlach, had not yet broken down; the deterioration in these relations accelerated following the Polish revolt of 1830. By the late nineteenth century, the Tsars' conservative ideology, and their disdain for Polish nobility, led them to blame the Jews for social tensions, particularly those that followed the emancipation of the serfs in 1861. In 1882 many hundred shtetlach were reclassified as villages as a way of trying to force the departure of the Jewish inhabitants who were no longer permitted to reside in rural and semi-rural communities. Jews therefore had to move to bigger towns and cities. This is precisely what happens to Sholem Aleichem's Tevye. Russian nationalism had turned the shtetl into a backward and impoverished place. But it was in the mid to late nineteenth century that the Yiddish literary tradition really got into its stride. By the time the great Yiddish writers wrote, the shtetl had seen much better days and nostalgia infused much of their writing.

One also needs to appreciate that for the most part Yiddish writers were *Maskilim.* A 'Maskil' is a term used to describe a Jewish person of central or eastern European background who was a follower of the Haskalah, a movement which was part of the European enlightenment. Maskilim had some exposure to western education; they might have travelled; they may have spoken one or two western languages; they loved learning; their horizons had been widened. As the *Jewish Encyclopedia* says: "'Maskil' usually denotes a self-taught Hebrew scholar with an imperfect knowledge of a living language (usually German), who represents the love of learning and the striving for culture awakened by [Moses] Mendelssohn and his disciples".[17] The Maskilim who wrote Yiddish fiction had emerged in their own lifetime from the world of the shtetl. They had complicated, sometimes contradictory, feelings about the world from which they had emerged. On one level, they felt a duty to open the eyes of those who continued to dwell in the shtetl about the insularity and backwardness of their existence. They therefore discouraged the use of Yiddish which they saw as a hindrance to

Jewish participation in wider culture, although they thought they might continue to use it, for a while, as a satirical self-destructive literature; they accepted religion as embodied in the Bible but rejected later rabbinic accretions; and they were very hostile to cultural mores that emphasised Jewish separateness. In short, the maskilic writers felt that the Jews of the shtetl should behave in society like educated middle-class Europeans but retain in heart and home the principles of Jewishness.[18] At another level, maskilic Yiddish writers felt a need to preserve through their writing a picture of a way of life they had known in their childhood and which they thought was at risk of disappearing. Abramovitsh is one of the best examples of this. He recognised that Jews of Eastern Europe were experiencing an alarmingly quick metamorphosis and felt a need to preserve an affectionate picture of that world through his writing, while remaining sensitive to its shortcomings. Nowhere is this better done than in his 'The Brief Travels of Benjamin the Third'. Other writers felt a need, perhaps boastfully, to depict the shtetl in a way which indicated how far they, as more educated men, had moved away from a world they thought primitive, and they used satire to achieve this.

By the late nineteenth century many literary treatments of the shtetl appealed to the nostalgia of their audience. Some of the Jews who moved to larger cities in the Russian empire, such as Kiev or Odessa, enjoyed nostalgic depictions of small towns which reminded them of home; some of the Jewish immigrants to America enjoyed the relatively unchallenging and nostalgic sentiments of some literary depictions which reminded them of the old country. After the Holocaust, there were various attempts to memorialise what was then a vanished world; perhaps some of the best examples of this are the stories and accounts assembled by S.Y. Agnon between 1945 and 1965. These depict the world of his shtetl Buczacz, which was the source of much of his inspiration, but which had been destroyed in 1941.

There are not very many memoirs that describe shtetl life in all its subtle complexity. One of the earliest, and most remarkable, is the autobiography of Solomon Maimon.[19] Maimon's work is described in George Eliot's *Daniel Deronda* as "that wonderful piece of autobiography", and we know that contemporary readers included Goethe, Hegel and Schiller. Solomon Maimon was born in 1753 in Żukowy Borek, a small town on a tributary of the Niemen River, near the city of Mirz in what was then the Polish-Lithuanian Commonwealth. His autobiography was published in Berlin, in two volumes, in 1792 and 1793. Maimon grew up as the grandchild of a Jewish leaseholder of the leading Polish-Lithuanian aristocrat Prince Radziwill. His background was traditional and observant; but he was prodigiously clever. He developed a very keen interest in the work of Moses Maimonides, particularly his *Guide for The Perplexed* written in about 1190. Young Solomon was so enthused by Maimonides' work that, as a mark of respect, he decided to adopt his surname. A discussion of Maimonides's work occupies a central place in Solomon Maimon's autobiography. Solomon Maimon travelled to Germany, became acquainted with Moses Mendelssohn and other figures in the Jewish enlightenment movement and became, through self-education, an important figure in philosophical circles. Immanuel Kant said of him that "none of my critics understood me and the main questions so well as Herr Maimon". Much of his autobiography continues to be of interest to philosophers, but it also provides an insight into many aspects of growing up in a shtetl, at a time when the shtetl was still functioning reasonably well.

The autobiography needs to be read with care because part of Maimon's purpose was to emphasise his achievement in escaping a very poverty-stricken and bleak background. Nonetheless, and among many other things, Maimon gives an insight into antisemitism that the family experienced, when a local priest, who he describes as a drunkard and ignorant simpleton, disingenuously accused his grandfather of murdering a Christian, as a way to extract revenge for the fact that Maimon's grandfather had decided to stop allowing the priest to have drinks on credit because he never paid for them.[20] Maimon also paints a vivid picture of the Polish nobility in his district, particularly Prince Radziwill: "Because his education had been neglected and he had no schooling of any kind he was one of the most depraved princes who ever lived. He had no constructive occupations and this, in turn, led him to become a devotee of alcohol, under the influence of which he committed the most senseless and insane acts."[21] Maimon vividly describes the poverty and squalor of the home of the leaseholder where he first worked as a tutor: "a sooty shack, blackened inside and out, with no chimney".[22] He also eloquently describes his journey to Germany and first encounters with members of the Jewish community there.[23]

Another valuable source of information about shtetl life is the so-called 'Yizkor' books. These are memorial books commemorating a specific Jewish community destroyed during the Holocaust. They are designed to be narrowly focussed on the experience of a particular place, and are often published by former residents of that place, or *landsmanshaft* societies. Most Yizkor books are written in Yiddish or Hebrew. The first Yizkor book was about the Jewish community of Lodz and was produced in New York City in 1943. More than 900 Yizkor books have since been produced. Most

Yizkor books were published in very limited quantities, but many of them have now been translated into English and are available online. In 1994 the Jewish family history website, JewishGen, established a Yizkor Book Project to make the contents of Yizkor books more accessible by translating them into English and compiling an index of names of victims and others mentioned in the books. Yizkor books are designed as memorials rather than works of history but can be very useful because they provide detailed information about particular places which are otherwise difficult to find out about.[24]

There is a Yizkor book about Pikeliai, but it is short. It tells us that Jews first settled in Pikeliai in the late eighteenth century; that at that time about two-thirds of Pikeliai was Jewish and that it supported a well-respected yeshiva; it says there was substantial emigration before the First World War, and a strong Zionist movement; it goes on to say that the Jews were exiled deep into Russia at the beginning of the First World War; it lists a number of distinguished residents. It concludes by describing the mass murder of Pikeliai Jews at Mažeikiai on 9 August 1941, which destroyed the entire community. There are few other documentary materials about Pikeliai. In trying to understand what life there was like in the last third of the nineteenth century, one has no real alternative but to infer what one can from the extensive documentary materials that exist about other shtetlach in the former Polish-Lithuanian Commonwealth.

We can be reasonably clear about what a shtetl looked like. At its centre was a market square. On one side of the square there was a Catholic church, built by the local landlord; it was a symbol of primacy. Many of the other buildings near the centre were owned by members of the Jewish community. There were synagogues, Jewish schools, *mikvot* (ritual baths), cemeteries and inns. Many Jews lived near the centre of the shtetl, and on the market square. For example, a study by Jerzy Motylewicz of an area called Przemyśl-Sanok, which was in the Pale of Settlement and is now in south-eastern Poland, shows that in the six towns he studied Jews occupied 119 of the 208 houses on the market square.[25] At the centre of the market square there were trading stalls, which were usually built of stone in the form of an arcade, imitating European market square galleries. The Jews tended generally to live interspersed with their Christian neighbours – there were no ghettos, as such. The ground floor and upper stories of Jewish homes were usually built of wood and reflected the fact that many Jews combined rural and urban activities. Many kept cows and goats so as to provide milk, cream, butter and cheese for their family, and for sale. And often the she-goat would share the same space as the family, an arrangement described in stories by Isaac Bashevis Singer and Shmuel Yosef Agnon. It seems that poor Jews were as poor as the poor Christian peasants in the shtetl, but Jews had proportionately more houses in unsatisfactory condition. About fifty per cent of their houses were unsatisfactory; and this compares with about one third of houses owned by Christians which were unsatisfactory.[26]

Middle class Jewish houses were rather different from those of their Christian neighbours in that they had often been adapted for business. The front room on the ground floor might serve as an inn, store or artisan's shop while the cellars were made of stone and served as a year-round refrigerator to preserve milk, cream and cheese. Many Jewish middle-class homes had been extended. Home improvement was one of the few possible investments in a world where Jews were prohibited from buying land or investing in other kinds of asset. Over time, therefore, Jewish middle-class homes tended to become the best houses in the shtetl. One of the sources for this is rather unlikely, namely the Russian military administration. Before army barracks were built from the late 1870s onwards, shtetl dwellers had the obligation to accommodate Russian soldiers – an obligation which was called 'quarter duty'. The Russian military strongly preferred to put up their men in Jewish homes because they were more comfortable. For example, Avrum Epelboim was a guild merchant from Vasylkiv. He housed part of a Russian sapper brigade. When he needed to renovate his home, he asked the military to move out, temporarily. They refused, making clear they did not want to be boarded in a "dark and uncosy inn" and that they found Epelboim's house much better![27]

Taverns were a major feature of the landscape of the shtetl. From the sixteenth century onwards, magnates granted Jews the right to produce and sell liquor, a right known as a *propinacja.* So many Jews became involved in the liquor trade that it came to be seen as the Jewish trade, par excellence. It has been estimated that at the time of the Third Partition of Poland in 1795 about 85 per cent of Jews permanently residing in the rural areas of eastern Poland were involved in tavern keeping.[28] Over the following century the Russian state became ever more dependent on income derived from selling liquor monopoly licences, to the extent that by the mid-1890s liquor trade revenues yielded a staggering 25 percent of Russia's annual budget.[29] Taverns were everywhere in the shtetl, and on the roads outside it. Some were drive-in: there would be big gates on the ground floor or a fenced-in adjacent yard into which a traveller could drive. There, the tavernkeeper's family would unharness the horses and unload the wagon. This served as a hostel for travellers, particularly for travelling merchants.

Other taverns were not drive-in, and simply provided drinks and snacks to local people. Over the course of the nineteenth century Russian Tsars increasingly attacked Jewish involvement in the liquor trade, harnessing the antisemitic trope that Jews corrupted the Russian peasantry by making them drunk. This culminated in introduction of a state monopoly on the liquor trade in 1894, which made several hundred thousand Jews destitute and contributed very considerably to the impoverishment of the shtetl.[30]

Many observers commented on the poor quality of the roads in and around the shtetl, particularly remarking on how muddy and pot-holed they were. A Russian army officer observed:

> Starokostyantyniv is dirty beyond any measure…to drive through the streets of the town is a real challenge, as there is no pavement. Stones once paving the road have long sunk into the soil. When it is raining, they do nothing but prevent movement." And Russian clerks wrote that: "it is extremely difficult to move when it is raining, impossible to move along the streets, the pits are filled with refuse."[31]

Those who observed the shtetl from the outside were often struck by the apparent strength of the Jewish family unit. People often married very young, particularly if they came from wealthy families. Solomon Maimon, for example, married at the age of 11 and became a father at the age of 14. Jews often lived in extended family units. There was a tradition of providing the son-in-law with board and lodging, a tradition known in Yiddish as *kest.* If he was a Talmudic scholar of any merit this was thought to reflect credit on the wider family. Jews had children out of wedlock much less frequently than their Christian neighbours. It has been estimated that in the 1870s out of every hundred new-born children, 4 per cent of Catholic babies were born out of wedlock, 3.4 percent of Protestant babies were born out of wedlock, and 3 per cent of Eastern Orthodox babies were born out of wedlock. The comparative figure for Jewish babies is that no more than 0.4 per cent of them were born out of wedlock.[32] Jews also seem to have had more children than their Christian neighbours. And Jewish women are often thought to have been more independent than their gentile neighbours. As well as raising children and keeping the house in order, they were often involved in running commercial activities from the home, such as selling groceries and liquor.[33] It seems that, in general terms, the Jewish family unit became less strong in the later nineteenth century. This was reflected in increasing rates of divorce, in the increasing numbers of *agunot* (abandoned women, who are unable to obtain a Jewish bill of divorce) and in the widespread feeling that domestic violence was becoming more prevalent. The weakening of the Jewish family unit stemmed, ultimately if indirectly, from policies of the Russian authorities. For example, they had abolished the *kahal* in 1844, which diminished the ability of Jewish communal elders to mediate in family conflicts. They had also sought to move trade out of the shtetl and into bigger towns, which in turn led to many Jewish men having to travel more for their business, with predictable consequences. It also led to migration from the shtetl to larger towns, and all the evidence indicates that divorce was far more common there than in the shtetl.

Jewish economic activity in the shtetl centred on trade. Trade was a niche which the Polish and Russian authorities had left open to Jews, in a way which might be compared to the way medieval Catholic Europe left a gap for Jews to be involved in moneylending.[34] Jewish approach to trade was characterised by energy. The Russian ethnographer Ivan Aksakov observed:

> Jews added to trade a particularly febrile agitation – they ran, hustled and bustled, accompanying each word with quick gesticulations... on each and every step they stop a visitor and offer him merchandise.[35]

The approach was also thought to be characterised by a willingness to do a reasonable deal, as opposed to holding out for the very best deal; in this, they were perhaps influenced by the wisdom of chapter 15 of the Book of Proverbs: "Better a little with the fear of the Lord than great wealth with turmoil". Observers were struck by the extraordinary variety of goods offered by Jewish traders. We know, for example, that in the early nineteenth century and in the relatively insignificant shtetl of Letychiv one could find locally produced lard, wax, soap, incense, clay and wooden utensils and also multi-coloured ribbons and female adornments. But this remote place also offered German wines from Gdansk and Leipzig, English beer, and French cognacs and champagne. In the shtetl economy, trade was overwhelmingly in the hands of Jews. In the 1850s, for example, Countess Radziwill considered that Jews had a tenfold predominance in trade around her family estates; but many of the customers of the Jewish tradesmen were the local Christian Lithuanians and indeed Jewish tradesmen arranged their business to fit with Christian religious holidays. In Letychiv, for example, there were five annual fairs and all of them fell on Eastern Orthodox holidays. In the course of the nineteenth century the Russian state became ever more hostile to trade in general and to Jewish involvement in it. Manufacturing and agriculture were considered preferable. The Russian state confiscated many shtetlach from Polish magnates and sought to conflate Jews with shady business practice. [36] Jewish trade diminished and shtetl life became more poverty stricken and precarious.

Jewish life in the shtetl was heavily dominated by religious observance. There were three key institutions. The first was the synagogue. It was intended as the shtetl's replica of the Temple in Jerusalem. Supporting the Holy Ark were two wooden pillars which symbolised the Yakhin and the Boaz, the columns guarding the Holy of Holies in the Temple in Jerusalem which the Romans destroyed in 70 CE; and the shtetl synagogue had a seven-branch candelabra and a wooden decalogue (the Ten Commandments) above the Ark further to remind worshippers of the Temple in Jerusalem. Prayers of at least a *minyan* (a quorum of ten men) were offered three times a day. But the synagogue also served as a meeting place where all manner of subjects might be discussed. As Abramovitsh said:

> Domestic secrets, the politics of Istanbul, the Sultan, the Austrian Kaiser, high finance, Rothschild's fortunes…were taken up in due order by a special committee of honourable and venerable Jews who [sat] there all the live-long day.[37]

The second key religious institution in the shtetl was the *mikveh* (pool or ritual bath). It was 'key' in a way in which the synagogue was not, namely that while prayer could be conducted anywhere, without a *mikveh* for the purpose of post-menstrual cleansing, Jewish women could not be sexually available to their husbands and therefore could not comply with the biblical commandment to "go forth and multiply". And the steam bath for men was not just a way of cleansing themselves but was also a way for them to fraternise on close terms with other Jewish men of the shtetl. The last key religious institution of the shtetl was the Jewish cemetery. Without this, Jews could not bury their dead and instead had to rely on the burial services of other communities, which was inconvenient and expensive, and placed a Jewish community in a state of subservience. Dan Miron comments on the way that Yiddish novelists often describe the cemetery, which he regards as a "metonymy available to those writers who regarded the shtetl itself as moribund".[38]

Celebration of the Sabbath and Jewish festivals was an important part of Jewish life in the shtetl. Elie Wiesel, the Romanian-born American Jewish writer and Nobel laureate reminisced about the importance of the Sabbath in his brief memoir *The World of the Shtetl*.[39] He emphasises how it contrasted markedly with the rest of the week: "*Shabbat* [the sabbath] helped people endure the other six days of the week, days that were often grey and dark and heavy with sorrow and anxiety". The coming of the Sabbath was much anticipated, with the housewife preparing special foods for the Sabbath meal, the men hurriedly concluding business, and rushing to the ritual bath, and the *shammes* [beadle] going from store to store and home to home shouting: "Jews, ready yourselves for the Sabbath!" Elie Wiesel also emphasised the communal solidarity and generosity to strangers which characterised the Sabbath: "It was forbidden to allow anyone to be alone for the *Shabbat* meal. Often, people would fight over a visitor. It was an honour to invite him or her to their table. I myself can hardly remember a Shabbat without an honoured guest in our home". The Jewish religious holidays marked the passing of the seasons: the early autumn saw the Jewish New Year and Yom Kippur; this gave way to the wetter, later autumn, with Sukkot and the bible readings of Genesis. The winter snows were associated with Hannukah and the readings from Exodus. Spring was associated with Purim and Passover. Shavuot marked the beginning of summer. Each holiday was associated with particular customs and moods: reflective and repentant in the case of Yom Kippur; joyful and celebratory in the case of Purim.

A longing for return to the Holy Land was a central part of shtetl existence and affected everyday activity. For example, Jews placed *kruzhki* – tin mugs or wooden charity boxes – on tables in their homes and on counters in their stores to collect charitable donations to support Holy Land communities. They illustrated communal books with images of mythological animals – including an ox, a leviathan and a deer – because these animals were thought likely to announce the redemption from exile and return to the Holy Land.

Many memoirs of shtetl life describe the emphasis placed on educating children in accordance with Jewish tradition, and they suggest there was a widespread and lifelong love of Jewish learning, and education generally. For example, Pauline Wengeroff, who was born in Babruysk in Belarus in 1833, looks back to her early childhood and describes how "we eagerly studied Pentateuch and the Prophets, for they gave us pride in our religion and its traditions and bound us to our people…My parents were God-fearing, deeply pious, and respectable people…Most of the day was spent on the study of Talmud, and only appointed hours were set aside for business…"[40] Elie Wiesel recalls the passion for learning in the shtetl in which he lived during his childhood: "I never saw my father or any of my uncles go anywhere without a book under their arms. What was the worst insult hurled at a person? That he is an *am-haretz*, an ignoramus. Who is respected? A *talmid khakham*, a scholar".[41]

Most Jewish boys attended a *heder* (elementary Jewish school) from the age of about five until thirteen. There, they learned the Hebrew alphabet, before progressing to the Pentateuch and Rashi's basic commentary and then to certain parts of the Talmud with traditional commentaries. After the age of thirteen the student moved on to deeper study of the Talmud, with guidance from a Talmudic scholar. This was designed to equip him for self-study or admission to one of the *yeshivot*. Most Jewish girls were educated at home, although a small number were studying in a *heder* by the end of the nineteenth century. There were several distinguished Lithuanian *yeshivot* including, particularly, at those towns known in Yiddish as Volozhin, Telz, Slobodka, Ponovez, Radin and Lida. Many of these had undergone far-reaching reforms in the course of the nineteenth century. R. Hayyim of Volozhin transformed and revitalised the Lithuanian yeshiva world: he was responsible for doing away with an old arrangement in which the yeshiva student had been housed and clothed by local families and instead arranged for benefactors to endow the yeshiva itself so that it could be responsible for students' board and lodging. R. Hayyim also discarded the old teaching system known as *pilpul*. This was a method of studying the Talmud through intense textual analysis in an attempt to explain conceptual differences or in an attempt to reconcile apparent contradictions presented from contrasting readings of different texts. In the eyes of its critics, *pilpul* had become a kind of casuistic hair-splitting. Solomon Maimon was deeply scornful:

> Fatuous investigations are pursued with the greatest mental exertions imaginable. For example: How many white hairs can a *red* cow have and still be a *red* cow?...Is it permissible to kill a louse or a flea on the Sabbath? (The former is allowed; the latter is a deadly sin.)[42]

R. Hayyim's innovation was to make the purpose of yeshiva study the attainment of true understanding of Talmudic texts by logical reasoning, without resort to seemingly absurd hair-splitting.

A particular feature of shtetl life was that Jews tended to conduct everyday communication with each other in their own language, Yiddish. Hebrew was reserved for worship and Jewish study. Yiddish is written in the Hebrew alphabet but its orthography (which is to say, the conventions as to how it is written, including its spelling, hyphenation and punctuation) is very different from Hebrew. For example, in Hebrew many vowels are represented only optionally by using a system of dots and points called *niqqud,* whereas Yiddish uses letters to represent all vowels. Yiddish is thought to have originated in the ninth century, although the first surviving written references date from the twelfth century. It emerged from Jews living in the Rhineland (particularly Mainz) and in the Palatinate (particularly Worms and Speyer). As a result of the twelfth century expulsion of Jews from German lands, and their subsequent emigration eastwards into Slavic speaking areas of central Europe, Yiddish gradually became isolated from mainstream varieties of the German language and developed organically, absorbing vocabulary and structural characteristics from Hebrew and Aramaic as well as from surrounding Slavic languages. The exact process by which this happened, and whether Yiddish should today properly be regarded as a German dialect, are subjects which remain hotly contested by scholars.[43] What is irrefutable is that the Yiddish language is principally a synthesis of German, Hebrew and Aramaic. For example: the word for 'sun' (*zun*) comes from German, the word for 'moon' (*levone*) comes from Hebrew and the word for 'probably' comes from Aramaic (*mistame*). Yiddish has a way of taking words from its donor languages and fine tuning them so as to give them a very particular Jewish meaning. For example, *gest* (from German) are any kind of guests, *orkhim* (from Hebrew) are poor visitors who need to be given Sabbath or Jewish holiday hospitality and *ushpizn* (from Aramaic) are the seven biblical figures who are believed in Jewish mysticism to visit the Sukkah during the festival of Sukkot, or the feast of Tabernacles.[44] The influence of Slavic languages on Yiddish reflects the everyday encounters between Jews and locals, and shows how boisterous those encounters could be. There is, for example, a remarkably rich variety of options for describing people as idiots and losers, such as: a *kaleke*, a *shlak*, a *parshivets*, a *bolvan*, a *yolep*, a *pentiukh*, a *propn*, a *zhlob*, and a *khlop.* All these words entered Yiddish from the Slavic world.[45]

Yiddish has two major forms, which are Western Yiddish and Eastern Yiddish. Western Yiddish was spoken west of the German-Polish border of 1939 and covered Holland, Alsace-Lorraine, Switzerland and most of Germany. Eastern Yiddish was spoken to the east of that line and had three principal dialects: North-Eastern Yiddish (Lithuanian-Belorussian), Central Yiddish (Polish-Galician-Eastern Hungarian) and South-Eastern Yiddish (Ukrainian-Romanian). The greatest difference between these dialects is in the sound of the vowels, although there are also differences in vocabulary and grammar. The use of Western Yiddish was in steep decline before the Second World War, as the communities which had used it rapidly acculturated; Eastern Yiddish, on the other hand, was still widely used. In 2012 the Center for Applied Linguistics based in Washington D.C. estimated that in 1939 the number of Yiddish speakers in the world was about 11 million. Since then, the number of native Yiddish speakers has fallen precipitously. It is thought that about 85 per cent of the approximately six million Jews murdered in the Holocaust were native Yiddish speakers. Post-war Soviet society strongly repressed the use of Yiddish. Zionists and the State of Israel generally disdained Yiddish as a worn-out relic of diaspora existence and instead promoted use of modern Hebrew, not least because this was a more neutral language choice for post-war Jewish immigrants to Israel from Middle-Eastern and north African countries. Jewish emigrants from eastern Europe to advanced economies in Europe and the new world tended to drop Yiddish in favour of the language of their host country as part of their rapid acculturation. Research by Rutgers University suggests that today there are only about 600,000 native speakers in the world, the majority of whom are *Haredi*, or ultra-orthodox.

The significance of the fact that Jews of the shtetl spoke Yiddish was twofold: first, it reinforced their sense of having a distinct identity as Jews, and this separated them from their neighbours; speaking Yiddish also gave many of them a facility with languages. They anyway had Hebrew from their religious devotions and the step from Yiddish to German was a relatively minor one. This was particularly the case in somewhere like Pikeliai, which was only a short distance from the Baltic ports with their substantial ethnic German populations and communities of Jews for whom German was their first language. Knowledge of German opened vistas to a wider world.

Jews in the shtetl had daily interactions with other Jews from their shtetl and they also met Jews from the surrounding area. In contrast with how shtetl life is depicted in many novels, most Jews also encountered gentiles. They might meet the local magnate who leased them property or other rights; they might encounter various faces of the Russian bureaucracy; from time to time Russian soldiers might be billeted in their midst; and they were likely to encounter local Lithuanians in the markets, the streets and indeed in the tavern. For most of the nineteenth century the relations between Jews and gentiles, while characterised by mutual suspicion and antipathy, did not lead to significant organised violence against Jews. Across the Pale of Settlement generally there was a period of relative peace for Jews until the 1880s when pogroms flared in the south-eastern part of the Pale, destroying 100,000 Jewish businesses, ruining 60,000 families, leaving 20,000 homeless, causing 10,000 rubles' worth of damage and leaving several dozen dead.[46] The calm that prevailed in Jewish-gentile relations in the nineteenth century Pale before the pogroms of the early 1880s was underpinned by a sense that, if attacked, Jews would fight back. They would give as good as they got. As Yohanan Petrovsky-Shtern puts it: "Violence put Jews on an equal footing with Christians long before any civil rights did, precisely because Jews in the shtetl were adamant about defending their own cultural space, independence, and dignity."[47] Samson the Nazarite explains how to deal with violence in Zev Jabotinsky's novel of the same name: "When they beat you with a bat, grab a real bat, not a reed one."[48] Self-evidently, by the early 1880s the threat of reciprocal violence was no longer effective in procuring peace for Jews of the shtetl. The shtetl had changed in a number of rather fundamental ways in the later nineteenth century.

Collective memory and literary fiction sometimes obscure the fact that life in the shtetl was undergoing very significant change in the course of the nineteenth century.

One of the fundamental causes of change was the *'Haskalah'*, the Jewish enlightenment. As has been said, devotees of this movement were known as '*Maskilim*'. The Haskalah can perhaps best be viewed as an extension of the eighteenth-century European enlightenment. Its aims were both to reform Jewish custom and also to reform the relationship between the Jewish world and Russian government and society. Haskalah favoured some acculturation, but strongly opposed full assimilation. It sought the continued existence of a distinct Jewish community, but one which was updated and reformed and which, it was hoped, would therefore have easier interaction with surrounding society. The origins of nineteenth-century Lithuanian Haskalah lay in the so-called 'early Haskalah'. This was an eighteenth-century movement. It consisted of some dozens of Jewish individuals, dispersed across Europe, who developed an interest in medieval Jewish philosophical and scientific literature as well as in eighteenth-century Enlightenment literature. Mendel Lefin (1749-1826) was one such man. He was born in Podolia (in the eastern part of Galicia), then under Polish rule, but spent time in Berlin, White Russia and other parts of Galicia. He wrote books, distributed translations of scientific material from European languages, popularised key Jewish texts, and submitted memoranda to the various authorities.[49] His two-fold objective appears to have been the reform of eastern European Jewry and its integration into wider society. The 'early Haskalah' prepared the ground for the so-called 'Berlin Haskalah', which developed in the late eighteenth century. A detailed expression of their outlook is to be found in 'Words of Peace and Truth' of

1782, by Naftali Hirz Wessely.[50] He drew a distinction between the Torah of God and the Torah of Man. The Torah of God is about divine revelation; it includes the Ten Commandments and is intended solely for Jews. By contrast, The Torah of Man is derived from human reason, is universal and includes all philosophy and science. Jews of his day had been cut off from the Torah of Man by discrimination and by persecution, but he was hopeful that more liberal government policy (such as the Edict of Tolerance issued by Joseph II in 1781) portended a brighter future. It was incumbent on Jews to respond by being willing to integrate into the social, economic and cultural life of their surroundings.

One of the central characters of the Berlin Haskalah was Moses Mendelssohn. He arrived in Berlin as a poor student. In 1750, aged 21, he was hired by Isaac Bernard, a wealthy silk merchant, as tutor for his son. But, Mendelssohn's real interest was in expanding his own intellectual horizons. He taught himself Latin, Greek, French and English; and his reading ranged across Spinoza, Cicero, Euclid, Aristotle, Plato, Montesquieu and Voltaire. Soon he came to befriend Gotthold Ephraim Lessing, playwright and journalist, and Friedrich Nicolai, bookseller and publisher. This group was thoroughly committed to the values of the enlightenment. Mendelssohn published a number of books, including *Letters on Sentiment* (1755) and *Phaidon, or The Immortality of the Soul in Three Dialogues* (1767). Mendelssohn became something of a celebrity, and intellectuals began to visit him from all over Europe. His renown was such that a zealous Protestant deacon from Zurich called Johann Caspar Lavater felt a religious compulsion to try to convert Mendelssohn to Christianity. He failed, but the experience caused Mendelssohn to reflect more deeply about reform of Jewish custom and about Jewish interaction with the wider world. He urged Jews to "Adopt the habits and constitution of the land in which you live but retain the religion of your forefathers". He translated the Psalms and the Pentateuch with the hope, which was realised, that this would bring about a revival of Hebrew poetry and literature. Mendelssohn strongly contended that Judaism had no tenets of faith that were inconsistent with human reason. His life appeared to embody the Jewish enlightenment. He was a Jew who was deeply learned in Jewish sources, but he was also a serious philosopher who was widely respected by prominent figures in the European enlightenment.[51]

Moses Mendelssohn deeply influenced the emergence of Haskalah in Russian-controlled parts of eastern Europe, including in Lithuania. Unsurprisingly, interest in Haskalah was always limited to relatively few people in Lithuania, and those of a strongly intellectual disposition. They were principally in larger urban centres such as Vilnius; such people were autodidacts.

Scholars have tended to divide the Lithuanian Haskalah into three phases: the first phase lasted from the early nineteenth century until the 1840s; the second phase lasted from the 1840s until 1855; and the third phase lasted from 1855 until the advent of the Jewish nationalist movement in the 1880s.

The first phase was characterised by a gradual emergence of interest in the ideas of the Berlin Haskalah in Vilnius and in up to thirty small centres spread across the Pale of Settlement. The ideas may have entered Lithuania from a handful of returning medical students who had trained in Italy, principally in the University of Padua, and from others who had received their training in Germany, particularly at the medical school in Frankfurt-am-Oder.[52] The spread of these ideas was facilitated by the relatively sympathetic attitude of the famous Vilnius rabbi and teacher known as the 'Vilna Gaon'. He had not forbidden the "external wisdom", and indeed had himself composed works on algebra, geometry and trigonometry as well as works about the geography of the Holy Land.[53] The second phase was inaugurated by appeals by *Maskilim* to the Russian authorities to institute reforms in Jewish life. In 1840 the Russian Minister of the Interior ordered the establishment of six district commissions in the Pale of Settlement to discuss reforms in education and culture. The policy was led by Serge Uvarov. He proposed that 'modern' Jewish schools be established with a view to reforming Jewish practice and particularly to diminish what he characterised as 'the damaging influence of the Talmud'. The proposals were controversial but some government schools were established in 1844. The languages of instruction were Russian and German and the first administrator was the well-known educationalist Max Lilienthal. Lilienthal became disillusioned, suspecting that the real, if undeclared, intention of the Russian government was to promote conversion. The numbers who attended such schools were small but their establishment did mean that, for the first time, some Jewish children were exposed to modern schooling. A third phase of the Lithuanian Haskalah began with the coronation of Tsar Alexander II in 1856. Initially, he was reform-minded. For example, he allowed Jews who the authorities regarded as 'useful' to live outside the Pale of Settlement. Such people included graduates of universities and technical colleges. The Maskilim regarded this as significant progress in that it appeared to give state recognition and approval to Jews who had been generally educated and to those who had chosen productive occupations. But these early hopes were to be disappointed. By the 1870s it had become clear that the Russian authorities were not going to remove the substantial body of discriminatory legislation against Jews or to rein in the rising wave of antisemitism. By then, Haskalah as a movement seemed to be losing momentum and interest shifted to Jewish nationalism. Many of the leading Maskilim and intellectuals became involved in Hibat Tsiyon and Hovevey Tsiyon, proto-Zionist movements that regarded emigration to Eretz Yisrael as the solution to the Jewish problem. This turn away from Haskalah is well-described by Moses Leib Lilienblum. Writing in 1881, in the wake of the pogroms, he says:

> My studies seemed a sin against my unfortunate people. I was thinking of entering the university... For years I had striven towards this. But now I am convinced that our misfortune is not the lack of general education but that we are aliens. We will still be aliens when we will be stuffed with education as a pomegranate is with seeds. I terminated my studies and with great dedication I began to prepare myself for my new ideal.[54]

The extent to which Haskalah had influence in a small community like Pikeliai is now unknowable. But it seems entirely plausible to suppose that Haskalah made inroads there, as it certainly did in other small shtetlach in northern and central Lithuania. In the first place this was because it was in the nature of Haskalah that it could be taken up by individuals or small groups in remote communities provided they had an enquiring mind and willingness to look beyond the religious books which were traditionally studied. The process is well described by Moses Leib Lilienblum, before his post-pogrom disillusion set in:

> I was weary and exhausted from studying the Talmud, its disputations and various absurdities. When I heard of something new that was rational, I was drawn to it. Every Haskalah book I came upon, I devoured like the fruits of summer...I had no teacher or guide in studying the literature of the Haskalah. In my town I was the first to show public interest in the Haskalah...Undiscriminating, I read everything that came into my hands...[55]

The ability of the Haskalah movement to exert influence in small communities was facilitated by its extensive use of the press. The Maskilim were the first in the Jewish world to use the press widely to disseminate information and to exchange ideas. By the end of the eighteenth century the periodical *Hame'asef* began to spread ideas emanating from the Berlin Haskalah among smaller communities in Lithuania. It is thought that in the generations before World War 1, 86 Jewish periodicals appeared in Lithuania, compared to only 62 Lithuanian periodicals during the same period.[56] Some of these Jewish periodicals were in Hebrew, such as *Hamagid* and *Hamelitz,* while others, such as *Razvet* and *Voshkod,* were in Russian. Publishing houses in Vilnius, particularly that of the Romm family, published books on a variety of 'new' subjects including social criticism, poetry, popular science, philosophy, grammar, history and geography. Many Haskalah books were also published in Warsaw, Odessa and Lwow and these books were then brought into Lithuania. In the second half of the nineteenth century books and periodicals of the Haskalah were appearing in the markets and among the goods offered by pedlars in the small communities of northern Lithuania.

The Haskalah also influenced Jews in northern Lithuania because it was relatively close to the Baltic ports where the German language was widely spoken and where German culture flourished. Liepāja/Libau, Klaipėda/Memel and Kaliningrad/Konigsberg all had strong German communities. Konigsberg became one of the great centres of the Berlin Haskalah. Indeed, it was there that *Ha-Me'asef* was published for about two decades.

The influence of Haskalah manifested itself in a great variety of ways in small communities like Pikeliai. It affected the question of which language people used: the Maskilim encouraged use of Russian as the language of the state and also encouraged use of German as the language, par excellence, of the European enlightenment; they encouraged use of modern Hebrew to facilitate access to modern literature and poetry. Many of the Maskilim disdained Yiddish as a garbled dialect which was symptomatic of a decayed culture but, because Yiddish was the language of the lower social classes and of women, ironically there was no alternative for the Maskilim but to use Yiddish as their linguistic vehicle for trying to persuade people not to use Yiddish. Haskalah influence affected the clothes people wore: controversially, the Maskilim supported government policies that prohibited the wearing of traditional Jewish dress. Haskalah influence was felt in gender relations: traditionally, men had married at the age of about thirteen and had then immersed themselves in religious study, leaving their wives to run the home and to provide for the family by running business from home. The Maskilim favoured a domestic model on more mainstream Christian lines in which the men became economically productive, leaving women to run the home, while also receiving proper religious education. The

Maskilim strongly encouraged Jewish men to branch out from traditional Jewish occupations and to become involved in trades and to pursue careers in the liberal professions, albeit in a place as small as Pikeliai this would almost certainly require a move to a larger town. The Maskilim encouraged parents to educate their children along more secular lines and to modernise religious practice. The perception that there was an urgent need for this modernisation of Jewish life is brilliantly captured in the diaries of the leading Hebrew poet, Judah Leib Gordon (1831-1892):

> Can we really continue the same way of life by the waters of Europe and other countries that we led by the waters of Babylon? If the Talmud with its pedantry, with its overlapping additions and rabbinic commentaries, becomes a guide for our people, then we will be like those who follow the pillar of clouds in the night and we will wander bewildered in the world...Woe to the tenant of a house where the ceiling is cracked and the builder does not repair it, because it will eventually collapse...[57]

There was a double paradox at the heart of the Haskalah movement: the influence of the movement was powerful and multifaceted, yet its greatest promoters and enthusiasts were usually isolated and weak. Typically, Maskilim were impoverished intellectuals, who tried to eke out a living as private tutors, and the like. They sought influence for their views by alliance with the Jewish communal elite and the institutions of the state, but such alliances were inherently unstable because wealthy Jews had limited enthusiasm for Haskalah's objectives, while the state was not at all interested in a Jewish renaissance, but simply in creating productive and loyal subjects. A second paradox was that the Maskilim hoped that their modernising influence would revivify and modernise Jewish practice; they absolutely did not intend that it should lead to assimilation and yet many of the leading figures of Haskalah found that their children moved a long way from traditional Judaism and that they assimilated. This has led some commentators to observe that Haskalah was often a one generation experience.

In the mid-late nineteenth century shtetl life was also being changed in a variety of ways by economic developments within the Russian empire. Following the emancipation of the serfs in 1867 the economy of the Russian empire went through a process of rapid industrialisation, a process which accelerated between 1894 and the outbreak of the First World War. During that period, coal production increased by 306%, oil production by 65%, gold production by 43%, copper production by 375% and iron and steel production by 224%. There were associated developments in transportation. Railways were built and improved, and steamships came into operation. Some parts of the Russian empire became much more industrialised than others and pockets of great poverty remained. The Russian author Alexander Afanassiev described conditions he observed in the area around Kaunas in about 1870:

> The Jews live in terribly crowded conditions, sometimes several families in a single room. Filth, inside and out, is the hallmark of their houses. The families of the poor craftsmen eat nothing all day, until the father comes home with part of his takings.[58]

Throughout the nineteenth century much of Lithuania remained rural, and lightly industrialised. Nonetheless, Jews were disproportionately involved in such industry as there was. This involvement was both as owners and as employees. For example, we know that of the 69 factories operating in the Kaunas province in Lithuania in 1864, 48 (or 69 per cent) were owned by Jews; and we know that of the 66,132 Jews employed in the Kaunas province in 1897, a full 22,024 (or 33.3 %) were employed in crafts and industry. A further 26% of all Jews in employment were employed in trade, with a mere 4% employed in agriculture. Just how remarkable these figures are becomes apparent when they are contrasted with the employment patterns of Lithuanians, a full 73% of whom were employed in agriculture with a mere 7.6% in crafts and industry and only 0.6% in trade.[59] Sectors of the economy in which Jews were particularly active included shoemaking, tailoring, flax, timber, leather, pig bristles (unlikely as this sounds), and printing. Much of the demand came from the need to supply equipment to the Russian army, particularly uniforms and boots. There were two particular areas of economic activity in which earlier generations of Jews had been much involved, but which declined markedly in the nineteenth century. These were the manufacture and sale of vodka, from which the Russian government had sought to remove Jews by legislative action, and transportation and haulage which changed fundamentally because of the opening up of new means of transport. The many wayside inns which Jews had run now found themselves short of clientele.

As my great-grandfather Myer Scher passed through childhood and adolescence in the remote northern Lithuanian shtetl of Pikeliai he must have become aware that, not very far away in what is now Latvia, on the Baltic coast, there were communities of Jews living a rather different existence from that which was possible in Pikeliai and beginning to take advantage of Russia's rapid industrialisation and trade with the wider world. The largest and most sophisticated Jewish community on the Baltic coast was in Riga but that was about 170 kilometres away, and the transport connections were difficult. Libau, as it was called in German, or Liepāja as it was known in Latvian, was about 80 kilometres away and the connections were easier.

Liepāja is situated on the eastern Baltic coast, between Riga and Danzig, in the province of Courland. The Duchy of Courland came into existence in 1608, when it was under Polish suzerainty, and then came under Russian control in 1795, at a time when it had several thousand Jewish inhabitants. The Russian government discriminated against Jews in Courland. For example, Jews were taxed more heavily than their gentile neighbours and Jews were subjected to petty restrictions, such as the fact that their children were denied the right to play on the Liepāja sands. Nonetheless, the presence of Jews was tolerated because of their supposed commercial acumen and the value of their tax contributions. In the late nineteenth century, Russia invested heavily in developing Liepāja because it was a warm water port; unlike other Baltic ports such as Riga, ice did not make Liepāja unnavigable during winter months. The maritime opportunities for Liepāja hugely expanded in 1880 with the opening of a railway line between Liepāja and Romny (near Poltava in modern Ukraine). This line passed through, and had stations in, areas of dense Jewish population in the Pale of Settlement, as well as in agricultural areas of Russia. The Liepāja-Romny line also connected with the railway line that carried freight from Kiev to Moscow. The combination of being an ice-free deep-water port and having good railway connections made Liepāja economically significant.[60] [61]

The Jewish community of Liepāja grew slowly: in 1797, it was a mere 19. In the early nineteenth century Jews arrived from Germany. They were quite secular and spoke German as their first language. In the later nineteenth century there was a substantial influx of Jews from Lithuania and Russia. These Jews tended to speak Yiddish and to be more religious. In 1890, the Russian government issued its 'Regulations on Passports'. This permitted only those Jews whose families were registered in the census of 13 April 1835 to remain in the port of Liepāja. It meant that some 400 families who did not possess valid documents were expelled but, despite these banishments, the community continued to grow and in 1897 it numbered 9,454.[62]

Jews were heavily involved in the industry and trade of Liepāja. The principal export trades were horses, grain, eggs, timber and, increasingly, people. In 1902, Major William Evans-Gordon, the MP for Stepney in the East End of London, visited Liepāja as part of his efforts better to understand, so as to oppose, Jewish emigration from the Baltic to the East End of London. He gave evidence to the Royal Commission on Alien Immigration, in which he said:

> The commercial harbour [of Liepāja] is convenient, and is being much improved. A very large export trade is carried on from here in the produce of the country – grain, wood, eggs, etc. – and this is entirely in the hands of Jewish merchants.[63]

It seems, on the basis of oral testimony given by one of my relations who is no longer alive, that in about 1890 Myer Scher was working in the small town of Vainode in what is now Latvia, just the other side of the border with Lithuania. He would then have been in his early twenties. He was working for a man called Joel Baskin, who lived in Liepāja and ran a business there. Joel was the uncle of the woman who was to become Myer's wife. A couple of points are intriguing about these circumstances: first, that Vainode was located on the Liepāja-Romny railway line, indeed that Vainode appears to have grown up around the railway station; and, secondly, that Myer was probably unable to live in Liepāja at this time as a consequence of the Regulations on Passports of 1890, which would have excluded him. These circumstances cast an interesting side-light on the way that life in Pikeliai, indeed shtetl life more generally, was evolving in the late nineteenth century. Perhaps one needs to think of the shtetl not just as poverty-stricken, remote and stuck in its ways (at one level, it was all those things), but also as occupying a hinterland to thriving port cities and these gave access to a wider world of learning and commercial opportunity.

Notes

1 Steven T. Katz, *The Shtetl: New Evaluations* (NYU Press, 2009), pp. 1–6.
2 Steven T. Katz, p. 7.
3 Yosef Hayim Yerushalmi, *Zakhor: Jewish History and Jewish Memory* (University of Washington Press, 2011).
4 Yerushalmi. Page 81.
5 Dan Miron, *The Image of the Shtetl and Other Studies of Modern Jewish Literary Imagination* (Syracuse University Press, 2000), p. 335.
6 Miron, p. 336.
7 Miron, pp. 1–5.

8 Steven T. Katz, pp. 179–92.
9 Steven T. Katz, p. 191.
10 Miron, p. 18.
11 Miron, p. 22.
12 Miron, p. 31.
13 Miron, p. 47.
14 Yohanan Petrovsky-Shtern, *The Golden Age Shtetl: A New History of Jewish Life in East Europe* (Princeton University Press, 2015).
15 Petrovsky-Shtern, p. 32.
16 Petrovsky-Shtern, p. 53.
17 *JewishEncyclopedia.Com: The Unedited Full Text of the 1906 Jewish Encyclopedia* (JewishEncyclopedia.com, 2002).
18 Miron, p. 53.
19 Solomon Maimon, *The Autobiography of Solomon Maimon: The Complete Translation* (Princeton University Press, 2020).
20 Maimon, p. 8.
21 Maimon, p. 45.
22 Maimon, p. 82.
23 Maimon, pp. 108–12.
24 Theo Richmond, *Konin A Quest,* (Vintage,1996). This work uses a Yizkor book to particularly good effect.
25 Steven T. Katz, p. 35.
26 Petrovsky-Shtern, p. 253.
27 Petrovsky-Shtern, p. 263.
28 Petrovsky-Shtern, p. 123.
29 Petrovsky-Shtern, p. 124.
30 Petrovsky-Shtern, pp. 144–47.
31 Petrovsky-Shtern, p. 268.
32 Petrovsky-Shtern, p. 228.
33 Petrovsky-Shtern, p. 219.
34 Petrovsky-Shtern, p. 96.
35 Petrovsky-Shtern, p. 92.
36 Petrovsky-Shtern, pp. 118–19.
37 Miron, pp. 36–37.
38 Miron, pp. 38–39.
39 Steven T. Katz, pp. 290–306.
40 Lucy S. Dawidowicz, *The Golden Tradition: Jewish Life and Thought in Eastern Europe* (J. Aronson, 1989), pp. 160–68.
41 Steven T. Katz, p. 298.
42 Maimon, p. 16.
43 Dovid Katz, *Words on Fire: The Unfinished Story of Yiddish* (Basic Books, 2004).

44 Dovid Katz.
45 Michael Wex, *Just Say Nu: Yiddish for Every Occasion (When English Just Won't Do)* (HarperCollins, 2008), pp. 145–55.
46 Petrovsky-Shtern, p. 173.
47 Petrovsky-Shtern, p. 163.
48 Petrovsky-Shtern, p. 180.
49 Bartal, p. 95.
50 Elisheva Carlebach and Deborah Dash Moore, *The Posen Library of Jewish Culture and Civilization, Volume 6* (Yale University Press, 2019), p. 223.
51 Amos Elon, *The Pity of It All: A Portrait of Jews in Germany 1743-1933* (Penguin UK, 2004), pp. 33–54.
52 Greenbaum, p. 116.
53 Levin, p. 95.
54 Dawidowicz, p. 129.
55 Dawidowicz, p. 123.
56 Levin, p. 98.
57 Dawidowicz, p. 135.
58 Levin, p. 83.
59 Levin, pp. 83–85.
60 Nicholas J. Evans, 'The Port Jews of Libau, 1880–1914', *Jewish Culture and History*, 7.1–2 (2004), 197–214.
61 David Cesarani, *Port Jews: Jewish Communities in Cosmopolitan Maritime Trading Centres, 1550-1950* (Routledge, 2014).
62 'Jewish Community of Liepaja | Databases – ANU Museum of the Jewish People'.
63 Evans, p. 202.

3

Emigration

In the early 1890s Myer Scher left the Baltic region and migrated to southern Ireland. In doing so, he became part of a great wave of movement of Jewish people. It is thought that in the roughly three and a half decades between 1881 and 1914 almost 2.7 million Jews migrated to the west from eastern Europe, being about one quarter of the entire Jewish population.[1] The overwhelming majority (perhaps 80 per cent) left eastern Europe for the United States. Others went to Argentina, Canada, South Africa, Palestine and a number of other European countries. So momentous did the year 1881 appear that it stirred Irving Howe, the great historian of eastern European migration to the United States, to suggest:

> The year 1881 marks a turning point in the history of the Jews as decisive as that of 70 AD, when Titus's legions burned the temple at Jerusalem, or of 1492, when Ferdinand and Isabella decreed the expulsion from Spain. On 1 March 1881, Alexander II, Czar of Russia, was assassinated by revolutionary terrorists; the modest liberalism of his regime came to an end and within several weeks a wave of pogroms… spread across Russia.[2]

From the late nineteenth century, both academic historians and Jewish families have tried to make sense of this extraordinary migration. In many ways their explanations followed a broadly similar trajectory, which one might call the 'traditional narrative'. It emphasised the severity of persecution, particularly the pogroms, to which Jews were subject in late nineteenth century eastern Europe. It described the misery and hardships of their journey. And it dwelt on the 'liberation' experienced in the Promised Land, whether that was the United States, South Africa or Palestine. Distinguished academic accounts which, very broadly speaking, follow this 'traditional narrative' include Samuel Joseph's *Jewish Immigration to the US from 1880 to 1910*, Mark Wischnitzer's *To Dwell in Safety: The Story of Jewish Migration since 1800*, Irving Howe's *World of our Fathers* and David Vital's *A People Apart*. Memoirs of Litvaks who migrated to Ireland

and which also (very broadly speaking) follow this 'traditional narrative', often with florid – indeed terrifying – accounts of persecution, include David Marcus's *Oughtobiography* and *The Noyek Story*, which was written by members of the Noyek family. It explains:

> Lithuania of the 1880's was subject to a tyranny more crushing than that which raged in Ireland. An entire people were being herded by the conquering Cossacks into slavery. Children were taken from parents for slave labour in the mines and to the labour camps of their Tsarist masters… [3]

Another memoir, one example among many, although in this case of a family who migrated to the United States, also describes this trajectory of persecution, through migration, to redemption in a promised land:

> In Czarist Russia of the 1870s and 1880s, life for the Jews had become intolerable. The vast ghetto, known as the Pale of Settlement ... had become a morass of overpowering poverty and the situation for the Jews had become intolerable … The new arrivals from Russia were ragged, poor, toughened by years of torment … My parents opened a grocery store…and worked very hard.[4]

From the 1980s onwards this 'traditional narrative' came under challenge from academics, for two particular reasons: first, it was pointed out that pogroms were comparatively rare in parts of the Pale of Settlement, including in Lithuania. The term 'pogrom' has no precise meaning, but the definition offered by the Encyclopaedia Britannica is helpful: "a mob attack, either approved or condoned by authorities, against the persons and property of a religious, racial, or national minority. The term is usually applied to attacks on Jews in the Russian empire in the late 19th and early 20th centuries." Defined in this way, academics agreed that most pogroms did not take place in Lithuania; they occurred further south. Scholars agreed that there was antisemitic violence in Lithuania and intense fear among Jews that pogroms might spread to Lithuania. However, pogroms in Lithuania were unusual and there is no particular correspondence between the incidence of pogroms and the places from which emigrants came.

This 'revisionist' school of historical writing also emphasises the economic motivations for emigration. Academic accounts which, very broadly, are influenced by this 'revisionist' approach include Lloyd Gartner's *Jewish Migrants en Route from Europe to America: Traditions and Realities* and Hasia Diner's *The Jews of the United States.* And this 'revisionist' academic approach affected how some Jewish family members reviewed memoirs of their ancestors. In 1985 Geoffrey Wigoder reviewed the 1935 edition of the memoir of his grandfather, Myer Joel Wigoder, who has left one of the fullest and most illuminating accounts of moving from Lithuania to Ireland:

> As I read through his [Myer Joel Wigoder's] works of memoirs I find no reference to antisemitic experience or to the atmosphere of pogrom and persecution which had been prevalent in Russia … various business ventures had not succeeded … so at the age of thirty-six he left his pregnant wife and four children and headed west.[5]

It is interesting to reflect on how both the 'traditional' and the 'revisionist' narratives came into being. Important background, of course, is that both narratives undoubtedly contain substantial elements of truth. Persecution in eastern Europe and the appeal of economic betterment in a promised land were important parts of the explanation as to why Jewish people emigrated, but both the 'traditional' and 'revisionist' narratives also contain elements of myth making. In collective memory the 'traditional' narrative appears heavily influenced by the biblical account of the exodus of the Israelites from slavery in Egypt, celebrated annually by Jews everywhere in the Passover ceremony on the 15th day of the Hebrew month of Nisan. Families may (perhaps unwittingly) have projected the biblical narrative of slavery in Egypt, followed by flight and redemption in the Promised Land onto their own modern family migration experiences. This was all the more likely to have happened in families who very quickly turned their backs on experiences in eastern Europe, leaving children and grandchildren largely ignorant of what had occurred. Barbara Lantin, an Irish-born Litvak, was not untypical in saying:

> The circumstances in which my grandparents left Lithuania meant that the connection was totally severed in a dramatic and painful way. In my imagination, Lithuania is a place of shtetls and pogroms, in no sense a homeland.[6]

It has also been argued that the 'traditional' narrative of persecution, flight and redemption may have served the purpose of unifying the Jewish people: that a large number of Jews, who came from different parts of the world, who spoke different languages and had hugely different life experiences, were turned into a recognisable, if not coherent, ethnic or national community by the narrative of exodus to a promised land.[7] The 'traditional' narrative may also have served the purpose of enabling Jews to express patriotism towards their new homeland – to embrace it as a land of the free, offering a generous welcome and diverse opportunities for immigrants. As Irving Howe put it: "America was safety valve and haven, place for renewal and source of support."[8]

The 'revisionist' account of Jewish migration is self-consciously at variance with the 'traditional' approach. It was developed by people who were understandably weary of seeing Jewish history written as a seemingly endless tale of persecution and suffering – what Salo Baron memorably described as the 'lachrymose' rendition of Jewish history.[9] Reaction against the 'traditional' approach led historians to emphasise (perhaps, to over-emphasise) the economic motivations behind migration. The 'revisionist' approach sought to make Jewish migration appear more normal, and more in line with other European migration experiences. Weariness with 'lachrymose' Jewish history intensified in the post-Holocaust years and a number of 'revisionist' accounts have valuably re-balanced a picture which was overly dependent on the 'traditional' narrative. (The work of Hasia Diner, which considers the history of Jews in America[10], and the work of Gur Alroey, which looks at letters written by potential and actual migrants to the new world[11], are both particularly valuable in this context.)

In the late nineteenth century my great-grandfather Myer migrated from Lithuania to Ireland. Late nineteenth century Jewish emigration from Lithuania to Ireland does not fit comfortably into either the 'traditional' or the 'revisionist' narrative. This Irish experience was a very marginal part of a much bigger picture of Jewish migration from eastern Europe, but in some ways the Irish-Jewish experience challenges, and subverts, conventional understanding and, in doing so, shines intriguing side-lights on that bigger picture.

The Jewish population of Ireland was always small. The decennial census of population suggests that the Jewish population of Ireland (North and South) rose from 285 in 1871 to 5,148 in 1911, and to 5,221 in 1936/7. It probably reached a peak in 1947, before falling back to 3,592 in 1971. Today, it is less than 2,000.[12] The reasons for Jewish people migrating from Lithuania to Ireland are complex, and sometimes obscure. At face value, Ireland was a very unlikely place for Jews to choose to migrate to. Approximately one million Irish people had died as a result of the Irish Potato famine between 1845 and 1852. There was long-standing and bitter sectarian conflict between descendants of English Protestant settlers and native Irish Catholics. Many Irish people found conditions in Ireland so grim that they left Ireland during this period. Between 1850 and 1911 more than 4.5 million Irish people emigrated from Ireland. As a proportion of the population, the rate of emigration from Ireland during this period was more than double that of any other European country with an average of about 13 people out of 1,000 leaving the country each year. As a consequence of this mass emigration, the Irish population fell from 6.5 million in 1851 to 4.4 million in 1911.[13]

Even its most fervent admirers would hesitate to characterise late nineteenth century Ireland as a 'promised land'. Many of the Jewish immigrants from Lithuania knew very little about Ireland before they went there, and the decision to go to Ireland was tentative and provisional. Economic motivation was not uppermost in their thinking. Moving to Ireland was a much less final and drastic decision than deciding to emigrate to the United States, South Africa or Palestine. It was more in the nature of hedging one's bets. Many may have gone to Ireland at short notice so as to get out of harm's way in Lithuania, perhaps with a view to returning when circumstances there improved. In Ireland, many of the recent Jewish immigrants initially continued a lifestyle familiar to them from Lithuania, often as itinerant pedlars in a rural Catholic community. Some Jews in Ireland retained close links with the Baltic, continuing to be supplied with goods from the region until the First World War made that impossible.

Before looking at how Jewish emigration from Lithuania can best be explained, it is important to be as clear as possible about the character of that emigration: how many emigrated, when they did so and what kind of people they were.

Our sources for this are imperfect. The best figures for the Jewish population within the Russian empire at the end of the nineteenth century are from the Imperial Russian census of 1897. The Russian authorities did not keep records of Jews who emigrated, but quite good immigration records were maintained by some countries of immigration, and notably, for the period after 1899, by the government of the United States. Our best estimate is that in the period 1881-1914 something between 2.4 million and 2.7 million Jews emigrated from Europe, and substantial numbers also moved from eastern Europe to western Europe.[14] A disproportionately large number of the migrants came from the north-western provinces of the Russia empire, including the provinces of Kaunas and Vilnius in Lithuania. The migratory wave appears to have begun in 1881 and to have increased over time, with a pronounced acceleration in the decade before the First

World War. Jews were far more likely to emigrate from the Russian empire than were other ethnic minorities who lived there. For example, in the year 1910 (a year for which good data is available) Jews left Russian-controlled territories at the rate of 8.4 per 1,000. The departure rate of ethnic Germans from the same territories was 4.1 per 1,000; for Poles, the figure was 3.5 per 1,000, and for Latvians and Lithuanians it was 3.3 per 1,000. In other words, Jews emigrated from Russian controlled territory at about twice the rate of ethnic Germans and at about two and a half times the rate at which Poles, Latvians and Lithuanians did so. Ethnic Russians emigrated at about two-hundredth of the Jewish rate.[15]

The Jewish migrants tended to be quite poor. The very poorest groups in Jewish society generally did not emigrate because they were unable to afford the cost of travel. The much better-off were disinclined to emigrate because they thought they had too much to lose. Jewish emigrants tended to be concentrated in crafts and trades which were modestly remunerated, such as domestic service, tailoring, carting and shopkeeping. Demographer Liebmann Hersch has established that 60 percent of Jewish immigrants to the United States worked in the tailoring industry, 15 percent in the building and furniture industries, 9 percent in the metal and machine industry, 7 percent in the food industry and the rest in the leather, paper and printing industries.[16] It seems that in their destination country immigrants did not invariably follow the occupation they had pursued in their country of origin. For example, many Jewish immigrants to the United States became tailors, reflecting the demand for labour in that area of business.

There was a family character to Jewish migration which distinguished it from the migration of other Europeans. In the case of other European migrants, the husband typically emigrated alone and, after he had saved money, either returned home or brought his family over to the destination country. With Jewish emigration, the most common pattern was for families to emigrate together, although in some cases the husband went on ahead with the intention that his wife and children follow shortly afterwards. This family character of Jewish migration meant that 44 per cent of all Jewish migrants to the United States were women, whereas the proportion of women among Italian immigrants to the United States, for example, was only 23 per cent.[17]

Where a Jewish man emigrated first, with the intention that wife and children follow, the general pattern was that wife and children did indeed join him, and in relatively short order; but in a significant minority of cases the woman and her children were left abandoned. An abandoned Jewish woman was likely, absent witness evidence of her husband's death, to be deemed by religious authorities to be an *agunah*. Such a woman was in a difficult, usually a desperate, position. She could not obtain a divorce because Jewish religious law provides that, for divorce to be effective, a man must grant his wife a *get* [a Jewish divorce document], and he must do this of his own free will. The effect of being an *agunah* was that, as well as being without financial support from her husband, the wife was unable to marry another man. This was the case irrespective of the circumstances of her husband's disappearance, and the length of that disappearance. If the *agunah* did have a child by another man, that child was deemed illegitimate, and was unable to marry another Jew. In practice, the *agunah* had two options. One was to ask friends, rabbis and charitable organisations in the destination country for help in finding her husband and in obtaining a divorce from him. The other was to save up and travel to the destination country, with her children, and try to find her husband there. The poverty and misery of an *agunah* in eastern Europe is captured in a letter by one Mashe Zilazne of Sjedletz to the IRO [Industrial Removal Office], seeking their financial support:

> It has already been nine months since [my husband] left me and my two poor children… and six months already that he has not sent us one letter. I don't have any way of feeding my children and I'm as miserable as can be… And the poor children miss their father. And I mourn my young years that I should – God forbid – end up an *Agunah*[18]

In the early twentieth century Jewish charitable organisations attempted a systematic analysis of why Jewish husbands abandoned their wives so as better to tackle the problem effectively. Of 561 husbands who were traced and questioned, approximately one-third were found to have left their wives to live with another woman they had met; one-third claimed incompatibility between themselves and their wives due to a difference of age or character. Most of the rest claimed, perhaps unconvincingly, that unemployment had forced them to move to other cities in search of work and this had necessitated breaking off contact with their families. The fundamental point was that, in many cases, mass emigration had led to a crisis in the structure of Jewish family life. Alone, in a new world, and in a more liberal environment, many men found new partners. In some cases, they did this because they were pleased to have distanced themselves from a failed relationship at home. In other cases, men simply succumbed to temptation, disregarding the dire consequences of their conduct for their abandoned wives and children in the old country.

There was another way in which late nineteenth and early twentieth century Jewish emigration differed from that of migrations of other European peoples; generally, once Jews left they did not return to their country of origin. An analysis has been carried out of the rate of return from the United States to migrants' original home country for the three-year period 1908–1910 (both years inclusive). The overall rate of immigrants returning to their original homes was high, reflecting the fact that 1908 was a year of economic crisis: the rate was 61 per cent for northern Italians and 56 per cent for southern Italians; it was 30 per cent for Poles, 25 per cent for Greeks and 20 per cent for Germans. For Jews, the figure was a mere 8 per cent.[19] One can only conclude that, however difficult conditions were in the United States, or in other destination countries, Jewish migrants felt they would be unwelcome if they returned to their country of origin and that prospects for them there were bleak. Those Jews who did return tended to do so only for a short time, often to visit a sick relative or to get married.

To leave home in Lithuania and move to a new country was, self-evidently, a major decision, with life-changing consequences. Some thought about this decision very carefully, others less so; for some, there would appear to have been a real choice, while for others the decision appeared to take itself. It is impossible to know precisely why Myer chose to emigrate, but one can identify a number of the questions and concerns that will have weighed with him, as they did with others, as they tried to decide whether to leave their home and chance their luck in a new country.

The first set of concerns was the policy of the Tsarist government following the assassination of Tsar Alexander II. As we have seen, Tsar Alexander II began his rule in relatively liberal fashion, but he became distinctly more conservative following the failed attempt to assassinate him by D. Karakozov, in 1866. On 13 March 1881, Tsar Alexander II was assassinated by the revolutionary group *Narodnaya Volya* (People's will), and was succeeded by his son Alexander III, who pursued hard-line nationalist policies. In doing so, Alexander III was heavily influenced by Konstantin Pobedonostev, Procurator of the Holy Synod and the Tsar's former tutor, mentor and trusted adviser. Notoriously, Pobedonostev was rumoured to have advocated dealing with 'the Jewish question' in Russian-controlled lands by forcing one-third of the Jews to emigrate, one-third to be baptised and the remaining one-third to be starved to death.[20]

In May 1882, Interior Minister Ignatiev introduced the so-called 'May Laws'. These were said to be only temporary, but this characterisation was essentially a device to obviate the need for Ignatiev to obtain the approval of the State Council, where he might have encountered opposition. The May Laws remained in effect until the Bolshevik Revolution of 1917. They were deliberately and strongly hostile to Jews in various ways: first, Jews were prohibited from doing business on Sundays and Christian holidays. Given that most Jews did not trade on their own Sabbath (Friday afternoon and Saturday), and that in many cases their businesses were only marginally economically viable, this trading prohibition was a body-blow.

Secondly, Jews were no longer permitted to acquire property, take out mortgages for farmland, enter into leases for landed estates or obtain powers of attorney to manage or sell such property. If Jews complied with these laws, their existence in agricultural areas became almost impossible; in practice, many tried to circumvent them by paying bribes. Disingenuously, Ignatiev continued to engage Jews to arrange the extension of leases on his own family estates long after enactment of the May Laws.

Thirdly, the May Laws further restricted where Jews could live. Without notice, marketplaces and hamlets were designated as villages where Jews were not permitted to live, even if their ancestors had lived there for generations.[21] [22] Over the next few years, further restrictions were imposed on the Jews. An old law, not previously enforced, which prohibited Jewish residence within 35 miles of the German and Austrian frontiers began to be enforced from 1884; and, in that year, the policy of encouraging Jews to enter the liberal professions was reversed. A commission under Count Phalen was established to look into 'the Jewish Question'. Some members of this commission went about their work in a comparatively fair-minded way. The Commission reported that it had identified an astonishing 650 different laws which restricted the freedom of Russian Jews. It was clear, even to those not known for possessing particular sympathy to Jews, such as Major Evans-Gordon, that: "In all legislation which affects the Jews there is an obvious intention on the part of the Russian government to suppress them and prevent them from taking their natural place in the social and official life of the country".[23] A majority of Phalen Commission members recommended a more liberal policy, offering Jews some economic freedom. However, their advice was over-ruled and the government instead accepted the reactionary position of a minority on the Commission. An imperial decree of March 1891 ordered the expulsion from Moscow of all Jewish artisans, brewers and distillers. Some 20,000 Jews were expelled from Moscow in short order, including many who had been born in Moscow and spent their whole life there. They were sent to the Pale of Settlement, often on criminal transports. This legislative brutality sent shockwaves through the Jewish community in Lithuania, and beyond.

A further set of concerns for Jews in late nineteenth century Lithuania was that many of them had an overwhelming sense that much of the local Lithuanian population disliked them, often intensely disliked them, because they were Jews; in other words, the Jews faced widespread antisemitism. The manifestations of this antisemitism, and its intensity, varied. The historian Michael R. Marrus proposed analysing antisemitism by reference to a model of three concentric rings. Vague, consistent, sometimes latent antipathy to Jews lies in the outermost ring. In the second ring there are expressions of more intense and changing antipathy to Jews, liable to become more intense in moments of crisis. In the central ring there is fanatical, ideologically-based antisemitism, which can exert influence over the outer two rings. This model is far from perfect, but is useful in that it distinguishes between different intensities of antisemitic feeling and acknowledges that at moments of crisis the character of the problem could materially change.[24] For the most part, late nineteenth century Lithuania was not significantly affected by the fanatically ideological, racial antisemitism which was beginning to gain ground in Germany and in other parts of central Europe. The root cause of Lithuanian dislike of Jews was religious. In a revealing interview at, the beginning of the twentieth century the politician Andrius Bulota said:

> The roots of this hostility to Jews, which is seen among us, should be sought in [religion], and in medieval survivals. The Lithuanian people, notwithstanding its revolutionary mood, remains deeply a religious people; and a good Catholic, who is in addition an ignorant man, naturally does not like Jews because they "crucified Christ".[25]

This Christian religious hostility to Jews had deep roots in a Christian sense of disappointment and grievance that Jews did not accept Christianity as the successor religion to Judaism. Many Christians believed that Judaism had been superseded by Christianity, and that it was obstinate and offensive of Jews not to accept this; Christian doctrine also held that Jews were, in perpetuity, responsible for killing Jesus. Many observers felt that Roman Catholic priests were more hostile towards Jews than the clergy of the Orthodox church. This hostility to Jews was rather closely connected to the enduring blood libel: this was the belief held by many Catholic Lithuanians that, during Passover, Jews would torment and kill a Christian child, usually a male, and use his blood to make Matzot (the unleavened bread which Jews eat during Passover). As many as 128 cases of this blood libel were recorded in Lithuania between 1881 and 1900.[26] The timing of the first appearance of the blood libel suggests that it was connected to the Fourth Lateran Council of 1215. This Council settled theological uncertainties about what happens in the Eucharist, determining that the bread and wine are 'transubstantiated' (transformed) into the body and blood of Jesus. The precise connection between the determinations of the Fourth Lateran Council and the emergence of the blood libel remains difficult, and highly conjectural. One psychological theory is that, at a certain level, the Eucharist was an act of cannibalism which forced Christians to seek protective psychological mechanisms, one of which was the 'projective inversion mechanism', whereby Jews were blamed for what Christians did and were ashamed of doing. The blood libel appears to have been particularly deeply entrenched in northern Lithuania. It was especially common in the spring, around the time of Easter and Passover. Mary Antin recalled: "the Gentiles made the Passover a time of horror for the Jews. Somebody would start up that lie about murdering Christian children, and the stupid peasants would get mad about it, and fill themselves with vodka, and set out to kill the Jews."[27] During these incidents Jews had little alternative but to seek support from local officials, but those officials frequently sided with the accusers.

With modernisation of the economy in late nineteenth century Lithuania, and accompanying social change, antisemitism acquired an economic character. Jews were disliked because they were thought of as intermediaries and competitors, but this antipathy was articulated in different ways. Jews were described as exploiters of Lithuanians (common epithets were that Jews were bloodsuckers, leeches, fleas, ticks, spiders). Jews were also characterised as dishonest in trade: they were accused of tampering with products, selling factory cast-offs as quality goods, and cheating in the measurement of goods. The Samogitian Bishop Valancius in his 'Book For Adults' warned the Lithuanian peasantry that in cooperative efforts or friendships "in the end, the Jew always cheats the other person". [28] Lithuanians were urged to engage in trade and crafts themselves, boycott Jewish stores, and buy only from other Lithuanians. A striking feature of this antisemitic economic discourse is how much of it originated with clerics, and the clerical press. Clerical accusations against Jews were summarised by the priest Antanas Maliauskas in his 1914 book "Jews: An Economic and Social Glance". He suggested Jews were by nature inclined to cheat and their most important goal was profit. They were parasitic, and chose only the easiest jobs, exploiting others, and morally corrupted the society in which they lived.[29]

Antisemitism acquired a political dimension too: the clerical press was at the forefront of claims that Jews controlled the world via banks, other financial institutions, trade and the press; Jews were criticised for being insufficiently supportive of the Lithuanian national movement and for being associated with the Left.[30]

Antisemitic legislation and the hostility encountered in everyday interactions with the local population made life difficult for Jews in Lithuania after 1881. What made life unendurable was physical violence, or the feeling that they were at serious risk of it.

Pogroms involved attacks on Jews and their property. The attackers were generally uneducated and unskilled; many of them were unemployed, and some came from the petty criminal classes. Pogroms went in waves. A great wave was set off by the assassination of Tsar Alexander II. The first in the wave occurred at what was then known as Elizavetgrad in the Kherson governorate on 15 April 1881. By the end of 1881 between 200 and 250 further pogroms had occurred in south-western Russia. In the following year, there was a well-documented pogrom in Balta in the Podolia governorate. Between 10 and 12 April 1882 nine Jews were killed and over 200 injured, some very seriously. About a thousand homes and a few hundred Jewish-owned shops, workshops and taverns were smashed. A journalist who worked for the antisemitic Russian newspaper *Golos* reported:

> Everything that had belonged to Jews had been demolished, destroyed, sacked ... Nothing remained standing other than the carcasses [of buildings], the walls and the roofs...The entire Jewish population of Balta at this moment lacks clothing, furniture, beds, household utensils, crockery...[31]

The first wave of pogroms lasted approximately between 1881 and 1884; there was then a lull, before a second wave in the early 1890s.

A striking feature of the pogroms is that, for the most part, they occurred in South-Western Russia, and not in Lithuania. Generally, they started in larger towns in South-Western Russia, and then spread to villages and small towns there. The causes of post-1881 pogroms have been much disputed: Simon Dubnow, whose magisterial *World History of the Jewish People* appeared between 1925-1929, was convinced the pogroms were instigated by Tsarist authorities, principally by Interior Minister Nikolai Ignatiev. He thought their purpose was to divert revolutionary sentiments away from the Tsar and towards the Jews because they were a less dangerous target. Dubnow appears to have been persuaded to this point of view (in part, at least) by first-hand accounts from Jews who lived through the pogroms. Most historians now think, contrary to Dubnow, that the pogroms were not planned by the Tsarist government but that the government was slow to put a stop to them. The delay flowed from a distinctly ambivalent attitude on the part of some within the Tsarist administration as to whether it was desirable to halt pogroms, but also from logistical difficulties in bringing them to an end. Other historians thought the pogroms were not organised by the central authorities, but by an organisation founded by high-ranking officials and called the Secret Alliance.[32] Others again have seen the pogroms as a spontaneous reaction by local non-Jewish populations to economic turmoil consequent upon the industrialisation of Russia. They suggest that antisemitic violence derived from the confusions and jealousies stemming from the fact that many Christian religious leaders encouraged their followers to see Jews as inferior, and yet some Jews had clearly succeeded in becoming wealthy and successful. Ordinary people, who had not been able to improve their lot after the emancipation of the serfs in 1861, were inclined to see the success of Jews as blatantly unjust.[33] They were particularly riled by the contrast between the Jews' inferior legal status and the perception that some Jews were nevertheless doing well economically.[34]

One might ask why there were fewer pogroms in Lithuania than in the South. It may have been directly connected with the personal outlook of Governor-General Totleben of Vilnius, the Tsarist official with responsibility for maintenance of order in Lithuania. He seems to have thought that Jews were relatively sympathetic to Russian cultural influence in Lithuania and could be regarded as more trustworthy and reliable than Poles and Lithuanians. He was mindful of the Polish uprising of 1863-4, and fearful that mob violence against Jews could, in the Lithuanian context, quickly develop into an anti-Russian movement. It should therefore be clamped down on. More prosaically, it seems he simply took the view that his job was to maintain order. On 6 May 1881, he gave detailed instructions to his subordinates about how they were to maintain order, and he provided for use of the army to assist with this task.

Although pogroms were much less common in Lithuania than further South, the fear that widespread pogroms would come to Lithuania remained intense. It was perhaps this fear that pogroms would break out, more than the actual experience of them, which most deeply disturbed the Jewish population and played a significant role in stimulating emigration. This intense fear is graphically described in a letter from an unidentified Jew in Vilnius to a newspaper editor in February 1882:

> We expected a pogrom during the Christmas holidays ... And now, our fears have not been allayed and we expect a pogrom at any minute...If someone gets into an argument with a Christian the latter immediately says: "Just wait, soon we'll settle all the scores. What kind of life is this? If I had the courage I would kill all those close to me and then myself ... If I do not, some drunken riffraff will come along, ravish my wife and daughter and throw my infant from the third-floor window ... What a miserable creature is a Jew?[35]

Another aspect of the pogroms in the South which particularly disturbed Jews both there and in Lithuania was the sense that they were not just facing mob violence, but that this violence gave the appearance at least of having the support of the Russian authorities. When the Phalen Commission report was published, its more fair-minded and liberal members ensured that its final form included wording which boldly stated that Jews faced deep unfairness which was enshrined in law. It said: "without granting [the Jew] equal rights, we cannot, properly speaking, demand of him civic obligations ... the discriminations and disabilities implied in these laws [the 650 laws prejudicial to Jews] are such that they have naturally resulted until now in making the life of an enormous majority of the Jews in Russia exceedingly onerous." It was not just law itself, but also the way in which it was enforced, that was also intensely hostile to Jews. The Governor of Odessa, for example, instructed his minions to punish Jews severely for the pogroms of which they were the victims. In November 1892, *The Jewish Chronicle* reported him as saying that it would be madness on his part to show any sympathy for the Jews since they drain the blood of the Christians; he went on to say: "I do not blame the Christians in the least for having attacked you; you fully deserve it. I am convinced the Emperor holds the same opinion." [36] It appears that the Emperor did, indeed, hold a broadly similar opinion. A delegation of Jewish notables was, after much delay, eventually granted an audience with Tsar Alexander III. This delegation requested that he publicly deny rumours that Jews had been involved in the assassination of his predecessor, Tsar Alexander II, and also that he deny rumours that he, as Emperor, had ordered punishment of Jews. Both requests were turned down flat. Instead, the Emperor used the short audience to rail against the iniquities of the Jews.[37]

The feeling that the Tsar, and the power of the Tsarist state, were hostile to Jews and were indifferent to, or supportive of, violence against Jews caused intense anxiety among Jews in Lithuania. Some of this anxiety may have been out of proportion to the real risk. Fear was magnified by rumours and by over-excited press comment. Nonetheless, detailed analysis of two pogroms which did occur in Lithuania in the 1880s, at Balbieriškis and at Prienai, strongly suggests that the anxiety was not wholly misplaced. The reason for the Prienai pogrom appears, in the opinion of the historian who has studied it most closely, to have been the 'pogrom atmosphere', that is, "the conviction of some Christians that the Tsar allowed them to beat up Jews and ransack their property". Such a conviction was strengthened by the fact that until August 1882 those accused of the pogrom in Balbieriškis remained unpunished.[38]

Jews did not react to pogroms by going on the attack. They scarcely ever initiated violence against local Lithuanians and did not ransack Christian property, let alone Christian places of worship. It has been suggested that this disinclination to be violent was because there was an informal social hierarchy in Lithuania, and that Jews knew their place within it. It may be more likely that Jews were dissuaded from going on the offensive because their rabbis and elders instilled in them a strong sense that such conduct would have been morally wrong. Nonetheless, Jews were prepared to defend themselves. A local newspaper reported that in the Jewish quarter of Vilnius, after the Warsaw pogrom, "each house is turned into a fortress; each shop is a fort ... and every Jewish citizen has become a commander-in-chief, his wife a commissary, his older children soldiers."[39] Jews also went to exaggerated lengths to avoid giving offence: the Jewish press explained that, as pogroms broke out, Jews tried to appear less in public, "walk on tiptoe", give way to Christians, and abandon certain religious practices so as not to create pretexts for assault. The most common response to violence was for Jews to appeal to local authorities for protection; that appeal might be bolstered by the suggestion that violence against Jews and their property also imperilled social stability more generally. Not infrequently, appeals for support from local officials were accompanied by the offer of bribes. But many local officials were unsympathetic and large numbers of Jews felt increasingly desperate. Fear of violence to themselves and their property was one of the main reasons that Lithuanian Jews began to contemplate emigration after 1881.

It is often thought that the desire to avoid conscription into the Tsarist army also led some Jewish men to emigrate. Military conscription was a subject which caused something approaching collective trauma in parts of the Jewish community in the Pale of Settlement. In Lithuania, in the 1880s and 1890s, there were still long memories of the experience under Tsar Nicholas 1 (who ruled between 1825 and 1855). Up to a point, the policies of Nicholas I had been motivated by desire to transform Jews into useful subjects, who were fully integrated into society. He consciously tried to follow a pattern set by enlightened European monarchies, such as that of Joseph II in Austria who had drafted Jews into the army to speed their assimilation. Tsar Nicholas I intended that, in the Tsarist army, Jews would learn Russian, acquire useful skills and crafts, and become loyal subjects. Initially, at least, some of the Maskilim were broadly supportive of the idea that Jews should serve in the Tsarist army. What caused the real upset was the conscription of young boys. In 1827, it was enacted that Jews would be conscripted on the same proportionate basis as all other subjects, and for the same period of twenty-five years. However, it was also enacted that, in the case of Jews, the minimum age for recruitment would be 12, and not 18 or 20, as for other recruits. In fact, some recruits were younger than 12. The boys were separated from the men and served in special 'Cantonist' youth battalions, before being posted to regular military battalions. No other ethnically or religiously distinct part of the population of the Russian empire was treated in this way. The obligation to find recruits was devolved to the Jewish community (specifically, to the *kahals*, which were dominated by richer families), with the consequence that the poor and uneducated bore the brunt of the draft. The task of finding Jewish child recruits was passed to the *khapers,* Jewish child recruit abductors, whose techniques for finding young boys included luring them with lies and abducting them from their homes.

The experience of witnessing the treatment of these young boys was described in his memoirs by Alexander Herzen, Russian writer and thinker, and founder of the movement for agrarian populism. The description is especially interesting being from someone who was not Jewish. Herzen recalls seeing a convoy of Jewish boys 'little fellows of eight and ten' being marched to Kazan to serve in a Cantonist battalion, 'sick children, uncared for and uncomforted, exposed to the wind which blows straight from the Arctic sea…marching to their graves'.[40] The historian S.M. Dubnov called on ex-Cantonists to write memoirs of their experiences of conscription; a handful did so, including Friedberg, Kotik, Berman and Itzkowitz. They describe desperate parents who hid their children in the forest, in Christian homes or in foreign countries if they could afford to; once abducted, children were temporarily housed in a local prison to wait for their enlistment; as their sons were being taken away, parents and other relatives followed the convoy through several cities in the hope of freeing their children or to catch a last glimpse of them; many ex-Cantonists recall the last words of their mother being a plea not to convert, to remember the Jewish laws, and to pray every day; Itzkovitz recalls how the officer in his battalion tried to force the young boys to convert: "Each night he forced [the Cantonists] to declare the 'Jews live in error and that Jesus was the true Messiah'... he demanded that the children agree to be baptised on the spot. Those who agreed were allowed to go to bed and supplied with new clothes and bread the next morning. Those who refused were kept kneeling on the floor all night long and would not get any food...The whole battalion was indeed baptised except for one 17-year-old Cantonist ... he was beaten every day..." When eventually, after long military service, Cantonists returned to their home-town they invariably felt alienated from their families because of their very different life experiences, and they encountered hostility from family and local community who were suspicious they had converted.[41]

Conversion was, indeed, common among Cantonists. While numbers cannot be precise, it seems probable that there were about 50,000 Jewish military conscripts during the reign of Tsar Nicholas I, most of whom were minors, and that about half of them apostatized. In the reign of his successor, Tsar Alexander II (1855-1881), hundreds of Cantonists who had been baptised under duress publicly rejected their baptism, reclaimed their Jewish names and identity, and organised protests about their treatment.[42]

The worst excesses of the recruitment system ended with the accession of Tsar Alexander II in 1855, and further reforms followed in 1874. From that time, the term of military service became much shorter and the decision as to who would be recruited became less arbitrary. The selection was made by ballot after central commissioners excluded certain groups on the basis of health or dependency. At the end of the nineteenth century Jews were fully represented in the Tsarist army. We know that in 1897 just over 1 per cent (53,194) of a total Jewish population of 5.2 million was serving in the army or navy. The total size of the armed services in 1897 (1,132,682 in a population of 125 million) implies that Jews were marginally over-represented in the Russian military at this time.[43]

This begs an important question. If the worst excesses of conscription into the Russian army were between 1827 and 1855, and if Jews were only marginally over-represented in the Tsarist army after 1881, is it likely that fear of conscription was a significant motivation for the great wave of emigration which occurred in the 1880s and 1890s? Self-evidently, fear of conscription was mainly likely to affect the thinking of young men directly at risk of being called-up. However, it could also have some knock-on effect on the thinking of that person's wider family. From the 1880s Russian law provided that the family of a Jew who evaded military service was liable to a fine of 300 rubles. For better-off families one option was simply to pay the fine. The less well-off were more inclined to encourage the young man's emigration so as to avoid the family being burdened with a substantial fine. Conscription could also have some impact on the thinking of the wider Jewish community. In the 1880s Jewish communities resorted to drastic measures to fill their quota of recruits for the army by, for example, seizing Jews within their districts who were without passports or who belonged to other Jewish communities. It is entirely possible that Myer, having moved away from home in the early 1890s, felt in danger of being forced to fill the conscription quota of the area to which he had moved.

It is clear from a number of memoirs that Jewish men resorted to desperate measures to avoid conscription. Some men went to elaborate lengths to change their names, to flee their home area, or deliberately to mutilate themselves.[44]

There were several connected reasons for this overwhelming desire not to be conscripted. At its root, there was a deep-seated trauma about conscription which derived from the brutal system which had existed between 1827 and 1855. The horror of that collective folk memory was aggravated by understandable concern that the regime of Tsar Alexander III might again extend the period of conscription to 25 years. Whether or not it did this, young Jewish men felt repelled by the prospect of spending a long time away from home and in an environment where there was no alternative but to break the Jewish laws of daily life. "A soldier often had to eat trefah [non Kosher food] and work on sabbath. He had to shave his beard and do reverence to Christian things."[45] Moreover, young Jewish men were not attracted by the prospect of giving up many of the best years of their life without obvious educational or career benefit, and in service of a regime which had introduced the May Laws and was suspected of not preventing pogroms and other violence against Jews. "On the person of a Gentile [the uniform of a soldier] was the symbol of tyranny; on the person of a Jew, it was the emblem of shame".[46]

How many of the Jews who emigrated from Lithuania after 1881 were primarily motivated by fear of conscription is now unknowable. Almost certainly, it was only a minority because only a minority of emigrants were men in the relevant age bracket. Nonetheless, for that minority, fear of conscription may well have been the decisive fact which caused them to move. Although one cannot be sure of this, I suspect Myer was among this group. A rather larger group of immigrants to different parts of the 'new world' developed, from the comfort of their new homes, a narrative about their own departure which placed somewhat exaggerated emphasis on fear of conscription. Not only did this seem a rather nobler reason for emigrating than economic betterment but it also became a kind of shorthand to describe all they had disliked about life under the Tsars: governmental persecution, forced baptism of young children, division within the Jewish world and poverty.[47]

Poverty and the desire to improve living standards was undoubtedly another great spur to emigration. A full and remarkably graphic English language account of turn of the century Jewish poverty in the Pale of Settlement is provided by Major W.E. Evans-Gordon MP. He is an unlikely source. He was public school educated and had a background in the British Indian Army. He became Conservative MP for the East-End constituency of Stepney, where many eastern European Jewish immigrants had settled. He was elected to Parliament on an 'anti-alien' platform. He was a member of the Royal Commission on Alien Immigration, which reported in 1903, and strongly advocated immigration restrictions. However, and in contrast to any of his colleagues, he took the trouble to visit Russia, Poland and Romania in an attempt to see what lay behind Jewish immigration to Britain. Some suspected him of antisemitism, but others, including no less a figure than Chaim Weizmann, were more sympathetic: "[he] had no particular anti-Jewish prejudices but he failed to see why the ghettos of London or Leeds should be made into a branch of the ghettos of Warsaw or Pinsk … [He] gave me some insight into the psychology of the settled citizen".[48] [49] In minutes of evidence to the Royal Commission, Evans-Gordon described the poverty of the Jews that he saw in Vilnius:

> the miserable dens and cellars in which the people live…the walls of the houses blistered and rotting, as if poisoned by the pestilent atmosphere within. Two or three families would be found in one miserable room or cellar… I was surrounded by a crowd of gaunt, curious, anxious faces - sad, careworn, hungry-looking people. Some openly begged arms.[50]

When he moved on to Lodz in Poland, Evans-Gordon described the way that:

> The conditions under which the work [in the textile trade] is done are appalling. I shall never forget the terrible places and rooms in which I saw this trade carried on. It would need the pen of Zola to do justice to them.[51]

A number of observers of Jewish poverty in eastern Europe commented that many Jews were not just poor in absolute terms, but that their poverty had different causes from that of their neighbours. Not only did the law discriminate against them, but the enforcement of the law was inconsistent. In practice, the way law was enforced depended on the ability of Jews to pay bribes to those Gentiles around them who occupied official positions. This was impoverishing. Mary Antin observed:

> If a Jew and a Gentile kept store side by side, the Gentile could content himself with smaller profits. He did not have to buy permission to travel in the interests of his business. He did not have to pay three hundred rubles fine if his son evaded military service. He was saved the expense of hushing the inciters of pogroms. Police favour was retailed at a lower price to him than to the Jew…[52]

The economic disparity between Jew and Gentile was especially marked in country areas and smaller towns. The contrast was drawn between the Russian peasant who, though poor, might at least be the proprietor of a small piece of land. The Jews, on the other hand, were unable to own land and by the late nineteenth century their position in rural areas was becoming almost impossible. Ba'al Mahshoves, a Yiddish literary critic, commented rather despairingly: "Jewish poverty is utterly without a cure; the Jew has no available means for improving his condition, which will remain abject as long as he lives among alien peoples."[53] In fact, the position was a little more nuanced than this. A majority of Lithuanian Jews were involved in trade, particularly in flax, timber, leather, pig bristles, cattle, geese and other fowl, and eggs. Generally, these people made a living, although sometimes a very precarious one. Other Jews were involved in crafts, typically as tailors, goldsmiths, furriers and tanners. The poorest craftsmen were those who had no place of employment and worked 'independently'. The census of 1897 identified 3,334 such unfortunate people in Lithuania. They included carters, porters, carriage drivers, rafters, pavers, agricultural workers, water-drawers, ragmen, woodcutters and ditch-diggers. The Russian author A. Sobotin described these people:

> The Jewish labourers stand all day in the marketplace without eating anything at all. They are looking for work, but often, after a day of idleness, have to return home where a hungry family awaits them… they work like oxen, dragging a two wheeled cart … Those who have not seen this picture for themselves will not be able to believe that Jews are able to bear such heavy burdens.[54]

There were also 1,402 Jewish industrial workers in Lithuania in 1897, who were generally employed in one of the 134 Jewish owned factories. They had no union to represent them, and often worked long hours in poor conditions for meagre pay.

Economic conditions became generally more difficult for Jews in Lithuania in the second half of the nineteenth century because of material increases in the size of the Jewish population. The Jewish population grew faster than in previous centuries and faster than that of the surrounding Christian population. The marriage rate among Jews was higher than among the Christian population and the marriage age was relatively low. Until the early nineteenth century it was rare for more than four children in each family to survive to adulthood, but improved nutrition and medical care meant that from the second half of the nineteenth century it became common for up to seven children to survive to adulthood. Inevitably, dramatic population growth imposed economic burdens on the family and made emigration seem desirable.

There were at least two other major reasons why economic conditions for Jews deteriorated at the end of the nineteenth century. The first is the great famine of 1891. This began along the river Volga and then spread as far as the Urals and the Black Sea. It is thought to have killed something between 375,000 and 500,000 people. The immediate cause of the famine was bad weather. A particularly dry autumn had delayed the planting of the fields. During the winter temperatures fell to minus 31 degrees celsius but, as little snow had fallen, seedlings were unprotected from frost. When the Volga flooded, lack of snow caused the water to freeze, killing more seedlings and destroying fodder used to feed the horses. There were deeper causes of the famine, including that the agricultural workers were still using medieval agricultural machinery, such as wooden ploughs and sickles; and Russia's very basic railway system was not capable of enabling redistribution of grain. Government policy almost certainly contributed to the crisis: grain exports were not banned until mid-August, and then merchants had a month's warning, which meant they could export their reserves. Famine quickly led to outbreaks of cholera, compounding the misery. It is true that the epicentre of the Great Famine of 1891 was east of Moscow, far from where most Jews lived. Jews in the Pale do not appear to have suffered directly from scarcity of food during the early 1890s, and in no small part because of their industry.[55] Nonetheless, the Great Famine caused a general economic downturn throughout Russian-controlled lands and made Lithuanian Jews poorer. This increased pressure on the Tsarist government to divert criticism by turning on a traditional scapegoat. Relief efforts from abroad, particularly those of the 'Russian Famine Relief Committee of the United States' may also inadvertently have been unhelpful to Jews because such efforts led to pressure to soften what had been vocal American criticism of Tsarist anti-Jewish policy. This famine relief committee sent generous support. It despatched a ship called 'Indiana', carrying 1,900 tonnes of food which arrived in Liepāja on 16 March 1892. The famine relief committee despatched a second ship called 'Missouri', carrying 2,500 tons of grain and corn flour, which arrived in Liepāja on 4 April 1892. If Myer and his friends contemplated the dockside in Liepāja where these ships from a different world discharged their cargoes of bounty, perhaps they began to wonder if their own lives would be better spent in lands capable of generating such riches.[56 57]

A second reason why economic conditions for Jews became distinctly more difficult in the early 1890s is that the May Laws began to be much more strictly enforced. If life for Jews had been difficult, but just about bearable, during the 1880s it was because many of the strict provisions of the May Laws were not being enforced. In February 1891 the United States Secretary of State, James G. Blaine, reported that the State Department had information that the cause of the recent upsurge in Russian Jewish immigration into the United States was generally not the result of new laws but, rather, it was caused by stricter enforcement of old ones.

The changed approach can be traced directly to the changed attitudes of Tsar Alexander III. The Tsar was involved in a railway accident at Borki in 1888 and around this time his attitude towards the Jews hardened. He began to welcome suggestions that Jewish emigration from Russia be encouraged. In 1888 the Governor of Podolya Guberniya argued in a report that the expulsion of the Jewish proletariat from his area would be very desirable. Alexander scrawled in the margin of his copy of the report: "And even useful". In 1890, Alexander wrote on a memorandum submitted to him in defence of Jews and Jewish rights that they deserved whatever happened to them because they had wanted the blood of Jesus to remain "on us and our children". The changed attitude and approach of Alexander III was also linked to the death in 1889 of Count Tolstoy, one of his principal advisers, who until then had been an important moderating influence. From 1891, the rules limiting where Jews could live were much more strictly enforced. On 23 April 1891, an edict was issued restricting Jewish residence in Moscow, as a result of which about 20,000 Jews were expelled from the city. Also, many Jews living in villages in the Pale of Settlement were expelled from their villages. These expulsions meant that economic competition between Jews in the towns where they were permitted to live became much more intense, making them poorer. The position of Jews in towns where they were permitted to live was made yet more difficult by the fact that the Jewish population was experiencing much more rapid natural growth than the Christian population. Also, no agency linked to the government would employ Jews. This point made a forceable impression on Major Evans-Gordon, as he toured the Pale: "No sort of employment, paid directly or indirectly by the state, is open to them. They can obtain no work from the municipality of the town in which they reside. The Government endeavours as far as possible to prevent them from obtaining any work over which it has control".[58] By the early 1890s, Jewish life in Lithuania had become extremely difficult.

Macroeconomic circumstances only go some of the way towards explaining the economic background as to why particular individuals emigrated. In the end, the decision to emigrate was intensely personal, and often motivated by personal financial misfortune. Two of the fullest memoirs of Litvaks who migrated to Ireland are those by Myer Joel Wigoder and by Lieb Berman and they both illustrate this point. Wigoder's account makes clear that a major reason for his departure was a fire which destroyed his house in Lithuania, as well as the Catholic church facing it, and much else in the centre of Viekšniai. Fires were not uncommon . In July 1894, *The Jewish Chronicle* reported "a very serious fire in the town of Plumgany, by which 800 families were totally without any shelter". Lieb Berman suffered a succession of business setbacks: his brother-in-law financed a venture as a brewer in Popalan but "he made it so good he lost heavily on every brew". He tried his luck in peddling, but "his horse ate up every groschen he had". Finally, his valuable cartload of smoked sprats was spoiled en route to Viekšniai market. This series of business setbacks appears to have driven him to the conclusion that he needed to emigrate.[59]

Because the financial position of many Jews was precarious, a setback which in other circumstances would have been minor quickly became serious: "The margin between life and starvation is so narrow that the least disturbance or crisis becomes a catastrophe..."[60] A period of ill-health, for example, involving medical and apothecary bills, could easily tip a Jewish family over the edge. Mary Antin explains that the long chapter of troubles which led to her father's emigration began with his own illness. When her mother also became ill "too much money was withdrawn from the business to pay doctors' and apothecaries' bills", and the family entered a crisis from which emigration seemed the only way out.[61]

Part of the explanation for Jewish emigration from Lithuania in the nineteenth century is that immigration law across much of the world did not prevent it. In principle, immigrants of the 1880s and 1890s could move to the English-speaking world - particularly to the United States, Great Britain and South Africa - without legal restrictions on entry in the destination country. In Britain, the nineteenth century was a time of free movement and open borders. There had been an Aliens Act of 1793 to control the numbers of French people entering Britain after the French revolution and the Napoleonic wars. This had reached a peak of 4,000 people a month in September 1792. The Aliens Act 1793 was intended to be only temporary, but was periodically renewed, before being abolished in 1836. Thereafter, there were no British controls on immigration other than a very loosely policed system of registration on entry. British immigration law began to tighten with the Aliens Act 1905, which was directed in fact, but not explicitly, at limiting Jewish immigration from eastern Europe. This Act provided that permission to enter the country could be withheld if the immigrant was unable to show that he had the means decently to support himself and his dependents, if he was a lunatic or otherwise diseased, if he had been sentenced to a crime overseas, or if he was already subject to an expulsion order under the Act. The Aliens Act 1905 was quite easily evaded. It did not require the immigration officer to give the would-be immigrant any permission in writing. Verbal permission sufficed. However, the 1905 Act was a turning-point. Thereafter, British immigration law tightened, particularly both before and after the First World War, with the Aliens Registration Act 1914 and the Aliens Restrictions Act 1919. By the late 1930s, when many Jews in Lithuania were desperate for a new home, immigration to Britain was all but impossible.

By far the most demanding immigration law requirements for the would-be Litvak migrant of the late nineteenth century were those imposed by the Russian authorities. To cross the Russian border legally and safely one needed a passport and exit visa. Russian law was unsuited to deal with a period of mass emigration, it varied from one region to another and its administration was mired in corruption. To obtain a passport, a prospective emigrant had to submit an identity card, a certificate from the police stating that there was no impediment to that person leaving the country and, if the applicant was male and between the ages of 18 and 21, a document certifying that he had reported to the army recruitment office. For many people, obtaining an identity card was difficult. If they were not registered in their place of residence they had no identity card. Even if they had an identity card, it might no longer be valid or it might fail to list all family members. To obtain a new identity card they had to travel to the municipality where they were registered, which might be far from where they lived. There were further bureaucratic obstacles in the way of women who wanted to join their husbands in the new country. These stemmed from the fact that in Russian law a woman could only get a passport with her husband's consent, and such consent was difficult if not impossible to demonstrate if the husband was in a far away country. The manifold difficulties inherent in assembling the paperwork to cross the Russian border in a lawful way meant that many chose to cross it unlawfully. The ICA (the Jewish Colonization Association) maintained an information bureau which collected data on total Jewish emigration before the First World War. It estimated that 80 per cent of total Jewish emigration before 1914 was illegal. What 'illegal emigration' generally meant in practice was crossing the Russian border, under cover of darkness, and with the assistance of people smugglers.[62]

This points the way to another important reason why so many Jews emigrated from Lithuania in the late nineteenth century; and that is that many companies and individual traders developed a strong commercial interest in the busines of facilitating the movement of Jewish people. Some of the businesses, including the major railway companies and shipping lines, were substantial and reputable. Others, including the agents and smugglers, who concentrated at the border crossings and pressed their services on anxious migrants, were tin-pot operations, and very far from reputable.

The ICA published many stories in *Der yidische emigrant* of emigrants who encountered smugglers and agents at the border. These people were prepared, for substantial payments, to take emigrants across the Russian border:

> When a Jew manages to reach the border village, the agent's cronies come and take more money from him for various services… Then comes the "border-crossing process". After midnight, drunken farmers …come and take the terrified wretches "under their protection," and they go with them to what seems to them a horrible place. They are afraid of the escorts and afraid of the border guards. And the drunkards take advantage of the emigrants' mood to abuse them and suck their blood and the rest of their money. (*Ha-zeman* 144)[63]

Whole industries developed in the major ports, including Liepāja, Hamburg and Bremen which were geared to accommodating and providing for the needs of migrants before they embarked.

Railways and shipping connections made it possible for Lithuanian Jews to emigrate. The railways and shipping companies had an economic motivation to move as many people as they reasonably could, and as efficiently as possible. Until about 1892 most Jews contemplating migration to Britain from Lithuania travelled by train to one of the north German ports, generally to Hamburg or Bremen. Most would have first travelled on the Liepāja-Romny railway line, mainly built between 1871-4 and opened in 1880. This served some of the most populous areas of the Pale, including Vilnius. From Vilnius, one could change onto other railways, including onto the Warsaw-St Petersburg line which had been constructed between 1851-1862; a branch of this line went via Kaunas to Eydtkuhnen (Wirballen), on the East Prussian border. For most emigrating Jews planning to go to Britain this was the border station through which they passed, although some crossed at Illowo (Mlawa) or at Prostken (Grajewo). The border station was remembered as a place of "terrible confusion", where emigrants were "driven from place to place like cattle". Emigrant aid associations provided assistance at the border and could make all the difference. Mary Antin describes the agent her family used as "the agent of our salvation".[64] Emigrants then proceeded by train from the border crossing to Hamburg or Bremen.

From there a steamer took them to England, typically to London, Southampton, Hull or Grimsby. For transmigrants, and for those contemplating onward migration to Ireland, there were effective communications linking the east-coast ports of arrival with west-coast ports of embarkation. The Wilson Line of Hull was one of the main shipping companies operating out of Hull, Newcastle and West Hartlepool. It had links with railways on the continent and in Britain, enabling it to provide an integrated transportation service. Passengers arriving on the east coast of Britain could be met and speedily transferred to the embarkation ports of Liverpool or Glasgow. The system became even more streamlined from 1907 with the building of the Riverside Quay in Hull. From then, passengers could walk straight down a gangway and onto waiting trains connecting Hull with Liverpool, Glasgow, London and Southampton. 100,000 European transmigrants passed through Hull in 1907 alone. These highly efficient integrated steamship and railway systems were necessary to enable British based companies such as the Wilson Line to compete effectively with the large ocean liners of the Hamburg-American Steamship Company and the Norddeutscher Lloyd which provided direct services from north German ports such as Hamburg and Bremen to the United States.[65] From about 1892 onwards a sea-route from Liepāja to Britain and the United States began to be a serious competitor to the railway route via the north

German ports. The sea route also involved a stop-over in the deep-water port of Cobh, which served Cork in southern Ireland.

In August 1902, Major Evans-Gordon observed and recorded the departure of Jewish emigrants from Liepāja, aboard the S.S. Kursk, which was bound for London. The ship carried 180 emigrants and 120 ponies, as well as a miscellaneous cargo of eggs and other produce. The voyage to London, via the Kiel canal, took four days. The price of a third-class ticket to London was 27 shillings and 6 pence, including food. There were fortnightly departures for Hull and weekly sailings to London. Evans-Gordon thought the departure was conducted in a quiet and orderly manner. The emigrants were evidently poor, but decent and respectable looking. There were some very old men among them, and a good many children and babies in arms. However, conditions on board were grim. The hold in which the emigrants were to travel was pitch dark and devoid of ventilation. Jewish emigrants slept on straw mattresses and lay alongside one another "like sardines in a tin". Evans-Gordon challenged the ship's Captain about how he managed with ventilation in bad weather. The Captain first denied that there ever was bad weather, but then acknowledged that in rough conditions it was customary to turn the vessel's head to the wind and wait until the sea moderated.

> "If I were to shut my hatches," said the Captain, "the ponies would die."
> "And the people?" I [Evans-Gordon] ventured to suggest.
> "Yes," he said, "and the people."
> But this was evidently an afterthought.[66]

The rather desperate Jewish masses, eager to escape their troubles in Lithuania, were valuable to large shipping and railway companies who were keen to transport them for their own commercial advantage. Indeed, it may be that the commercial ambitions of these big companies not only contributed to the overall numbers who emigrated, but also had a direct influence on precisely where the migrants went.

This connection has been rather clearly established in the case of Lithuanian Jews going to South Africa. In the late 1880s the Union Line, a large shipping company owned by Donald Currie, ordered 24 new ships. Each ship was capable of carrying between 100 and 150 third-class passengers, in addition to several hundred steerage passengers. The intention was that these ships should carry former Cornish tin miners to South Africa. There had been a collapse in the Cornish tin industry because it had become much cheaper to produce tin from Malaysia by washing it out from alluvial deposits rather than from deep quartz workings. Gold mining in Johannesburg was by now based on deep ore working so it seemed sensible for the Union Line to take Cornish tin miners to South Africa to work in the gold mines there. About 200 Cornish tin miners were transported in 1886/7; this climbed to an annual peak of about 4,000, but then collapsed. It seems that Cornish tin miners did not enjoy gold mining in South Africa, and nor did their wives. The gold rush subsided. The miners returned home to Cornwall, leaving Donald Currie with ships for which he needed to find another purpose. From 1893, Donald Currie began sending cheques to the Temporary Jews Shelter in London's East End. This housed eastern European Jews on a temporary basis before they travelled on to other countries. From 1893 onwards the Shelter was in receipt of regular cheques from Donald Currie personally and from the Castle and Union Lines (which amalgamated into the Union Castle Line). Before about 1895 there is little evidence of passengers passing through the shelter en route to South Africa. Then the figures jump: in 1893, 453; in 1894, 500; in 1895, 880 and in 1896, 2,134. There seems little reason to doubt that an important reason why many Litvaks emigrated to South Africa was that Donald Currie had cleverly found an alternative way of filling ships he no longer needed for Cornish tin miners disillusioned with the prospect of earning a living by gold mining in South Africa.[67]

Some Jews who wished to emigrate tried to inform themselves and take the initiative in deciding where to go. Others, almost certainly a majority, were passive in such decision-taking. In larger family groups, the elderly and the children had little influence, and a wife's views sometimes carried weight, but often they did not. It might be, therefore, that in an emigrant family group of, say, six or seven people, only one or two were actively involved in deciding which part of the world the family should emigrate to. Some of the decision-taking that took place was based on very limited information. Such as it was, it might derive from letters from family members and former residents of their home community who had already migrated (this was likely to carry considerable weight), from newspapers or from the information bureaux founded for Jewish emigrants. Six of these were founded in the early twentieth century: the information bureau of the Jewish Colonization Association (ICA) was founded in 1903; two Zionist bureaux were established, one in in Odessa in 1905 and another in Jaffa in 1906; the information bureau of the Jewish Territorial Organization (ITO) was established in Kiev in 1907; the information bureau of the Industrial Removal Office (IRO) in the United States was established in 1901; and the

Central Office of Migration Affairs was established in 1904 by the Hilfsverein, the Alliance Israelite Universelle and the ICA. The main tasks of these bureaux were to provide prospective emigrants with information about possible destination countries, assist with obtaining the necessary documentation and warn of dangers that the prospective emigrants might encounter on their journey.[68]

Much of the correspondence between would-be emigrants and the Information Bureaux survives. It is difficult to dip one's toe into this vast sea of documentation without immediately being struck by just how little many emigrants knew about their destinations. One letter, among many, serves as an example. Written by four would be emigrants from Plonsk in 1905. They ask the information bureau:

1. A single man of eighteen. He is familiar with the textile trade... Where in America should he go so that he can earn a living and learn the language?
2. A single man of twenty-three, a pattern designer, fluent in three languages. Where in America should he go to earn a living?
3. A single man of twenty...Where in America should he go so that he can enrol in a technical school?
4. A single man of eighteen, an agricultural worker, where should he go to be able to earn his living in agriculture?[69]

One cannot be precise about the numbers of Jews who migrated, and where they went, because the records kept were only partial. However, Jacob Lestchinsky has conservatively estimated that 4,020,000 Jews migrated from central and eastern Europe in the period 1840-1947. Of these, 3,011,000 (74.9%) went to the U.S. and to Canada; 295,000 (7.3%) went to Argentina and Brazil; 95,000 (2.4%) to other South American countries; 434,000 (10.8%) to Palestine; and 185,000 (4.6%) to all other countries.[70] Two particular points stand out from these figures: the overwhelming popularity of the United States as a destination, and the absence of specific reference to Britain. The absence of Britain reflects the fact that it was a different kind of destination to the others. Generally, migrants going to the United States, Palestine or other places intended to stay there. Some of those going to Britain intended to settle there, but others intended to 'transmigrate' (although this is not a term they would have recognised), which is to say they intended to enter Britain before moving elsewhere. Some intended to stay in Britain for a period of time, perhaps of uncertain duration, so as to earn enough money to pay for their onward journey. Some just did not know when they entered Britain whether they intended to settle permanently or to transmigrate. The figures we have for Jewish immigration to Britain do not distinguish between the permanent settler and the transmigrant, and so figures for Jewish immigration to Britain are unreliable and tend not to appear in comparative tables.[71] [72]

How to choose where to go? First of all, there had to be economic opportunity. A chance to live comfortably and to make oneself wealthy attracted migrants to a number of countries, but particularly to the United States. It had fast-expanding new industries, including petrol refining, steel manufacturing and electrical power. Its railroads brought remote parts of the country into a national market economy. Between 1881 and 1914 about 22 million immigrants from different countries entered the United States, perhaps 10 per cent of them Jews. Mary Antin's family was one of them. She describes receiving a letter from her father. She was still in Polotsk, he was journeying to America. She opened the letter with her mother: "as we read the letter together in the darkened room ...there was an elation, a hint of triumph as had never been in my father's letters before. My father was inspired by a vision. He saw something - he promised us something. It was this 'America.' And 'America' became my dream".[73]

Alongside large-scale economic opportunity, Jews sought a liberal and constitutional, often a democratic, regime. It was important that the rule of law should apply; that there should be no pogroms or other violence against Jews and that they should be able to practise their religion freely, without molestation. It was also important that they go somewhere where they could educate their children properly. Evans-Gordon reported:

> Of all the questions one hears discussed among the Jews in Russia, none arouses keener feeling than this of education. It has an important influence upon the Hebrew exodus ... I came across several instances of Jewish workingmen [who] said that although they were comfortable enough they could not bear to deprive their children of education ...[74]

Such requirements tended to push Jews in the direction of English-speaking countries.

For some Jews considering emigration, their ideology and principles, or their views about religious practice, might influence their choice of emigration destination.

The most obvious example of ideologically motivated emigration is Zionism, albeit that in the 1880s and 1890s the Zionist movement was still in its infancy. In 1882, Leon Pinsker in his book "Auto-Emancipation" had urged Jews to seek a national retreat, preferably on the banks of the Jordan. In 1896 Herzl published his book Der Judenstaat ("The Jewish State"), urging Jews to seek their national home in Palestine. Five years later, in 1901 Herzl had an audience with the Sultan in which he argued, in vain, that the Sultan should cooperate in promoting Palestine as a national home for the Jewish people. In the 1880s and 1890s Palestine remained an impoverished and backward province of the Ottoman empire. There was very little economic development in Palestine and much of the land was barren. The regime was arbitrary and despotic. Communal Jewish authorities were rather repressive. Nonetheless, some intrepid pioneers were sufficiently inspired by the dream of a Jewish homeland to give it a try: around 35,000 Jews went to Palestine in the period 1840-1900, and a further 76,000 did so in the period 1901-1925. In each period this was approximately 3.5 per cent of all Jews who migrated from central and eastern Europe.[75] An indication of the difficulties and frustrations these pioneers encountered is that of the 90,000 Jews who went there between 1881 and 1914 (almost all of whom intended to stay, and not to transmigrate) only about 45,000 actually stayed.[76]

Religious belief and practice influenced the pattern of migration in two principal ways. First, it seems that the very devout were somewhat less likely to wish to emigrate. For many of the strictly orthodox what really mattered was belief in God and punctilious religious observance. Where one did this was secondary, but many rabbis feared that new lands would offer dangerous temptations and that strict religious observance would diminish there; they felt that a truly pious Jewish life was best lived in eastern Europe. Rabbi Israel Mayer Kagan Poupko, known as the Hafetz Haim, wrote a book known in English as "The Dispersed of Israel". It is a religious guide for emigrants. He argued that, if a person must emigrate, they should leave their children behind, as long as the children are old enough to care for themselves. Having emigrated, they should save money in their new land so as to return in prosperity to Eastern Europe and "walk there in the ways of the Lord". A second way in which religious belief and practice affected the pattern of migration is that some migrants chose to go to a particular place on the basis that a rabbi who was known to them personally or by reputation was living there, surrounded by a community which the prospective migrant expected to find congenial.

Finally, but importantly, practical considerations connected with the journey determined choice of emigration destination. Above all, how was the prospective emigrant to travel and was the cost of the journey affordable? Once arrived in the new country, would the emigrant be able to retain contact with friends and family in eastern Europe or to arrange for some of these people to join them in the destination country?

We have seen that these various economic, political, ideological and practical considerations pulled Eastern European Jewish immigrants in a variety of different directions, but overwhelmingly towards the United States and other English-speaking countries. A small number of emigrants went to Ireland. Why?

In collective memory, the fact that Jews chose to emigrate to Ireland is often characterised as a result of trickery practised on them, or their own foolishness. The Jews were said to be trying to reach the United States, but somehow or other landed up in Ireland. Being an Irish Jew was therefore a kind of accident, albeit one which had a funny side, and from which amusing anecdotes could be spun. These anecdotes take three main forms: the first claims that Jewish migrants were tricked into landing at Queenstown (later known as Cobh), the port for Cork, by dishonest ships' captains who had double-booked their onward passage to New York; the second suggests that migrants disembarked thinking they were in the United States having mistaken cries of 'Cork' for 'New York', or 'Ireland' for the Yiddish *aier land* (your land). The third maintains that the ship's supply of kosher food had run out and the strictly observant Jews preferred to stay in Ireland rather than starve or eat non-kosher food.[77]

The last of these stories is probably the one most based in reality. There were occasions when ships carrying migrating Jews bound for the United States had to put into Cork for repairs. Transatlantic shipping lines did not carry kosher food on board so when travellers' supplies ran out they were left with nothing to eat. In October 1891 passengers from one such ship were found wandering the town of Passage (between the port of Cobh and the city of Cork). About five hundred Jews were found on board "in a most pitiable state, some of them almost starving, and in a state of nudity". Some of these people had been driven from their homes at short notice as part of the expulsion of Jews from villages and from Moscow. Jews living in Cork came to their assistance.[78]

How then is one to account for these stories of the accidental origins of Irish Jewry? There can be no definitive answer. It is worth noting that not dissimilar stories exist in relation to other provincial British Jewish communities. A part of the answer may be that the stories do reflect, in a distorted way, a kind of underlying reality, in particular that the immigrants did face a measure of trickery and double-dealing from agents and others on their migratory journey and that some who stopped in Ireland may have done so in order to save money for an onward journey to the United States, but then for one reason or another decided to stay in Ireland. Some almost certainly stayed in Ireland because they had found conditions on the sea-voyage they had taken so unpleasantly over-crowded and sickness-inducing that they simply could not bear to take to sea again for the longer Atlantic sea-crossing. The stories of accidental origins may also reflect an underlying embarrassment on the part of second and third generation descendants of the immigrants seeking to explain to themselves and others why their parents chose to migrate to Ireland when they might have migrated to the United States or to South Africa, which were obviously much more prosperous destinations. It is also possible that stories of the accidental origins of Irish Jewry were, consciously or otherwise, part of an exercise in concealment. Perhaps the whimsical and amusing anecdotes were, at one level, designed to conceal from the Irish (or at least not draw attention to the fact) that Jews came to Ireland as a result of policy on the part of the Jewish establishment to disperse Jews around Britain and Ireland, and to which it was thought politic not to draw attention; and amusing anecdotes about the accidental origin of Irish Jewry may also have served to obscure the fact that some Jews actually chose to go to Ireland, perverse as this may sound, because they perceived there were particular economic opportunities for those willing to be pedlars in an impoverished rural environment. In Ireland, there was relatively little competition for Jewish pedlars from the indigenous population. Peddling required little start-up capital or English language skills. Litvaks knew how to do it – it was "a calling they brought with them from their homeland".[79] It offered some chance of socio-economic advancement and gave those involved in it the opportunity to return home each week to observe the Sabbath and Jewish festivals. In contrast to the United States, there was no glut of Jewish pedlars in Ireland.

Nonetheless, it may be that Jewish immigrants did not wish to draw attention to the fact that they were choosing to come to Ireland to peddle and a variety of amusing stories about accidental arrival in Ireland may have helped provide a useful smokescreen.[80] If stories of accidental arrival in Ireland contain a large element of myth-making it is clear one needs to look beyond them in order to find a convincing explanation as to why Jews went to Ireland.

Important background is that in the later part of the nineteenth century there was growing concern that Jewish migrants from the Pale were tending to concentrate in particular locations. That there was concentration of settlement is undeniable. Before the First World War about 60-70 per cent of immigrating Jews settled in London, mainly in the East End. Overall, about 80 per cent of Britain's Jews lived in just three places, London (180,000), Manchester (30,000) and Leeds (20,000). And the communities in Liverpool (8,000), Glasgow (7,500) and Birmingham (6,000) accounted for another 7 or 8 per cent.[81]

Concern about this geographic concentration of Jews was strongest among non-Jews, and was often most forcefully articulated by those closest to the principal areas of settlement. Major Evans-Gordon set out the concerns very clearly. He thought the influx of Jews created severe overcrowding in areas where they concentrated and that this led much of the native population to move out of the area and sometimes left those people with much longer journeys to their place of work. He argued that this concentration of Jews caused substantial increases in rents, and sharp practice on the part of some Jewish agents. The pleasant gardens and open spaces which used to abound "have nearly all disappeared, and these are now too often occupied by sweaters' workshops or are receptacles in which rags and garbage are piled."[82] The willingness of Jews to work long hours for low wages had the effect of depressing wages of local non-Jewish workers and placing undue pressure on them to work ever-longer hours. There was concern about observance of Sundays: "The day of rest has become a day of unrest .. there is a veritable babel of hawkers' cries"[83] and East End churches were "continually being left like islands in the midst of an alien sea".[84] Evans-Gordon expressed concern that these circumstances would stir up politically extreme feelings in the local native population. Moreover, he sought to draw a sharp distinction between Jewish immigrants from the Pale and earlier waves of non-Jewish immigrants to England, notably Huguenots and other persecuted Protestants. He thought Jewish immigrants were unassimilable: "Cleanliness, tradition, a sort of historical fear of separation from their co-religionists, their obligation to observe peculiar ritual ordinances", all of these kept Jews apart. "And the native folk cannot assimilate this element, for intermarriage with Gentiles is forbidden by the precepts of the Jewish faith and is opposed to the Hebrew ideal."[85]

Evans-Gordon thought the answer to what he thought was the problem of the concentration of Jews was to control immigration, encourage repatriation and onward migration and, significantly, to disperse immigrants around Britain and Ireland. He said: "this 'ghetto habit'... impels and tempts Jewish immigrants to congregate in crowded quarters of populous cities [and it is this] from which all the dangers and evils ... spring ... If they were scattered and, as it were, sprinkled among the 40,000,000 of people in England few would take heed of their presence."[86]

With the passage of time Evans-Gordon's anxieties have come to seem over-heated, indeed plain wrong. Within a generation or two many East End Jews had moved to the suburbs, which relieved over-crowding. Many Jews had established their own businesses, substantially increasing overall net employment for the wider community and making Evans-Gordon's economic analysis appear an example of what economists now term "the lump of labour fallacy". By the early twenty-first century, descendants of immigrant Jews had become highly acculturated, and a majority were not choosing to marry Jewish partners. The unassimilable were assimilating.

Even if mistaken, Evans-Gordon clearly articulated a number of concerns which non-Jews felt about Jewish immigration from the Pale and to which the older-established Anglo-Jewish community felt bound to respond. One of the main responses was to attempt to anglicise the new immigrants as quickly as possible, concentrating on rapid anglicisation of their children. Many of these efforts were ineffectual and some were rather strongly resented.[87] There were a variety of instruments for this process. One was the Jewish Lads Brigade, which its founder Colonel A.E. W. Goldsmid said was for "ironing out the ghetto bend" so as "to instil all that is best in the English character". Another instrument for anglicisation was the Jews' Free School, established in 1732. Moses Angel, its headmaster from 1842-1897, thought his pupils were drawn from "the refuse population of the worst parts of Europe" who needed to be "anglicised or humanised".[88]

Another response of the established Anglo-Jewish community to concerns of the kind Evans-Gordon raised was to attempt to disperse immigrant Jews around Britain and Ireland. These efforts were discreet, informal and relatively minor. They are now difficult to trace, but there are a few indications of this activity. The Jewish Board of Guardians appears to have organised the voluntary transfer of some Jewish immigrants from London to Ireland in the early 1870s.[89] Charles Booth, the great investigator of the condition of the London poor, conceded in 1887 that "The Jewish Board of Guardians are fully cognisant of this deplorable state of things [that parts of the East End are 'overrun'], and have made great exertions to check the influx and to send back or send further those who have come."[90] E.N. Adler, son of Chief Rabbi Nathan Adler, recalled that his late father had made a pastoral visit to Ireland in 1871, following which he had expressed the desire to induce Jews to settle in Ireland.[91]

In some countries to which Jews migrated there were organisations which more openly encouraged the dispersal of migrants. In the United States the Jewish banker Jacob Schiff established the Industrial Removal

Office (IRO) for this purpose, and in France the Alliance Israelite Universelle actively encouraged dispersal. In Britain and Ireland the policy of dispersal was pursued very quietly until the early twentieth century when the activities of the Jewish Congregational Union's Dispersal Committee made the policy more open. With hindsight, one might question whether dispersal was a good idea. In the first years of the twentieth century, *The Jewish Chronicle* is full of reports of provincial Jewish communities which found it difficult to attract good Rabbis, which worried about the Jewish education of their children, which were in perilous financial circumstances and whose young adults tended to move away in search of better employment opportunities and more chance of finding a suitable marriage partner.[92] In time, most of the smaller provincial Jewish communities in Britain and Ireland withered and many of them died out.

It seems, therefore, that by the 1870s a handful of Litvaks had arrived in Ireland, through a combination of accidental landing and a very discreet dispersal policy on the part of the Jewish Board of Guardians and a handful of authority figures in the Anglo-Jewish establishment. Within a short time, the originally small Eastern European presence triggered a 'chain migration' of relatives, friends and *landsmen*. This chain migration was a very common feature of Jewish migration from the Pale of Settlement. By way of comparison, for example, 94 per cent of the Jewish immigrants to the United States between 1899 and 1914 reported that they were joining a relative.[93] Most of the Lithuanian Jews who migrated to Ireland from 1881 onwards were joining a relative or family friend. The point is well-made in a piece in *The Jewish Chronicle* by its Dublin correspondent called 'Halitvak' (E.R. Lipsett) in 1906:

> The entire Hebrew community of Dublin, excluding the few - very few so-called 'Englische Yidden' - are as one family, coming from the same stock, and knowing each other from home, down to many generations past. With a few isolated exceptions they all hail from the Government of Kovno, and some time ago it used to be said that the town of Okmyan [Akmene] had emptied itself out into the arteries of the South Circular Road, Dublin.[94]

It is striking that the small towns and shtetlach from which Litvaks emigrated to Ireland were all located in the same small corner of northern Lithuania (the Kovno *guberniya* in Tsarist times), bordering the Courland region of Latvia. As well as Pikeliai, the towns and shtetlach included: Viekšniai, Akmene, Žhagarė, Šiauliai, Papile, Klykoliai, Židikai, Telšiai and

Kuršėnai. None of these places were more than about fifty kilometres from any of the others. 9 These towns and shtetlach were small and most of them had a majority Jewish population. According to the Russian census of 1897, 56% of Viekšniai was Jewish, 71% of Šiauliai was Jewish and 73 % of Židikai was Jewish. The Schonbergs report on Lithuanian Jewish communities says that Akmene's Jews were engaged in small businesses, crafts and agriculture; Židikai's Jews were small scale traders and pedlars in the villages of Courland and Klykoliai's Jews were "pedlars going out to neighbouring villages on Sunday and not returning until Sabbath eve."[96]

'Chain migration' therefore involved Jewish immigrants who came from a handful of small towns and shtetlach in northern Lithuania, and who knew each other through family ties and trading connections, following each other to Ireland and, at least initially, continuing to engage in a similar kind of small-scale trade and peddling that their families had been involved with in Lithuania. Those who were already established in Ireland felt a certain obligation to look out for and assist the new arrivals. When Myer Joel Wigoder arrived in Dublin from Viekšniai in 1890, a Litvak boy he met in the street took him to the house of Mr. Eppel who gave him the addresses of other Viekšniai immigrants. In Jessie Spiro Bloom's home by the Grand Canal near Portobello in Dublin "there was a constant stream of people passing through…and many of them would stop over at our home ..."[97]

For 'chain migration' to work effectively a number of favourable circumstances need to apply: first of all, there needs to be a means of communication between the immigrant in the destination country and their friends and family back home in the country of origin. In the late nineteenth century steamships were regularly travelling between Liepāja and Cobh (the port for Cork), and so letters could be exchanged regularly, albeit this process was slow. Secondly, the immigrant needs to feel that there will be a way to travel affordably to the proposed destination country and, once there, to earn a living, even if modest; peddling, unglamorous to say the least, was nonetheless an activity familiar to many Jews, and without real barriers to entry, which could be pursued in southern Ireland. Above all, there needs to be a sense that the immigrant will be safe in the destination country, that the indigenous people will be mainly respectful to the incomer, and treat them decently.

There was a feeling among many Jews in late nineteenth century Lithuania that the British and Irish establishment, while being far from unanimous in welcoming Jewish immigration, was nonetheless basically fair-minded and likely to afford a generally courteous welcome. Some Litvaks had heard that there had been a great public meeting in London at the Mansion House on 1 February 1882 under the auspices of the Lord Mayor of the City "to express public opinion upon the outrages inflicted upon the Jews in various parts of Russia and Russian Poland". The Earl of Shaftesbury, the Bishop of London, and Cardinal Manning all attended the Mansion House in person and spoke at length. Messages of support from the Archbishop of Canterbury, the Duke of Westminster, the Master of Balliol College Oxford, the Poet Laureate (Lord Tennyson) and other notables were read aloud. Such a public display of sympathy and support from the highest echelons of the British establishment left a powerful impression.

Newly arrived Jews in Ireland reported to their family and friends in Lithuania that they had received a generally favourable reception from the local Irish community. In 1980 Larry Elyan had an article published in *The Jewish Chronicle* called 'From Zhogger to Cork'. It is about his grandfather, the Reverend Meyer Elyan, known to him as 'Zeida' (Hebrew for grandfather), who moved to Cork in 1881, as the community's first Rabbi. Larry Elyan recalled how touched his grandfather was by the reception he received:

> .. to be able to go about unafraid was ... a new-found pleasure ... Zeida spoke glowingly of the many acts of kindness they received from their Catholic neighbours. "We couldn't speak a word of English", he said. "You understand, not a word, adding with unabashed pride: they used to raise their hats to me, a foreigner...

Meyer Elyan became friendly with a Protestant minister called Reverend Kerr and a Catholic priest called Father O'Leary.

> It was the first time that either of them had ever met a rabbi in the flesh. As Zeida recalled what these two had done for him, his eyes would light up as if he were recalling having seen Moses coming down from Mount Sinai. A wondrous miracle. These two clergymen had collected money from their parishioners in aid of the poor Jewish community of Cork.[98]

There would certainly be some tensions in relations between Jewish immigrants and native Irish in the years after 1881. There were boycotts of Jewish traders and occasional scuffles; but, these difficulties were as nothing compared to Jewish experiences in Lithuania. Overall, the Jewish perception was that the native Irish were welcoming. There is an interesting letter from the Mayor of Cork published in *The Times* on 15 March 1888 which sheds light on some particular reasons as to why this was so. The main purpose of the letter was to counter suggestions that two members of the Cork Trades Council had been hostile to local Jews and "to say that we entirely repudiate sympathy or connection with attacks on Jewish people". The Mayor goes on to say that Irishmen are "proud of the fact that theirs is the only country in Europe in which Jews have never been persecuted". He emphasises that the Irish are particularly well placed to empathise with the predicament of Jews: "We fully appreciate that the wanderers who are driven abroad by oppression [Jews] are in the very same position as the evicted Irish emigrants who have been obliged to leave here for England, America and other colonies ..." Although he does not quite say this, one is left with the impression that the Mayor is almost proud that Jewish people should have chosen his country and city in which to settle, given that Europeans in the nineteenth century did not generally choose Ireland as a country to which to migrate.

By the early 1890s my great-grandfather Myer was ensconced in Cork. Definitive evidence as to the reasons for his migration from northern Lithuania, and his means of bringing it about, remains elusive, but the following account, admittedly based on some speculation, seems to me most likely.

Myer and his family's life had become ever more difficult in northern Lithuania following the Tsarist regime's more rigorous enforcement of the May Laws at the end of the 1880s. Edicts which expelled Jews from Moscow and villages added to their woes by substantially increasing economic competition. Stricter enforcement of the May Laws created difficulties. Myer was of the age to be concripted for military service. He did not want to serve in the Tsar's army because it would waste five years of his life for no useful purpose. He would be sent far from family and friends where he would be unable to observe Jewish dietary laws and would be unable to observe the Sabbath and Jewish religious holidays. Some soldiers with whom he would have to serve were likely to be hostile to him because he was Jewish. He had a deep-seated reluctance to serve a regime responsible for so much legislation which discriminated against Jews and which quietly encouraged, or turned a blind eye to, anti-Jewish violence elsewhere in the Pale of Settlement. As he was avoiding conscription, he was unable to obtain a passport to leave Russia. He and his family knew other Jewish people from the surrounding shtetlach and small towns who had moved to Ireland, including members of his family. They reported back that, by peddling, one could just about make a living in Ireland and that the local people were, for the most part, friendly enough. Myer did not have strong personal or family connections with Jewish people who had migrated elsewhere and, besides, he could not afford to travel to the United States straightaway. At the time of deciding to go to Ireland he was unsure whether he would stay there permanently or move on to the United States; that would depend on how things worked out. If he did decide to move on to the United States he would, by moving to Ireland, be well on his way and, because Cobh is a deep-water port and trans-Atlantic steamers stopped there, there would be no shortage of ships to take him onwards. He may have secured an understanding from people he worked with in Lithuania and Latvia that they would supply him with furniture and other items to sell in southern Ireland. He took the Libau-Romny railway from Vainode, changing in Vilnius. From there, Myer made his way towards a north German port, crossing the Russian-German frontier without a passport, unlawfully, and at night. He took a ship from Hamburg or Bremen to Hull, crossed England by train from Hull to Liverpool and from there took a further ship to Ireland, perhaps passing through Dublin en route to Cork.

This account, if broadly correct, is not exactly flight from pogrom to a promised land; nor does it exactly amount to a search for economic plenty in a promised land. The story is rather more nuanced than that. It is a decision to move, taken tentatively and in haste, to avoid the imminent danger of conscription. It is predicated on continuing links with the Baltic. Above all, it suggests an attempt to keep doors open. It allows for the possibility of return to Lithuania if circumstances improve, or of onward migration elsewhere, most obviously to the United States, if life in Ireland proved too difficult.

Notes

1 David Vital, *A People Apart: A Political History of the Jews in Europe 1789-1939* (OUP Oxford, 2001), p. 298.
2 Irving Howe, *World of Our Fathers: The Journey of the East European Jews to America and the Life They Found and Made There* (Phoenix, 2000).
3 Cormac Ó Gráda, *Jewish Ireland in the Age of Joyce: A Socioeconomic History* (Princeton University Press, 2016), p. 13.
4 Scott Ury, 'Migration as Redemption: The Myth and Memory of Jewish Migration from Eastern Europe to the New World', *Jewish Culture and History*, 20.1 (2019), 3–22.
5 Gráda, p. 16.

6 Gráda, p. 9.
7 Ury, p. 6.
8 Howe Chapter 1.
9 Salo W. Baron, Ghetto and Emancipation, 1928.
10 Hasia R. Diner, *The Jews of the United States, 1654 to 2000* (University of California Press, 2006).
11 Gur Alroey, *Bread to Eat and Clothes to Wear: Letters from Jewish Migrants in the Early Twentieth Century* (Wayne State University Press, 2011).
12 Gráda, p. 11.
13 Timothy J. Hatton and Jeffrey G. Williamson, 'After the Famine: Emigration from Ireland, 1850–1913', *The Journal of Economic History*, 53.3 (1993), 575–600.
14 Vital, p. 298.
15 Vital, p. 309.
16 Alroey, p. 11.
17 Alroey, pp. 10–11.
18 Alroey, p. 72.
19 Vital, p. 308.
20 Greenbaum, p. 187.
21 Hugh Seton-Watson, *The Russian Empire 1801-1917* (Clarendon Press, 1967), p. 493.
22 Greenbaum, pp. 190–91.
23 William Evans-Gordon, *The Alien Immigrant* (BiblioBazaar, 2016), p. 56.
24 Michael R. Marrus, 'The Theory and Practice of Anti-Semitism', in *The Origins of the Holocaust* (KG Saur, 2011), pp. 172–84.
25 Vladas Sirutavicius and Darius Staliunas, *A Pragmatic Alliance: Jewish-Lithuanian Political Cooperation at the Beginning of the 20th Century* (Central European University Press, 2011), pp. 77–118.
26 Darius Staliunas, *Enemies for a Day: Antisemitism and Anti-Jewish Violence in Lithuania under the Tsars* (Central European University Press, 2015), p. 23.
27 Mary Antin, *The Promised Land* (West Margin Press, 2020), p. 14.
28 Staliunas, p. 71.
29 Staliunas, p. 73.
30 Staliunas, pp.79–83.
31 Vital, p. 283.
32 Staliunas, p. 85.
33 Antony Polonsky, *The Jews in Poland and Russia: Volume II: 1881 To 1914* (Littman Library of Jewish Civilization, 2019), p. 5.
34 Benjamin Nathans, *Beyond the Pale: The Jewish Encounter with Late Imperial Russia* (University of California Press, 2002), p. 321.

35 Paul R. Mendes-Flohr and Jehuda Reinharz, *The Jew in the Modern World: A Documentary History* (Oxford University Press, 2011), p. 388.
36 *The Jewish Chronicle*, 17 November 1882.
37 Vital, p. 293.
38 Staliunas, p. 113.
39 Staliunas, p. 123.
40 Vital, p. 159.
41 Adina Ofek, 'Cantonists: Jewish Children as Soldiers in Tsar Nicholas's Army', *Modern Judaism*, 1993, 277–308.
42 Michael Stanislawski, *Tsar Nicholas I and the Jews: The Transformation of Jewish Society in Russia, 1825-1855* (Jewish Publication Society of America, 1983), pp. 22–25.
43 Gráda, p. 28.
44 Carole Malkin, *The Journeys of David Toback: As Retold by His Granddaughter* (Schocken Books, 1981).
45 Antin, p. 17.
46 Antin, p. 163.
47 Yohanan Petrovsky-Shtern, *Jews in the Russian Army, 1827-1917* (Cambridge Unioversity Press,2009).
48 Chaim Weizmann, *Trial and Error: The Autobiography of Chaim Weizmann* (Harper, 1949), pp. 90–92.
49 Evans-Gordon, p. 108.
50 Great Britain Parliament House of Commons, *Royal Commission on Alien Immigration. Minutes of Evidence Taken Before the Royal Commission on Alien Immigration. Vol. II.* (House of Commons, 2007), pp. 451–66.
51 Commons, p. 459.
52 Antin, p. 25.
53 Vital, p. 303.
54 Levin, p. 90.
55 Evans-Gordon, p. 80.
56 Allan Spetter, 'The United States, the Russian Jews and the Russian Famine of 1891–1892', *American Jewish Historical Quarterly*, 64.3 (1975), 236–44.
57 Eric M. Johnson, 'Demographics, Inequality and Entitlements in the Russian Famine of 1891', *Slavonic & East European Review*, 93.1 (2015), 96–119.
58 Evans-Gordon, pp. 61–62.
59 Gráda, p. 16.
60 Evans-Gordon, p. 62.
61 Antin, p. 101.

62 Alroey, pp. 44–63.
63 Alroey, p. 58.
64 Antin, p. 124.
65 Nicholas J. Evans, 'Work in Progress: Indirect Passage from Europe Transmigration via the UK, 1836-1914', *Journal for Maritime Research*, 3.1 (2001), 70-84
66 Evans-Gordon, p. 103.
67 Aubrey Newman, 'The Poor Jews' Temporary Shelter: An Episode in Migration Studies', *Jewish Historical Studies*, 40 (2005), 141–55.
68 Gur Alroey, 'Information, Decision, and Migration: Jewish Emigration from Eastern Europe in the Early Twentieth Century', *Immigrants & Minorities*, 29.01 (2011), 33–63 (p. 37).
69 Alroey, pp. 131–32.
70 Mark Wischnitzer, *To Dwell in Safety: The Story of Jewish Migration Since 1800* (Jewish Publication Society of America, 1949), p. 295.
71 Lloyd P. Gartner, 'Notes on the Statistics of Jewish Immigration to England 1870-1914', *Jewish Social Studies*, 1960, 97–102.
72 Cecil Bloom, 'The Politics of Immigration, 1881-1905', *Jewish Historical Studies*, 33 (1992), 187–214.
73 Antin, p. 104. There is no doubting the vigour of Mary Antin's writing. Some Jewish critics, however, have decried her fulsome gratitude towards the new land; while others have insisted that her attitude needs to be read in the context of her campaign against restrictive immigration laws.
74 Evans-Gordon, pp. 72–73.
75 Wischnitzer, p. 295.
76 Lloyd P. Gartner, 'The Great Jewish Migration 1881-1914: Myths and Realities', *Shofar*, 4.2 (1986), 12–21.
77 Natalie Wynn, 'The History and Internal Politics of Ireland's Jewish Community in Their International Jewish Context (1881-1914)' (unpublished PhD Thesis, Trinity College Dublin, 2015), pp. 94–95.
78 *The Jewish Chronicle* 30 October 1891.
79 Hannah Berman and Melisande Zlotover, *Zlotover Story: A Dublin Story with a Difference* (Hely Thom Limited, 1966).
80 Gráda Chapter 2.
81 Todd M. Endelman, *The Jews of Britain, 1656 to 2000* (University of California Press, 2002), pp. 129–30.
82 Evans-Gordon, pp. 10–11.
83 Evans-Gordon, p. 13.
84 Evans-Gordon, p. 13.
85 Evans-Gordon, p. 7.

86 Evans-Gordon, p. 253.
87 David Feldman, *Englishmen and Jews: Social Relations and Political Culture, 1840-1914* (Yale University Press, 1994).
88 Wynn, p.75.
89 Gráda, p. 25.
90 Vital, p. 319.
91 *The Jewish Chronicle* 31 March 1905.
92 *The Jewish Chronicle* 30 May 1884 and 30 September 1898.
93 Charlotte Erickson, 'Jewish People in the Atlantic Migration, 1850-1914', *In Patterns of Migration*, 1850-1914, 1–18.
94 Referred to in Wynn, pp.93-94.
95 Gráda, p. 23.
96 Nancy Schoenburg and Stuart Schoenburg, *Lithuanian Jewish Communities* (Rowman & Littlefield, 1996).
97 Gráda, p. 23.
98 *The Jewish Chronicle* 26 September 1980.

4

Lithuania 1896-1921

By 1896 Myer was established in Cork in southern Ireland. It is not clear where he first lived, but he probably stayed with family in Hibernian Buildings before finding more permanent accommodation. By the summer of 1901 he was residing in North Main Street, Cork.[1] This was in the heart of medieval Anglo-Norman Cork, a historic neighbourhood although since the 1820s North Main Street had been rather overtaken by St Patrick's Street as the main business street of the city. The Cork Jewish community was small, and initially Myer knew only a handful of its members. Much of Myer's extensive family and his circle of friends remained in the Baltic, mainly in Lithuania. Their aspirations and travails continued to be a central part of his life.

Lithuanian Jewish life continued to be dominated by the fact that the government was in the hands of an autocratic Tsar. The character and policy of the Tsar profoundly affected Jewish life. Nicholas II succeeded as Tsar in 1894. He strongly believed in *Samoderzhetsvo*, the principle of absolute, God-given autocratic power. He married Alix of Hesse, who became known as Alexandra Feodorovna. When the couple's fifth child, a son called Alexander, proved to be a haemophiliac, the Tsar's family became surrounded with 'holy men' of whom the most powerful and best-known was Grigory Rasputin. Both the Tsar and Tsarina came under Rasputin's influence, but Rasputin turned the Tsarina in particular into a religious fanatic and mystic. Tsar Nicholas II was strongly antisemitic. When workers went on strike in St.Petersburg in 1896 he appointed Plehve, a known reactionary and disciple of the antisemitic Pobedonostsev, as his Minister of the Interior with instructions that Plehve suppress the uprising. With the Tsar's support Plehve adopted antisemitic policies, promising to put down the uprising "in the blood of the *zhidi*" (the pejorative Russian term for Jews).[2]

Count Witte, who became Prime Minister in 1905, published three volumes of memoirs which, among other things, provide a valuable insight into Tsar Nicholas II's private views of Jews. Witte saw the Black Hundreds for what they were: gangs of thugs who were responsible for killing and raping countless numbers of Jews in pogroms. However, Witte reported that Nicholas II and his wife greatly admired these thugs, and indeed regarded them as "the pride of the nation". The Okhrana, which was the Tsar's own secret police force, knew the Black Hundreds to be thieves and murderers; these were people "with whom decent Russians do not shake hands". Witte described this period as one of continuous and widespread persecution of Jews; he thought that never before had Jews been subject to such abuse in Russia and he expressed deep concern that this attitude to Jews had become a prerequisite for conservatives in Russia to achieve political advancement: "One who is not a Jew-hater cannot achieve a reputation as a true conservative."[3]

Jewish life in Lithuania continued to be characterised by abject poverty, caused or exacerbated by the combined effect of the 650 Tsarist laws discriminating against Jews which had been identified by the Phalen Commission. A number of contemporary accounts dwell on the clearly rather shocking extent of this poverty. The Phalen Commission itself said: "About 90% of the entire Jewish population is an insecure mass living in poverty and misery". A more extensive description of the poverty of everyday life of Lithuanian Jews is provided by Julius Brutzkus's contemporary reports. Brutzkus, who went on to become Minister for Jewish affairs in the Independent Republic of Lithuania, said: "In 1911 two-thirds of the Jewish population of Lithuania earned their living by serving as 'hewers of wood and drawers of water', coachmen, brickmakers, and in other servile capacities. Poverty was endemic, sanitary conditions extremely primitive. More than one third of the Jews depended on charity; money forwarded by relatives provided some with their sole income."[4] The American Jewish Committee's Report on "The Jews in the Eastern War Zone", which was drawn up in 1916, said:

> The results of repressions and persecutions are known…the Jewish population imprisoned in the Pale has festered in misery. The merchants have been obliged to resort to fearful competition. Workingmen, overcrowding their industries, have been compelled to work for starvation wages. Most of the Jewish homes in Russia are miserable hovels, with little air or light. In the great cities, the proportion of paupers amounts to approximately a fifth of the Jewish population. In Odessa in 1900, of a population of 150,000 Jews no less than 48,500 were supported by charity; 63 per cent. of the dead had pauper burials, and a further 20 per cent were buried at the lowest possible rate.[5]

If anything, the poverty of Jews increased in late nineteenth century Lithuania, as laws restricting where they could live were more rigidly enforced which increased competition among Jews in those places where they could live. Lithuania was also adversely affected by agricultural crisis. Western European markets were flooded with cheap grain from the United States, making it harder for Lithuanians to export, and reducing the price of agricultural produce and therefore of farmers' incomes. The situation was aggravated by differential tariffs which encouraged grain export from central provinces of the Russian empire. This agricultural crisis bore most directly on agricultural labourers, but their distress had knock-on adverse economic consequences for Jews in Lithuania.[6]

Lithuanian Jews also had to endure hostility from the local ethnic Lithuanian peasantry, which periodically erupted into violence directed against Jews and their property. A study has been made of anti-Jewish violence in the northern Lithuanian districts of Panevėžys and Šiauliai in June and early July 1900.[7] Three pogroms took place (at Deltuva on June 4, at Linkuva on June 18 and at Pašušvys on June 25), two incipient pogroms were put down by the police and Cossacks (at Žeimelis on June 29 and at Deltuva on July 2) and there was one small outbreak of anti-Jewish violence which would probably not have developed into a full-blown pogrom, even though one Jew died from the wounds he sustained (at Pamūšis on June 30). These pogroms are interesting to study precisely because they were comparatively 'normal', which is to say they were not triggered by wider political crisis, as happened with pogroms in 1881 after the assassination of Tsar Alexander II and with the pogroms in 1905 at the time of the Russo-Japanese war. The pogroms of 1900 involved violence against Jews and against their property. Their character becomes clear by looking at the relatively typical example of what occurred at Pašvitinys, near Linkuva, on 25 June that year. It was a Sunday and a large number of Lithuanian peasants had gathered in town. Some went to church, but others stood in groups in the town square. After mass ended at around 1:00 pm several Lithuanians attacked an elderly Jew named Movsa Makhat, but he managed to escape. Then, a mob of between 500 and 1,000 attacked Jewish houses around the square with sticks and stones. Later, the mob moved along the mainly Jewish Linkuva Street and returned towards the square to damage the remaining Jewish houses (a total of 53 houses were affected). Several Jews were beaten. Premises of the Jewish apothecary and the synagogue were damaged. Religious books in the synagogue were torn to pieces, and damages were suffered to the value of 326 rubles and 75 kopeks. The pogrom ended at about 4:00 pm.[8] By the standards of what was to occur in later years this was a minor event. Nobody was killed. Nonetheless, it was seriously unsettling for the Jews of Pašvitinys and the surrounding area.

One should try to be as clear as possible about the characteristics of those who took part in anti-Jewish violence at Pašvitinys. The underground Lithuanian press called them "farm lads" or "striplings". Police records of the questioning of the accused and the charge sheets suggest they were young people from neighbouring villages, economically dependent on others, unmarried, and illiterate. Approximately two-thirds of them were less than 30 years old. Many earned their living as hirelings, or as millers or bricklayers. Court records suggest that many of the accused, and many witnesses, tried to ascribe blame to one of the oldest participants, Juozapas Eidukas, who had already been convicted of bodily harm in relation to another incident. His doctor thought him mildly insane. Others blamed the brothers Julius and Jonas Pocius. They had a previous conviction for theft and were to go on to murder a Jewish tradesman, Leizer Shokhet, during an attempted robbery in 1902. Such people were marginal characters. They may indeed have played a prominent part in the violence, but the fact remains that as many as 1,000 people took part in the pogrom in Pašvitinys. This was a substantial proportion of the local young male Lithuanian population. It may be that many who were charged in subsequent proceedings found it convenient to treat Eidukas and the Pocius brothers as scapegoats, believing they would be unable to defend themselves effectively, and moreover that the authorities would deal leniently with Eidukas, recognising he was not entirely sane.[9]

The obvious question begged by the pogrom at Pašvitinys in 1900, and by similar incidents, is why Lithuanians behaved in this way to their Jewish neighbours.

A fundamental part of the answer is that many Lithuanian Catholics continued to disdain Jews because they regarded every Jew as being responsible, in perpetuity, for the killing of Jesus. In addition, Jews were suspected of kidnapping and killing Christian children at the time of Passover so as to use their blood in the baking of *matzot* [the unleavened bread eaten by Jews during Passover]. Extraordinarily, this seems to have been widely believed among Catholic Lithuanians and is a recurring feature of pogroms at this time. Local officials investigating the pogrom in Deltuva in 1900 said that tales of Jews stealing Christian children for religious purposes were something babies imbibed with their mothers' milk and naughty children were routinely warned that they "would end up in Jewish *matzot*".[10] Many Jews believed that Catholic priests and the Catholic press were central to the dissemination of these ideas. Two Jewish witnesses from

Deltuva said that they visited local priests after rumours spread of a coming pogrom. They were met with the priestly response: "Is it not true that Jews need Christian blood? Read the newspapers, there was such a case in Vilnius not long ago".[11] The newspaper *Ūkininkas* described the wave of pogroms in northern Lithuania around 1900 and had no doubt that religious hatred towards Jews was being spread by the Catholic church. It seems that common religious identity drew the mob together helping bond them into what has been called a 'socio-confessional community'. Jews, as the 'other', were vital to this bonding.

There was nothing very new in turn of the century Lithuania about the fact that some Catholics disliked Jews. Other ingredients were needed to convert this underlying disdain into violence.

It is sometimes thought that one such ingredient may have been the growth of Lithuanian nationalism. At a practical level, nationalists needed to define who was and who was not a part of the nation. The large cultural, religious and linguistic gap between Jews and Lithuanians made it difficult for Jews to be accepted as fully part of the Lithuanian nation, even if they were Lithuanian speaking and wore Western clothes. The Panevėžys and Šiauliai districts were important centres of the Lithuanian national movement, although less important than other parts of northern Lithuania such as the border regions of Raseiniai and Telšiai. If national consciousness was the main driving force behind these pogroms, one might expect to find more pogroms in those areas. Moreover, it seems that Lithuanian nationalists were often more exercised about the presence of ethnic Russians than of Jews. In other words, national feeling may have contributed to a pogrom atmosphere but it was only one of the ingredients: Jews were not at the top of the hierarchy of enemies of nationally aware Lithuanians.

Economic competition between Jews and ethnic Lithuanians also contributed to the pogrom atmosphere. This competition had intensified in turn of the century Lithuania because of the general downturn in the economy, combined with the fact that Lithuanians were beginning to become involved in trading activities which had traditionally been the preserve of Jews alone. As industrialisation began to infiltrate remote northern Lithuania, Jews and Lithuanians began to come into direct economic competition. This led to a host of accusations to the effect that Jews were engaged in unfair economic activity, were exploiting poor Lithuanians and that they cheated. Economic competition and resentment contributed to the smashing of Jewish-owned shops in the pogroms of 1900. The liberal newspaper *Ūkininkas* counselled against such action on the basis that "by destroying and smashing some Jewish shop, people will not get their own shops and free themselves from the Jews who, being more skilled in general in commercial matters, always show the way to backward Lithuanians."[12]

Rumours spread fast and mutated quickly among the uneducated Lithuanian population. Rumours seem to have played an important role in creating the pogrom atmosphere of 1900. The pogromists' counsel, Jonas Vileisis, said during the trial relating to the Pamūšis incident: "Intellectuals believe rumours too, so what can we say about simple ignorant folk – this is the sole source of their knowledge of external events". During the pogroms of 1900 the rumours appear to have been of two kinds: first, that Jews had done harm to Christians: there were endless variations of the story that Jews kidnapped and killed Christian children and young people so as to use their blood in Jewish festivals, and particularly at Passover. Secondly, there were rumours to the effect that the Tsar and Tsarina had issued a decree allowing the beating of Jews with impunity. In Deltuva there were rumours that the authorities permitted the beating (even the putting to death) of a Jew but that a price of three kopeks had to be paid. Other rumours said that three kopeks had to be paid for killing a village Jew, five for a town Jew and fifteen kopeks for a rabbi. An 'opposite rumour' suggested that the government would pay the person who killed a Jew. It is striking how often the figure three recurs in these rumours and it has been speculated that this may refer to the thirty pieces of silver Judas received for betraying Jesus.[13] A number of authority figures suggested that stories about missing children and the Tsar's decree were spread as part of a malicious plan. The Governor of Kaunas claimed that the rumours stemmed from "secret agitation" and the Deltuva police officer blamed "malicious persons". Because the rumours were so varied and mutated so quickly it seems improbable that they were centrally organised. It is more likely that they evolved, like 'Chinese whispers'. The rumours circulated among uneducated people predisposed to believe, and to embroider, what they heard.

There were isolated and spontaneous Jewish efforts at self-defence: Josef Vilenskii, the assistant chemist at the chemist's shop in Pašvitinys, poured sulphuric acid out of the window and onto the attackers below. In Pamūšis a man called Gruber attempted to oppose the mob and struck one member of it "with an iron glove", an action which further enraged the mob and cost Gruber his life. The problem for the Jewish community was that such acts of self-defence tended to be counter-productive; they simply made the mob more angry. The fundamental difficulty was the absence of any effective self-defence organisation. As it was, Jews had little alternative but to rely on the goodwill of local officials, which was often in short supply. At the margins, bribery of officials could provide some protection. Otherwise, the best tactic seemed to be to hide from the mob and hope their fury would subside.

The Lithuanian pogroms of 1900 should be kept in context. They were far less extensive than pogroms in southern Russia during the period between the assassination of Tsar Alexander II in 1881 and the outbreak of the First World War in 1914. The reasons for the relative lack of pogroms in Lithuania at this time are not entirely clear. Explanations can only be tentative: it may be that in the period immediately following Tsar Alexander II's assassination the conduct of Governor Totleben was decisive in preventing pogroms in Lithuania and the habit of engaging in pogroms did not therefore develop as happened in the south. Later, the fact that Lithuanian nationalists regarded Russians and Poles as their principal national antagonists may have assisted Jews by pushing them down the list of Lithuanians' ethnic rivals and potential enemies. It is also noteworthy that Lithuania was comparatively undeveloped economically and this meant that intra-communal economic rivalries were less intense than was the case further south. Whatever the reasons for the comparative lack of pogroms in Lithuania, events further south almost certainly influenced behaviour in northern Lithuania. The example of pogroms in the south encouraged some in northern Lithuania to contemplate the possibility of 'copycat' attacks.

The fear and resentment generated by pogroms in the summer of 1900 created a toxic atmosphere, and this endured. In a circular of 8 July the Governor of Kaunas said: "the mood of the Jews is suppressed and frightened, and that of the Christian population is fervent and threatening". The investigations and legal proceedings that followed the pogroms meant that intra-communal tension persisted.

As we have seen, my great-grandfather Myer became a naturalised British subject in 1901. As he contemplated the predicament of family and friends left behind in northern Lithuania he must have reflected on their misfortune of being subject to poverty and hostility from the local population and that, in practice, only a handful of alternatives were available to them.

The most obvious alternative was to emigrate. Myer appears to have encouraged his family to do this, and he met with success. Most of Myer's siblings did emigrate. Myer's parents had lived in Pikeliai and he and his six siblings had been born there. The death notice for Myer's mother, known as Zisse, appeared in *The Jewish Chronicle* on 18 February 1910.[14] It is clear from this that, by 1910, Myer's father and two of Myer's siblings had died. Myer, Zisse and two of Myer's other siblings (Philip and Jacob) were living in Ireland. One sibling (Aaron) had emigrated to South Africa. Only one of Myer's siblings (Hiya Henna) remained in Lithuania, probably because her husband had commitments there. Tragically, she was murdered by the Nazis in Kaunas in 1941.

Myer's family experience was not untypical. The period between the mid-1890s and the outbreak of First World War saw a substantial increase in Jewish emigration from Russia. Of the approximately 1.6 million Jews from the Russian empire who emigrated between 1880 and 1914 almost two-thirds left between 1903 and 1914, triggered in particular by the wave of pogroms that swept Russia between 1903 and 1906 and also by the economic disruptions caused by the Russo-Japanese war and the Russian revolution of 1905. Jews made up almost 50 per cent of all people emigrating from the Russian empire during the period of greatest emigration between 1903 and 1907.[15] The Aliens Act of 1905, designed to restrict immigration to Britain, seems to have had a limited effect. Only the First World War stemmed the flow.

There were Lithuanian Jews who chose not to emigrate or were unable to do so for one reason or another, and instead turned to different kinds of ideology in the hope it would improve Jewish life. Some turned to Zionism. Others turned to Socialism. The historian Simon Dubnow thought that from the mid-1890s onwards Jews in the Tsarist empire searched with new dynamism for answers to the predicament in which they found themselves:

> The entire gamut of public slogans rang through the air, all bearing testimony to one and the same fact: that the era of national prostration had come to an end, and that the vague longings for liberation and regeneration had assumed a conscious endeavour pursuing a well-defined course.[16]

Jews appeared particularly attracted to Socialism. There were many varieties: the Mensheviks, the Bolsheviks, the Social Revolutionaries, the Polish Socialist Party, the Social Democracy of the Congress Kingdom and Lithuania, and the General Jewish Workers' Alliance, otherwise known as the Bund. Jews were found in the leadership and among the followers of all these groups.

It is well-known that a number of the founding fathers of Socialism were Jewish, by ancestry if not by religious observance. Such people include

Karl Marx, Rosa Luxemburg and Leon Trotsky. The question of whether it is merely a coincidence that such people were Jewish is intriguing. Isaac Deutscher thought it was not:

> I think that in some ways they [and other innovative thinkers such as Spinoza, Heine and Freud] were very Jewish indeed. They had in themselves something of the quintessence of Jewish life and of the Jewish intellect. They were *a priori* exceptional in that as Jews they dwelt on the borderlines of various civilizations, religions, and national cultures. They were born and brought up on the borderlines of various epochs... They lived on the margins or in the nooks and crannies of their respective nations. Each of them was in society and yet not in it, of it and yet not of it. It was this that enabled them to rise in thought above their societies, above their nations, above their times and generations, and to strike out mentally into wide new horizons and far into the future.[17]

Jews were attracted to Socialism for a variety of reasons: for some, it seemed a way to break out of Jewish isolation and to begin a process of integration into wider society; others were attracted to Socialism, consciously or otherwise, because it represented a secularised version of age-old Jewish messianic longing; others became Socialists from a sense of horror at the extreme poverty of the Jewish masses they witnessed around them.[18] And Jews were also attracted to Socialism as a reaction to their oppression by the Tsarist government.

This last point is well-made in the diaries of Theodor Herzl. In 1903 Herzl visited Russia and was granted an audience with Count Witte, the comparatively liberal Minister of Finance. Witte suggested to Herzl, probably exaggeratedly, that while Jews made up only seven million out of a total population of 136 million, about fifty per cent of the membership of the revolutionary parties was Jewish. Herzl then asked Witte whose fault that was. Witte replied, with disarming candour: "I think it is the fault of the government. The Jews are too oppressed."[19]

There was, however, a rather fundamental difficulty about Jews being Socialists, namely that swathes of the Russian peasantry, who Socialists wished to represent, were antisemitic, and sometimes sympathetic to pogroms. This problem came to the fore at the end of the nineteenth century. The leaders of Russian populist and other Socialist movements were generally not strongly antisemitic, but they wished to identify with every kind of peasant revolt. They were reluctant to restrain poor

Lithuanians' anti-Jewish behaviour for fear of alienating their constituency. The leaders took refuge in rather specious arguments that all revolt in Russia had to start as anti-Jewish rioting but that this could become a gateway to a full-scale revolution and that, anyway, the popular fury was directed against Jewish shopkeepers and money-lenders and should therefore be regarded as a respectable form of class war.

In 1904, similar arguments were used in the Socialist revolutionary press in answer to a direct appeal by the Bund for armed support to defend Jews against those participating in anti-Jewish violence. The Socialist Revolutionaries declined to provide support, saying: "How can we do so? ... after all, the main mass of the pogrom-makers will consist of those same destitute toilers whose interests socialists are pledged to defend…is it really to be expected that we, the socialists, should go forth and beat up our admittedly blinded brothers, but brothers all the same, hand in hand with the police? Or, at best, hand in hand with the Jewish bourgeoisie armed in the defence of its property?"[20]

The Bund was one of the main Socialist groups which appealed to Jews. It was established in Vilnius in September 1897. Its aims were twofold: to struggle for political reform in Russia on behalf of all the peoples of Russia but, additionally, it was to undertake the particular task of defending the interests of Jewish workers, carrying on their struggle for civil rights and, above all, combating the laws which discriminated against Jews. There was always an uneasy tension between the Bund's general Socialist objectives and its specifically Jewish objectives. This tension came to a head at the Second Congress in 1903. Lenin and his supporters maintained that the Bund's demand for Jewish autonomy in matters connected with propaganda and organisation amounted to 'nationalism', and that this was incompatible with Marxist internationalism. The Bund thought that Lenin's group, *Iskra,* had set out to destroy the Bund and was merely using the charge of 'nationalism' as a device. It seems reasonable to regard the charge levelled by Lenin as being substantially false in that the Bund did not put the narrow national interests of Jews before wider social democratic interests. The real point of difference between Lenin and his supporters and the Bund was that Lenin was committed to the idea that a revolutionary party should be run by a cadre of professional revolutionaries (including himself, needless to say). The Bund, by contrast, thought that the party should be more broadly based, and more generally reflective of the views of its members. This quarrel between the Bund and Bolsheviks was important because the factors which divided the two in 1903 metamorphosed into a similar division between the Bolsheviks and the Mensheviks in the succeeding years. The history of the Bund after 1903 closely paralleled the history of the Mensheviks. Both were trying to uphold principles of social democracy which they believed were at risk of being destroyed by Lenin. Many more Jews were Mensheviks than Bolsheviks. For example, at the party congress of 1907 about one fifth of delegates who followed the Menshevik line were Jewish, whereas only one tenth of delegates who followed the Bolshevik line were Jewish.[21] Again, this division reflected the fundamental disagreement among Russian Socialists as to whether Marx had intended that the impetus for revolution should come from the workers themselves or from an outside group of professional revolutionaries acting, so they claimed, in the interests of the workers. Instinctively, most (but by no means all) Jews tended to the Bund and the Menshevik position.

None of this is to deny that at the time of the October revolution some Jews were active in Bolshevism. Trotsky, Zinoviev and Kamenev were among them. By 1917 five of the 25 full members of the Central Committee of the Communist Party were Jewish, and Jews were active in lower levels of the party machinery. It is nonetheless absurd to conflate Bolshevism and Jews, as antisemites often did during the inter-war period. As has been said, most Jews sided with Mensheviks, not Bolsheviks. Many of the prominent Jewish Bolsheviks (including Trotsky, Zinovyev and Kamenev) were eliminated during the 1920s, and Stalin led what can only be called a widespread assault against Jews who were Bolsheviks in 1937 and 1938. Jews who served the Bolsheviks became victims of a new kind of nationalism they had failed to foresee, dressed up in the clothes of international Socialism.[22]

As we have seen, some Jews who did not emigrate from Lithuania became swept up in various ideologies, particularly those connected with Socialism and Zionism, in the years immediately following my great-grandfather Myer's emigration in 1896. The outbreak of the First World War in August 1914 was to change everything.

On 28 June 1914 Archduke Franz Ferdinand (heir to the Austro-Hungarian empire) and his wife Sophie were in Sarajevo to inspect the Austro-Hungarian imperial forces in Bosnia-Herzegovina. 19-year-old Gavrilo Princip and fellow members of the Young Bosnia Movement had learned of the Archduke's planned visit. They acquired weapons from 'the Black Hand', a secret Serbian society and terrorist organisation, and travelled to Sarajevo, intending to assassinate the Archduke. Their first effort failed. One of the nationalists threw a bomb which rolled off the back of the Archduke's vehicle, wounding an army officer and a few bystanders. Later in the day the imperial car took a wrong turn into a side-street where

Princip happened to be standing. Seizing his opportunity, Princip fired into the royal vehicle, seriously injuring both the Archduke and his wife. They died within an hour.

Emperor Franz-Joseph of Austria-Hungary was outraged; he wrote a personal letter to Kaiser Wilhelm in Germany, seeking his support. On 6 July 1914 German chancellor Theobald Bethmann Hollweg informed Austrian officials that Germany would, indeed, stand by Austria-Hungary. On 23 July 1914 the Austro-Hungarian ambassador to Serbia therefore delivered an ultimatum to Serbia. It must take steps to eliminate terrorist organisations operating on its territory, suppress anti-Austrian propaganda and accept an independent investigation by the Austro-Hungarian government into Archduke Franz-Ferdinand's assassination, or face military consequences. Serbia appealed to Russia for help. The Tsar's government began the rather slow process of mobilising its army, in the belief that Germany was using this crisis as a pretext to launch a pre-emptive war in the Balkans. Austria-Hungary declared war on Serbia on 28 July. On 1 August, in response to news of Russia's general mobilisation, Germany declared war on Russia. In accordance with its long-standing strategic military plan known as the Schlieffen Plan, the German army launched an attack on Russia's ally France, intending to knock it out of the war before turning its full might eastwards to concentrate on Russia. Germany attacked France through Belgium, violating its neutrality, and so bringing Great Britain into the war as well. The Schlieffen Plan did not work. Instead, Germany became bogged down in a long war of attrition against France and Britain on what became known as 'the western front'.

The story on the eastern front was very different. Here, in 1914 and 1915, German armies enjoyed a record of almost unbroken success against the armies of Tsarist Russia. In late August 1914, acquiring foreknowledge of Russian plans by reading radio signals dispatched *en clair*, and as a result of bold leadership by the German corps commander General von Francois, Germany won a stunning victory at the Battle of Tannenberg, characterised by the distinguished military historian Sir Michael Howard as "one of the greatest military victories of all time."[23] In 1915, Erich von Falkenhayn, the German Chief of the General Staff, created a new Austro-German army group under the command of General August von Mackensen to attack Russian positions in Galicia in the region of Gorlice-Tarnów. This operation was another spectacular German success, with 100,000 prisoners taken, and the Russian lines penetrated to a depth of eighty miles.

At the outbreak of war, the Russian frontline had passed on a north-south axis through Lithuania, just east of the Lithuanian border with East

Prussia. By the end of 1915 Russian forces had withdrawn hundreds of miles eastwards, all the way across Lithuania until, by the end of 1915, Russian armies managed to halt the German-Austrian advance and stabilise the position on a new line: Riga-Jēkabpils-Daugavpils-Baranavichy-Pinsk-Dubno-Ternopil. This remained the front line of the eastern front until the Russian collapse in 1917.

For much of 1914 and 1915, therefore, Lithuania was on the front line of the war between Germany and Russia. This situation was obviously difficult for the local Lithuanian Jewish population. It was severely affected by substantial economic setbacks: industrial plants were relocated to the Russian interior, depriving many Lithuanian Jewish workers of their livelihood; many Jews were ruined when their homes or places of work were damaged in battle; the mobilisation of reservists meant that many families lacked a breadwinner; and, on account of the war, financial assistance from émigrés almost dried up, bringing substantial financial hardship to many Lithuanian Jewish families who had depended on remittances from abroad.[24]

Generally speaking, Lithuanian Jews seem to have responded to the outbreak of war with what one might regard as surprising displays of patriotic allegiance to Tsarist Russia. Large numbers of Jews served in the Russian army: 350,000 according to an estimate made by the Mayor of Saint Petersburg before the Conference of Russian Mayors in August 1914; or, 400,000 according to an estimate made by the Jewish Colonization Association in Saint Petersburg.[25] Thousands of Jewish students who had studied at foreign universities (because an onerous Jewish quota system had closed Russian universities to them) returned to enlist in the Russian army. Jewish soldiers served despite the fact that under Russian law Jews were not permitted to achieve a rank higher than corporal. Other Russian laws discriminated against Jewish soldiers, including one to the effect that, if a Jew defected, then his whole family (including parents and relatives by marriage of the person accused) was liable to a penalty of 300 rubles. Russian Jewish soldiers won medals. Over 1,000 received the Medal or Cross of St. George, awarded for distinguished valour in the face of the enemy. Jews who stayed at home opened and equipped hospitals for wounded soldiers from all backgrounds and contributed generously to public funds.

Most parts of the Jewish press forcefully articulated patriotic support for Russia. The 'Novyi Voskhod' said:

> We were born and brought up in Russia. Our ancestors are buried here. We Russian Jews are bound to Russia by ties which cannot be

> broken, and our brothers who have been driven beyond the ocean by cruel fate cherish their memories of Russia all through life…At this historical moment, when our country is threatened by foreign invasion, when brute force has taken up arms against the great ideals of humanity, the Jews of Russia will bravely go forth in battle and will fulfil their sacred duty…[26]

There were voices in the Russian Jewish community who offered a more nuanced view of the appropriate Jewish response to the war. The great Jewish historian S.M. Dubnov said: "I did not share the unconditional patriotism of some representatives of our society. I was of the opinion that if slaves are driven into battle together with citizens, then the slaves must declare loudly that they fight only in the hope of winning for themselves equality and freedom…" But such voices were marginal. Most Jewish opinion seems to have been strongly supportive of Russia, perhaps hoping this was an opportunity for Jews to be more accepted.

Such hopes were quickly disappointed. The Commander-in-Chief of the Imperial Russian Army was Grand Duke Nikolai Nikolaevich. He was a Romanov and cousin of Tsar Nicholas II. The Chief of Staff was General Nikolai Yanushkevich. Both men were fanatically antisemitic. Yanushkevich had long sought the expulsion of Jews from the Russian army on the basis that their presence 'offends against the Russian people'. Now, Yanushkevich encouraged his officers to place Jewish soldiers in the vanguard of every attack and, in retreat, to place Jews in the last rows so that they would be the first to be killed by enemy fire.[27]

In September 1914 the Tsarist army under the command of General von Rennencampf suffered an embarrassing defeat in the First Battle of the Masurian Lakes in East Prussia. There were over 100,000 Russian casualties. The Russian front line was pushed back and the Russian army was rendered incapable of mounting serious operations for many months.

A scapegoat was needed. Allegations were made that Jews were communicating secretly with the German invaders and providing them with valuable intelligence. According to Minister of Finance P.V. Bark, Yanushkevich became "obsessed with the idea of spies and spying"[28] and thought that Jews were primarily responsible. The similarity of the German and Yiddish languages gave superficial plausibility to such allegations and so, by an order of July 1915, Yanushkevich prohibited postal and telegraph communications in Yiddish in the military area he controlled, being almost the entire area in which Jews were permitted to live. The American Jewish Committee observed:

> By this order the Russian government not only branded the entire Jewish people as spies and traitors, but also prevented hundreds of thousands of Jewish soldiers at the front from communicating with relatives and friends, because many of the soldiers had been prevented by educational restrictions from learning to read and write Russian...[29]

Parts of Catholic Lithuanian society stirred up anti-Jewish sentiment, taking advantage of the well-known antisemitic views of the Russian military. The Jewish press thought that Lithuanian clerics and the newspaper *Viltis* were responsible for this. There were absurd stories that Jews were filling geese with gold coins and smuggling them across front lines to the Germans; that Jews were putting fortress plans in bottles and floating them down the river Neman to the Germans; and that Jews were sending secret messages to Germans by flags or by windmills or by small radios concealed in their beards.[30]

This hysterical association of Jews with spying for the Germans led the Russian military authorities to a policy of expulsion of the Jewish population of Lithuania. The policy started gradually. From July 1914 until January 1915 there were a handful of expulsions of Jews from the area near the front line. Jews were sent to the interior of Russia. These expulsions do not appear to have been official policy formulated by senior officers but, instead, were carried out piecemeal on the instructions of individual officers in the field.[31] A wider expulsion needed a pretext. This was provided by a minor incident at Kuzhi, near Šiauliai, on 28 April 1915. It was a small village, and only six Jewish families lived there. When the German army captured the village eight German soldiers visited several Jewish homes in search of food, water and other provisions, and then left. The Russians recaptured the village two days later. The Jews warned the Russian troops of the proximity of German forces. The Germans shelled the village and the Jews were then accused by the Russian military authorities of having given German forces the information they needed to destroy Kuzhi. The incident attracted great publicity and was debated by the Fourth Duma (the Russian parliament) in May 1915. A commission under Alexander Kerensky was established to conduct an in-depth investigation. The Kerensky commission found the military authority's account of what had occurred at Kuzhi to be a total fabrication. Nonetheless, the damage was done. This, and other incidents were the background to a series of orders expelling Jews from Lithuania. Jews were expelled from Courland in April 1915 and from Kaunas, Grodno and Suwałki in May 1915. The expulsions from Kaunas and Courland affected between 150,000 and 200,000 Jewish people, and only the rapid invasion of this territory by the German army prevented the complete expulsion of all Jewish inhabitants of Lithuania. Generally, the Jewish population was given less than 24 hours to leave. In a speech delivered in the Duma, the non-Jewish deputy Dzubinsky said:

> As a representative of our 56th Siberian division I was myself on the scene and can testify with what incredible cruelty the expulsion … took place. The whole population was driven out within a few hours during the night. At 11 o'clock the people were informed that they had to leave, with a threat that anyone found at daybreak would be hanged…Old men, invalids and paralytics had to be carried on people's arms because there were no vehicles …[32]

The expelled Jews were scattered across wide areas of the interior of the Russian empire including in the counties of Bakhmut, Mariupol, Yekaterinoslav, and Poltava. The consequences of these expulsions were many and varied. Most significantly, perhaps, they led to great hardship on the part of the expelled. The expulsion orders applied to all Jews, whatever their age. Hospital patients, handicapped people living in care homes and elderly people living in old-age homes were not spared. They had to travel for days at a time in freight cars, or on foot, to places hundreds of miles from their homes. Almost as soon as the Jews left, their former neighbours began looting their homes; as they travelled, they had to try to avoid the advancing and withdrawing Russian and German armies, which was sometimes very difficult. There were several districts of Lithuania, particularly around Vilnius, which changed hands nine times. On their journeys, they had to throw themselves on the goodwill of Jewish relief organisations, particularly the so-called 'Yekopo', or on the goodwill of local Jewish people. This was not always forthcoming as there were plenty of long-standing tensions between Lithuanian and Polish Jews. Once they reached their destination the expelled Jews tended, at least initially, to be dependent on local Jewish communities and communal organisations such as the "Hevrat Mefitzei Haskalah". Many Christian residents greeted the arrival of expelled Jews with dismay. They feared that refugee Jews would over-burden local social services; many associated the Jews with the German enemy or blamed them for fomenting revolutionary movements. Above all, they were wary that Jews might bring with them diseases such as scarlet fever, diphtheria, typhus, dysentery and cholera acquired in the unsanitary freight cars in which they had been compelled to travel.[33]

The Russian military's encouragement of spy mania and its subsequent expulsion of Jews from Lithuania had a number of consequences which, from its own perspective, were counter-productive: by branding the entire Jewish population as traitorous, the Russian military heightened distrust between populations and made the fighting area of much of the Eastern front a quagmire for Russian armies. Troops could no longer decide who to trust or distrust. Expulsions of Jews from Lithuania led to a severe economic shock to the local economy, depriving it of many industrialists, contractors and army suppliers. Moreover, the expulsions brought about a *de facto* end to the Pale of Settlement, scattering Jews across a vast expanse deep inside Russia. In August 1915 the Council of Ministers sought to gain kudos by legitimising what was by then a fait accompli and, in the context of trying to secure overseas aid, formally permitted Jews to live outside the Pale of Settlement. As Duma deputy Skobelev observed: "the question of the Pale was brought up in the Council of Ministers only when the wave of Jewish refugees had already swept away this medieval dam".[34] Above all, expulsions of Jews were counter-productive for the military and the right because they stirred indignation in liberal circles in Russia and beyond, bitterly dividing Russia at a critical moment during the war. Many outraged voices were raised in the Duma. For example, professor Milyukov, leader of the Constitutional Democrats said: "The foul play upon the obscure racial prejudices of the masses, with the customary weapon of this kind of strife - antisemitism - has been exercised with unparalleled effrontery. Under the mask of military precaution, measures worse than credible are taken against crimes that are imaginary".[35] Many public officials, cities, trade and professional organisations and well-known Russian writers also voiced strong criticism.

By 10 May 1915 around 75-80 per cent of the Jewish population of Lithuania had been expelled. Reaction in liberal circles in Russia and overseas was highly critical. The policy appeared to be backfiring, and was suspended. The last deportation took place on 10 May 1915. Jews were permitted to return to their homes, but few were able to do so while war continued.

Yanushkevich's thinking became rather schizophrenic in the days immediately before suspending the policy of expelling Jews on 10 May. Briefly, he ordered a scorched earth policy in selected areas of retreat, ordering the deportation of the entire population to the interior, *except Jews*. He said that Jews were so corrupting and burdensome that it would be better to leave them for the Germans. This policy was reversed three weeks later. In addition, Yanushkevich briefly replaced the policy of driving Jews into the interior by a policy of driving them across the frontline into the hands of the Germans.

The policy of expelling Jews was replaced by a policy of taking some Jews hostage. Prominent rabbis and Jewish community leaders were seized and imprisoned. The Jewish population was then informed that these hostages would be hanged in the event of "even the smallest act hostile to the fatherland or generally, or any assistance rendered to the enemy by any members of the Jewish population."[36] Taking hostages from among one's own population was almost unknown in modern warfare. It is true that hostage-taking had occasionally been used in pre-modern Muscovite warfare and during the wars in the Caucasus in the nineteenth century, but by 1914 it was widely regarded as brutal and anachronistic. We will never know how many hostages were taken, but a leading authority on this subject suggests "the total number taken during the war probably should be estimated in the tens of thousands."[37] The scale of hostage-taking declined by the end of 1915; this was partly because Yanushkevich was replaced as Chief of Staff by the somewhat more moderate Alekseev, and also because a new front-line was stabilised further east. Nonetheless, army commanders retained the right to expel Jews from the immediate front-line area, and to take hostages, right up until the February revolution of 1917. The Lithuanian Jewish communities which had survived the expulsions, or were modestly reconstituting themselves from mid-1915 onwards, therefore continued to live under the threat of their local leaders being executed at the whim of a local official or army commander.

It would be difficult to over-state the calamitous impact of the May 1915 expulsions on the Jewish communities of northern Lithuania. Pikeliai was quite typical of the area. We know that the all-Russian census of 1897 showed that, at that time, 1,758 people lived in Pikeliai. 1,206 (68%) of these people were Jewish. By 1921, the Jewish population had decreased to 286. It was to decrease again to about 30 families on the eve of the Holocaust.[38] It is reasonable to assume that the Jewish population had shrunk between 1897 and 1915 on account of emigration; but the expulsions of May 1915 removed all Jews from Pikeliai, inflicting a blow to that community from which it never really recovered. A handful of Jews returned to Pikeliai following the German conquest of the area in summer 1915 and a few more did so at the end of the First World War but, by then, the Jewish community was a shadow of its former self. It seems probable that the Jewish population was reluctant to return to a place where, in May 1915, Lithuanian neighbours had occupied their homes and looted their property.[39]

Between summer 1915 and autumn 1918 northern Lithuania was administered by a German military administration (the *Ober Ost*). Šiauliai and Liepāja had been occupied by the German army by early May 1915; Kaunas fell to the Germans on 18 August, Grodno on 3 September and Vilnius on 19 September. By late summer 1915 a great strip of land with a population of about three million people was under German military administration. It was to remain so until the first Lithuanian government was established on 5 November 1918.[40]

During this period of German military administration a small number of the Jews who had been expelled from their homes attempted to return home. Many found their homes had either been destroyed or seized by the local population. Many Jews found their way to Vilnius. In 1916, it was estimated that about 22,000 Jews who had been expelled from their homes were living in Vilnius.[41] Other Jews remined scattered across Russia and Ukraine, generally in larger towns.

Initially, Jewish hopes for the *Ober Ost* were high. There was a feeling that the Russian government had made their lives intolerable and that the Germans would surely be better. The German military administration set out to encourage pro-German sentiment among the Jews. The German Chief of Staff, General Ludendorff, made positive noises in one of his early manifestos: "*Meine Liebe Juden:* We have come to change your lives!"[42] Early gestures designed to encourage Jewish support included making official announcements in yiddish, authorising the reopening of a yeshiva in Slobodka (a neighbourhood of Kaunas) and licensing the publication of a Jewish newspaper, *Letzte Nayes.* German Jews, serving in the German military, were put to work as advisers and intermediaries to work with Jews in Lithuania. Many German Jews viewed their eastern co-religionists with condescension and were more than happy to try to educate them in German ways. German Jews were tasked with establishing German-speaking high schools for the local Jews. For example, Dr Joseph Carlebach was appointed as director of a technical high school (*realschule*) in Kaunas, and a cultural programme was developed. Leading roles were played by Herman Struck, a German Jewish artist who headed the 'Jewish department' of the German army, and by the writer Leo Deutschlander, who was put in charge of Jewish education in Lithuania. At the time of Jewish festivals, Jews in the German army prayed in Lithuanian synagogues, strengthening informal ties between German Jews and their Lithuanian co-religionists.

However, the encounters between non-Jewish German soldiers and Lithuanian Jews were less happy. Many contemporary reports suggest that German soldiers were revolted by Lithuanian Jews. They saw them as poor and unhealthy, squalid in appearance and manners. For example, the *Zeitung der 10. Armee* (Newspaper of the Tenth Army), published in December 1915, told its readers:

> Filthy Jews, with full beards in the lightest red to the darkest black, stand in their ragged kaftans amongst pale women and young girls. Dirty children crouch on wooden stairways. Unwashed, uncombed they are all – and over all of them the smell that gives the whole city its atmosphere pervades.

A slightly later edition of the same army newspaper commented on:

> a certain kind of strangeness in the language and habits, and, by German standards, unbearable uncleanliness [of Lithuanian Jews]… an often apparent disposition towards dishonesty and to what we call haggling spirit, and finally the not infrequent desire to achieve certain aims by bribing officials ...[43]

It gradually became clear that the German military authorities were determined to run Lithuania so as to advance German interests, particularly military interests, and largely irrespective of the impact of their policy on the local population. It was annexation. German rule became a colonising mission, self-consciously drawing inspiration from that undertaken centuries before, and in the same area, by Teutonic knights. This was underpinned by a strong sense of the backwardness of the local population. Even in late 1917 the *Deutschen Verwaltung für Litauen* (the administrative arm of the military) was insisting that the Reich had brought "the spirit of order and peaceful work even to enemy territory."[44] One of the first and most graphic signs of Germanisation was a deluge of orders and decrees, affecting almost every area of daily life. This was amusingly satirised in a memoir by Joseph Buloff:

> Whoever owns a horse must cut the hair from its tail and mane and present it to this and that collection centre. And a bit later the same day: 'Along with the cut hair, the owner must also present the horse'. From this it became apparent that the Germans were …simply out to drive the city crazy.[45]

The German military authorities engaged in requisitioning of food and supplies to meet their army's needs. They forced the export of certain goods to Germany. And they conscripted labour. Many Jews were deported as labourers to coal mines in the Ruhr and in upper Silesia and others were forcibly employed on the docks at Tilsit and Klaipėda. An aspect of occupation policy which affected the Jewish population particularly adversely was the German attempt to restructure the economy. Jews were to be excluded from trade by establishing cooperative societies. The German authorities well understood that cooperatives were inefficient, but their introduction was deliberately to squeeze Jewish merchants out of business.[46] Conditions for Jewish people in Lithuania quickly became atrocious. In Vilnius an estimated 50-60 people starved to death each day.

There were few strategies available to the Jewish population. One possibility, at least in theory, was to emigrate to the United States. This was only really available during the early war years to a small minority of well-off Jews and it became effectively impossible after America's entry into the war. Another possibility for those required to provide forced labour, and who possessed sufficient means, was to buy their way out of it. A payment of 600 marks placed a Jew in one of the categories exempt from forced labour, such as Talmudic student, physician, pharmacist and teacher. A further possible strategy, and for most Jews the most practical one, was to seek support from Jewish charitable organisations. The principal ones were the *Hilfsverein der deutschen Juden* and the American Jewish Joint Distribution Committee (also known as "the Joint"). It became much more difficult for American charitable organisations to provide assistance after America's entry into the war on 6 April 1917, although some limited assistance did continue after that date, channelled through Holland. The Joint transferred a total sum of $1,439,635 for the assistance of impoverished Jews in the *Ober Ost* and for Lithuanian Jews who were refugees elsewhere. An indication of the extraordinary extent to which the Jewish community came to depend on charity at this time is that by 23 February 1917 some 57,000 Jewish people had registered with charitable societies in Vilnius alone.[47]

Germany's military position worsened in 1917; and the hold of the German military authorities in Lithuania became more tenuous. The Lithuanians were given permission to convene a kind of National Council, called the 'Taryba', but Jewish representatives were not permitted to play a part in this. On 16 February 1918 the Taryba declared Lithuania an independent and democratic state, although at this stage it continued to rely on German support. In November 1918 the German military recognised defeat. The armistice was signed, ending World War 1.

Observing the first twentieth century encounter between a German military administration and Lithuanian Jews in the period between 1915 and 1918 one is bound to reflect on whether there was continuity between German policy towards Jews during the *Ober Ost* and German policy towards Jews following German reoccupation of Lithuania from June 1941 onwards. This has become highly controversial. In *Hitler's Willing Executioners* the American historian Daniel Goldhagen argued that the Holocaust happened because the German perpetrators were filled with "a demonological antisemitism" that "was the common structure of the perpetrators' cognition and of German society in general". Because Hitler and the Germans were "of one mind about the Jews, he had merely to "unshackle" or "unleash" their "pre-existing, pent-up" antisemitism to perpetrate the Holocaust. As Christopher Browning has put it: "Daniel Goldhagen is arguing that virulent, lethal antisemitism is the veritable *Leitmotiv* not only of Hitler's ideology but of 150 years of German history."[48] Christopher Browning, and others, take a more nuanced view. They emphasise that the character of German antisemitism evolved substantially during the inter-war years. They also emphasise that the willingness of Germans to murder Jews during the Holocaust depended on the particular circumstances in which they were placed; and that there were plenty of Germans who declined to commit atrocities and others who participated in them very unwillingly.

What is one to make of these different arguments? It seems clear that many German soldiers who encountered Lithuanian Jews during the period of German administration 1915-1918 reacted strongly against them. They disliked their poverty, feared the diseases they might spread, found their style of doing business unattractive and thought many of them were politically radical and dangerous. The *Ober Ost* adopted some policies which were deliberately prejudicial to Jews, including the effort to squeeze them out of trade, and so pauperise them, by establishing cooperative societies. Nonetheless, this was a very long way from a policy of murdering Jews, so vigorously pursued by parts of the German military and administration after June 1941.The most that can sensibly be said is that some of the policies of the *Ober Ost* towards Lithuanian Jews were hostile; indeed, one could see them as a chilling harbinger of what was to follow in the Second World War. However, there was no straight line between the discriminatory but sometimes chaotic policies of the *Ober Ost* and the genocidal fanaticism of the Nazis. Christopher Browning is right that Germans did not display "an undifferentiated, unchanging…single, monolithic cognitive outlook – that is at the heart of Goldhagen's interpretation".

At the end of the First World War, Europe was in chaos. In Russia, there had been two revolutions, the February 1917 revolution and the Bolshevik revolution of October 1917. There was to be protracted civil war between Whites (supporters of the Tsar) and Reds (Bolsheviks) for control of former Tsarist Russia. The defeat of Austria-Hungary and Germany in 1918 gave would-be nation states the opportunity to establish themselves on the territories of those former empires. Both Poland and Ukraine sought to do so.

The Taryba had declared Lithuanian independence in February 1918 and in March 1918 Kaiser Wilhelm II recognised independent Lithuania, provided it enter an "everlasting alliance" with Germany and help finance the cost of the war. The Lithuanian crown was offered to Wilhelm of Urach, the Catholic Duke of Württemberg, to govern under the name of King Mindaugas II. The offer was rather quickly withdrawn and questions about the form of government referred to the constituent assembly. It favoured a republican structure. On 11 November 1918 the Taryba instructed Augustinas Voldemaras to form the first provisional Lithuanian government.

This government faced immediate military threats to its sovereignty both from Soviet Russia and from newly-independent Poland. It needed all the support it could muster, including from the Jews. In December 1918 the Taryba decided to establish a stronger provisional government under Mykolas Sleževičius. He established a very broad coalition, representing most strands of Lithuanian political opinion and declared his readiness to grant Jews equality, full political rights and cultural autonomy. This appeared to be a decisive breakthrough for Lithuanian Jews.

In its war against Poland, Lithuania lost control of Vilnius, and made Kaunas the capital city of Lithuania in its place. Vilnius was very briefly restored to Lithuania in October 1920 before the Polish army, under General Zeligowski, captured it again. In December 1918 and January 1919 the Soviet army invaded Lithuania and quickly occupied much of the eastern part of the country before having to re-deploy hastily in Russia to concentrate on its battle against the Whites. Russia and Lithuania reached a peace treaty on 12 July 1920, under which Russia renounced all claims to Lithuanian territory and recognised Lithuanian independence. Russia agreed to make a financial contribution towards construction of a new Lithuanian state. By late 1920 Lithuania was independent and the immediate military threats from both Poland and the Soviet Union had been repulsed.

Because of the mass deportation of spring 1915, the Lithuanian Jewish community was still widely scattered when the First World War ended. It is estimated that about 200,000 Jews had been deported fron Lithuania and

Courland. A handful trickled back to Lithuania from the summer of 1915 onwards; more returned following the Armistice in November 1918. A provision of the July 1920 peace treaty between Russia and Lithuania gave Lithuanians in Russia the right to choose between Lithuanian and Soviet citizenship. Those opting to return to Lithuania were taken by train to Obeliai in eastern Lithuania, where they were kept in quarantine for a few days and their papers were checked. They were then free to return home. Jews continued to return in this way for two or three years after the peace treaty with the Soviet Union. Poland's annexation of Vilnius and the surrounding region, which was confirmed by the League of Nations in March 1923, cut off about 70,000 Jews in Vilnius from their friends and relations in the rest of Lithuania. They were permitted to cross the 'demarcation line' just once a year, at the time of the fast of the Ninth of Av.

We know a certain amount about the demographics of the Jewish population of Lithuania in 1923 because Lithuania conducted its first official census on 23 September that year. There were then 153,743 Jews in Lithuania, 7.6 percent of the total population. They were the largest minority, substantially larger than the Poles (3.2 percent of the population) and the Russians (2.5 per cent of the population). Nonetheless, the Jewish population was very much smaller than it had been pre-war, when it had constituted 13.8 per cent of the total population. Almost two thirds of the Jewish population lived in four cities (Kaunas, Panevėžys, Šiauliai and Ukmergė) and in 33 towns. There were 109 Jewish women for every 100 Jewish men, reflecting male deaths in the war and that men sometimes emigrated before women. Most Jewish men continued to earn their living from trade and crafts, and the craftsmen were typically involved in tailoring and textiles, or shoemaking and leatherwork.

Life was usually very difficult for those Jews who returned to Lithuania at the end of hostilities. Often their homes and stores had been looted or destroyed, as we know happened in Pikeliai. Jewish neighbours and friends were no longer around. Some Jewish men had resorted to smuggling and some Jewish women turned to prostitution. Julius Bielskis reported in his 'Delegates Trip to Lithuania' that when he went to Kaunas (albeit in 1916, before the end of the war) he was conscious that:

> there were many signs with the words "Bier Stube"- miserable holes in the wall where they offered beer and...well, girls. Those joints were run by Jews and frequented almost entirely by soldiers. This was almost the only way for Jews to make a living. The girls at those

> bars were also Jewish. There was no money to be earned in the city and the poor people suffered greatly.

Some Jews were able to get back on their feet quickly, assisted by their energy and facility for trade. Tadas Daugirdas, an archaeologist and then director of the Kaunas City Museum, kept a diary in which he described how:

> there are many returning Jews, Kaunas residents coming back from Vilnius, and those coming from surrounding towns from which they have been expelled. The Jews quickly resumed commerce: arriving only today, by the day after tomorrow they had already opened their shops. Today, I noticed tens of newly opened Jewish stores...[49]

Many other returning Jews remained dependent on remittances from family in the West or on charitable support, provided particularly by Yekopo, the Joint and by the American Joint Reconstruction Foundation, a body for economic reconstruction set up after World War 1, and known as 'the Foundation'. It built 1,333 new houses and rebuilt 356 others in 75 settlements; it also granted 83 loans in the sum of $166,066 for these purposes.[50]

Many observant Jews felt that the experience of deportation or flight in the First World War had made it difficult for traditional, observant Jews to practise their religion and this had led to a kind of crisis about how to remain Jewish. Hayim Ozer Grodzienski returned to Vilnius from exile in Yekaterinoslav in 1919. He said:

> The terrible days of war came and the whole world was thrown into confusion...I was shocked to see when I returned to Lithuania that it was twice stricken; its physical and spiritual foundations were torn asunder, and the spiritual destruction was even greater than its physical destruction...[51]

Rabbi Ya'akov Landa had been forced into the interior of Russia in 1915. After his exile he toured refugee Jewish communities and was so shocked by the decline of traditional observance he witnessed that he composed a report which he sent to Rabbi Shalom Dov-Ber Schneerson of Lubavitch. Rabbi Landa noted that the exiled Jews were neglecting Sabbath observance; traditional Jewish schooling had been abandoned; there was an absence of ritual baths, and a shortage of rabbis and ritual slaughterers.

Local synagogues in Russia's interior had insufficient room for the newcomers. Rabbi Landa was particularly vexed that this sudden fall-off in religious observance was not caused by the seductive pull of secular ideologies on Jewish youth (which had been a long-standing challenge to traditional observance), and nor was it the trend among well-to-do families seeking to imitate the mores of the non-Jewish bourgeoisie. Instead, it had been caused by economic and material pressures brought about by Jews being exiled to Russia's interior. Jews who had no objection in principle to traditional observance were caving in to these pressures:

> While one son is employed in the shop of a non-Jew and does his work on the Sabbath as on any weekday, the second son [works] for one of the [native] Jewish residents and does his work on the Sabbath as on any weekday, and sometimes their father, too, is like that. It should thus not be surprising that the feelings of holiness of the Jewish people on the Sabbath day are lost from their memories…[52]

Rabbi Landa's concerns encouraged Orthodoxy to undergo substantial educational reform, which it had previously resisted. Reform included the introduction of secular subjects, changes in the teaching of sacred subjects, the opening of schools for girls and various other hygienic and pedagogic improvements. It also encouraged Orthodoxy to emerge as a political force in most countries which had a large Jewish population. Perhaps ironically, many historians of Jewish religion have come to see Jewish Orthodoxy as a modern phenomenon. In particular, they emphasise the transition from an unselfconscious, traditional society to a self-consciously traditionalist one.[53] This had a number of causes including the challenge of the Reform and Haskalah movements, as well as the destruction of the heartland of traditional Judaism in the Second World War. However, it also seems that the forced dispersal of Jews in 1915 played a key role in this process of the emergence and renewal of the modern concept of Jewish Orthodoxy.[54]

Other Jewish organisations and movements in Lithuania, religious and otherwise, were profoundly affected by the experience of the World War and its violent aftermath. For example, there is substantial evidence that Zionism changed rather fundamentally as a consequence of the dislocations and trauma which Jews suffered in eastern Europe during these years. Of course, these were anyway momentous years for the Zionist movement: the Balfour declaration in 1917 and the granting to Britain of the mandate for Palestine at the San Remo Conference of April 1920, subsequently approved in July 1922 by the League of Nations. Recent research suggests that

Zionism changed fundamentally during these years, becoming, for the first time, a genuine mass movement. Before the war, Zionist circles had been consumed with a rather arcane discussion about the nature of Jewish nationhood and pioneering efforts in Palestine. During the war and in the immediate post-war period Zionism evolved to become concerned with aiding starving populations, organising soup kitchens, establishing orphanages, schools, kindergartens and hospitals and organising self-defence groups. This was the context in which Zionism moved from being somewhat marginal and overwhelmingly bourgeois into a genuine mass movement, which inspired and drew in thousands of Jewish people across Lithuania.[55]

Some Jews who had lived in Lithuania before 1915 made their way back to Lithuania, if not to their homes, after the war ended in November 1918. But many others remained, at least for a while, stranded or trapped in the areas to which they had been expelled, in Russia and in what is now Ukraine. Some had no means of getting back to Lithuania; others felt they had no particular reason to go back there. These Jews became caught up in a terrible wave of pogroms between 1918 and 1921 as conflicting armies fought each other in this area. Whites fought Reds in the Russian civil war; Ukrainians and Polish nationalists fought Russians. But, or so it often seemed, all armies were prepared to attack Jews when it suited them. It is estimated that 100,000 Jewish people were killed, maimed or tortured in the pogroms in Ukraine between 1918-1921. There were about 1,000 pogroms in some 500 different towns and villages across Ukraine.

What happened in Ovruch might serve as a microcosm for what happened in Ukraine as a whole.[56] Ovruch is 155 kilometres north-west of Kyiv. In 1917 it had a population of 11,000, including 3,000 Jews. Soldiers from the Russian imperial army were billeted in the city during the First World War, and were demobilised in December 1917. When that happened, they looted Jewish-owned shops. In 1918 a Bolshevik faction, supported by Red Army units, managed to gain control of the city, by force. There were a handful of Jews among the Bolshevik leaders. Opposition to Bolsheviks mounted in Ovruch, and the Ukrainian peasant leadership sent word to the anti-Communist "Directory" that they needed military assistance. This assistance was provided by a paramilitary partisan detachment (of Cossacks), led by Oleksii Kozyr-Zirka. He had served in a dragoon regiment during the World War and was an early recruit to Petliura's Ukrainian nationalist army. Kozyr-Zirka was sadistic; and he "took the Jews and the Bolsheviks to mean the same thing", as one aid worker reported. In the marketplace his troops seized ten Jewish girls, dragged them to an inn and raped them. In one house the men found a father and three sons sitting at a table; they led all four out into a yard and shot them one after the other. When Kozyr-Zirka's troops arrived at the house of a lawyer called Glossman they took him and his elderly father into the street. When the old man refused to abandon his son, the Cossacks beat the old man with whips in the course of which they struck out his only eye and they shot the younger Glossman on the spot. In mid-January 1919 Bolshevik forces massed to the north of the city. Kozyr-Zirka realised he would shortly need to evacuate the city and, by way of a parting shot, ordered his troops to round up Jewish men and bring them to the station. These Jewish men were compelled to sing and dance the *mayufes* – a Sabbath table song that Polish nobles had sometimes forced Jews to sing and dance for their amusement – as they were force-marched towards the station. When the procession arrived at the station other militants attacked the Jews with sabres and revolvers. They killed 34 Jews before departing the city by train.

Pogroms in Ukraine between 1918 and 1921 were more extensive, and more vicious, than the nineteenth century and early twentieth century pogroms which preceded them. Explaining such violence, apparently so mindless and cruel, is very challenging. The desire for loot is part of the explanation: there was a pogrom in Tetiiv, approximately 135 kilometres south-west of Kyiv, on 25 December 1919. One of the victims, Aron Sery, has left a detailed account of what happened. About ten Cossacks and one Chechen fighter barged into the family home, yelling: "Jews, Money!" Sery's father offered some money, but the Cossacks were not satisfied and struck him in the face. Sery handed over a silver watch and all the money he had on him. The soldiers ordered Sery and his father to place their hands on the table and they raised their sabres in mock execution. The Cossack intruders left, taking clothing and valuables, and helping themselves to three geese from the yard, as they departed.[57] At the end of the First World War peasant soldiers on all sides were poor and hungry. Food shortages had been exacerbated by difficulties in cultivating fields during the later war years. Peasant soldiers from the countryside had a long-standing animus against town-dwellers and a sense of the Jews as 'the other' and therefore as 'fair game'.

Another important reason many soldiers attacked Jews is that they thought of Jews as being Bolshevik. In Ovruch, one observer, Hillerson, thought that "the pogrom took place under the slogan 'beat the Jews because they are Bolsheviks'".[58] However, he went on to say that: "the attitude of the masses in Ukraine toward the Jews is such that any other slogan would be suitable for a pogrom as well". Undoubtedly, there was some association between Jews and Bolshevism. Many in eastern Europe were aware that Leon Trotsky, one of the most prominent Bolsheviks, was Jewish by background. And during the civil war period Bolsheviks did make a strategic decision to try and crack down on antisemitic violence, not least as a way of seeking to attract Jews to their cause. This met with some success. One memoirist wrote of "Jewish youth [who] leave the shtetls and run to Kyiv for one purpose – to get into the Red Army. However: "They are not Bolsheviks; they go to the Red Army because there one can die with a 'gun in hand.'"[59] In other words, many Jews were drawn to Bolshevism because it appeared generally more sympathetic to Jews than did the other warring parties.

However, it would be misleading to suggest that the Bolshevik armies invariably behaved well towards Jews. We have remarkable contemporaneous accounts by Isaac Babel, including his '1920 Diary,' which provide a record of his time spent with the Bolshevik army in Ukraine and in Poland in 1920. He did not reveal that he was Jewish to the Bolshevik soldiers around him (although some probably guessed his antecedents). He witnessed how other armies behaved towards the Jews. For example, during the Soviet-Polish war his division arrived in the Polish town of Komarów:

> We found the Jewish population robbed of everything it had…In the pitiful huts that had been razed to the ground, seventy-year-old men with crushed skulls lay naked in pools of blood, infants, often still alive, with fingers hacked off, and old women, raped, their stomachs slashed open, crouched in corners, with faces on which wild unbearable desperation had congealed.[60]

But Babel well-understood that the Soviet army could be every bit as hate-filled and cruel to Jewish civilians; reflecting on Soviet behaviour to Jews in Komarov, Isaac Babel observes rather despairingly: "The hatred is the same… the Cossacks just the same, the cruelty the same, it's nonsense to think one army is different from another. The life of these little towns. There's no salvation…"

Babel well describes the sense of the Jews' disappointment at how Soviet armies deeply let them down by behaving as terribly as other armies. Babel describes the Bolshevik entry into Sokal in August 1920:

"The Sokal cobbler is a proletarian. The cobbler had looked forward to Soviet rule - and what he sees are Jew-baiters and looters, and that he won't be earning anything… he is dismayed and looks at us mistrustfully ... "[61]

Religious hatred was another reason for the pogroms. A witness to the Proskurov pogrom, for example, described how in a house on Sobornaya Street, where 21 people were massacred: "before the murder, the Cossacks demanded that the Jews cross themselves. In the event of a refusal or indecision they killed with the cry "Die, Jew". Later the same day about 20 Jews engaged in a study session in the synagogue were murdered when soldiers barged in.[62] Overall however, religious motivations for murder seem generally not to have been mentioned as often as the desire for loot and the association of Jews with Bolshevism.

Various thinkers have sought to explain how people behave in crowds by reference to group psychology. In 1895 Gustave Le Bon suggested that in a large group individuals become part of "a sort of collective mind which makes them feel, think, and act in a manner quite different from that in which each individual of them would feel, think and act were he in a state of isolation".[63] Freud, on the other hand, thought that apparently uncharacteristic ways in which people behave in crowds are embedded within the individual, but usually repressed. In other words, the crowd does not make them behave in a way which is alien to their true self, but the crowd merely brings out that deeper self. In a crowd: "the individual is brought under conditions which allow him to throw off the repressions of his unconscious instincts"; Le Bon would have thought that people became antisemitic in crowds whereas Freud would have said that, being in a crowd, enabled individuals to throw off previously repressed antisemitic feelings. It is difficult to judge which psychological explanation is more plausible but what is clear is that, in a crowd, Ukrainians, many of whom were very young, behaved with extraordinary violence and cruelty to their Jewish neighbours, many of whom were, as has been said, Lithuanian Jews who had been expelled from Lithuania in 1915 and had been relocated in Ukraine. During the following years these pogromists continued to live side by side with Jewish people they had attacked. In many cases, their behaviour seems to have been deeply a part of them and was capable of re-emerging, and did re-emerge, shortly following the German invasion in 1941. It seems the habit of mob violence was learned, at a deep level, in the 1918-21 period and then buried for many years. Interestingly, in Lithuania, where there were fewer post First World War pogroms, German officers initially found it harder to set off pogroms, after the German invasion of June 1941. The German officer in command of the operation noted: "To our surprise it was not easy at first to set in motion an extensive pogrom against the Jews."[64]

By 1921 my great-grandfather Myer had been settled in Dublin for more than fifteen years. He had late adolescent and grown-up children of his own. His business had flourished despite the disruption of the First World War. But he must have been very conscious of the difficulties of Jewish life in the Baltics. His wife's family were in Liepāja. His sister was in Kaunas, the new capital of Lithuania. Many of his friends and family brought news of the difficulties of the Jewish community of Pikeliai and the surrounding area of northern Lithuania. Myer must have been all too conscious of the deportation of that community in May 1915 and that, by 1921, some had struggled back to Lithuania but that many had not done so and had encountered horrific pogroms in the general turmoil that accompanied the collapse of great empires at the end of the First World War. His anxiety may have been increased by the difficulty of obtaining accurate information about where Jewish family members and friends actually were in the Baltics, and what precisely had befallen them since May 1915.

Nonetheless, in 1921 the outlook for Jews in Lithuania seemed more hopeful than it had been for many years.

Notes

1 We know this from his Naturalization Certificate (reference HO 334/32), available from the National Archives, in Kew.
2 Greenbaum, p. 197.
3 Greenbaum, p. 203.
4 Greenbaum, p. 204.
5 American Jewish Committee, *The Jews in the Eastern War Zone* (American Jewish committee, 1916).
6 *The Vanished World of Lithuanian Jews* (BRILL, 2004), p. 68.
7 Staliunas, p. 129 et seq.
8 Staliunas, pp. 130–31.
9 Staliunas, pp. 147–48.
10 Staliunas, p. 136.
11 A reference to the Blondes blood-libel case, held in Vilnius, in 1900.
12 Staliunas, p. 157.
13 Staliunas, p. 144.
14 *The Jewish Chronicle* 18 February 1910.
15 Simon Kuznets, *Immigration of Russian Jews to the United States: Background and Structure* (Routledge, 2017), pp. 42–43.
16 Semen M. Dubnov, *History of the Jews in Russia and Poland: From the Earliest Times Until the Present Day* (Jewish Publ. Soc. of America), Vol iii p. 41.

17 Isaac Deutscher, *The Non-Jewish Jew: And Other Essays* (Verso Books, 2017), p. 27.
18 Polonsky, *The Jews in Poland and Russia*, pp. 31–32.
19 Theodor Herzl, *The Diaries of Theodor Herzl* (Victor Gollancz, 1958), p. 395.
20 Leonard Schapiro, 'The Rôle of the Jews in the Russian Revolutionary Movement', *The Slavonic and East European Review*, 40.94 (1961), 148–67 (p. 155).
21 Schapiro, p. 160.
22 Schapiro, p. 167.
23 Michael Howard, *The First World War* (Oxford University Press, 2003), p. 42.
24 Greenbaum, p. 210.
25 American Jewish Committee Location 405.
26 American Jewish Committee Location 391.
27 Louis Stein, *The Exile of the Lithuanian Jews in the Conflagration of the First World War (1914-1918)* (www.jewishgen.org/yizkor/lita/lit0089).
28 Eric Lohr, 'The Russian Army and the Jews: Mass Deportation, Hostages, and Violence during World War I', *The Russian Review*, 60.3 (2001), 404–19 (p. 407).
29 American Jewish Committee Location 661.
30 Staliunas, p. 205.
31 Lohr, p. 409.
32 American Jewish Committee Location 726.
33 Jeffrey Veidlinger, *In the Midst of Civilized Europe: The Pogroms of 1918-1921 and the Onset of the Holocaust* (Pan Macmillan, 2021), p. 40.
34 American Jewish Committee Location 183.
35 American Jewish Committee Location 857.
36 Lohr, p. 412 Quoting Tumanov to Kovno governor, 10 May 1915.
37 Lohr, p. 414.
38 Schoenburg and Schoenburg, p. 215.
39 Staliunas, p. 207 and Footnote 161 .
40 Jürgen Matthäus, 'German Judenpolitik in Lithuania during the First World War', *The Leo Baeck Institute Yearbook*, 43.1 (1998), 155–74 (p. 156).
41 Levin, p. 109.
42 Greenbaum, p. 215.
43 Matthäus, pp. 163–64.
44 Matthäus, p. 160.
45 Joseph Buloff, *From the Old Marketplace* (Harvard University Press, 1992), p. 263.
46 Matthäus, p. 167.

47 *The Jewish Chronicle* 23 February 1917.

48 Christopher R. Browning, 'Daniel Goldhagen's Willing Executioners' *History and Memory*, 1996, Vol 8, No.1 pages 88-108.

49 Referred to in 'The Jews of Kaunas' (2022) p.46. This multi-authored book was translated and edited by Darius Suziedelis, and published by Vsl "Kaunas 2022" to mark Kaunas being 'European Capital of Culture' in 2022.

50 Levin, p. 135.

51 Andrew N. Koss, 'War within, War without: Russian Refugee Rabbis during World War I', *AJS Review*, 34.2 (2010), 231–63 (p. 243).

52 Koss, p. 232.

53 Moshe Samet, 'The Beginnings of Orthodoxy', *Modern Judaism*, 8.3 (1988), 249–69.

54 Koss, p. 262.

55 Jan Rybak, *Everyday Zionism in East-Central Europe: Nation-Building in War and Revolution, 1914-1920*, (Oxford University Press, 2021).

56 Veidlinger, p. 96.

57 Veidlinger, p. 276.

58 Veidlinger, p. 104.

59 Veidlinger, p. 198.

60 Isaac Babel, *The Complete Works of Isaac Babel* (W. W. Norton, 2005), p. 372.

61 Isaac Babel, *1920 Diary* (Yale University Press, 2002), p. 81.

62 Veidlinger, p. 146.

63 Gustave Le Bon, *The Crowd: A Study of the Popular Mind* (T.F. Unwin, 1926), pp. 29–30.

64 Veidlinger, p. 360.

5

Inter-War Lithuania

Before the First World War my great-grandfather Myer had traded with the Baltic states, particularly with Liepāja. War disrupted that business fundamentally. Like many others, he hoped that the coming of peace and the declaration of Lithuanian independence would bring better days.

Post-war stability and independence came slowly to Lithuania. The Lithuanian National Council (Lietuvos Taryba) proclaimed Lithuania an independent state on 16 February 1918. But, at the end of 1918 the Red Army invaded Lithuania and occupied most of its territory. When Vilnius fell to the Bolsheviks the Lithuanian government moved its capital to Kaunas and appealed to its citizens to help defend the country. The Lithuanian government mobilised an army of between 5,000 and 6,000 men and by mid-1919 had driven back the Red Army. The principal concern of the Soviet leadership at this time was to win the civil war against the Whites. They therefore put out peace feelers to Estonia in August and to Finland, Latvia and Lithuania in September 1919, effectively recognising the independence of these countries. Lithuania reached a formal peace agreement with the Soviets in July 1920. However, after settling with the Soviets, Lithuania was almost immediately threatened by Poland, also trying to re-establish itself as an independent state. On 9 October 1920 'mutinous' Polish forces under General Zeligowski seized Vilnius and established an authority called Litwa Srodkowa (Central Lithuania), separating it from independent Lithuania. There were intensive international efforts to return Vilnius to Lithuania, but in such negotiations Lithuania was never likely to prevail. The rebirth of Poland had been one of the main war aims of the Entente during the First World War. Poland had been officially invited to attend the Paris Peace Conference and enjoyed the special protection of France. Vilnius was finally incorporated into Poland in February 1922, and was to remain a part of Poland for most of the inter-war period. This annexation became the source of lasting tension between Poland and Lithuania.

By the early 1920s Lithuania was independent for the first time since the late eighteenth century and was at peace, even if the peace with some of its neighbours was distinctly cold.

Hopes that there would be better times for Jews in post-war Lithuania grew out of wartime Jewish-Lithuanian discussions. Fundamentally, the proposed bargain was that Jews would support Lithuanian independence in exchange for a measure of autonomy in an independent Lithuania. The discussions at the 1919 Paris Peace conference led to an eight-point Lithuanian pledge concerning Jewish national rights. The promises included that there would be a cabinet-level department to represent Jewish interests, Jews were to have civic equality, proportional representation in parliament, Yiddish and Hebrew were to be recognised as official languages, and Jews were to be free to enjoy unfettered observance of the Sabbath and Jewish holidays. Many of these commitments were honoured during the first three years of Lithuanian independence but, in an indication of how the mood was changing, the Lithuanian constituent assembly declined to incorporate them into the constitution adopted in 1922.

Between 1919 and 1922 the Lithuanian government appeared to welcome the idea of Jewish autonomy. A Minister for Jewish Affairs was appointed, a Jewish National Council was established (headed by Shimon Rosenbaum) and the Jewish community was permitted to run its own religious and social affairs. However, Jewish autonomy was not to last because, with the end of the wars against Russia and Poland, and the loss of Vilnius to Poland, it seemed that support from the Lithuanian Jewish community, and in particular the hope that they might influence overseas Jews, was no longer of much importance.[1] It became clear that the increasingly nationalist Lithuanian political leadership no longer needed minority support "and it proceeded to turn the country from a federation of autonomous nationalities into a Lithuanian ethnocracy."[2]

Early post-war and newly independent Lithuania faced substantial problems. The first of these was serious tension with some of its larger and more powerful neighbours. Lithuania was a small independent state, surrounded by larger hostile powers. Relations with Poland were embittered by Poland's seizure of Vilnius and failure to return it. The border between Lithuania and Poland was closed, and a state of 'no peace no war' prevailed. A siege mentality developed in Lithuania, and this led to heightened Lithuanian nationalism. It drew Lithuania closer to those powers seeking to overturn the Versailles agreement, as it affected eastern Europe. Notwithstanding this, tensions between Lithuania and Germany rose after 1923. In January that year Lithuanian troops seized the port of Klaipėda, Lithuania's main Baltic Sea port, which had been ceded to the allies by the Germans in The Treaty of Versailles. This action stirred up great patriotic fervour in Lithuania, particularly because it occurred against the backdrop of the perceived humiliation of losing Vilnius to Poland. Initially, the German government acquiesced in its loss and in May 1924 the League of Nations agreed to Klaipėda becoming part of Lithuania. However, with the death of German chancellor Gustav Stresemann in 1929, Germany became more insistent in its demands for return of Klaipėda. And these demands were pressed even more forcefully when Hitler came to power in January 1933.

Another difficulty for newly independent Lithuania was that, as Russia had become Bolshevik in 1917, Lithuania found itself cut off from its traditional economic markets in Russia.[3] This seriously hampered Lithuanian trade with Russia but, as significantly, it also diminished other countries' interest in Lithuania as a country with which to do business. In the immediate post-war years, the British government provided naval support and military equipment to the Baltic states to support them in their fight against the Bolsheviks and the German army and in the hope that Britain might develop a flourishing trade with the Baltic as a bridge to the Russian market. Timber and flax were two of the main commodities to be traded. But, as Lithuania remained cut off from the Russian market, the interest of the British government waned. Some enterprising businessmen, including the financier and industrialist Richard Tilden Smith, developed schemes to trade Baltic flax and timber and establish a state bank in Lithuania. Such plans did not progress. By the mid-1920s British and other commercial interests turned away from Lithuania, Latvia and Estonia and instead came to regard Finland as a more trustworthy and valuable trading partner for commodities such as timber and flax.[4]

Jews faced particular challenges in post-war Lithuania. The conflict between Lithuania and Poland over Vilnius, which led to Vilnius being seized and administered by Poland, cut off Jews in Lithuania from their co-religionists in Vilnius. This was a heavy blow. Vilnius had been one of the great centres of the Jewish world, the 'Jerusalem of the North'. After 1922 Poland and Lithuania had no official contacts. Jewish families were split, unable to visit each other and barely able to communicate with each other. As postal agreements were cancelled, even correspondence had to be routed through a third country. Rail and other transport connections were cut.[5] The Jewish population of post-war Lithuania seemed very shrunken compared to what it had been pre-war. By far the largest number (31,428) lived in Kaunas, the new capital of independent Lithuania. Most of the rest of the Jewish population lived in urban centres. Only 0.5 per cent of the Jewish population lived in villages and rural areas.[6] The days when significant numbers of Jews lived in Pikeliai and similar villages seemed to have passed.

Jews in post-war Lithuania were also very divided among themselves. Very broadly speaking, there were three main political groupings. There was the Folkist-Communist camp, itself divided into the Folkspartei, Po'alei Zion Smol and the Communists. These were highly polemical and confrontational. The Folkist parties declined with the collapse of the autonomist experiment. In the 1920s Communism was very much a minority movement but in the early 1930s it attracted radical young people who were alarmed by the rise of Fascism and the lack of economic opportunities. The second main group was the Zionists. This was also divided into different factions. There was General-Liberal Zionism, Socialist Zionism, Nationalist Zionism and Religious Zionism. Each faction had a number of different parties and youth movements. And, finally, there was the religious ultra-Orthodox camp. The Orthodox retained considerable influence and the major Lithuanian yeshivot all flourished in the 1930s, particularly those at Telšiai, Panevėžys and Slobodka. Divisions within the Lithuanian Jewish world were profound and were often articulated in a strident and divisive way. A particular problem was that parts of the ultra-Orthodox community cultivated close links with the increasingly unpopular Smetona regime. The ultra-Orthodox sought Smetona's support for opposing the plan to consolidate religious elementary schools with the general Jewish primary system. They hoped they and Smetona could find common ground in trying to prevent young Jewish children growing up as 'leftists' or of being at risk of falling prey to other dangerous influences. The perceived closeness of the ultra-Orthodox and the Smetona regime embittered relations between the ultra-Orthodox and other parts of Jewish society.

By the mid-1920s the experiment of Lithuanian democratic government, and Jewish autonomy, was in trouble. Perhaps expectations had been set too high and were unrealistic. Lithuanians had hoped that, if granted autonomy, Jews would help them acquire Vilnius and Klaipėda, attract Belarus to a multinational Lithuania and reconcile Germans to Lithuanian rule. It was beyond the capability of the Jewish world to deliver such things, even if it had been more united than it was. After 1922 the Lithuanian party most supportive of Jewish autonomy, the Nationalists, was excluded from power. A body blow was delivered on 4 April 1926 when the Vatican decided not to include the dioceses of Vilnius and Sejny in a new ecclesiastical province, thereby recognising de facto Polish control of this area. This undermined support for the nationalist Christian Democrats party, driving many nationally-minded Lithuanians further to the right, and beyond the realms of democratic politics. On 17 December 1926 the government was overthrown by a military coup; a radical right-wing regime was established, with Smetona as 'state leader' and Voldemaras as prime minister.

A hard right-wing regime was self-evidently not in the interest of Jews, although it should be said that the regime was welcomed by parts of the ultra-Orthodox community who now called for the return to their control of Jewish hospitals, homes for the elderly, *mikvaot* and cemeteries. The new regime was unsympathetic to Jewish autonomy, although parts of the Jewish private school system and the Jewish cooperative banking system did continue to survive.

Between 1926 and 1940 Jews faced the difficulty that the Lithuanian government was run to promote the interests of ethnic Lithuanians. Jewish interests were secondary, although Jews were not the most disdained ethnic minority. Loss of Vilnius, and conflict over Klaipėda, intensified anti-Polish sentiment and anti-German sentiment and made ethnic Poles and ethnic Germans in Lithuania especially unpopular, particularly as they were thought to have dangerous foreign backers. There is debate about whether the post-1926 Smetona regime should be characterised as 'fascist'.[7] Many on the left are clear that it should be thought of in that way, emphasising that fascism can differ from country to country. It is true that the regime was ethnocentric, had a kind of *Fuhrenprinzip* and an element of worship of the past, not least in its cult of Grand Prince Vytautas the Great. But the Smetona regime was very different from, and milder than, the regimes of Hitler, Mussolini or even Pilsudski. Smetona himself was not overtly antisemitic, and on several occasions made speeches in which he made comments about Jews which were regarded as friendly. In 1934 he said: "The Jews are Semites… and how great has been their impact on mankind. They gave us the bible". In 1938 he made a speech in which he said that for the nationalist ideal to remain alive it must include "a basis in universal human values" and that it would be "impoverished by narrow nationalism".[8] On balance, it seems the word 'fascism' mischaracterises the Smetona regime. It is more helpful to see it as ethnocentric, hostile to the interests of all minorities, cool towards Jews and influenced by fascist regimes elsewhere in Europe, but very different from them.

Much of the inter-war hostility towards Jews was concentrated in Lithuanian social organisations formed to strengthen 'national consciousness', to combat 'foreigners' and oppose the supposed negative influences of ethnic minorities. These included the Riflemen's Union and the Lithuanian Businessmen's Union. Both were strongly hostile to Jews, and published periodicals featuring anti-Jewish material.[9]

Antisemitism in inter-war Lithuania was stimulated by three particular circumstances. The first was that Jews and ethnic Lithuanians came into increasingly direct economic competition. At the end of the nineteenth century, Jews and Lithuanians had occupied different economic spheres, in which they tended not to compete directly with each other. For the most part, Lithuanians were peasants. The Russian census of 1897 in the province of Kaunas and in the districts of Suwalki and Vilnius shows that 93 per cent of those who described themselves as Lithuanian were peasants, 4 per cent city dwellers and 3 per cent landowners. Jews, on the other hand, tended to live in towns and cities and were involved in trades, crafts and the professions. In the inter-war years, Jewish domination of trade and industry was undermined by development of big agricultural cooperatives. By 1939 there were about 2,000 of these. Some, such as Linas, a flax producers' and exporters' cooperative, and Pienocentras, which handled dairy produce, grew into very large enterprises and established monopolies in foreign trade. The agricultural cooperatives controlled 77 per cent of Lithuania's exports in 1939.[10] They came to dominate areas of business which had previously been mainly in the hands of Jewish middlemen. Lithuanians also became more active in small trading. In 1923, 83 per cent of the country's commercial and retail enterprises were owned by Jews, and only 13 per cent by ethnic Lithuanians. By 1936 ethnic Lithuanians owned some 43 per cent of the country's commercial and retail establishments and those in Jewish hands had decreased by about one tenth.[11] From the perspective of ethnic Lithuanians there may well be something to be said for the state's support for the previously disenfranchised majority's economic advancement, but the growing ethnic Lithuanian share of the non-agrarian economy necessarily came at the expense of others, and principally of the Jews. Also, the fact that ethnic Lithuanians and Jews were increasingly in direct economic competition with each other increased the scope for tensions, and for associated antisemitism. The journal of the Lithuanian Businessmen's Union reflects this. In its December 1938 issue it called for "laws which would regulate the Jewish question" and for the establishment of Jewish quotas in employment and business "until such time as the majority percentage of Lithuanians is also reflected in commerce". Jewish involvement in the Lithuanian economy remained considerable. In 1939 Jews are thought to have been responsible for 20 % of Lithuania's export trade and 40 % of its import trade and in 1937 more than 40% of the country's doctors and lawyers were Jewish. However, as ethnic Lithuanians moved into parts of the economy historically dominated by Jews, tensions between Jews and ethnic Lithuanians markedly increased.

These economically based tensions were aggravated by a second major difficulty which affected inter-war Lithuania, namely the world-wide Great Depression, which followed the Wall Street Crash of October 1929. Across the world, international trade fell by more than 50%. Unemployment rose, and gross domestic product fell by an estimated average of 15%. Tensions between Jewish factory-owner and Lithuanian worker were given a harder antisemitic edge by the hardships that flowed from the Great Depression. This happened, for example, during a dispute in 1935 between Lithuanian workers in Vilkaviškis, who wanted to be released from Sunday work, and the Jewish factory owners who employed them, who threatened to dismiss the workers if they persisted with their demands.[12]

Finally, antisemitism developed in Lithuania in the 1930s under the influence of racist propaganda emanating from Nazi Germany. Tensions with Germany because of disagreements over Klaipėda almost certainly limited the penetration of Nazi ideas in Lithuania, but nonetheless fascist ideas did make headway, and particularly influenced a group called the *Gelezinis Vilkas* (Iron Wolf). This was a secret paramilitary organisation, protected by Voldemaras. Many of its members were army and air force officers. Other young people seem to have been drawn to it by what they regarded as its romantic secrecy and the fact that its members could carry revolvers. Lithuanian university students seem also to have been attracted by aspects of Nazi ideology coming from Germany. For example, in March 1938 there were disturbances at the University of Kaunas, which were marked by attacks on Jewish students and distribution of the Nazi antisemitic paper *Der Stürmer.*

By the late 1930s Lithuania had become very nationalist. In 1938, Articles 73 and 74 of the constitution (which had assured minorities of autonomous rights in education, culture and welfare) were repealed and attacks on Jews became more common. For all this, antisemitism in inter-war Lithuania needs to be kept in perspective. Unpleasant and depressing as it was, it was trivial compared to what was happening in Germany, or even in Romania or Poland. There were no pogroms as such, and serious anti-Jewish violence was rare. Emigration was attractive but difficult due to unwillingness of potential destination countries to admit Jews. Nonetheless, some Jews did leave. Between 1928 and 1939, 13,898 Jews emigrated from Lithuania, of whom about 35% went to South Africa and about 25% to Palestine. But most Jews had no option but to stay and try to make the best of it.

One way of 'making the best of it' might be seeking to integrate fully into Lithuanian life and culture but without losing their separate identity as Jews: acculturation. Generally, Jews in Lithuania acculturated much more slowly than Jews in the west. In 1937, for example, 98 % of Lithuanian Jews who declared themselves as 'Jews by religion' also described themselves as 'Jews by nationality', and less than 1 per cent described themselves as of 'Lithuanian nationality'. [13] The first step towards acculturation was to acquire the Lithuanian language. Before independence, most Jews in Lithuania rarely spoke Lithuanian. Yiddish was the vernacular language, Hebrew the language of prayer and ritual. German and Russian were the languages of high culture. Polish was a language which facilitated communication with Polish landowners. A few words of Lithuanian might help with trade in the marketplace. Some Jews spoke it rather better, depending on where they lived and on what their occupation was, but generally Jews did not make a great effort to master Lithuanian. This changed with independence, when quite suddenly proficiency in Lithuanian became important. The Lithuanian language became compulsory in Jewish schools, and Lithuanian history and geography were introduced into their curriculum. An increasing proportion of Jewish children began to attend Lithuanian schools. Indeed, 20 per cent of Jewish children were being educated in Lithuanian schools by the mid-1930s.[14] The Lithuanian language became the language of instruction in Vytautas Magnus University. A measure of the growth of the Lithuanian language among Jews was that two Jewish journals were set up which used the Lithuanian language, *Žydų balsas* (The voice of the Jews) and *Apzvalga* (Review). In July 1938 Jokubas Goldbergas said in an interview in *Apzvalga*: "Young Jewish people use Lithuanian among themselves not only in public places but at home as well. It is not a rare occasion nowadays to hear Jewish children speaking Lithuanian among themselves."[15]

Acquisition of Lithuanian language skills enabled Jews to take an interest in traditional Lithuanian culture, and particularly in its folk art. For example, Elijah Goldschmidt and Uriah Katzenelenbogen compiled collections of prose, poetry and translations which they published in a journal called *Lite*. Katzenelenbogen published translations of Lithuanian folk songs in a Kaunas yiddish daily newspaper that carried extensive descriptions of his project for collecting Lithuanian folklore. There were signs in inter-war Lithuania, particularly in pockets of the Jewish intelligentsia, of a burgeoning interest in traditional Lithuanian folk culture.[16] There were also early signs of Jewish interest in Lithuanian literature. In August 1929 the nationalist daily *Lietuvos aidas* said:

"A few years ago it was difficult to find a Jew who could speak Lithuanian and was acquainted with Lithuanian literature, but now we can see among the Jews young philologists who easily compete with young Lithuanian linguists."

This was some way from real acculturation, but it hints at the early development of a fertile cultural exchange, tragically cut short by the Holocaust.

An indication of the relative lack of acculturation of Lithuanian Jews is the infrequency of intermarriage and conversion. The census of the Lithuanian population of 17 September 1923 suggests that of the 155,125 individuals in Lithuania who were born Jewish all but 35 followed the Jewish faith at the date of the census. 15 were evangelical Lutherans, eight were Karaites, seven were Catholics, three were Orthodox, and two were evangelical reformers. In almost all cases the principal motive for conversion was the desire to marry a Christian partner. And in almost every case the conversion and intermarriage caused a stir in local communities, with the matter extensively reported in the local Lithuanian press. The reporting was usually in terms designed to reflect badly on the Jewish community, often suggesting criminal misconduct on their part. It is clear from the reports that the local Jewish community felt real consternation at the prospect of one of their members marrying out of the faith. For example, on 29 October 1933 the *Žemaičiu prietelius* reported that a 19-year-old Jewish man called Naika Leizeris planned to marry a young Catholic lady from the village of Padegliai. The report explained:

> Having found out the news the Jews are in uproar and have taken to following him [Leizeris] day and night. On one occasion he was seized, severely beaten, and locked in a cellar, but the police found out and he was released. Nevertheless, the Jews began to assault him even more often, attacking him both during the day and night...[17]

Generally, Lithuanian Jews seem to have acculturated less than the neighbouring Polish Jewish community. For example, the Polish census of 1921 showed that only 73.8 per cent of all Jews in Poland identified themselves as Jews in terms of religion. Almost all Lithuanian Jews at that time identified themselves as Jews by religion.

There are various and complex reasons why Litvaks acculturated more slowly than other European Jewish communities. It was partly a consequence of the fact that Tsarist laws had kept Lithuanian Jews separate and discriminated against for many years and that Lithuania was a poor and backward place; but it also seems probable that Jews were not very enthused by the prospect of acculturating into a small, often hostile and seemingly backward peasant culture. This was a much less appealing prospect than acculturating with Russian, German or British cultures which, in different ways, offered the prospect of easier access to the world's greatest literary and scientific achievements.

For the most part, then, Jews did not assimilate in the sense of losing their distinct identity and becoming an indistinguishable part of Lithuanian society, but they did make a major contribution to inter-war Lithuanian culture. There was, briefly, a sudden outpouring of cultural activity. Much of this was centred on Kaunas, the new capital.

Jews were involved as architects, engineers, and contractors in constructing some of Kaunas's most striking modernist buildings, which changed the face of the city and continue to attract architectural interest. They include the Central Post Office, the Officers' Club and the Kaunas Sports Arena. The headquarters of the dairy company Pienocentras and the city's great War Museum are acclaimed art deco buildings. International and local Jewish musicians played in Kaunas, including Jascha Heifetz, Chaim Potashinsky and Vlado Perlemuter. A vibrant artistic scene developed, particularly around Arbit Blatas, Max Band, Jacques Missene, Zale Beker, Chaim Feinstein and M.L. Ginsburg. A number of Jewish writers, many inspired by the legacy of Abraham Mapu, worked in inter-war Kaunas. Among many others, they included Markas Zingeris and Lea Goldberg. Lea Goldberg went on to become a well-known novelist, poet and children's author in Israel. Her 1946 novel *Vehu Haor* (And this is the Light) captures the frenetic modernism of inter-war Kaunas, trying to establish itself as a modern capital of a new state, while standing uncertainly on precarious foundations. The novel is set in the summer of 1931. It describes the impressions of Nora who returns to her native Kaunas after university studies in Berlin:

> The new post office, like all the new government buildings in that small state [Lithuania], was a little more splendid than it had to be. And even though it didn't go beyond bourgeois taste, something in it bordered on the absurd, because of the search for a 'special style' that had the pretence of coordinating the demands of modern man in a technical age with big, vaulted Venetian windows and pink marble columns like both Renaissance and ancient buildings.[18]

There are not many English language accounts of life in Kaunas during the inter-war period. But there is one remarkable exception: the diaries of Robert Wayne Heingartner.[19] Heingartner was the United States consul in

Lithuania from 1926 until 1928 and stayed in contact with Lithuania and friends he made there after he was posted elsewhere. He was born of German-American ancestry in Canton, Ohio. He had consular postings in Carini, Italy (1904), Trieste (1904-1906) and Vienna (1907-1917), before returning to Vienna after the First World War where he married Lily Kraus, daughter of a well-to-do assimilated Jewish family. Heingartner describes well how simple, even primitive, he found the physical condition of Kaunas when he arrived in the mid-1920s: "Kaunas has no water works and no money to construct a water system. All water is drawn from the wells in every backyard. There is also no sewage system." (18 September 1926). At that time, there seemed to be little new construction: "little or no building is going on in Kaunas and hardly any public improvements are being made. I am told that nobody, not even government, cares to invest money here because of the city's uncertain future" (11 September 1926). Many of the cultural artefacts of the city had been removed. His wife Lily was a painter and she thought that Kaunas Art Gallery contained "many interesting pictures by Lithuanian artists, but the collection is small because... German soldiers took all the best works of art back to Germany with them" (7 November 1926). Much of the diplomatic world in which Heingartner circulated regarded Kaunas as a dull and provincial posting. He remarked of a diplomatic gathering shortly after his arrival "As usual everybody asked me with a sardonic smile how I would like Kaunas and when I told the British vice consul that I thought I would like it, he answered that he had been here for five years and does not like it yet" (20 September 1926). A French minister to whom Heingartner spoke claimed that "the three worst diplomatic posts are considered to be Ankara, Tirana and Kaunas" (24 September 1926). Heingarter describes the distinct lack of confidence about the future of independent Lithuania which was openly articulated in diplomatic circles in Kaunas. He reports a conversation with the Papal Nuncio in Lithuania, Monsigniore Faidutti:

> The Monsigniore is very sceptical as to the future of Lithuania. He remarked to me that the political leaders quarrel among themselves, that they have no experience in politics, and that the people are entirely unfit for self-government. He thinks the only solution for this country is its absorption by Poland and that this is inevitable because of the higher Polish culture.

Heingartner was struck by the number of Jews in Kaunas and by how they dominated retailing and trades. His diaries are full of references to the inconvenience of Jewish holidays which led to "most of the shops" being closed. He was also struck by the efforts made by many Jews to leave Lithuania. His consular responsibilities, which included responsibility for matters relating to immigration and citizenship, gave him particular insight into this. He confided to his diary that rabbis made up such a large proportion of those seeking to immigrate to the U.S. that he doubted the bona fides of some of them and he came to wonder if they might be Lithuania's chief export (9 December 1926 and 28 July 1927).

It is particularly interesting to read how the opinions of Heingartner and his circle evolved. By the mid-1930s they had come to recognise that the physical environment of Kaunas had undergone remarkable development. And there was a much more flourishing cultural life. By the mid-1930s, after he had been away from Kaunas for a few years, he recorded his friend Mr. Kuykendall telling him:

> I [Heingartner] would not recognise the place [Kaunas] now with its asphalted streets and tall buildings along the main street. There is a six-storey apartment building on the main street and many of the wooden houses in the business section of the city have been replaced by up-to-date buildings of brick or concrete and having such conveniences as elevators and steam heat... A good motorbus service has taken the place of the horse-drawn street carline of our time...

Heingartner's contemporaneous diaries and notes record how for a few brief inter-war years Kaunas grew and prospered, despite an ever-present sense of vulnerability, before Lithuania and its Jewish population were again plunged into crisis, this time by the onset of what was to become the Second World War.

During the inter-war years my great-grandfather Myer appears to have had mixed feelings about Lithuania. His business involved continuing trade with the Baltic, and he maintained contact with a handful of commercial tradespeople. He did not return to Lithuania or to Latvia, apart from on a single occasion in the late 1930s when he attempted, unsuccessfully, to recover a substantial debt. There were family and friends with whom he corresponded. According to those who knew him in old age, his feelings at this time were complex: a mixture of resentment, generally not publicly expressed, at having had to leave the land where his family had lived for generations and in which he grew up, coupled with anxiety about the increasingly dangerous international situation. The growing risk of war threatened his business and the wellbeing of his family and friends in the

Baltic. He was relieved that, in Ireland, he seemed to be out of immediate harm's way, but felt guilty at being powerless to help family who sought his help to leave the Baltic.

Notes

1 Mark Levene, 'The Balfour Declaration: A Case of Mistaken Identity', *The English Historical Review*, 107.422 (1992), 54–77. This article illustrates how during the First World War, and in the decade following it, there were widely-held, if mistaken, assumptions about the power of Jews to influence international diplomacy.
2 Yivo Institute for Jewish Research, Article on Lithuania by Dov Levin.
3 Merja-Liisa Hinkkanen-Lievonen, *British Trade and Enterprise in the Baltic States, 1919-1925* (SHS, 1984).
4 Esa Sundbäck, 'The Baltic States, Finland, and British Economic Expectations in the Early 1920s', *Journal of Baltic Studies*, 33.3 (2002), 307–21.
5 Dawidowicz, pp. 28–50. Lucy Dawidowicz describes her stay in Vilnius in 1938. She found it steeped in history, but provincial: "To me Vilna was the very epitome of the Old World, a storied place with a storied past.... Vilna's streets and buildings were emanations of the past..."
6 Levin, p. 130.
7 Romuald J. Misiunas, 'Fascist Tendencies in Lithuania', *The Slavonic and East European Review*, 48.110 (1970), 88–109.
8 Polonsky, *The Jews in Poland and Russia*, p. 230.
9 Šarūnas Liekis, ChaeRan Y. Freeze, and Antony Polonsky, *Jews in the Former Grand Duchy of Lithuania Since 1772* (Littman Library of Jewish Civilization, 2013), p. 246.
10 Polonsky, *The Jews in Poland and Russia*, pp. 227–28.
11 *The Vanished World of Lithuanian Jews*, p. 125.
12 *The Vanished World of Lithuanian Jews*, p. 128.
13 Antony Polonsky, *The Jews in Poland and Russia: 1914-2008* (Littman Library of Jewish Civilization, 2010), p. 226.
14 Ezra Mendelsohn, *Jews of East Central Europe*, (Indiana University Press, 1983) p. 235.
15 Liekis, Freeze, and Polonsky, p. 301.
16 Liekis, Freeze, and Polonsky, pp. 166–82.
17 Liekis, Freeze, and Polonsky, pp. 229–43.
18 Lea Goldberg, 'And This Is the Light' www.google.co.uk/books.
19 Robert W. Heingartner *Lithuania in the 1920s: A Diplomat's Diary* (Rodopi, Amsterdam and New York 2009)

6

To the Edge of the Abyss

As the 1930s progressed Jewish life in Lithuania became more difficult. An important turning point occurred in March 1933 when the National Socialist Party under Adolf Hitler came to power in Germany. Lithuanian nationalists and some ethnic Germans living in Lithuania were emboldened by the world's weak response to the Nazi seizure of power and its subsequent antisemitic actions. The credibility of the Nazi regime received a substantial boost when the Vatican signed the 'Concordat' with it in July 1933, and right-wingers in Lithuania took due note of the lack of strong and coordinated world reaction to the introduction of the Nuremberg racial laws in 1935.

Nazi seizure of power in Germany emboldened General Petras Kubiliūnas, chief of the Lithuanian General staff between 1929 and 1934, to attempt a military coup in Lithuania in June 1934. Most participants in the coup were extreme right-wingers, followers of the nationalist leader Voldemaras, and many were involved in the 'Iron Wolf' organisation. Generally, coup plotters had considerable support among the approximately 100,000 ethnic Germans living in Lithuania, particularly from those in and around Klaipėda. The attempted coup did not bring Kubiliūnas to power, and a military tribunal sentenced him to a term of life imprisonment. Notwithstanding the failure of this coup attempt, Kubiliūnas and his supporters did succeed in one of their main objectives, which was to galvanise extreme right-wing opinion. He helped set off a strident antisemitic press campaign, infused with racial elements, and which was strongly influenced by the Nazi example. For example, local newspapers such as *Lietuvos Aidas* and *Verslas* proposed plans for a kind of racial discrimination against Jews. Among other things, they suggested that Jews be forbidden from employing Christian women as servants, that Jews be excluded from holiday resorts and that they be restricted to bathing on separate, fenced-off beaches.[1]

In the late 1930s the Lithuanian state tried ever more vigorously to favour Lithuanians in the economy and to restrict Jewish economic influence. To implement this policy the state used import and export taxes, credit and consumer cooperatives, subsidies and exemptions which favoured Lithuanian-owned establishments.[2] The Lithuanian state, the country's largest employer, exercised great influence on the job market but was loath to employ Jews. In 1934 only 1.35 percent of 31,091 state employees were Jews and by 1935 neither the government nor any private Lithuanian business would hire Jews. Emigration appealed to many Jewish people but was very difficult as most potential destination countries put up barriers.

In March 1938 Lithuania agreed, under strong Polish pressure, to renounce its claim to its historic capital Vilnius (occupied by Poland since 1922). From then on, one of the main uses which leading Lithuanian politicians saw in the Jewish community, its supposed ability to exert international diplomatic influence, was much diminished. A further low occurred in March 1939 when Germany annexed Klaipėda (or Memel as Germans called it).

Klaipėda was a city-enclave of approximately 1,000 square miles on the Baltic coast; it had belonged to Germany until 1919 when, pursuant to the Treaty of Versailles, it was ceded to the allies on the basis that it was to be administered by France. In early 1923 Lithuania seized Klaipėda, claiming a need for an outlet to the sea, and forced the evacuation of the French garrison. This matter was referred to the League of Nations which, following extensive negotiations, concluded the Memel Convention of 1924. This provided for local autonomous government, with the governor of Klaipėda appointed by the President of Lithuania. However, more than half the population of 141,000 spoke German: they looked to Germany as their homeland and to the German government as their protector. Germany was unwilling to accept the loss of Klaipėda. By 1938 Klaipėda's local administration was in the hands of local Nazis and in December 1938 the Nazis won 25 out of 29 seats in elections to the Memelland legislature. Many Jews saw the writing on the wall: following the December 1938 election 8,000 Jews fled from Klaipėda to other parts of Lithuania. Lithuania and Germany signed a non-aggression pact in January 1939 and ten weeks later, on 23 March 1939, Nazi Germany occupied Klaipėda, unopposed, and incorporated it into the Reich. Hitler arrived on a battleship, accompanied by a fleet of warships, to celebrate this further expansion of the Reich. For the Jewish population of Lithuania this was a deeply alarming moment: it brought the Nazi regime to their doorstep and it indicated that swathes of the Lithuanian population regarded this development with equanimity, if not with unalloyed delight.

Flight of Klaipėda's Jews to surrounding Lithuanian towns and villages led to Lithuanian nationalist groups (Verslas prominent among them) making increasingly strident calls for restrictions on economic opportunities for Jews. It also led to an increasing number of physical attacks on Jews and their property. There was much window-smashing and arson in many smaller Jewish communities.

Five months after the German occupation of Klaipėda, on 23 August 1939, the Soviet and Nazi regimes signed the Molotov-Ribbentrop Pact, a so-called non-aggression treaty which secretly partitioned eastern Europe into Russian and German spheres of influence. It placed the three Baltic states in the Soviet sphere. Nine days after signing this pact, Germany invaded Poland, so beginning what was to become the Second World War. On 18 September 1939 the Red Army occupied the part of eastern Poland that it had secretly agreed with Germany should be within its sphere of influence. In October 1939 the Soviet Union proposed that Lithuania sign a mutual assistance agreement under which the Red Army would be permitted to garrison 50,000 soldiers on Lithuanian territory and to build and use air bases in Lithuania. A very tempting quid pro quo was offered: the return of Vilnius from Poland to Lithuania. In any case, Lithuania was in no position to resist, or even seriously to negotiate, the terms of this Soviet proposal. The Soviets now dominated Lithuania but did not yet occupy it. While the Soviets tried to charm Lithuanians with fine words about their limited intentions, the NKVD (the Soviet secret police agency and forerunner of the KGB) was drafting a top-secret document issued under Order 001223 which prescribed the arrest and deportation to the USSR of all anti-Soviet 'elements' in all three Baltic states.

The return of Vilnius and its surrounding area to Lithuania increased the Jewish population of Lithuania. A wave of Jewish refugees fled to Lithuania from the parts of western Poland which had been occupied by Nazi Germany. This brought the Jewish population of Lithuania to a peak of approximately 270,000, more than 10 % of the total population. This increase in the Jewish population was unwelcome to many Lithuanians and led to serious anti-Jewish riots in Vilnius and Kaunas. 200 Jews were wounded in riots in Vilnius on 31 October 1939.

The Communist party of Lithuania (the "CPL") was jubilant at the signing of the Mutual Assistance Agreement with Moscow; local Communists tried to stir up political unrest. They accused the Lithuanian government of kidnapping two Soviet soldiers in Vilnius and of various other provocations. The CPL accused the Lithuanian government of "attempting to sabotage the mutual assistance pact with the USSR."[3] Relations between the Lithuanian government and the Soviets deteriorated. Allegations of sabotage were really just a pretext for wider ambitions. On

14 June 1940 the Soviet government delivered an ultimatum. This required Lithuania to dismiss several cabinet ministers alleged to be responsible for 'provocations' against Soviet troops, form a pro-Soviet government and allow free entry of an unlimited number of Soviet troops into Lithuania. The Soviets gave the Lithuanian government ten hours to reply to this ultimatum, during which time it was informed that 200,000 Soviet troops had massed along the Soviet-Lithuanian frontier and would enter Lithuania the next day, irrespective of the response to the ultimatum. The Smetona government remained ignorant of the secret provisions of the Molotov-Ribbentrop Pact which had given the Soviets a free hand to treat Lithuania as being in its sphere of influence and to deal with it as it saw fit. In fact, Smetona's government decided to accede to the demands set out in the ultimatum, but on 15 June 1940 the Soviets invaded nevertheless. President Smetona left the country for Germany the same day. Lithuanian independence was at an end.

Between June 1940 and June 1941 Lithuania was occupied by the Soviet Union. In effect, it was a satellite. The experience was unsettling, sometimes traumatic, for much of the ethnic Lithuanian population. Two particular aspects of the Soviet occupation go some way to help explain how relations between Jews and Lithuanians deteriorated during that year and how that affected the way the Holocaust occurred in Lithuania.

The first noteworthy feature of the Soviet occupation between June 1940 and June 1941 was that many Lithuanians came to see Jews as being very closely connected with communism.

In June 1940 many ethnic Lithuanians believed, and some have continued to believe, that Jews generally welcomed the Soviet invasion, were disproportionately inclined to be sympathetic to Soviet communism, and that they played a significant role in the administration of the Soviet regime in Lithuania between June 1940 and June 1941. The nature and extent of the Jewish connection with Soviet communism has become important in trying to understand the behaviour of ethnic Lithuanians during the Holocaust and their subsequent coming to terms (or not coming to terms) with that behaviour.

Obviously, there was no contemporaneous polling of Jewish attitudes to the Soviet invasion of June 1940 and so it is impossible now to be entirely clear what Jewish Lithuanians collectively really thought about it. Diaries and memoirs suggest that some young Jewish people greeted the Soviet troops enthusiastically, while older people tended to be much more circumspect. For example, conservative historian Zenonas Ivinskis described this mixed reaction:

> Disorganised gangs of young Jewish boys and girls, not older than 15-18 years…welcomed each passing [Red Army] vehicle, shouting "hurray!" and singing and shouting and waving their arms…Only the young Jews showed such joy. The older Jews disapproved. They just watched and kept silent.[4]

There were some solid reasons why Lithuanian Jews might welcome the Soviet invader: first, and most importantly, Soviet rule was perceived as being preferable to Nazi rule – it was much the lesser of two evils. This feeling grew stronger as Jewish refugees from Nazi occupied Poland brought accounts of Nazi atrocities towards Jews in parts of Poland, such as Czestochowa and Wyszków. The point is forcefully made by a resident of Slonim (a town in Belarus), who wrote:

> Who cared about communism? Who paid any attention to theoretical problems of national economy, when one faced an immediate danger to life? The question of whether the regime was good or bad was irrelevant. There could hardly be any doubt that the entire Jewish population, poor and rich, workers and factory owners, was relieved when the Red Army entered our town [because it offered protection from Nazism].[5]

Another reason some Jews welcomed the Soviet invader was that, even if they were not Communist, they were attracted by Soviet promises to end anti-Jewish discrimination and harassment. Many accounts emphasise the immediate feeling of relief experienced by many Jews. A wealthy Jewish mill owner said: "There was no racial or national persecution and, for the first time, the Jew was not a second-class citizen." Tanya Fuchs said: "Jewish children move without fear…they go to school and cross the road without looking round with terror in their eyes."[6]

Many Lithuanians came to think the whole Jewish population, in an undifferentiated way, was enthusiastically pro-Soviet and pro-Communist. There were some understandable reasons why they might have thought this: they were conscious of the large numbers of Jews who fled to Lithuania from German-occupied Europe in 1940 and early 1941 and may (mistakenly) have thought such people were mainly attracted by the Communist regime, rather than by the more basic point that Lithuania was not occupied by the Nazis; they were conscious that some Jews were involved in the Communist Party of Lithuania and in some parts of the Soviet bureaucracy and they were also conscious of, and perhaps especially aggravated by, the increasing and conspicuous presence of Jews in occupations previously closed to them as Jews. Many Lithuanians were devout Roman Catholics and were strongly influenced by their priests. There was deep antipathy to Communism because it was atheistic. Its atheism made it offensive and the idea that many Jews were sympathetic to Communism transferred that hostility, in a rather un-nuanced way, from Communism to Jews generally.

This raises the question of whether, during the Soviet occupation, Jews were generally sympathetic to the Soviet regime and whether they made a disproportionate contribution to serving it.

It is clear that there were substantial parts of the Lithuanian Jewish world which opposed a Bolshevik takeover. Unsurprisingly, conservative and religious Jews tended to oppose Bolshevism: for example, in late May 1940 the chief rabbi urged Lithuania's rabbis to support the Lithuanian government and denounce Jews who supported the Communist party. It also seems that better-off Lithuanian Jews strongly opposed the Communist party, not least because its actions were strongly contrary to the interests of such people: of 1,593 firms nationalised in Soviet Lithuania 1,320 belonged to Jews; of 986 workshops taken over by the state, 560 had been in Jewish hands.

Despite some Lithuanian views to the contrary, it seems Jews were not heavily over-represented in the administration of the regime which ran the Lithuanian Soviet Socialist Republic (the LSSR). Of the fifty members of the central committee that ran the new government only two were Jewish; of the twenty commissars and forty assistant commissars only one was Jewish; and of the many thousands of senior government and municipal officials, fewer than thirty were Jewish. Some of those prominent in the NKVD, such as Todes, Dembo and Finkelstein, may have been Jewish by background, albeit not practising or identifying as such. But it appears that some Lithuanians often assumed senior members of the NKVD were Jewish, on the basis of their appearance or name, when actually they were not. Indeed, there was a compelling reason why the Soviet authorities did not want many Jews involved in administering Lithuania, which was that they well understood that antisemitism was pervasive, and that the presence of large numbers of Jews in administration of the Communist regime would turn the Lithuanian masses away from Communism.

During the Soviet occupation of Lithuania the seemingly paradoxical position arose that, to quote Masha Greenbaum "Jewish involvement in the new leadership of the LSSR was very small", but many Lithuanians thought it was very substantial and they intensely resented it.[7] At the end of June 1940 Zenonas Ivinskis wrote in his diary:

> Most of the people (at least those whom I meet) are simply craving for the Germans to come. And then the real slaughtering of Jews would start. Fury at the Jews for their outrageous sympathies to the Bolsheviks, for their internationalism, and for their arrogance is great.[8]

Evidence suggesting relative lack of Jewish involvement in the administration of the Lithuanian Soviet Socialist Republic between June 1940 and June 1941 is, in Masha Greenbaum's words, "highly significant in view of subsequent allegations by Lithuanian antisemites that Lithuanian collaboration with the Nazis in the murder of Jews during the Holocaust had been provoked by massive Jewish support of and identification with the hated Communists during the Soviet occupation."[9]

Far from being closely tied up with administering the Soviet regime in Lithuania it seems, on the contrary, that Jews were generally more oppressed by it than the ethnic Lithuanian population. Some Soviet policies specifically targeted Jewish activity: for example, Yiddish newspapers (with two exceptions) were shut down. Official efforts were made to discourage religious observance and synagogues were converted to 'more social' uses; Jewish museums and libraries, including the YIVO institute and the Strashun library in Vilnius, were also forced to close. Other Soviet policies ostensibly affected the whole Lithuanian population, both Jewish and non-Jewish, but in practice bore much more heavily on Jews. Imposition of heavy taxes on small shopkeepers, and seizure of their business, affected Jews particularly severely because this was a very typical Jewish occupation. By June 1941 only ten percent of formerly privately-owned shops remained in their owners' hands. Larger commercial enterprises were nationalised from autumn 1940 onwards and 57 per cent of such enterprises had belonged to Jews.[10]

The Soviet occupation set off intense intra-Jewish tensions. The Jewish Communists tended to despise the "clericals" (as they called all religious Jews), and were hostile to Zionists, Bundists and other Jewish socialists. Synagogues were closed, use of the Hebrew language was restricted and leaders of non-Soviet Jewish groups were sent to Siberia.

In June 1941 many Lithuanians seemed to feel an intense need to blame Jews generally as responsible for the hardships of the Soviet occupation. This remains difficult to explain. There seem to have been a number of ingredients: in the final analysis, Jews were more sympathetic to the Russians than to the Germans because of the intensity of Nazi antisemitism; Lithuanians, on the other hand, tended to be more sympathetic to Germans than to Russians because they thought Germans were more cultured and they despised the atheism that was an important part of Bolshevism and the hardships that Russian occupation brought them. These different views about Russians and Germans created a wedge between Jews and Lithuanians. It is also clear that some Lithuanians were outraged by the prominence of a small handful of Jews in the higher ranks of the NKVD, men such as Gladkov and Todes. Lithuanians were generally disorientated and resentful of the fact that, under the Soviets, Jews occupied some government positions from which they had been excluded in the past; they found this 'uppity'. Depressingly, if inevitably, Lithuanians may also have felt a need for a scapegoat for the horrors and trauma which Soviet occupation brought them: the Lithuanian historian Albert Kalme calculated that the one year period of Soviet occupation resulted in the death, injury or disappearance of 52,000 Lithuanians.[11]

A second aspect of the Soviet occupation of Lithuania which was to have a lasting impact on Jewish-Lithuanian relations was that most ethnic Germans, and a few ethnic Lithuanians, who had been living in Lithuania fled to Germany in autumn 1939 and spring 1940. It is thought that about 52,000 people were "repatriated' to Germany from Lithuania following the signing of the Molotov-Ribentrop Pact in September 1939. Of these, about 35,000 were ethnic Germans. The other 17,000 comprised Lithuanians who were "Germanising", and ethnic Lithuanians who the German authorities thought might prove useful to them.[12] Among the ethnic Lithuanians who fled to Berlin were about 1,000 former Lithuanian government officials, army officers, political party leaders and members of the Lithuanian Security Police. In November 1940 many of these people, from different political backgrounds, coalesced around Kazys Škirpa, a former colonel in the Lithuanian army, to form the Lithuanian Activist Front (LAF). The LAF espoused a political ideology based on nationalism, Christianity and 'social justice'. Above all, Škirpa and his associates strongly believed that Lithuania must regain its independence and that only German backing would enable Lithuania to free itself from Soviet domination. The LAF therefore aligned itself very strongly with the Nazi regime. Its statements became more and more radical and antisemitic. This was partly from conviction but also from the calculation that such statements would enable it to curry favour with the Nazi regime. In March 1941 the LAF published a leaflet which said: "Inform the Jews that their fate has been sealed and that those who are able to flee should start leaving Lithuania now to avoid unnecessary harm." Five days later, in *"Instructions for the Liberation of Lithuania"*, the LAF elaborated on this theme: "The hospitality that Vytautas the Great offered to the Jews in Lithuania has been revoked for all times for the ongoing betrayal of the Lithuanian nation." [13]

The LAF was not simply a front organisation for the Nazis. It saw itself as an independence movement. In spring 1941 Škirpa and his associates negotiated with a number of different German agencies as to how Lithuanian independence was to be re-established. There was clandestine wooing of the Abwehr (German military intelligence) and, separately, with the Wehrmacht at their headquarters in Konigsberg. But the LAF deceived itself in thinking that the Germans were committed to Lithuanian independence. On 20 April 1941 Hitler appointed Alfred Rosenberg as Reich Minister for the *Ostgebieten* (the Occupied German Territories), with responsibility for the affairs of the Baltic region. His files relating to the intended organisational structure of the *Ostgebieten* were later captured intact by the allies. They have become known as 'the Rosenberg Files'. These papers make clear that there was extensive cooperation between Rosenberg and other parts of the German administration, and that the clear plan was that Ostland should become a 'German protectorate' "after Germanising racially possible elements and transforming the area into part of a greater German Reich". Far from allowing it to regain independence, the German plan was that Lithuania become a colony for German settlement.[14] With the benefit of hindsight, it is difficult to avoid the conclusion that Škirpa and his LAF associates were utterly deluded about the willingness of the German authorities to reinstate Lithuanian independence. Mistakenly, they thought Germany would be grateful for the military support that Lithuania could contribute to its campaign against the Soviet Union; they thought that the fait accompli of proclaiming Lithuanian sovereignty would tie Germany's hands; and, naively, they believed Hitler was committed to the right of Lithuanian self-determination.[15] The LAF became ever more stridently antisemitic as part of its effort to solicit Nazi sympathy and support. The extent of Škirpa's miscalculation of German intentions only became clear to him after the Nazi invasion of the Soviet Union. The Germans placed him under house arrest and did not allow him to return to Lithuania. In 1944 he was sent to a concentration camp in Bad Godesberg. In September 1941 the LAF sent an angry memorandum to Hitler complaining that, despite its vociferous support for Germany, Lithuania was being treated as an occupied territory. The response was rapid and emphatic: the headquarters of the LAF was stormed and its then leader, Leonas Prapuolenis, was arrested. He was sent to Dachau concentration camp and the LAF disintegrated.

There were two particular ways in which the activities of the LAF were adversely to affect the Lithuanian Jewish community: the LAF succeeded in creating a significant network of followers in Lithuania and their noisy rhetoric inflamed antisemitic sentiment there, predisposing the population to behave in a hostile way towards Jews. Also, some groups associated with the LAF in Germany were trained for infiltration into Lithuania on the eve of the German invasion, and they were later involved in mass killings. For example, Pranas Lukys, convicted by a West German court in 1957 for the murder of Jews and Communists near Tauragė, was trained in 1940 with a group of 50 men near Tilsit, later stationed near Klaipėda, and sent across the border on the night of 21-22 June 1941.[16]

Almost the last act of the Soviet occupying forces before the German invasion of June 1941 was the deportation of thousands of "anti-Soviet minded" Lithuanians, and their families. This occurred in the last week of Soviet rule, 14-21 June 1941. Those arrested were deported by train to Siberia and to other parts of Soviet Asia, where they were interned in forced labour-camps and compelled to undertake manual labour. Many were put to work in coal mines; others were made to fell timber. About 35,000 Lithuanians were deported that week. The Soviets and Jews were widely blamed for these deportations (Jews collectively were blamed, it seems, because two Jewish Communists, Gladkov and Todes, were involved, among others, in organising the deportations). The Red Army also committed outrages against the civilian Lithuanian population as it retreated in the face of the advancing German army. For example, a Russian tank drove to the Pravieniškės concentration camp and, for no obvious reason, mowed down women and children with machine guns.[17]

On the eve of the Nazi invasion of Lithuania, some parts of the Lithuanian population were in a frenzy of rage against Jews. They were beyond the point of being capable of making distinctions between Orthodox Jews, bourgeois Jews, Zionist Jews, Bundists and Communist Jews. Instead, they indiscriminately categorised all Jews as Communists, and as being collectively responsible for betraying Lithuania to the hated Soviet occupier.

Notes

1. Levin, p. 182.
2. Karen Sutton, *The Massacre of the Jews of Lithuania: Lithuanian Collaboration in the Final Solution, 1941-1944* (Gefen Pub., 2008), p. 48.
3. *Kommunistas* [The Communist], journal of the CPL Central Committee, no. 6 (Vilnius, June 1960), p.31
4. Polonsky, *The Jews in Poland and Russia*, p. 389.
5. Polonsky, *The Jews in Poland and Russia*, p. 387.
6. Polonsky, *The Jews in Poland and Russia*, p. 388.
7. Greenbaum, p. 292.
8. Robert van Voren, *Undigested Past: The Holocaust in Lithuania* (Rodopi, 2011), p. 58.
9. Greenbaum, p. 292.
10. Sutton, p. 89.
11. Albert Kalme, *'Total Terror. An Exposé of Genocide in the Baltics'* (New York: Appleton-Century-Crofts, Inc, 1951) p. 94.
12. Zvi Gitelman, (ed) '*Bitter Legacy; Confronting the Holocaust in the USSR*'. Indiana University Press, 1997, p.96
13. Voren, p. 62.
14. Sutton, p. 112.
15. Sutton, pp. 104–5.
16. Voren, p. 64.
17. Sutton, p. 94.

1. My great-grandfather Myer (front row, left) celebrating his golden wedding, in 1948.

2. Myer standing on the left.

3. My grandfather JD (left) on his wedding day, in 1932.

4. My father Michael.

5. A photo of Liepāja taken in 1912 showing the Great Synagogue, St. Joseph Cathedral and the Market.

6. A photo showing the port of Liepāja, from which emigrants embarked for a new life.

7. An old building in Pikeliai where Jews probably lived and worked.

8. Another old building in Pikeliai where Jews probably lived and worked.

9. A photo of Jewish traders in Vilnius taken by the German army during World War 1.

10. A photo of the Meeting Room of the Lithuanian Seimas taken in 1926.

11. The site of the old synagogue in Pikeliai.

12. The site of the old cemetery in Pikeliai. Many of the gravestones were removed in the post-war period, probably for re-use as building materials.

13. Massacre of Jews in Lietūkis Garage in Kaunas in June 1941.

14. Abba Kovner (back row, centre), among other members of the United Partisan Organisation during the Vilnius ghetto uprising of 1943.

15. A Lithuanian soldier guarding a group of Lithuanian Jews in Vilnius in July 1941.

16. A pit at Ponary, just outside Vilnius. About 70,000 Jews were murdered at Ponary. The pit was used to burn corpses that had been exhumed in an effort to destroy evidence of mass murder.

17. Site of the mass grave in Mažeikiai where most of the murdered Jews of Pikeliai are buried.

7

An Outline of the Holocaust in Lithuania

It was very uncomfortable for my great-grandfather Myer, grandfather JD, and other wider family members to follow from afar the German invasion of Lithuania in June 1941. They were anxious anyway about Britain's war against Germany and the extent to which Britain still risked being invaded. There were concerns about the bombing of London, which brought war horribly close to home. Anxiety about the invasion of Lithuania was of a different kind: a sense of foreboding about the fate of Lithuanian Jews under German occupation, aggravated by a lack of information about what was really happening and the virtual impossibility of obtaining such information.

The way the Holocaust unfolded in Lithuania was distinctive. What happened there was subtly if significantly different from what happened elsewhere in Europe. It was the first country in which the Nazis pursued a policy of killing the entire Jewish population, and this objective was largely achieved. It is estimated that about 96 per cent of the pre-war Jewish population of Lithuania was murdered. The killing was mainly carried out by shooting (not by gas van or gas chamber), and much of the shooting was carried out by local Lithuanians, albeit this was often, but not always, under the direction of Germans. The way in which Lithuanians have faced up (or not faced up) to complicity in the Holocaust during the post-war period has been complicated, and often controversial.

At the risk of stating the obvious, it is difficult – if not impossible – to explain the Holocaust in Lithuania. A sensible writer approaches such a task with humility. All I can do is offer some general observations: first, in this chapter, to provide a broad outline of what happened; then, in chapter 8 and as a way of trying to make this wider story more "human", to provide an account of the experiences of a survivor who, among many others, has written a powerful memoir. In chapter 9, I offer some thoughts about how and why the Holocaust in Lithuania occurred by considering it, in turn, from the perspective of perpetrators, bystanders and victims.

We cannot know the precise number of Jews who lived in Lithuania on the eve of the Nazi invasion of June 1941 because no census was taken at that time. Reasonable, but conservative, estimates suggest that at the end of the first half of 1940 (in other words, during the period of the first Soviet occupation) there were about 225,000 Jews living in Lithuania. This comprised about 145,000 Jews living within the pre-Second World War Lithuanian borders together with about 65,000 Jews in Vilnius and the surrounding area which again became part of Lithuania at the end of October 1939. These numbers were supplemented by about 15,000 Jewish refugees who arrived in Lithuania after September 1939 from German occupied Poland. The number of Jews in Lithuania declined in the period between the first half of 1940 and the eve of the German invasion in June 1941 for three particular reasons: first, about 5,000 Jewish refugees from Poland migrated to other countries, mainly to Palestine, the United States and the Far East; secondly, about 3,000 Jews were deported to the deep interior of Russia because the Soviet authorities regarded them as "anti-Soviet elements"; and thirdly about 12,000 Jews fled into the Soviet Union during the first days of the German invasion. These numbers suggest that approximately 205,000 Jews remained in Lithuania after the Germans invaded in June 1941.[1]

It is helpful to divide the Holocaust in Lithuania into three distinct periods: the first period lasted from the German invasion on 22 June 1941 until December 1941. This was a period of mass murder of Lithuanian Jews. About 80 per cent of them were killed during this time. The second period lasted from January 1942 until March 1943 and can be thought of as a relatively quiet period, during which German policy concentrated on exploiting Jews for their labour having first enclosed them in ghettoes in Vilnius, Kaunas, Šiauliai and Švenčionys. The third period began in April 1943 and lasted until July 1944. It was characterised by the gradual liquidation of the existing ghettoes and of the surviving Jewish population by a mixture of murder and deportation to camps in Germany.

The first period began on 22 June 1941 when Nazi Germany launched Operation Barbarossa, its surprise attack on the Soviet Union, with which it had concluded a non-aggression pact in 1939. Some 3.3 million German soldiers were involved in Operation Barbarossa, divided into three army groups. Army Group North, which entered Lithuania, was the most important army group in the initial phase of the invasion because its principal objective was to conquer St Petersburg as quickly as possible. The Soviet army in Lithuania was caught by surprise. It withdrew in great haste, barely engaging with the invading German army. It should not have been so surprised. As early as August 1940 British intelligence had received indications that there were German plans to attack the Soviets and these warnings were passed to the Soviet Union. Stalin's distrust of the British, and his suspicion that their warnings were merely a device to bring the Soviets into the war on their side, led him to ignore these warnings. In early 1941 Stalin's own intelligence services and American intelligence gave further repeated warnings of an impending German attack. These were given added veracity by reports from the Soviet spy Richard Sorge. Again, Stalin failed to react to warnings of a likely German invasion. His lack of response may in part have been so as to avoid the risk of provoking Hitler but it was also because Stalin simply disbelieved the warnings. Behind a public display of bravura, senior members of the Nazi party were disconcerted that the Soviet army had withdrawn rather than engaged with their invading armies. On 27 June 1941 Joseph Goebbels said: "We are all afraid the Red Army will retreat prematurely and not enter into the battle of annihilation."[2] The German high command had not anticipated the rapid retreat of the Red Army to lines further east, and this contributed to later German difficulties.

For a few weeks following the German invasion of 22 June 1941 there was a lack of any effective government in Lithuania. Most of the Jewish population was terrified. A few were offered transport into the Soviet Union by the departing Soviet authorities, but many declined this offer because their children were away at 'Pioneer' camps (party-sponsored summer camps) or because they felt a need to remain with their own parents. Some Jews tried to follow the Red Army and reach Russia on their own, but many of them ran into armed Lithuanian bands and were brutally murdered. About 12,000 were successful in escaping to Russia in the days after the German invasion, usually by train, although this means of escape was complicated by the fact that the Germans bombed trains and railway tracks. Some Jews in small towns sought safety by moving to larger centres, while others took the opposite view and moved from larger towns to villages.

The majority of the Lithuanian population greeted the Nazi victory over Soviet forces and the occupation of their country with pleasure, and some with elation. German forces under General Friedrich Wilhelm von Kuchel marched into Kaunas in an orderly parade and were welcomed by cheering and flag-waving crowds. Archbishop Juozapas Skvireckas, prelate of the Papal palace, broadcast greetings to "the brave German soldiers and their leader, Adolf Hitler," and offered prayers for their wellbeing. There was an outpouring of savage violence against Jews. In Kaunas, Lithuanian partisans murdered 4,000 Jews in the two days between the invasion and the arrival of German forces in the city. A particularly brutal attack took place in the Kaunas garage of the Lietūkis cooperative where some 60 Jewish men, chosen at random, were taken to the garage and savagely beaten to death as a large crowd observed, and cheered. In Slobodka, partisans went from house to house searching for Jews to murder. Over two nights between 600 and 1,000 Jews were murdered. On 25 June partisans decapitated the Chief Rabbi of Slobodka, Zalma Ossovsky, placing his severed head on display in the front window of his home, while leaving his decapitated body in a nearby room next to the open volume of Talmud he had been engaged in studying.

It is clear that some of these horrific attacks on Jews occurred *before* the arrival of the German army. It is now thought there were at least 40 villages where Lithuanians attacked Jews before the arrival of the Germans and that about 18,000 Jews, mostly men, were murdered in mass shootings before the end of July 1941.[3] Other estimates suggest there were as many as 150 localities which became '*Judenrein*' (free of Jews) 24 hours before the German occupation forces arrived.[4] It seems these pogroms were not entirely organised by the Germans but they were incited and encouraged by them. There had been a number of meetings, in Berlin and at Pretzsch Castle, in early June 1941 at which Heydrich addressed senior personnel in the *Einsatzgruppen* and verbally conveyed the message that Jews were to be killed in the forthcoming invasion. It is possible (but not certain) that during these meetings Bruno Streckenbach told the assembled *Einsatgruppen* leaders that Hitler had expressly ordered the liquidation of Jews in the Soviet Union.

An important German motivation was to channel the energy of local people against Jews to distract Lithuanians from trying to fight for their independence. In addition, Germans wanted to portray local people as the sole initiators of chaotic attacks on Jews so that Germans could present themselves as a force for stability and order. Five days before the invasion, on 17 June 1941, Reinhard Heydrich, head of Reich Security's main office, brought together the commanders of Einsatzgruppen and Einsatzkommandos, as evidenced by his letter to the four heads of the Einsatzgruppen dated 29 June 1941:

> With reference to my oral remarks made in Berlin on 17 June, I remind you: 1) not to place obstacles in the path of the self-cleansing aspirations of anti-Communist and anti-Jewish circles in the areas we are about to occupy. On the contrary, trigger them, but without leaving any traces, intensify them, if necessary, and steer them in the right direction, without enabling the local 'self-defence circles' to claim later that we gave them the orders or gave them assurances with political concessions…[5]

One might wonder why oral remarks made on 17 June needed to be evidenced in writing twelve days later. The most likely explanation is that it was necessary for the Einsatzgruppen to have something in writing to show officers of the Wehrmacht to explain why civilians and Jews, in particular, were being attacked behind the front-lines. The Einsatzgruppen needed to be able to demonstrate they were acting on orders from above.

Many Lithuanians needed little encouragement from Germans to attack Jews. There was an orgy of killing and plunder:

> Many of the killings and lootings were carried out in broad daylight amid acquiescent, often cheering witnesses. When they attended mass in church, the partisans were praised by the priests for their courage and patriotism. The Nazis were blessed and lauded as the liberators of Lithuania, worthy of the eternal gratitude of the country and the Church.[6]

The Jews of Pikeliai fell victim to these attacks in the very early days following the Nazi invasion. During July 1941 Jews in Pikeliai were abused by their Lithuanian neighbours and many of their belongings were stolen. On 5 August 1941 they were transferred to the Latz barns near Mažeikiai. Men were put to work digging pits at the southern end of the Jewish cemetery and were then shot. Women and children were imprisoned in the barns along with women from Mažeikiai and the surrounding areas. On 9 August they were taken to the pits next to which the men had been murdered a few days earlier. Women were forced to undress and were then shot by Lithuanians. Many of the children were thrown into the pits and buried alive. This was so as to save bullets. Jews from a number of nearby towns were murdered at the same site. These towns include Akmenė, Viekšniai, Židikai, Tirkšliai, Klykoliai and Seda.[7] The number of Jews murdered at Mažeikiai is thought to be at least 2,500 and probably between 3,000 and 4,000. About 100 of these came from Pikeliai.

We have an eye-witness account from a survivor called Khonon Reif who came from Viekšniai, a small town near Pikeliai, whose Jewish residents were also murdered in Mažeikiai. Reif's testimony was given while he was in a displaced persons camp in November 1946.[8] It seems probable that what happened to the Jewish residents of Pikeliai was broadly similar to what happened to the Jewish residents of Viekšniai.

Reif begins his account by explaining that he had lived in Viekšniai for about fourteen years before the German invasion of June 1941. About 700 Jews lived there at this time. In a modest way, Jews had been involved in developing local industry. Viekšniai was well-known for its potteries. It had a fine Jewish theatre. Reif maintains that, before the war, Jews had generally got on reasonably well with their Lithuanian neighbours. When war broke out, all the Jews in town tried to flee to the Soviet Union, but only five Jewish families succeeded in doing so because "armed Lithuanian bandits, calling themselves 'partisans'" began shooting at fleeing Jews. On the way back to their homes, armed Lithuanians robbed Jews of their clothing and valuables. On 28 June 1941 'partisans' drove all the Jewish men out of their homes and assembled them in the marketplace where they were forced to perform deliberately demeaning tasks, such as pulling out grass growing between cobblestones and cleaning Lithuanians' outhouses. While the Jews were doing this work, the Lithuanians mocked them and beat them. When the work was done, the Jewish men were forbidden from returning to their homes, but were forced to sleep in the synagogue, which was guarded by 'partisans'. "There were no Germans in town at that time. Generally, they [the Germans] drove through town without even stopping." At 3:00 am on 1 July 1941 the Jewish men were told to leave the synagogue and ordered to run back to their homes. Armed Lithuanian 'partisans' stood next to every Jewish home. Jews were ordered to assemble enough food for three days and prepare to travel to Poland. The Jewish men were herded together in the marketplace, and women and children were forced into the synagogue. The men were lined up in rows. The director of the Lithuanian gymnasium placed the rabbi in front of all the Jews, cut off his beard with a pair of scissors and cut a crucifix into the hair on his head. The rabbi stood with his head bowed, weeping. The Lithuanians then ordered the town doctor, Khayim Lipman, to point out the Communists among the Jews. Dr. Lipman responded that there were no Communists among the Jews of Viekšniai.

One German SS officer was present, and he beat Jewish men with a whip. The "Lithuanian murderers" compelled the rabbi to get on to a horse, and then forced a younger assistant rabbi to pour a bucket of water on the rabbi's head. The town's entire 'Lithuanian intelligentsia' stood on a nearby hill next to the study house, dressed in their holiday clothes, alongside simple peasants. All of them watched as their Jewish neighbours were tormented, and they enthusiastically clapped 'as if they were watching a circus'. The Jewish men were again lined up and all their knives, watches, gold rings and similar items were taken away. For several weeks the men were kept in empty stores and the women and children were detained in the synagogue. In the early days of this imprisonment the Jews had a little food, but they then became very hungry. The women were stripped naked and searched, and meanwhile were bullied and mocked. At 4:00 am on 5 August 1941 the 'Lithuanian bandits' drove the Jewish men out of the stores and the women and children out of the synagogue. They were forced to march nine kilometres to large barns at a mill compound near Mažeikiai. This mill was owned by local ethnic Germans. Elderly Jewish men who paused for rest during this march were shot. When the Jewish men from Viekšniai were forced into the barns they found various scraps of food and clothing that had belonged to Jewish men from Mažeikiai who, they correctly deduced, had been murdered. "They [the men from Viekšniai] realised why they had been brought to the barns".

At 7:00 am on 5 August 1941 'the Lithuanian murderers' ordered 130 healthy young Jewish men out of the barns. They were given spades and shovels. Under heavy guard from Lithuanians armed with machine guns these Jewish men were taken to the Mažeikiai Jewish cemetery about one kilometre from the barns. Reif was one of these 130 young Jewish men. He names many of the Lithuanians who stood guard as the Jews were compelled to dig pits near the cemetery. These Lithuanians were clearly well-known to him. Near the new pits was a half-filled pit where the men from Mažeikiai had been shot. At noon, the German commandant of Mažeikiai, an SA man, arrived at the cemetery, took various measurements and indicated how long the second pit should be. A group of strong young Jewish men from Akmenė was brought in. Some of the weaker Jewish men, including Reif, were taken back to the barns, where they told others what they had witnessed and said what they thought what was going on:

> Rabbi Kalmen Magid ordered everyone to recite the Jewish confessional prayer, and did the same himself. Everyone sat hopelessly, recited psalms and wept. In the second barn the women tore their hair out of their heads, kissed their small children, wept bitterly and wildly, and took leave of one another.

Khonon Reif saw that at the barn gate there was a Lithuanian he recognised. This man, Kerys Antanas, had been a client of his leather goods store before the war. Reif asked Antanas to let him fetch a bucket of water from a pump situated about forty metres from the barn. Antanas agreed and accompanied Reif to this pump, quietly putting down his rifle beside the pump. Reif seized this moment to run off in the direction of the Jewish cemetery and grain fields. Antanas shot at him, but missed. Reif hid in a field of potatoes. For some time, there was shooting in his direction, but then the commotion died down. At 6:00 am the following day Reif heard the first group of men taken from the barns to the pits. The shouts of men could be heard: "Help, save me! My little children!" Immediately afterwards, shouting and moaning could be heard. Reif set off in the direction of Šiauliai. Walking only at night, it took him three nights to reach Šiauliai.

Jews there were still living in their homes and were almost entirely ignorant of what was happening to Jews in the Lithuanian countryside. Reif gave a detailed account of his experiences to two members of the Šiauliai Council of Elders. They found it difficult to credit what Reif told them, and thought he must be mentally ill. Later, after the shooting of the Jews of Šiauliai began, these members of the Council of Elders started to believe what Reif had told them. Reif then entered the ghetto in Šiauliai, with other Jews from that town. He was exceptionally fortunate to survive the war and therefore be in a position to recount his experiences to Leib Koniuchowski, a Lithuanian Jew who survived the war and collected testimonies from other survivors in the immediate post-war period.

Several aspects of Khonon Reif's account are worth emphasising. It is striking that Germans were not present during most of the events that Reif describes and, when they were present, there were only very few of them. There was, nonetheless, a sense that Germans were encouraging and directing things in the background. Many of the Jews who were killed were personally acquainted with the Lithuanians who were rounding them up and killing them. They were their neighbours and people with whom they had done business. Only a minority of Lithuanians were involved in murder, but there was a 'carnival' type atmosphere and many Lithuanians appeared to derive pleasure from the sight of their Jewish neighbours being humiliated and assaulted. Much of the treatment of Jews was highly sadistic. Much Lithuanian behaviour was motivated by the prospect of stealing the personal property of Jews. There had been great propaganda efforts to conflate Jews with Bolshevism, but the overwhelming majority of Jews were, for a variety of different reasons, unsympathetic to Bolshevism. Some of the deep-seated disdain for Jews derived from Christianity. The Jews were generally taken by surprise by the immensity of the hostility they encountered. They felt bewildered by the extraordinary level of violence and hatred they encountered and were unclear how to react. The rabbinical advice they received did not encourage fighting back so much as confessing sins and preparing for death.

In July 2022 I visited the pits in the southern part of the old Jewish cemetery in Mažeikiai, where the Jews of Pikeliai were murdered. It is a bleak place. There is a simple black stone monument engraved in Yiddish and Lithuanian, and a plaque with a very short statement in English about the history of Jews in Mažeikiai and the surrounding area. One of the most striking features of the cemetery is that there are a few tombstones for non-Jews murdered at this site, but there are no tombstones for any of the Jews murdered here, probably because the Jewish communities were almost totally eradicated, and after the war the Soviet regime did not acknowledge the Jewishness of the victims and made it all but impossible for relations of the dead to travel there to pay their respects and organise fitting memorials. The old pre-war Jewish cemetery today lacks many of the pre-1941 tombstones because, during the Soviet era, they were stolen by local people to use as building materials. Bodies of the murdered Jews remain in the pits in Mažeikiai. This contrasts with the position in many other parts of Lithuania. There, pursuant to the so-called *Sonderaktion* 1005, a top-secret Nazi operation was conducted between June 1942 and late 1944. So-called *Leichenkommandos* ("corpse units") were forced to exhume mass graves and burn the bodies of murdered Jews as a way of trying to hide evidence of Nazi mass murder. It seems *Sonderaktion* 1005 simply did not have time or resources to complete their work and therefore bodies in the Mažeikiai pits remained unburned at the time of Soviet reconquest of the area at the end of the war.

For a few weeks following the German invasion of Lithuania in June 1941 there was chaos and an absence of effective government. On 23 June the Lithuanian Activist Front (LAF) purported to set up a far-right provisional government. Colonel Škirpa, still in Berlin, was named Prime Minister and General Raštikis, a known German collaborator and Hitler supporter, became Minister of Defence. This provisional government announced that it was restoring capitalism and private property rights. Its policies towards the Jewish population were distinctly hostile. The Jews of Lithuania were disenfranchised and subjected to the restrictions of the Nuremberg Laws. Jews who had fled with the Soviet forces forfeited the right to reoccupy their homes. Jews were prohibited from walking on pavements but were, instead, required to walk in single file near the gutter. Jews were forbidden to sit on benches in public parks and gardens and were barred from using public transport. Jews were forbidden to own radios or sell their property. [9] Unsurprisingly, many Lithuanians thought the LAF provisional government was actively encouraging them to abuse their Jewish neighbours, albeit the actual position of the LAF provisional government may have been less clear-cut. There are reports that in a meeting with Nazi generals defence minister Raštikis argued for the campaign against Jews in Kaunas and elsewhere to be toned down. The Nazi generals refused this request and one of them unexpectedly poured a jug of cold water over Raštikis's head as he left the meeting. From the outset, the provisional LAF government had uneasy relations with the German authorities. It hoped Germany would support full Lithuanian independence. It was to be disappointed. On 17 July 1941 Berlin informed the provisional LAF government that Hitler had decided that the Baltic states would not have independence. On 5 August the provisional LAF government was forced to suspend its activities and was outlawed. Some of its leaders were arrested. The Germans took full control of Lithuania.

German administration of Lithuania was rather muddled. Nominally at its head was Alfred Rosenberg. He had authority to coordinate the affairs of the Baltic, Belarus and the eastern part of Poland. The Rosenberg Files (the contents of which the LAF Provisional government was not aware of) make clear that Rosenberg never intended that Lithuania be independent but should instead be a colony for settlement, principally for Volga Germans but, he went on to say, "there might also be the possibility of the settlement of Danes, Norwegians, Dutch, and after the war has been brought to a victorious end – of Englishmen too." The Rosenberg Files show that there was extensive discussion of policy with other parts of the German administration, including the OKH (Army High Command), the OKW (Armed Forces High Command), the ministries of Economy, Labour and the interior, the SA and the SS.[10] On 17 July Heinrich Lohse was appointed Reichskommisar for Ostland and Theodor Renteln was appointed general commissar for Lithuania. They were part of the civilian political administration, but both were members of a secret group directed by the most senior Nazi authorities in Berlin that had been directed to prepare plans for the Final Solution of 'the Jewish problem'.[11]

By early autumn 1941 the Germans were in effective control of the government and economy of Lithuania. They were in a position to organise the mass murder of Jews in Lithuania and proceeded to do so with such ruthlessness that it is estimated that by December 1941 only about twenty per cent of the pre-war Jewish population remained alive. Given that Jews in Germany and some other parts of German occupied Europe were not at this time being murdered with such ruthlessness a number of historians have keenly debated why Germans sought to eradicate Lithuanian Jews in autumn 1941.

Some historians, including Arūnas Bubnys, argue that this was because German policy, as conceived by Alfred Rosenberg, was to colonise and Germanise the Baltic countries:

> Because Lithuania had a common border with Germany and Lithuania was supposed to become ground for German colonisation after the war, Lithuanian Jewry had to be shot immediately, that is, as Nazis understood it, this strategically important territory had to be cleansed of undesirable elements and prepared for colonisation.

Bubnys also argues that the Germans were concerned that Jews, behind German front lines, were likely to 'cause disturbances' for German troops.[12]

An eminent German historian, Christoph Dieckmann, argues that German ferocity against Lithuanian Jews was mainly motivated by a different and more practical consideration: when in late summer of 1941 it became clear that war against the Soviet Union was likely to last longer than German war planners had anticipated, military commanders became concerned that they would be unable to feed their troops as well as the civilian population. Hard choices had to be made. Jews and Soviet prisoners of war were anyway despised and so it was decided to kill them as a way of reducing the number of 'useless mouths' to feed. Dieckmann contends that German planners were strongly influenced by the idea that Germany had lost the first world war because of food shortages and consequent instability on the home front; to avoid the risk of instability on the home front in this second world war, it was felt imperative to feed the army and the people at home. Two pre-war plans had been drawn up and approved by the Nazi leadership: a so-called 'hunger plan' ("the Back'sche plan") which involved starving to death up to thirty million people, most of them ethnic Russians; and also a so-called 'decapitation plan' which involved murder of the Soviet leadership, bureaucrats in high positions and Jewish men in the expectation that this would bring about the implosion of the Soviet state. Dieckmann thinks that these plans were adapted in early autumn 1941 when it became clear that the Soviet Union was not collapsing as quickly as military planners had anticipated. The priority then became to get rid of 'useless eaters' and so it was decided, as a first step, to kill all Jews and Soviet prisoners.

The historian Yitzhak Arad disagrees with Dieckmann. He acknowledges that Nazi leaders welcomed the fact that killing Jews reduced the total number of mouths to feed but argues that

> this was not the decisive reason for the resolution. The decisive reason was the racist anti-Jewish Nazi theories and their relation to the Soviet Jews as bearers of Communist ideology and [the belief that] Jews were the mortal enemies of Nazi Germany".

Arad believes that there was a decisive shift in German policy following a meeting at Hitler's headquarters on 16 July 1941, which was attended by the top Nazi leadership. At that time, the expectation among Nazi leaders was that the Soviet Union would collapse quickly. The meeting discussed the administration and political future of the occupied territories. Hitler and Himmler thought they should seize the opportunity to carry out the murder of all of the Jews, under cover of war. They believed such total murder would be much harder, if not impossible, in peacetime because public opinion across the world, particularly in America, would be difficult to face down. This was what lay behind the mid-July 1941 change in Nazi policy from the murder of young and middle-aged Jewish men to the wholesale murder of the entire Jewish population.[13]

A further line of argument suggests that an important part of the explanation for the rapid murder of Jews in Lithuania in autumn 1941 is the willing participation of some of the local Lithuanian population in the murder. Donald Bloxham suggests that Lithuanian nationalists gave the Germans "a policy guide in extremism, since, at brief but seminal moments, non-Germans showed how murder could be expanded in scope."[14] Proactive and willing Lithuanian involvement in murder not only showed Germans how Jews could be killed quickly but also showed that this could be done without having to use many Germans in the process. Germany managed to administer Lithuania with remarkably few Germans. Arūnas Bubnys has shown that at the beginning of 1944 there were only about 660 German officials in the civil administration of Lithuania, compared to some 20,000 ethnic Lithuanians. Also, there were only about 60-100 Germans in the political and criminal police compared to 800-900 Lithuanians.[15]

It seems clear that from mid-July 1941 onwards the character of the murder of Jews in Lithuania changed. Until that time much of the murder was carried out by Lithuanians, sometimes but not always directed by Germans, and the murder was mostly of young men. From mid-July there was a step-change and from then until December 1941 there was an orchestrated and systematic assault on the entire Jewish population, including women and children, which led to most Lithuanian Jews being killed by December. How is one to reconcile the conflicting explanations and best explain this change of approach?

One should first say something about why there have been so many different opinions on this point. Hitler and other leading Nazis deliberately tried not to leave documentary evidence about the murder of Jews, communicating instructions verbally where possible and using code words and euphemisms where orders were given in writing. This approach became more sophisticated and deliberate as a result of lessons learned in the so-called T4 action, being the campaign to kill the seriously ill. In summer 1939 Hitler directed staff to consult medics and academics to come up with a procedure for extending euthanasia to seriously ill adults in the event of war in order to free up hospital beds for military casualties. Those consulted wanted assurance that their advice was not unlawful. Chancery officials therefore sought and obtained from Hitler his written authorisation for this. Those involved in the T4 campaign were duly reassured that they were immune from criminal prosecution. But there was a substantial public backlash against murder of the seriously ill. A number of Protestant leaders spoke out and then, crucially, so did Clemens Graf von Galen, Catholic bishop of Munster.[16] Fearful of adverse public opinion, Hitler formally ended the first phase of the T4 Action on 24 August 1941, by which time between 70,000 and 80,000 people had been killed.[17] It seems a decision was taken not to give instructions in writing about the Holocaust which could be traced back to top Nazi officials, including Hitler. Lack of clear written instructions about the Holocaust from Hitler and other senior Nazis complicates the historian's task of understanding the decision-making process and goes some way to explaining the plethora of different interpretations.

A further reason for the variety of such opinions has to do with the nature of decision-taking in Hitler's Germany. There were different power centres, with ill-defined, overlapping and sometimes competing jurisdictions, lacking clear written instructions from the top. Different parts of the power apparatus often sought to curry favour with more senior officials by taking the initiative at a local level to do things they believed would meet with approval. This sometimes meant that policy was incoherent and makes it difficult for historians to agree on why things happened as they did.

The main reasons for escalation in anti-Jewish policy in late summer 1941 may be something like this: the Nazi leadership had always been strongly and ideologically antisemitic. Some of the originators of Nazi ideology came from the Baltic, notably Alfred Rosenberg. Lithuania abutted Germany, had a long history of German settlement, was comparatively fertile and relatively empty of people. The local people were thought unlikely to be able to prevent the elimination of the Jews, even if they had wanted to do so. Lithuania seemed a natural place for implementing the policy of 'lebensraum', the idea that Nazi Germany should acquire more 'living space' by expanding the territories it controlled in the east. The relatively small number of Jews in Lithuania (compared to Poland, for example) and the preparedness of parts of the Lithuanian population to shoot Jews made it possible in mid-July 1941 to imagine that the Jews of Lithuania could be totally eliminated, enabling Hitler to fulfil the 'prophecy' made in his Reichstag speech of 30 January 1939 that 'if … Jewry … should succeed in plunging the nations once more into a world war, the result will be … the annihilation of the Jewish race in Europe'. In mid-July it seemed, from a German perspective, that the war in the east was going well, and there was a possibility the war would end quickly. It would be easier to eliminate Jews under the cloak of war than once peace returned, when powerful countries overseas, particularly America, were very likely to make difficulties. The decision to eliminate all Jews quickly was taken in a mood of celebration, even euphoria, at early German successes. Within a few weeks the mood darkened as German leaders came to realise that the retreat of Soviet armies, and their unwillingness to engage the German army, might present military difficulties and the war might last longer. But this did not change the fundamental calculation about eliminating Jews quickly. Indeed, from late July 1941 there appeared to be additional reasons for killing all Lithuanian Jews quickly. These were that, if left alive, Jews would consume food that would otherwise be available for German military personnel and the local population. Shooting Jews seemed more straightforward than trying to starve them to death. There was concern that Jews, now living in impoverished and overcrowded conditions, might spread epidemic disease, putting German soldiers at risk. There was also a fear that Jews, who had every reason to oppose the German military, might become active in partisan activity against the Germans behind their front lines. Moreover, if some Jews were allowed to survive, there was the risk that in time they would seek revenge. In October 1943 Himmler reflected on the decision to kill Jewish women and children too. He told Nazi Party leaders in Posen:

> What about the women and children? I did not consider myself entitled to exterminate the men and to let avengers in the form of their children grow up for our sons and grandchildren. The severe decision had to be made to make this people disappear from the earth.[18]

Most Lithuanian Jews were murdered between August and December 1941, but the Holocaust developed in rather different ways in the countryside and in the larger towns. In the countryside most of the murder was carried out by mobile killing units. The most significant were the Ypatingasis būrys in the Vilnius area and the Hamann Rollkommando in the Kaunas area. There was a third killing unit, part of the fourteenth Batallion in Šiauliai, commanded by Romualdas Kaloksa, but this was smaller and less is known about it.[19] The Hamann Rollkommando is the best-known mobile killing unit. It consisted of 8-10 members of Einsatzkommando (EK3) and a Lithuanian battalion commanded by Lieutenant Bronius Norkus; this had eighteen Lithuanian officers and 450 men. The Hamann Rollkommando was commanded by Joachim Hamann. He was of Baltic German parentage but had spent most of his pre-war life in Kiel in north Germany. Hamann trained as a chemist but, unable to find work in his field, had to make do with low paid farm work. He joined the SA in 1931 and the SS in 1938. He was a devoted Nazi and fiercely antisemitic. He invariably attended killings carrying a whip. The Hamann Rollkommando killed tens of thousands of Jews around Kaunas and in southern Lithuania. It travelled to places where Jews had been gathered together by Lithuanian policemen and volunteers, known as 'white armbanders' and where pits had been prepared. Sometimes these pits were dug by Jews, sometimes by Soviet prisoners of war. A report by Karl Jager to his superiors in Berlin explains that 137,346 Jews had been shot by 25 November 1941. With some pride, he details the process of how Jews were murdered in the Lithuanian countryside:

> The implementation of such actions is first and foremost a matter of organisation…The Jews had to be assembled…Depending on the number of Jews the site for the required pits had to be chosen and the pits excavated. The marching distance from the assembly point to the pits was on average 4 to 5 kilometres. The Jews were transported in detachments of 500 to the execution site, with a distance of at least 2 kilometres between them. The following example demonstrates the difficulties.
>
> In Rokiskis 3,208 people had to be transported 4.5 kilometres before they could be liquidated. In order to get this work done within 24 hours, over sixty of the eighty Lithuanian partisans had to be detailed for… cordon duty. The rest, who had to be relieved constantly, carried out the work [i.e. shooting the Jews] together with my men.[20]

Most Jews in the Lithuanian countryside were shot in autumn 1941 and were buried in pits. Young children were often thrown alive into the pits, rather than being shot. They were buried alive. This was to save bullets. All the bodies were covered with earth and lime. Many witnesses report that they saw the earth move for up to three days after the shootings, perhaps reflecting efforts to escape of those who had been buried alive.

Jews in some larger Lithuanian towns were treated rather differently. By autumn 1941 the priorities of different parts of the German civil and military apparatus collided. None were sympathetic to Jews, but it became evident that Jews comprised the bulk of the skilled workforce in Lithuania and performed services that the German authorities badly needed. In autumn 1941 some Germans realised that if all of the Jews were killed immediately the Lithuanian economy would collapse.

There is a striking example of the impact of these economic considerations from Šiauliai. This was the third largest town in Lithuania. In 1877 Chaim Frankel had founded a tannery there, and two years later he added a leather goods factory. Frankel took advantage of Šiauliai's convenient communication links and his business was early to embrace opportunities provided by steam boilers and electricity. He died, in 1920, a very wealthy man. His leather goods and shoe business continued to flourish after his death to the extent that it became one of the largest businesses of its kind in the Baltic and in Soviet Russia. A memoir by Eliezer Yerushalmi explains how Frankel's leather goods and shoe factory played a crucial role in the survival of some Jews throughout the period of Nazi occupation.[21] Yerushalmi explains that, before the Nazi invasion, the factory's top managers, department heads and about half the workforce were Jews. When the Germans arrived, local Lithuanians wanted to replace the entire Jewish management of the factories and all the Jewish workers with (non-Jewish) Lithuanians. On 30 June 1941 "when the Jewish workers and employees came to work the Lithuanians forced them to clean the toilets and cesspools, jeering and ridiculing them. Afterwards they drove all the Jewish employees out of the factory." However, much of the work in a leather goods and shoe business requires highly skilled labour.

> The Germans soon realised that they could not run the factory only with Lithuanians, and [this] forced them to recall the experienced Jewish employees. First, they reinstalled the former director of the factory, Eliyahu Mordel, the former factory manager Max Lipshitz, the chief engineer Patruch, the chief chemical engineer Kron…and others. All of them brought back other factory employees with them, releasing 110 people from prison.

Yerushalmi believed that what he calls "this Jewish 'conquest' of the factory made [some] Lithuanians wild with resentment", not least because it frustrated their efforts to steal Jewish possessions, which they knew was common practice elsewhere. This resentment led some Lithuanians, including Antanas Stankus (Šiauliai deputy for Jewish affairs until February 1942) to treat Šiauliai Jews who were not working in the Frankel leather goods and shoe factory with additional harshness. Yerushalmi says that Stankus "grabbed half the residents of the old-folks' home and sent them to Žagarė". Nonetheless, Jews in Šiauliai appear to have succeeded in persuading the German authorities that Jews alone had the necessary skills to support the vital leather goods industry and this put a check on German efforts to murder all Lithuanian Jews as quickly as possible. It goes a considerable way to explaining how some Jews from Šiauliai survived long into the period of German occupation of Lithuania.

In autumn 1941 there was misunderstanding and disagreement between different parts of the German military and administrative apparatus as to whether economic considerations should be allowed to have any bearing at all on the policy of exterminating Jews. We know that Joachim Hamann arrived in Šiauliai in September 1941. He complained that the policy of killing Jews in Šiauliai was 'a dirty mess' (*ein Saustall*), by which he meant it was proceeding too slowly. He insisted that all Jews in the city be liquidated as soon as possible. He visited Hans Gewecke, the Gebietskommisar in the city, who strongly disagreed. Gewecke explained he needed Jews because they were skilled workers. Infuriated, Hamann argued that this was none of Gewecke's business, and that economic considerations did not matter and were of absolutely no concern to him. Gewecke seems to have prevented Einsatzkommando 3 from completing its mass killing in Šiauliai. This bitter row was referred up to Generalkommisar Renteln. Gewecke was required to justify his conduct in a formal written report to Renteln. He explained the importance of Jews in the economy: "it is impossible to carry on work without Jews. This is especially the case in the leather tanning industry. Every single artisan in the leather tanning industry is Jewish. " But Gewecke's report tried to provide reassurance that he was co-operating with the policy of killing Jews to the extent consistent with the economic needs of the Reich: "You may be convinced that we have acted on the Jewish question in the Schaulen region [Šiauliai] with the necessary intensiveness and with National Socialist stubbornness."[22] Disagreements between different parts of the German administration are significant because they help explain the apparent confusion of German policy towards Jews in Lithuania in autumn 1941 and why expedited mass murder became more gradual. In particular, they help us understand how the Holocaust unfolded in the largest towns, Vilnius and Kaunas, during the 'first period', which is to say the period between June and December 1941.

Vilnius had the largest Jewish community in Lithuania, and before the war had been a great centre of Jewish cultural life. Many Nazis saw it as a "centre of Judeo-Bolshevism". Soviet troops departed the city on the night of 23 June, and the first German troops arrived on 24 June, but most German troops passed through or by-passed Vilnius in pursuit of the retreating Soviet army. Power in Vilnius was initially in the hands of Lithuanian partisans, remnants of the 29th Corps of the pre-Soviet Lithuanian army and the pre-Soviet Lithuanian police. They seemed primarily interested in giving "Vilnius a purely Lithuanian character, by decorating the city with eye-catching Lithuanian flags"[23] and their ethnic hostility was initially aimed at Poles as much as at Jews. Within a few days the SS arrived in Vilnius. *Einsatzgruppe* A was commanded by Franz Walter Stahlecker. The *Sonderkommando* of *Einsatzkommando* 9 had a Lithuanian unit, the Ypatingasis būrys. This group roamed the streets of Vilnius in search of young Jewish men who, when caught, were never seen again. These young Lithuanians were known to the Jews as "catchers" or "chappers"(in Yiddish). Noah Shneidman describes them in her memoir, *Jerusalem of Lithuania:*

> I was startled and shocked to learn about the fate of those approached by the catchers, the more so since among the catchers were several young Lithuanians that I knew. They were former students of the local Lithuanian high school and members of a well-known basketball club. I was astonished to learn how little time it took to unleash the evil instinct in those who were previously regarded as decent young men.[24]

In early July anti-Jewish measures were introduced in Vilnius which, among other things, required Jews to wear yellow stars, prevented them from walking on the main streets and limited the amount of food that shops could sell them. From mid-August the mass murder of men, women and children began. With just one day's notice Jews were enclosed in ghettos in Vilnius. As a part of this process, some were taken to Paneriai forest, just outside Vilnius, where they were shot. A further change in German policy occurred in mid-September 1941, from when it seems that some Jews working in economically important areas were to be temporarily spared, together with their immediate families. Two ghettos were established in Vilnius: ghetto I for 'productive' Jews, being those who were to be kept alive for as long as their labour was considered useful and ghetto 2 for the remaining 11,000, which included children, the elderly and those regarded as unfit for work, who were to be killed as quickly as possible.

Most of the killing took place at the Paneriai forest, just outside Vilnius. The pits next to which the Jews were to be shot and into which they were to be buried were dug near a railway station so as to facilitate the transport of Jews to the killing sites. The pits were in a densely wooded area, in the hope that local people might not understand what was going on. Most of the shooting was done by Lithuanian volunteers, members of Ypatingasis būrys, with some, rather minimal, German supervision. There are slightly varying estimates of the number of Jews killed at Paneriai before the end of 1941, but Yitzhak Arad calculates that about 33,500 Jews from Vilnius were murdered there before the end of December 1941.[25]

On the eve of the Nazi invasion my great-grandfather Myer had a sister living in Kaunas. No doubt he was anxious as to what was happening to her and to other Kaunas Jews but communication between Britain and Kaunas was virtually impossible. Lack of knowledge bred anxiety and distress. We now have a reasonably full picture of what happened; in many ways, what took place in Kaunas was not dissimilar from what occurred in Vilnius. Within a few of days of the German invasion, local Lithuanians, encouraged by German military and security police, began a 'pogrom' in Vilijampolė, a suburb of Kaunas. Rabbi Ephraim Oshry explains:

> That Wednesday evening at dusk, Lithuanian Nazis, accompanied by mobs of ordinary Lithuanians, marched into the Jewish section of Slobodka [Yiddish for Vilijampolė] with axes and saws. They began the Slobodka pogrom ...moving from house to house, from apartment to apartment, from room to room, killing every Jew they encountered, old and young alike ...[26]

Between 600 and 1,000 Jews were massacred in the pogrom of 25-27 June 1941. The killing then moved to the centre of Kaunas. A further pogrom took place there on 27 June at the former Lietūkis garage. From 30 June 1941 Jews began to be executed away from the city centre of Kaunas, at the Seventh Fort. This was one of a number of forts built by the Tsarist authorities in the 1880s as part of a network of fortifications designed as a means of defence against possible German attack. In the inter-war period the fort was repurposed for civilian use. In summer 1941 some 5,000 Jews were taken there and killed. The fort was chosen as a killing site because, as it was a little removed from Kaunas, it was possible to attempt to conceal from the civilian population the mass murder that was taking place there. In August 1941 Jews of Kaunas were required to live in the ghetto. On 18 August 1941 over 18,500 Jews were taken to the Fourth Fort and murdered in what became known as the "Intellectuals' action". On 26 September and 4 October 1941 another 3,500 ghetto inhabitants were murdered as a result of smaller "actions" and then, on 28-29 October 1941, there was a so-called "Great Action" which led to the death of about 10,000-12,000 people. The selection process seems to have been designed to kill all the Jews in the ghetto who were unable to work. William Mishell, an eye-witness, explains what he saw on Democratu Square in the Kaunas ghetto:

> The morning was very chilly, a typical autumn day with a thin layer of snow covering the ground. It was still dark and the air was extremely damp ... one could see mothers with children in their

> arms, old people who could barely walk, small children holding the hands of their mothers, grown-ups supporting their elderly parents or grandparents, and even invalids supported by canes. Some people who were unable to walk were carried out on stretchers. Everybody tried to make it out of the house to avoid being shot…
>
> Suddenly Rauca [Hauptscharführer in Einsatzgruppe A] appeared on the plaza and an air of doom overcame everybody…With an unusual calmness he directed people to the right or to the left [those directed to the left being selected for immediate death], totally ignoring family composition. At will and with obvious delight, he separated parents from children, husbands from wives, and children from mothers …[27]

After this selection Lithuanian police chased the Jews who had been selected into the small ghetto from where they were marched to the Ninth Fort. Two youngsters escaped from the Ninth Fort, returned to the ghetto and gave the Jewish Council an eye-witness account of what they had seen. The Jews were separated into groups of one hundred, ordered to undress and they were then shot by Lithuanian units who were supervised by a small number of Germans. The slaughter lasted a day and a night. The victims' clothes were collected, to be later repaired, cleaned and sent to Germany. The Lithuanian killers divided their victims' valuables among themselves. After the "Great Action" the Kaunas ghetto settled into a period of relative calm. About 15,000 Jews remained alive in the Kaunas ghetto. It seems the Nazis were satisfied that the only Jews remaining alive in Kaunas were those needed to work for the German war effort.[28]

By the end of November 1941, the great majority of Lithuanian Jews had been murdered. Karl Jaeger, commander of Einsatzkommando 3, made secret reports dated 25 November and 1 December 1941 in which he said: "There are no Jews in Lithuania anymore, except those needed for work and their families. Their numbers are 15,000 in Vilnius, 15,000 in Kaunas, and 4,500 in Šiauliai. I intend to kill off these working Jews too, but the civil administration and the Wehrmacht need them and their families for the war effort."[29]

Some Jews lived in the ghettos of Vilnius, Kaunas, and Šiauliai from autumn 1941 until late summer 1944. What was Jewish experience of life in the ghetto?

When Jews were first forced into city ghettos many of them were remarkably unaware of the Nazis real attitudes towards them, or what lay in store for them. Older Jews remembered that, in World War 1, German armies had usually behaved civilly towards them, more so than had the Tsarist armies. Germans used elaborate techniques of deception to obscure their real intentions from Jews. In Kaunas, for example, Germans tried to persuade a delegation of prominent Jews that it was in the Jews' own best interests to enter the ghetto quietly because the ghetto would afford effective protection against the Lithuanian mob. Also, many Jewish leaders, at this early stage, simply found it impossible to credit that Germans were capable of behaving with the barbarity which some people (particularly those aware of the Germans' harsh treatment of Polish Jews) were beginning to ascribe to them. Einsatzgruppe Report 20 of 12 July 1941 says: "The Jews are remarkably ill-informed about our attitude toward them. They do not know how Jews are treated in Germany or... in Warsaw... they believe [mistakenly] that we shall leave them in peace if they mind their own business and work diligently."[30]

When Jews were first incarcerated in city ghettos, their lack of understanding about what was happening to them was frequently made more complicated by the fact that many were trying to come to terms with traumatic loss of close family members. Often, fathers and sons had been murdered. Sometimes, family members had just vanished, creating anxiety about what had happened. Christoph Dieckmann, who spent many years reading different materials written by Jews in ghettos, found that concern about family was their principal concern:

> Many people were mainly loyal to their families. They didn't care so much about Jewish religion, Zionism or socialism. The guiding question ... for all those difficult decisions and choices they had to make was whether it was good or bad for their families, whether it would help the family to survive or not.[31]

The ghettos were very over-crowded. Often, there were five to seven families in one small house or apartment, sharing one kitchen and an outhouse toilet. Each family cooked for themselves, on a tiny stove. The main room tended to be divided by sheets hanging from the ceiling. During the day mattresses were piled up in the corner and at night laid on the floor. Many people slept in the same bed, so if one turned over in the bed it woke up others. The living quarters were very noisy.

There was very little food. The Germans wanted to control how much Jews ate and did so by means of rationing. For example, in August 1942, Jewish workers in Kaunas were entitled to: 1,400 grams of bread, 250 grams of meat, 100 grams of fat, 0 grams of cheese, 75 grams of a food substitute, 0 grams of sugar, 0 grams of marmalade. Jewish nonworkers in Kaunas were entitled to: 700 grams of bread, 125 grams of meat, 75 grams of food surrogate, and nothing else.[32] Jews were not provided with eggs, milk or sugar. Very occasionally, horse meat was delivered, but Orthodox Jews would consume horse flesh only when faced with starvation and ordered to do so by their Rabbis, and sometimes not even then. Responsibility for delivering food to the ghettos lay with the administrations of the Lithuanian cities, and they discharged this obligation by using the cooperatives. They were supposed to deliver food to the ghettos' Jewish councils, which were then to distribute food in accordance with the ration cards. However, the cooperatives often did not have enough food to deliver. In October 1941 a cooperative called Sodyba informed the German civilian administration responsible for the Vilnius ghetto that it was unable to deliver the requested quantity of vegetables to the Vilnius ghetto because it had not received enough vegetables from Lithuanians. On 16 October 1941 Murer, the German representative of the civilian administration responsible for the Vilnius ghetto, advised Sodyba that it was only to deliver vegetables to the Vilnius ghetto if it had food left over after it had satisfied all other requirements.

Jews could only survive by smuggling food into the ghettos. The Jewish councils appear to have organised about 40 per cent of food smuggling into the ghettos. If members of the Jewish council were caught smuggling food, they were highly likely to be killed. Children and teenagers also smuggled food into the ghetto; and chimney sweeps smuggled food into the Vilnius ghetto by climbing onto roofs with the buckets divided into two sections, one of which was designed to conceal food.

The dire shortage of food, the smuggling and attempts to trade with Lithuanians on the outside are well captured in the 2017 recollections of Judita Mackeviciene, a survivor of the Kaunas ghetto:

> What I remember most from life in the ghetto was the constant fear, the incredible hunger, the tortuous longing and loneliness. My father tried to trade for food, but there was no way to transport the produce. But [some Lithuanians] traded with us. We'd usually exchange clothing for food...That food kept us from dying of starvation.[33]

Electricity was also rationed. From 6:30 am until 10:30 am and again from 4:50 pm until 9:00 pm there was no electricity in the Vilnius ghetto. These were times of day when electricity would have been most useful for preparing breakfast and dinner. There was no electricity in the ghetto hospital. The ghetto was dark and cold, especially during the winter of

1941-2 when Jews had to give away their furs and warm clothes for the German army in the Soviet Union. There was a constant risk of the spread of epidemic disease although, in fact, there were few serious epidemics. This was mainly because the Jewish councils gave strict instructions that Jewish inhabitants of the ghetto were to wash, go to the bathhouse and not leave rubbish lying about.

Much of the administration of the Jewish ghettos was carried out by the Jewish councils and by the Jewish police units. The Germans set up Jewish councils mainly so that German personnel would not have to deal directly with Jews. They sought compliance from the Jewish councils by killing those they thought most likely to resist and by taking hostages, telling the Jewish councils that if they did not obey then the hostages would be killed. Most Jews did not wish to serve on the Jewish council. There are records of a meeting of Jews in Kaunas on 5 August 1941, attended by about 30 people. The Germans wanted a council selected by this body to act as the Jewish council. Jews did not volunteer, thinking it would be shameful to take on such a task. Eventually, Rabbi Schmukler begged doctor Elkhanan Elkes to lead the Jewish council of salvation, a role Elkes took on with great reluctance. Other council members were chosen because they spoke German or knew members of the Lithuanian political elite. The Jewish councils were required to collect goods and valuables belonging to Jews including gold and silver jewellery, electrical appliances and new shoes. They were also required to establish administrative departments to keep the ghetto running smoothly. These were tasked with matters such as overseeing food distribution and they were also responsible, among other things, for health, sanitation and police.

The Jewish councils were supported by Jewish police units. Some of these policemen have been criticised for, in effect, collaborating and lacking integrity but it seems unwise to make sweeping moral judgements. Most of these policemen were not highly sophisticated but did their best in impossibly difficult circumstances. Much of the criticism of their conduct derived from post-war Soviet trials which were hastily conducted and contaminated by ideological and antisemitic motivations. The context for the behaviour of these policemen is provided by pleas in mitigation submitted by relations of the accused in those trials which emphasise, for example: that the Jewish policemen were trying to assist the Jewish council keep the ghetto going by providing labour for the Germans, without which Jews in the ghetto would have been killed; at great risk to themselves, Jewish policemen helped Jewish partisans arm themselves and escape to the forest, and they tried to pass Jewish children to people outside the ghetto; most

Jewish policemen lost almost their entire families to the Holocaust; and when the Germans evacuated the ghetto, policemen thought it better to die than take their chances with the departing Germans. The wife of a policeman concludes her defence of her husband's conduct by asking rhetorically: "Can such a person, someone who was confined to the ghetto and condemned to death, be considered an accomplice of his enemies? "[34]

There is a difficult question about the treatment of Jews in the ghettos between autumn 1941 and liquidation of the ghettos in autumn 1943. As has been said, Germans appear to have kept Jews alive in ghettos for the principal purpose of exploiting their labour to assist the German war effort. But: the Germans kept Jews in conditions of such over-crowding, hunger, and terror as to make it very difficult for them to work effectively. One might have thought it would have been more in German self-interest to improve living conditions somewhat in order to derive more benefit for the German war machine from Jewish labour. There are no easy explanations for this. This, and questions like it, perplexed Jews in the Lithuanian city ghettos at the time and they remain perplexing. The best answer seems to be that there were different agendas within different parts of the German war apparatus but, in the final analysis, fanatical loathing of Jews trumped all other considerations. And, above all, no more food was to be given to Jews than was strictly necessary for the survival, for a while, of some key Jewish workers.

On 21 June 1943 Heinrich Himmler ordered the liquidation of the ghettos in Lithuania. They were to be replaced by concentration camps for the small number of Jews whose labour he thought was still needed. Before this order, about 40,000 Jews remained alive in Lithuanian ghettos. Himmler's order had a long background. Since summer 1942 he had been trying to take over authority for the ghettos and transform them into concentration camps administered by the SS. He thought this would enable tighter control over Jews and so help prevent revolts. His concerns grew during the first half of 1943 with the deterioration of the German position on the eastern front, and the lifting of the siege of St Petersburg. The immediate background to Himmler's order to liquidate the Lithuanian ghettos was the Warsaw ghetto uprising of April-June 1943. This took the Nazis by surprise and it alarmed them. They came to believe that the objective of Jews involved in the Warsaw ghetto uprising was not so much their own survival as dying with dignity and avoiding murder in Treblinka. Himmler persuaded himself that Jews in ghettos had become a major security risk. In the process of putting Jews from Lithuanian ghettos into concentration camps a further one third of the approximately 40,000 still alive were to be killed. It was decided to kill off those who might be dangerous and those who consumed food but were not providing productive labour. Two-thirds of the Jewish population to be kept alive were to be moved to Estonia, particularly to a labour camp at Vaivara. The worsening military position had created an urgent need for manpower in Estonia to build fortifications, construct roads and work on extraction of oil shale, which became a priority when the German army appeared to be losing control of oil-rich eastern Ukraine.

In August and September 1943 the SS took control of the Lithuanian ghettos from the German civil administration, although disputes about whether the SS or the civil administration should keep income generated from Jewish labour continued until the end of the German occupation.[35]

The ghetto in Vilnius was liquidated in September 1943. There had been 18,000–19,000 Jews still alive before the liquidation. In September about 11,000 Jews deemed fit for work were deported to concentration camps in Latvia and Estonia. About 3,500 of those regarded as unfit for work, including children and the elderly, were murdered at the Paneriai Forest just outside Vilnius and at the Sobibor death camp. About 1,000 Jews escaped to the forests surrounding Vilnius and joined the partisans or went into hiding in or around Vilnius. Roughly 2,600 Jews then remained alive in Vilnius and were used as forced labour. They worked in three main places: about 1,500 worked at the Kailis fur factory, about 1,000 worked at the HKP repair garage for military vehicles and a small handful worked at the Spanish hospital in the Antakalnis neighbourhood.[36] Before the German retreat from Lithuania in late summer 1944 the Lithuanian concentration camps were liquidated. About 2,000 of the remaining Jews in Vilnius were taken to the Paneriai Forest and shot.[37]

The Šiauliai ghetto was also officially converted into a concentration camp in autumn 1943 and its area reduced. Of the 4,000-4,500 Jews still alive, about 1,500 were sent to labour camps around Šiauliai and about 800 children and the elderly were murdered on 5 November 1943. The remnant, about 2,000, stayed in Šiauliai. Eliezer Yerushalmi wrote a vivid description of the so-called *kinderaktion* (children's action) of 4/5 November, 1943. He explains that Commander Schleef told the Jewish Council: "I inform you that I have received orders to remove from the ghetto all children up to the age of 13, all elderly and those not able to work…" He goes on to describe how 31 German soldiers, accompanied by Ukrainian units, entered the ghetto with trucks, pistols and machine guns. They broke into houses and stole what they liked. On the town square they divided the Jews into two groups, with the young children, old and sick to one side and those capable of work on the other side. There was great brutality, with beatings and screaming everywhere. Yerushalmi explained that on 4 and 5 November about 800 people were taken away from Šiauliai to be murdered, 506 being children under ten, 68 children between ten and thirteen, 56 elderly men and 35 elderly women. After the children's action many of those who were left felt that morale in the ghetto collapsed. Understandably, Yerushalmi felt that nobody cared much about anything anymore. [38] After the children's action about 2,000 Jews were left alive in Šiauliai. In May 1944 it became clear that the Red Army was approaching. The Germans ordered that packing materials and machinery from the leather factories be taken to Germany and that the surviving Jews from Šiauliai be taken to the concentration camp at Stutthof in East Prussia, from where many were sent to other camps in Germany. On 22 July, 1944 the last Jews were removed from the Šiauliai concentration camp and it was set on fire by the Germans. The desperation of departing Jewish residents is reflected in a note by Frida Niselevich, which she buried in the ground in the hope someone would find it later:

> 11 July 1944. On leaving [Šiauliai] and taking the step between life and death, I left behind a few photos of my dearest ones in the hope somebody would find them someday while digging and searching in the soil, and that this person would be so kind as to send them to one of my relatives in America or Palestine, if any of them are left...[39]

On 25 October 1943 the Kaunas ghetto was turned into a concentration camp and put under the command of Wilhelm Goecke of the SS. In October 1943 about 2,750 Jews were deported to camps in Estonia, mainly to Vaivara, and 5,000-6,000 were sent to camps elsewhere in Lithuania. About 7,000-8,000 remained in Kaunas in a concentration camp on the site of the former ghetto. They worked in and around Kaunas, including at the Petrašiūnai brick factory. Jews in Kaunas had heard about the murder of children in Šiauliai and so great efforts were made to hide children with Lithuanian families. About 500 were hidden in this way and survived. On 27 March 1944 there was an *Aktion* against children and the elderly, as a result of which about 1,800 were either deported to Auschwitz or murdered in the Ninth Fort in Kaunas. As the Red Army approached in the summer of 1944 Jews from the Kaunas concentration camp were deported, women to Stutthof and men to Dachau, and from there many were sent on to camps elsewhere in Germany. About 1,500 Kaunas Jews had gone into hiding in so-called 'malines' (being elaborate hiding places, in attics, basements and the like) but these people were mainly killed when German soldiers burned down or blew up the houses in which they were hiding before the final German retreat of 12-14 July 1944. By the time Kaunas was reoccupied by the Red Army following the so-called 'Kaunas Offensive' of 28 July-28 August, 1944 only a small handful of Jews in Kaunas remained alive. They crawled out of the malines where they had been hiding: 18 Jews survived in the sawmill and 20 in a pottery workshop. 24 Jews had hidden in a maline in the sewer under the public toilets, but conditions there were so desperate that only four of them remained alive. Baruch Sedak, an officer with the Red Army, went into the ghetto and discovered a note left by his brother, Hirsch:

> Humans! They chased us here like animals. For seven days we hid from the henchmen without water in horrific heat. Then they threw grenades on us and the house burned down. We crawled into the cellar while the house burned above us… Comrades, take revenge for us. There were over 40,000 Jews in Kaunas, now we are among the last…[40]

As a result of Himmler's order of 21 June 1943 the Vilnius ghetto was totally liquidated in September 1943, whereas many Jews in the Šiauliai and Kaunas ghettos remained alive until summer 1944, although those ghettos ceased to be ghettos as such and became concentration camps under the authority of the SS. How to account for the different treatment of the Vilnius ghetto? It seems the SS regarded the Vilnius ghetto as more dangerous. It appeared a potential centre of resistance and therefore had to be liquidated completely, and by surprise, so as to prevent resistance and mass escape.

In some respects the Holocaust in Lithuania was unique. It was the first country in which the Holocaust took place. The destruction of the Jewish community in Lithuania was almost total, with approximately 96 per cent of the pre-war Jewish population destroyed, and this was facilitated by substantial collaboration from parts of the local population.[41] It is worth reflecting on how any of the pre-war Lithuanian Jewish community survived. Survivors fell into several distinct categories: first, there were those Jews who, as events turned out, had the good fortune to be deported deep into the Soviet Union in the few days before the German invasion. Their numbers were supplemented by some Jews who successfully fled the invading German forces, managed to avoid Lithuanian partisans who were out to kill them, and successfully crossed into the Soviet Union before the arrival of the advancing German army. It is thought about 15,000

Lithuanian Jews were deported or escaped, of whom about 12,000 survived the war. Most of the 3,000 who died were soldiers in the Sixteenth Lithuanian Division in the Soviet army and they fell in battle. A second category of survivors consists of those Jews who were evacuated from the Lithuanian concentration camps to Germany, principally to Stutthof or Dachau, on the eve of the German retreat in July 1944. Perhaps 7,000-8,000 Lithuanian Jews survived this way. Only about 1,700 Lithuanian Jews survived the German occupation in Lithuania. This is less than 1% of the pre-war Lithuanian Jewish population. Of these 1,700, about 900 were partisans in the forests. Part of the explanation as to why there were not more Jewish partisans is that other partisan groups were often hostile to Jewish partisans, both because they were Jewish and because Jewish partisan groups sometimes consisted not just of fighting men, but of women and children too. The remaining 800 or so Jewish survivors had survived by hiding in malines, with the help of Aryan documents or with support from exceptionally brave local Lithuanians, some of whom have since been recognised by Yad Vashem in Jerusalem as being among the "Righteous among the Nations".

Only a tiny handful of Lithuanian Jews survived the German occupation of Lithuania between 1941 and 1944. The big picture is that the long and rather distinguished history of this community was brought to an abrupt and terrible end. Not only were over 200,000 Jews murdered but, to all intents and purposes, a civilization was obliterated.

Notes

1 *The Vanished World of Lithuanian Jews*, p. 176. These numbers are cited by Yitzhak Arad; they are lower than those cited by other authors, notably Dov Levin.

2 Christoph Dieckmann and Rūta Vanagaitė, *How Did It Happen?: Understanding the Holocaust* (Rowman & Littlefield, 2021), p. 64.

3 Dieckmann and Vanagaitė, p. 95.

4 Greenbaum, p. 307.

5 Dieckmann and Vanagaitė, p. 96.

6 Greenbaum, p. 307.

7 'Yizkor Book Database' www.jewishgen.org/yizkor/database.

8 Leyb Koniuchowsky, *The Lithuanian Slaughter of Its Jews: The Testimonies of 121 Jewish Survivors of the Holocaust in Lithuania, Recorded by Leyb Koniuchowsky, in Displaced Persons' Camps (1946-48)*, 2020, p. 146.

9 Greenbaum, p. 309.

10 Sutton, p. 111.
11 Greenbaum, p. 311.
12 *The Vanished World of Lithuanian Jews*, p. 214.
13 *The Vanished World of Lithuanian Jews*, p. 183.
14 Donald Bloxham, *The Final Solution: A Genocide* (OUP Oxford, 2009), p. 8.
15 Voren, p. 73.
16 The Bishop declined, however, to speak up against deportation of Jews, apparently regarding them as dangerous agents of modernity and Bolshevism.
17 Peter Hayes, *Why?: Explaining the Holocaust* (W. W. Norton & Company, 2017), p. 121.
18 Speech by Himmler to Party leaders in Posen on 6 October 1943
19 Dieckmann and Vanagaitė, p. 193.
20 Dieckmann and Vanagaitė, p. 198.
21 'The Destruction of the Jews in the Šiauliai Ghetto and Surrounding Towns' by Eliezer Yerushalmi, translated by Andrew Cassel, and originally published in *Lita*, vol 1, pp 1767-1832
22 Sutton, p. 142.
23 *Einsatzgruppen* report number 17, 9 July 1941
24 N. N. Shneidman, *Jerusalem of Lithuania: The Rise and Fall of Jewish Vilnius: A Personal Perspective* (Mosaic Press, 1998), p. 48.
25 Yitzhak Arad, *Ghetto In Flames* (KTAV Publishing House, Inc.), pp. 209–17.
26 Ephraim Oshry and Efroim Oshry, *The Annihilation of Lithuanian Jewry* (Judaica Press, 1995), pp. 1–4.
27 William W. Mishell, *Kaddish for Kovno: Life and Death in a Lithuanian Ghetto, 1941-1945* (Chicago Review Press, 1999), pp. 90–91.
28 Greenbaum, p. 325.
29 Cited during the trials at the Nuremberg International Military tribunal of 1945-6, and the trial of Major German War Criminals. Jaeger's reports omitted to mention that there was also a small ghetto at Svencionys, which was not liquidated until April 1943.
30 Sutton, p. 150.
31 Dieckmann and Vanagaitė, p. 218.
32 Dieckmann and Vanagaitė, p. 222.
33 *The Jews of Kaunas*, (VsJ "Kaunas 2022"), p.159.
34 Alain Blum, Thomas Chopard, and Emilia Koustova, 'Survivors, Collaborators and Partisans?: Bringing Jewish Ghetto Policemen before Soviet Justice in Lithuania,' *Jahrbücher Für Geschichte Osteuropas*, 68.2 (2020), 222–55.

35 Dieckmann and Vanagaitė, p. 311.

36 Dieckmann and Vanagaitė, p. 313.

37 *The Vanished World of Lithuanian Jews*, pp. 175–99.

38 'The Destruction of the Jews in the Šiauliai Ghetto and Surrounding Towns' by Eliezer Yerushalmi, translated by Andrew Cassel, and originally published in *Lita*, vol 1, pp 1767-1832

39 Dieckmann and Vanagaitė, p. 319.

40 Dieckmann and Vanagaitė, pp. 325–26.

41 David Cesarani, *The Final Solution: Origins and Implementation* (Routledge, 2002). Dina Porat: "The Holocaust in Lithuania: Some Unique Aspects"

8

A Survivor's Experience of the Holocaust in Lithuania

I do not have a memoir from a member of my family who was a witness to the Holocaust in Lithuania. However, there are a number of moving eyewitness accounts of aspects of the Holocaust in Lithuania from Jews who did survive, including, notably, from Rivka Lozansky Bogomolnaya.

Rivka Lozansky Bogomolnaya was born in 1919 in Butrimonys (Butrimantz in Yiddish) in the municipality of Alytus. Butrimonys is about 83 kilometres south-west of Vilnius and about 69 kilometres south-east of Kaunas. Rivka lived in Butrimonys with her parents and three sisters until 1941, part of a pre-war Jewish community of about 2,000. In late summer and autumn 1941 most of the Jews in Butrimonys were murdered. Rivka, her mother and a sister and brother-in-law survived three years of German occupation by hiding in nearby forests and pits. After the war Rivka married Avraham Bogomolnaya and they lived together in Vilnius. She had no children. In the 1990s, during extended stays in hospital, Rivka began to write down memories of her wartime experiences in Lithuania. She wrote in exercise books and in Yiddish. In 2000 a book was published, edited by Susan Logan, which contains a translation into English of Rivka's description of her wartime experiences.[1]

All eyewitness accounts need to be approached cautiously. Memory fades. Judgement can be distorted by many different emotions, including bitterness. Eyewitnesses describe what they have experienced, invariably only part of a wider story. Nonetheless, Rivka's description of her wartime experiences is unusually compelling. It provides a counterbalance to a big picture discussion of the Holocaust in Lithuania, emphasising the personal and human dimension of the tragedy. Rivka wrote many years after the events she witnessed and it is clear she remained haunted by those events. Despite this, her account is of particular value because she lived in Lithuania throughout the period of German occupation, witnessed first-hand a number of different aspects of the Holocaust, continued to live in Lithuania post-war and was an intelligent woman able to convey her experiences and opinions in a clear and forthright way.

Rivka begins her account with a short description of Jewish life in pre-war Butrimonys. As well as the 2,000 Jewish inhabitants, there were Poles and Lithuanians. Tatars lived nearby. The Jews lived "a quiet, calm, and poor life". Almost every family lived in a little wooden dwelling. Quite a few of these had holes in the roof and some even had no floor. Almost every house had a shop of some kind in it. Lithuanians from nearby villages came to town to buy necessities. Many of these people were desperately poor. Rivka describes how it was common for them to possess only one pair of shoes and these were to last a lifetime: "for going to market they would walk the whole way barefoot and only when near the village would they put their shoes on". Often, the Lithuanians would buy on credit and not repay their debt, even though the impoverished shopkeeper had himself bought on credit and had to repay the debt on the due date for payment.

Some of the Jews had trades. There were shoemakers, tailors, capmakers, quilters, blacksmiths and coachmen. The coachmen used to transport merchandise from Kaunas for the shopkeepers. They were on the road from Sunday afternoon each week and would take a break at the half-way point at Prienai, at a Jewish inn. The journey was hard because the roads were muddy and pot-holed and often the horses would get stuck. For much of the way the driver would help the horses by pushing the wagon. Jewish religious life centred around three study houses, one for old people, a second one for younger householders and the third was a handsome brick building for the entire community. The rabbi was Avrom-Moyshe Vitkind. "He used to settle disputes among the Jews and would always bring peace amongst the disputants". There was an elementary school which was maintained by the government. There were also evening classes for those who wanted to achieve the entrance requirements for the *gymnazya*, and an excellent library "containing all the best Yiddish and Hebrew books". There was a village policeman, apparently rather ineffective, because the main punishment available to him was the issue of fines which, as he was illiterate, he was unable to impose. All government positions, such as telegraph operator and postman, were restricted to ethnic Lithuanians only.

Until the early 1930s relationships between Jews and ethnic Lithuanians, Poles and Tatars were quite good. "In the beginning of the nineteen-thirties, when hooligans from surrounding towns tried to create a pogrom, every person in Butrimonys stood up to stop it …The villains were defeated that time. They ran away as far as they could, until the summer of nineteen forty-one."[2]

Although Rivka wrote *Wartime Experiences in Lithuania* more than 50 years after the war, it is clear that, at the time of writing, she remained traumatised and very angry about the wartime treatment of the Jewish community of Butrimonys. She likes to refer by name to members of her extended family and other Jews in Butrimonys who were murdered, perhaps hoping that, by doing so, she will save them from vanishing into oblivion. For example, she describes her brother-in-law's family: "I constantly see before my eyes the Shenker family; there were four sons, Shmuel, Tevya, Gershon and Hillel, and one daughter, Basya…Every morning the family could be seen setting out for work, led by their father Aaron Shenker." When Rivka mentions Jews' gentile neighbours in Butrimonys she frequently comments on how they participated in murdering Jews, and she observes how grasping and callous they were in stealing possessions belonging to Jews. For example, when discussing education in pre-war Butrimonys, Rivka mentions that "nearly all the teachers participated in annihilating the Jews", remarking acidly that "they provided a good example to their students." Special venom is reserved for some of the priests, mainly because Rivka feels they should have known better. She describes the behaviour of a priest called Lastakauskas: "the wealthy Jews entrusted to him almost all of their most valuable possessions, believing the honesty of one who is in the service of God. They believed that such a priest would return these valuable items to their rightful owners, who hoped that at least someone in their family would survive." Lastakauskas left for Alytus, taking six loaded wagons of [Jewish owned] goods with him. But when he returned the following day he fell into dispute with his church organist who could not see why the priest should have the benefit of all the Jewish owned goods, but felt that he too should share in the plunder. Rivka concludes: "How foolish it was of the Jews to trust that their possessions would be safely guarded".

Rivka describes the German invasion of 21 June 1941. There was a brief opportunity for her family to flee into Russia. "The youth of the village begged father to lead them [to Russia] in order to save their lives". Rivka's father decided against fleeing because he felt duty-bound to remain with family members who were unable to leave: "Basya and Nechama were still in Kaishadar [now Kaišiadorys]. Tzila and her husband were living in Pen [now Penkiniai]", and also because "the advice of wealthier Jews was to remain put; they still believed in justice. We didn't have anything to do with politics… We believed that the innocent ones would not have anything wrong done to them." Rivka recalls the first sight of Germans: "The Germans were all tall and handsome as though one mother had given birth to them all. They sang as they marched through." Within a very few days the German front had moved east, and then Rivka and her family saw very few Germans. Rivka's family believed the Soviets would quickly repel the German advance and their safest course of action would be to hide for a few days in bushes near the village until the Soviets had regained control. They took a Lithuanian neighbour with them. But, "As soon as we rode into the bushes Lithuanian motorcyclists appeared with white armbands. They warned the [local] Lithuanian and Polish inhabitants not to allow any Jews to enter their homes, not even their fields or roads. If they found any Jews hidden they would burn their dwellings. Shooting as they went, they hurried from one peasant to the next giving this warning." Rivka's father asked a close Lithuanian friend to hide his family. The friend was prepared to look after their valuable belongings but was too frightened to hide Rivka's family. Rivka's father and his Lithuanian friend "kissed each other and parted in tears as though knowing that this was for the last time. Even his best friend couldn't hide us for a day or two. We had to return home, not knowing what was going on in the village."[3]

When Rivka's family returned to Butrimonys they found very few Jews in their homes. Most were hiding in side streets. Many locals who knew Jews well had chased them away and stolen their belongings. The locals understood that, with the arrival of the Germans, Jews had no rights. "Lithuanian criminals" wearing white armbands, armed with whips with iron studs sewn in to increase the pain and damage to the body of the victim, forced all the Jews they found in the street to undress and then they beat them. Rivka explains how Lithuanians broke into Jewish homes and took whatever they liked, saying that the Jews were now without rights. "There were no Germans in the village. It was only Lithuanians who conducted the atrocities." She goes to considerable lengths to name the principal Lithuanians involved, emphasising that many had middle-class occupations. She identifies teachers and a former police official. Rivka explains that some of the neighbours, who again she names, stuck notes saying '*Jews live here*' on the doors of Jewish homes and orders were posted in the village to the effect that Jews had no rights. These orders stipulated, for example, that Jews could not walk on the pavement, but only in the gutter; that they could only shop between specific hours and they were not allowed to leave the village. "There was only one penalty for not following the last of the aforementioned and that was the death penalty."

Rivka had a sister called Nechama. Nechama had blond hair and was fluent in several languages, including Lithuanian. Nechama wanted to run away to somewhere where nobody knew her: "She could have hidden her identity, getting away with not looking Jewish". Rivka says: "Oh how difficult it is for me to confess that I, in my great love for her, held her back, pleading with her not to abandon us at such a terrible time. I, with my own hands, was the cause of my sister's death…I cannot forgive myself throughout my entire bitter life".

Rivka describes how, seven days after the start of the German occupation, many Jewish men in the village were arrested at night. She thought the people arrested were "those with more education, communists, anyone who would have been capable of organising any resistance". They were all tortured and beaten without being told why. A few were let go to create the impression that only 'guilty' ones were being singled out.

From the first days of the German invasion refugees were driven through the village. Rivka glimpsed them though a top window. They were naked, barefoot and exhausted. On one occasion some members of the Lithuanian Activist Front caught a refugee disguised in peasant-style clothing. As a punishment they cut out his tongue and "let him run off into the village to see who would have pity on him and offer him food". Nechama, who was sympathetic to the poor man's suffering, took a pail and inside it placed a cup of milk with bread, but she was observed doing this by a local woman who reported Nechema's behaviour to a Lithuanian Activist called Yoseliunas. That evening, Yoseliunas and some assistants drove the disguised refugee to the edge of the village, forced him to dig a pit and buried him alive. "Nechema paid with her young life for this sin".

Rivka describes events of 12 August 1941. All Jews aged between 15 and 60 were forced to assemble in the town square. A selection was made of young adult men, who were taken away and shot. Another selection was made of children and teenagers, including Nechama. As she was being taken away, she repeatedly said to Rivka: "You will live, please take care of my *gymnazya* uniform and my diploma and remember me as a High School student. I gave my life for it". She was then taken to a pit with other youngsters where she was shot. After the war Rivka met one of the Lithuanians who had severely beaten Nechama near the pit. He told Rivka he respected Nechama because even though he had beaten her very badly she did not cry and she accepted death with dignity. Rivka is utterly unforgiving. In italics she writes: *"If there is a God let him not spare them. May they also have a bitter end. Blood can only be avenged with blood."*

Rivka explains the elaborate lengths to which the Germans and the Lithuanian White Armbanders went to try to deceive the Jewish population about what was happening to Jews who were taken away. They arranged for Lithuanian neighbours to tell Rivka and her family that Nechama had been seen alive working on the roads and had been seen returning from work with a loaf of bread. On the basis of these lies, Rivka first told her Jewish neighbours that they should not cry, but instead wait calmly for their loved ones to return. However, Rivka and her mother became suspicious about what they had been told. They therefore walked across fields to visit an acquaintance, the son of Rivka's mother's good friend who was a teacher in Varėna. He showed them a document he possessed as a result of his having participated in the killing of some Russian soldiers as they were retreating from Lithuania. From this document, and from discussions with this man, Rivka and her mother came to understand that Nechema had been shot. Rivka even learned the name of the Lithuanian who had shot her sister. He was a man called Prashkus who lived in a village about four kilometres away. Rivka describes the torment in her family: "The Jews in our town went around in a confused state, not washing, not eating on time, hysterically yelling at one another...My father didn't want to remain alive without Nechama...his face got swollen and his eyes got bloodshot".

Rivka describes an occasion when some German troops stopped in her village, on their way eastward. The Germans required all Jews aged between 15 and 60 to stand in the town square from 4:00 am until sunset. The German commander said that, since all Jews were lazy and had never worked, they must now work for Lithuanians without pay. Rivka summoned the courage to ask, in German, if she needed to learn to work when the muscles of her arms and hands were swollen from work. The German commander heard her and said: "Fine, you'll be my translator, it's impossible to communicate with the Lithuanian animals". Through this Commander Rivka got to know another German officer called Pluschke, a 29 year old married pharmacist from Magdeburg, who was unsympathetic to Nazis. He gave Rivka a little food and warned her that the Lithuanians had "been given the right to murder [the Jews]". After a few days, however, he came with a pack of butter to say farewell, explaining that his unit had been ordered to march on Moscow. The departure of this unit left Lithuanians in charge in Butrimonys.

On the night of 21-22 August 1941 the Director of Police, Kasperunas, together with other Lithuanian policemen, barged into Rivka's family home. Kasperunas demanded that all money and gold which the family possessed be placed on a table. The police assistants dragged the Jewish men in the household naked from their beds. Rivka was ordered, with a revolver pointed at her heart, to hand over keys to the chest of drawers and cupboard. "They emptied the contents of the chest of drawers and the cupboard into sacks which they had brought with them." Then they searched everyone individually. "The men were led out of the house. I saw my father then for the last time. He was driven naked from the house, carrying his trousers in his hands… As soon as they were taken out I started to look for my mother. I found her lying in the bedroom on the floor unconscious." Every local Jewish family had similar stories to tell: on the night of 22 August, 1941 the Lithuanians had gathered all the men of the town and only the very few who had managed to hide remained. All those arrested were driven into the yard of the prison, about 100 men and 15 women. The rabbi was tortured more than others. Half his beard was shorn off. He was stripped until half naked and his cap torn off and put on a short man, a glazier. The other men were terribly beaten with whips and hail shot. They were all taken to a forest near Alytus, where pits had been dug. Some were shot and thrown into pits, others were thrown into the pits and buried alive. Before death, these people were forced to write letters home requesting food and clothing, as part of a scheme to deceive survivors about what had happened to their menfolk. Their clothing was sent away for disinfecting. Rivka says her neighbour Vaytisch brought her a letter from her father. In his letter he asked for cigarettes and clothing. Vaytisch even offered personally to take these things to Alytus and give them to Rivka's father. Rivka confesses that, at first, she was duped into thinking her father was still alive. She even helped other local Jewish women prepare parcels.

At different points in her narrative Rivka erupts in fury at the behaviour of certain priests. She describes the behaviour of a man called Radziavitshius who was the priest in a tiny village, Punia (Pun in Yiddish), where members of her wider family had lived. After the war, Rivka went there. She approached the priest, with a couple of soldiers for protection. "On the priest's windows hung our curtains. He himself was wearing a light fur coat with black trimmings that belonged to mother. A cross had been sewn on to a lapel. In my anger I tore my mother's fur coat off him and the cross came with it…" Rivka also discovered from a local Lithuanian villager that, towards the end of the war, a few days after the Russians had liberated them, the villager had gone to the priest to obtain *mishas*, a Catholic prayer for the dead. She had entered through the kitchen to find three Jewish people, Mendka, Roza and their two-year-old child, in a pool of blood. Rivka supposed they had been killed by the priest with the assistance of a handful of others. She comments that "at that time the Lithuanians killed whoever they wanted". Rivka's strong suspicion is that the priest and other Lithuanian neighbours knew that Mendka and Roza were fully aware they had stolen a great deal from Jewish families, and they did not want the Soviet authorities to be told about this. Sadly, Rivka concludes: "Thus the guilty ones went unpunished."[4]

Rivka goes on to say how at the end of August 1941 the Jews of Butrimonys and Punia were forced into a ghetto before being taken to another ghetto in Alytus. Extraordinary violence accompanied this ghettoization. People were beaten with whips, their hands tied together with wire, and they were heaped on the ground: "When they were brought out it was impossible to recognise them. They were bloodied and swollen." As Jews were being ghettoised, much of the local Lithuanian population was very eager to steal their possessions: "Strangers came [to Rivka's family home] uninvited; a wealthy peasant woman... carried out chairs and silverware from the buffet...[Her] daughter immediately asked for Nechama's things..[Other neighbours, including], Gitzvichius... started to load their wagon with whatever they could lay their hands on. They carried out things from the cupboard. We couldn't prevent them because we had no rights..." As ever, Rivka displays outrage at the failure of moral leadership on the part of those in the Lithuanian population who she feels should have known better:

> I saw near the [Jewish] study house a long wagon drawn by two horses, and the priest of Pivashun [now Pivašiūnai], Kaushila, in his black priest's frock... bareheaded, carrying our furniture from the synagogue. His organist, Stanulionis, was helping him. The best furniture of the wealthy Jews had been stored in the synagogue by the police. The leaders of the slaughterers were dividing the furniture amongst themselves. I still believed in the honesty of God's servants so I asked my mother's friend, Ettel, 'How is it possible that priests should also be criminals?' She replied that it couldn't be the case and that he probably wanted to hide it for us. This is how the Jews foolishly believed and lost their lives. [Kaushila] was arrested after the war ...

Rivka describes the terrible overcrowding in the ghetto. In the house there were about ten families, each family consisting only of old people and children, the result of five round-ups…Under the table was the 'apartment' of Shayna Lerman, the sexton of the synagogue..." In the ghetto, one thing above all gave Rivka strength "and that was how devoted our people were to Jewish traditions. In such a catastrophe, how religiously and honourably they conducted themselves ..."

Rivka describes how she felt in the very last days before the liquidation of the ghetto. She was conscious of the efforts of local Lithuanians to deceive Jews about what was going to happen to them. For example, she and her mother hid for two nights in a barn owned by a man called Gutzevitsch, a neighbour but also one of the shooters. He tried to calm Rivka and her mother and even gave them something to eat, but Rivka felt strongly this was merely a ruse to try and win their trust and so obtain more of their belongings. In his barn Rivka read a Lithuanian paper which said that the question of Jews and Gypsies would be settled first; then, the Russian and Polish presence would be "taken care of". It followed with the comment that Lithuania must remain only for the Lithuanians. Any lingering doubts Rivka may have had about what lay in store for her and her mother were settled by a conversation she had with Dr. Gabay, a Jewish doctor who had been treating the Chief of Police, Kasperunas. When Rivka bumped into Dr. Gabay he told her that the rest of the Jewish population was going to be shot the following day. Rivka suggests that, in the very last days before the liquidation of the ghetto, many Jews had a strong sense that they were going to be murdered, but they were simply unable to absorb and process this information because it seemed so monstrous. At that time their predominant feeling was one of disgust at how local Lithuanians were so desperate to steal their possessions: "At the Lesctshinsky's place (..my mother's old good acquaintance) we saw our tablecloths on the table and our curtains hung at the windows. Even our dresses had been altered. In front of us they began to hide our stuff..."

The ghetto was surrounded by armed Lithuanians. Jews were taken to two huge pits, about two kilometres from Butrimonys. Even when they saw these pits many Jews managed to deceive themselves: 'They must be for storing potatoes for wartime'. Escape was difficult because of the guards and because many adults like Rivka were looking after young children or had elderly relations for whom they felt responsible. Rivka asked her friend Freydal Kalamitzky to run away with her, but Freydal pointed to her child and said it would be impossible to run away with a three-year old. There was a great deal of noise and confusion. Local people who lived near the pits "watched the sad procession and were astonished at our catastrophe". Amidst all this confusion Rivka and her mother managed to cross the street and disappear into bushes.

The Jewish men were first driven to the pits. They had been beaten up and were half-naked. They had been starved of food and drink so that they would go to their deaths without resistance. They were lined up half a foot from the edge of the pit and shot from behind, the shots being aimed at the brain. The wife of the guard master Germanavitshius was responsible for stripping the women and sorting their clothes. "She kept all the best things for herself and divided the rest amongst those who did the shooting... Germanavitshius's wife gave the men [the shooters] a bucket of beer after every round of shooting". When they heard shots, the Jewish women screamed loudly and cried. A few gave birth beside the pit. When asked to undress and stand beside the pit "they asked the wife of Germanavitshius at least to allow them to remain in their knickers…but even this was not granted to them. The women were pushed into the pit while still alive. A policeman went down into the pit to lay the women out so that more could be put in. The women grabbed him by the hair and tore at his face until he was barely dragged out alive with a rope". "The children were thrown into the pit while still alive; Astrauskas hammered nails into a long stick and with this pierced the living children and threw them into the pit." Rivka concludes her description of the mass murder of the Jews of Butrimonys with a bald italicised statement:

> *For several days the mass grave did not rest; the earth heaved. The earth was reluctant to accept all the bodies.*

After the Jews of Butrimonys were killed, Rivka and her mother tried to hide in the forest. They decided they would be safer near Polish villages: "We headed [towards] Polish villages because very few of the Poles were criminals". Nonetheless, Rivka and her mother were very aware that they could hardly trust anybody, not least because there were terrible penalties for anyone found helping Jews. For a few days they stayed in the barn of a man called Vavioris, who she characterised as a "rich Pole but a bandit". Rivka thought his and his wife's motivation for helping them was theft: "His wife brought us something to eat and took note of what we were wearing. She came over to me and removed the shawl from my head; she told me that the following day I would be murdered so I wouldn't need a head shawl, but she would be able to go to church in it." Rivka and her mother moved on and found temporary shelter in another barn, owned by an ethnic Lithuanian man called Mikhail Shestakovsky, to whom Rivka's father had extended some kindness before the war. It was from him that Rivka learnt in detail:

> the terrible news about the [Butrimonys] Jews. How brutally our entire town of [Butrimonys] had been mercilessly murdered by the Lithuanian neighbours. How they were tortured before death. How young children were stabbed and thrown into the mass pit. How one fellow who came up with a better method of torture, and excelled in his ability, was applauded. One threw children with a powerful blow onto a tree until their blood and brains were spurting out. After that they were thrown into the pit…The Germans arrived only at the end.

> They only filmed ... the efficiency with which the Lithuanians were executing and burying their victims and how they covered the half-alive bodies with lime so that they wouldn't last long and so that after the war they would be able to deny their actions.

Hiding in the forest or in barns became increasingly dangerous because gangs of Lithuanian activists, self-styled 'self-defence' units, had been formed to search for Jews. Savage punishments were meted out to Jews found alive and to those found protecting them. Shestakovsky dug a pit in the floor of his workshop in which Rivka and her mother could hide. A little iron pipe provided light and air. The pit was small, just large enough for two people to lie down and there was a board on which to sit. "The pit was suffocating. The walls were damp from the fresh lime paint. The sweat poured from us. We stripped practically naked but that didn't help us either…From the bad air and troubling thoughts our heads started to ache…Late at night, when the neighbours were asleep, [they] would come out for fresh air and for necessary bodily functions."

It became too dangerous for the Shestakovskys to continue to hide Rivka and her mother. Rivka was "in danger of being caught and then, not being able to bear the torture ... might reveal where [we] had been hidden. It was the custom of the police not to shoot the captured one on the spot but first to cut off their fingers and poke out their eyes, so they would reveal who had helped them". They decided to escape to the forest, where they lived rough. At night they scrounged for bread, walking a considerable distance from where they were hiding. Even in the forest they were hunted. On more than one occasion they survived only by running into a swamp known as 'Devil's Swamp'. There they had to jump from one bush to another, in spite of sharp-edged grass, because there was otherwise a risk of sinking deep into mud, from which there would have been no rescue.

Rivka became aware that Jews were being caught in the forest and came to think that she and her mother would be safer hiding in fields of rye by the road-side, near the property of someone known to the family. They depended on scrounging for scraps of food from people they thought they should be able to trust. On one occasion they knocked on the door of an acquaintance called Asakavitsh. "Asakavitsh's wife was lying in bed in my nightgown. She had seen me dressed in a coat… with great agility [she] jumped out of bed, ran over to me and started to remove my coat. I pleaded with her to take into consideration that she had a roof over her head while I was at the mercy of the naked sky". Asakavitsh interceded on Rivka's behalf, but his wife "told him to shut up... She told him the coat was still a good one and could be altered for the children. To me [i.e. Rivka] she said she knew the police weren't far away, 'if I tell them, you won't need anything any more'".

Rivka and her mother somehow staggered on. They continued to eke out an existence on the edge of fields of people they knew near Butrimonys, where they believed everyone they knew had been murdered. "In the homes lived the criminals who were now out to murder every last one of us, so that no memory of us would remain on Lithuanian soil ... At night I would leave mother alone and go looking for bread."

Eventually, Rivka and her mother realised that the Russian armies, which were advancing westwards, must be getting closer. Hopes began to rise that they might soon be freed. "The tumult of armaments kept getting louder and louder. Bombs were exploding near us... The non-Jews cherished their lives so they hid from the bombs" but the attitude of Rivka and her mother was different: "the bombs and planes were the harbingers of freedom and very dear to us; we ran to them with fervour. They exploded close to us."[5]

The final part of Rivka's memoir describes, in some detail, her feelings about being liberated and about life in post-war Lithuania. She was overwhelmed by a sense of being alone: "It's hard to describe the terrible pain we felt once we were free, knowing we were free but had to live with the loss of our dear ones. We knew there was nobody waiting for us." This sense of loneliness was aggravated by a feeling of guilt that she had been indirectly responsible for deaths of family members. She felt guilt because she had discouraged her father from running away to the forest when he had the opportunity to do so, and she continued to be plagued by the idea she had inadvertently contributed to the death of her sister Nechama by discouraging her from running away. Rivka returned to Butrimonys. "The Germans had given our homes to the bandits who had helped murder us. They had sold whatever they could from inside, even the bricks from the ovens". Her family home was an uninhabitable wreck. Lithuanians were now keeping pigs there. Lithuanians in Butrimonys "went about in the streets dressed in Jewish clothing and even went to church dressed in the best of Jewish clothes and they pretended not to know us when they saw us, even though we had known one another all our lives."

Rivka felt an obligation to visit and put in order the two mass graves of the Jews of Butrimonys. The site was about two kilometres from the shtetl, on Klidj Road. On her first visit, there was no sign of graves, because they were unmarked, but when she found them "I fell upon the grave site and couldn't tear myself away. I couldn't cry though my heart ached." She made later visits to the graves, accompanied by her husband. He thought it prudent to visit the graves armed with a gun to protect Rivka and himself from the possibility of attack by locals. This weapon had been provided by the mayor because he knew local people had been digging up bodies in the mass graves to search for gold crowns in the teeth of corpses and strongly suspected that they would find Rivka's attention unwelcome. Rivka was also tormented by the fact that the graves were very shallow: "I couldn't live in peace when dogs were dragging around the bones of my dear ones and cows and horses were feeding off their graves. I knew it was my duty to make proper twin graves and erect a monument." With advice and support from a sympathetic priest called Andrikonas, "whose hands had not been bloodied", and from three Jewish men, including her husband, they opened the graves and reburied the bodies:

> We erected a modest-size monument, with an inscription in Yiddish and Russian, for the Jews who had perished so tragically to the eternal disgrace of their murderers. My heart didn't permit me to make an inscription in Lithuanian because that was the language spoken by their murderers.
>
> Our government tore down the inscription and replaced it with a tiny inscription in Lithuanian, stating that on this spot Soviet citizens had died. The truth was that our Jews had died on 9 September 1941, having been put to death by Lithuanians.

Rivka's memoir is punctuated by her reflections on different parts of the population with which she came into contact. She says a little about Jewish survivors she encountered after the war. "Gradually, Jews who had miraculously survived showed up from surrounding villages. They found nobody in their villages so they came to us for a short time". Most of the Jews who Rivka met had served in the 16th Lithuanian Division. "None of them found anyone in their families", and they did not find Jews alive from their villages. Rivka's mother helped care for them for a short while, but almost all then left the country, many for what was then Mandatory Palestine. At times, Rivka seems surprised that she stayed in Lithuania: "I never forgot what I had said to myself while hiding in the pits before running away – that if anyone survived and returned and tread on this soil, they should be cursed – yet here I am living until the present time in this very place, so I am cursed". She does not manage to say what exactly made her stay. One is left with the impression that she stayed because she wanted to be near those who had died, to put their graves in order and try to bring the murderers to justice. It may also have been because her mother and husband were in Lithuania and had their own reasons for not wanting to leave.

It is striking that Rivka barely comments about Germans. Apart from the time in June 1941 when the advancing German army passed through her village, she seems hardly to have encountered them. As has been said, most ethnic Germans had left Lithuania before the war and she seems to have seen very few German soldiers. It may also be that, for Rivka, Nazi attitudes and behaviour towards Jews were beyond words.

Rivka was touched by the kindness shown by Russian officers after the Soviet reconquest of Lithuania in 1944. She took the Russian commander to her empty house.

> He sat down and asked all kinds of questions, such as who was responsible for all the murders, and how we had manged to run away. I noticed that as he was talking to us he took out a white handkerchief and wiped his eyes…before he left he gave an order to let us stay with the army staff.

Rivka says a good deal about local ethnic Poles. Generally, she regards them as more compassionate and sympathetic than Lithuanians. Quite frequently, she makes the contrast:

> When we were in hiding we had feared every single Lithuanian. When we went looking for bread, we would first listen to hear what language was being spoken in each house. If we heard Lithuanian we would quickly move on. If we heard Polish we would knock. The mean Pole who wouldn't give us bread would not denounce us. From the Lithuanians though, anything was expected. They were capable of offering us bread and detaining us while they contacted the police to come and take us to certain death.

Rivka gives the impression that the great majority of Lithuanians were very hostile to Jews. For example, she says: "If all the Lithuanians were lined up and every second one sentenced, and then lined up anew, there would still have remained bandits." She makes a distinction between what she calls 'Shaulists', being nationalist paramilitary, and the Lithuanian population more generally. Although Rivka may not have known this, some of the Shaulists had been directed by the German SS before the invasion of June

1941. Her greatest animus is often directed towards ordinary Lithuanians, those who had lived in relative harmony with their Jewish neighbours before the war, but who turned on them viciously. Rivka's explanations for such conduct seem to be that these people were simple and easily-led; that they had been told that, following withdrawal of Soviet forces, Jews had no rights and therefore they could do as they liked to them and could take their property. Many priests, to whom many Lithuanians looked for leadership, were disdainful of Jews and gave the impression they supported this policy, implicitly or otherwise. The desire to steal property which belonged to Jews was a very strong motivation for local Lithuanian people. Many of the murderers were drunk on beer or vodka when they committed murder. Once a number of Jews in a village had been killed, many locals became anxious that surviving Jews might take revenge and that they might demand that their stolen property be returned. This led to an intensification of Lithuanian hostility towards those Jews who survived.

Rivka goes out of her way to note the support she received from some Lithuanians and describes her efforts to repay their kindness. In particular, she mentions three brothers in the Maldanis family. These brothers had helped Rivka and her mother while they were hiding in the forest. After the war, the Soviet authorities arrested the brothers. Rivka went to the Russian officer in charge and "I fell to his feet and told him he must… tell me how I could rescue them. I begged him until I had convinced him." The brothers were released. "They came with a gift to thank me. I didn't want any gifts because for doing a *mitzvah* one doesn't take money. Nevertheless, they left it and went away. The gift was a small old cow which could only eat hay." This cow produced five litres of milk per day.

It is clear that Rivka thought the immensity of the wrong done to the Jewish community of Lithuania meant that forgiveness was out of the question. Indeed, her narrative is punctuated by repeated, italicised cursing when she refers to a particularly odious killer. Her preferred curse is: '*may his name [and memory] be blotted out*'. Rivka wanted to take revenge but needed to be attentive to the risks in doing so. Of the 2,000 Jews in pre-war Butrimonys only 10 survived. "The other [9] tried to scare me, saying that after all the torments I had lived through until the liberation I shouldn't risk my life trying to exact revenge, since the guilty ones were as plentiful as grains of sand." Such warnings were not without substance. At one time, her house was burned down. Rivka's revenge took the form of private satisfaction at the pain and difficulties of those who had caused such suffering and destruction to her community. For example, she discusses Germanavitshius's wife who "had been capable of undressing women completely naked before they were shot, not even allowing them their underwear. She had kept many of the belongings for herself... and after the war her sons would come to the cinema dressed in the rabbi's and the *chazan's* clothes, enjoying themselves." After the war this woman died from cancer. Far from being sympathetic, Rivka simply says: '*May her name be blotted out*'. Beyond this, Rivka's revenge took the form of trying to act as a "'one-person memorial committee and vengeance squad', locating the mass graves throughout Lithuania and attempting to bring the murderers to justice".[6]

When Rivka's strength recovered after the war she obtained a job as a salesperson in a shoe store and used this as an opportunity to question customers about their experience of wartime atrocities and their knowledge of the whereabouts of those responsible. She made detailed notes of what she learned. Rivka also found she quite often encountered, or found herself in close proximity with, people she knew had killed her family and neighbours. For example, she describes efforts to bring to justice a man called Vitkevich. Rivka says his son "was also guilty of killing Jews. He is presently living in [Vilnius] in the same building where I live!" On another occasion, while walking on the Kolvor bridge in Vilnius she met Yanas Yeirushavitshius, the man who had taken away her father and who she had witnessed stealing valuables from her home. Before the war, his family and Rivka's family had been on friendly terms: "Our murderers had at one time been our good friends." When Rivka identified people who had been involved in committing atrocities she passed on this information to the authorities and used every effort to try and make sure they were brought to justice. She found this demoralising work because, again and again, she encountered reluctance to institute legal proceedings and, when action was taken, the sentences seemed absurdly lenient in relation to the gravity of the offences committed, and often the sentences were not served. Yoseliunas, for example, was sentenced to death for his part in mass murder. Rivka thought him almost unique in receiving so severe a sentence. However, a few years later one of Rivka's acquaintances spotted Yoseliunas alive and well and going for a walk in a small town. It transpired that Yoseliunas had been freed on account of his ill health. Acidly, Rivka reflects: "The state of health of our murdered people had never been taken into consideration."

Rivka does not comment in detail on why so few of the guilty were brought to justice in post-war Lithuania. The nearest she comes to offering an explanation is in the context of the trial of Yanas Yeirushavitshius:

> The case was dealt with at the time of the so-called doctors' plot in Moscow.[7] Day and night innocent people [mainly Jewish people]

> were arrested. Jews feared for their lives so I was warned it wasn't the right time to go to court regarding bandits. Our lives were in danger and we were on death's doorstep. But there was no way back. To forgive the murderers of my father and all the men from my shtetl could not be justified under any circumstances.

The feebleness of efforts in post-war Lithuania to bring the guilty to justice was, as Rivka suggests, partly a reflection of an antisemitic climate in Stalin's post-war regime. It perhaps also reflects the lack of survivors such as Rivka determined to press for justice to be brought. It was difficult to find witnesses because most of the Jews were dead and "for Lithuanians to be witnesses for the deeds of their own brothers was risky [for them]". In addition, the Soviet authorities did not regard bringing Lithuanian murderers to justice as a priority. They were more concerned with the regime's primary objective of stabilising Lithuania as a compliant Soviet satellite.[8]

As with all eye-witnesses, Rivka's testimony needs to be approached with caution. She was clearly, if understandably, very angry and she wrote when she was an old lady, many years after the events she witnessed. Nonetheless, her account is unusually powerful and not least because she was witness to many different aspects of the Holocaust in Lithuania. She gives voice to the voiceless, to those who were killed and were therefore unable to articulate what happened to their families and to their civilization.

Notes

1 Rivka Lozansky Bogomolnaya, *Wartime Experiences in Lithuania* (Vallentine Mitchell, 2000).

2 Riva Lozansky, *If I Forget Thee—: The Destruction of the Shtetl Butrimantz* (Remembrance Books, 1998), pp. 20–21.

3 Lozansky Bogomolnaya, pp. 17–24.

4 Lozansky Bogomolnaya, pp. 32–43.

5 Lozansky Bogomolnaya, pp. 65–94.

6 Myra Sklarew, *A Survivor Named Trauma: Holocaust Memory in Lithuania* (SUNY Press, 2020), p. 177.

7 1951-3: a Soviet campaign against Jewish doctors, and other Jews, who were accused of a conspiracy to assassinate Soviet leaders. After Stalin's death in 1953 the new Soviet leadership admitted these allegations were entirely false.

8 Lozansky Bogomolnaya, pp. 97–145.

9

Trying to Explain the Holocaust in Lithuania

How can one explain the Holocaust in Lithuania ?

Attempts to explain the Holocaust are still influenced by a book by Raul Hilberg called *Perpetrators Victims Bystanders* which was published in 1992.[1] In his memoirs, published in 1996, Hilberg describes the background to his writing this book. In 1961 he travelled through Europe for the first time since the end of the Second World War. Because he was interested in Renaissance portrait paintings, Hilberg made a point of visiting the Rijksmuseum in Amsterdam. As he viewed the triptychs of the Christian trinity an idea came to him: to seek to explain the Holocaust by writing three seemingly separate sections which, by the end, formed a single unit. Many historians have found his analysis of each of the three categories of perpetrator, victim and bystander a useful mechanism for seeking to understand the Holocaust, although some think the boundaries between the categories are too rigid. Concern centres on use of the term 'bystander'. Some writers think Hilberg's tripartite categorisation fails to recognise important differences between state-sanctioned violence and individually motivated acts of violence; there is concern that his use of the term 'bystander' encompasses too great a variety of attitudes to anti-Jewish violence that people observed around them; and that for many people the status of being a bystander was only a transitional position before becoming a perpetrator, in one form or another. There is also concern that the term 'bystander' wrongly puts the person concerned outside a proper moral and legal framework. Mary Fulbrook has written:

> "perpetrator" is both a legal and moral category, with implications for justice. [Recognition as a] "Victim" may be implicated in terms of justice, reparations, compensation, entitlement to some form of "making good again". It may be argued that "bystander"... implies that one is somehow outside this legal and moral framework. But this is not necessarily the case even in terms of legal systems. It is certainly not so in moral terms.[2]

No doubt one could use other categories and devices for seeking to explain the Holocaust. By way of example, Mary Fulbrook suggests that the category of 'bystander' could be sub-divided into 'collaborators', 'beneficiaries', 'functionaries' and 'facilitators'. In this chapter, I propose to stay with Raul Hilberg's simple tripartite categorisation: perpetrators, victims, bystanders. It is a blunt instrument and has its shortcomings but, treated carefully, it remains a helpful and straightforward tool for trying to understand the Holocaust.

The starting point is to consider how it was that some Germans became perpetrators of the Holocaust. An informed and dispassionate observer looking at the international scene before 1914 would almost certainly have thought Germany one of the European countries least likely to launch a murderous assault on its Jews and the Jews of Europe. Russia, with its history of antisemitic legislation and pogroms, or France, still reeling from the effects of the Dreyfus case, would have appeared more likely to do so. In trying to understand how some Germans became perpetrators in the Holocaust one has first to seek to understand something about the long history of antisemitism in Christian Europe.

The word 'antisemitism' first appeared in 1879 and is thought to have been coined by Wilhelm Marr. The word implies that those professing the belief are not against Jews per se but are instead against something called 'Semitism'. The term 'antisemitism' derived from linguistics. Antisemites claimed to combat speakers of the semitic family of languages, which differed in syntax and grammatical structure from the Indo-European family of languages. However, this claim was misleading because antisemites were not against all semites. They were not against Arabs, despite the fact that Arabic is a semitic language. Neither were antisemites against modern speakers of Aramaic, also a semitic language. They were actually, and very specifically, against Jews and, by using the pseudoscientific and invented word 'antisemitism', were trying to differentiate Jews from others and to base their hostility in the nature and thought processes of Jews, and to suggest that their opposition to Jews needed to be dealt with politically.[3]

The reasons given for being against Jews differed over time but many scholars and theologians think the root cause is that 'anti-Judaism was deeply embedded in Christian theology, fostered and sustained by the New Testament itself'.[4] It is important to acknowledge that some of the language in the New Testament which is apparently most hostile to Jews may derive from conflicts within the Jewish world among the followers of Jesus in the early years after his death. These conflicts centred on the question of whether or not his teaching should be taken beyond the Jewish world. In other words, what appear to be attacks on Jews may actually have been attacks on those Jews who wanted the teaching of Jesus to be reserved exclusively for Jews by other Jews who thought his teaching should also be taken to a gentile audience.

There are three particular grounds for thinking anti-Judaism was embedded in Christian theology: the first is 'supersessionism'. This is the view that Christians have superseded or replaced Jews as God's covenantal people. The authors of the New Testament believed the Torah to be the word of God, but they also believed that, since Jesus, the term 'Israel' referred not to the Jewish people but only to those Jews and gentiles who believed in Jesus. Everyone – including Jews – could participate in the covenant with the God of Israel only by believing in Jesus. As a result, an elaborate theology evolved that saw Judaism as a moribund and spiritless religion that was destined to die out over time. "Such descriptions and the supersessionism on which they are based contributed to the denigration of Jews and Judaism well into the twentieth century."[5]

The second ground for thinking that anti-Judaism is embedded in Christian theology is the association of the Jews and Satan. The association appears to come from two particular places. The first is the Book of Revelation 2:9 and 3:9. 2:9 says: "I know the blasphemy of them that say they are Jews and are not, but are the synagogue of Satan" and 3:9 says: "I will make those of the synagogue of Satan who say that they are Jews and are not, but are lying – I will make them come and bow down before your feet, and they will learn that I have loved you." Both verses have given rise to arcane theological debate about their precise meaning, although the main point that there is an association between the Jews and Satan seems plain enough. There is also a verse in the Gospel of St. John which apparently associates the Jews and Satan. The key verse is John 8:44, in which Jesus tells a group of Jews: "You are from your father the devil, and you choose to do your father's desires. He was a murderer from the beginning and does not stand in the truth, because there is no truth in him." John appears to be saying that by murdering and lying, the Jews demonstrate that they are not the children of God, but the children of the devil. As Jesus states in John 8:42 "If God were your Father, you would love me, for I came from God and now I am here." It is argued that because Jews do not accept Jesus (8:43), the Jews cannot be God's children but rather must have the devil as their father.[6]

The third reason for thinking anti-Judaism is embedded in Christian theology derives from the so-called 'deicide charge', the idea that Jews, in perpetuity, are responsible for killing Jesus. The synoptic gospels of Mark,

Matthew and Luke give, in their last few chapters, a broadly similar account of the events leading to the death of Jesus. This is known as the Passion Narrative. Judas betrays Jesus to the authorities; Jesus is cross-examined by the high priest and convicted of blasphemy; he is taken to Pontius Pilate where he is further questioned; Pilate is reluctant to take further steps against Jesus but, under pressure from Jewish authorities, Pilate reluctantly agrees to send Jesus for crucifixion. The Gospel of John adds an account of a further incident: after the dramatic resurrection of Lazarus (John 11:38-44) many Jews who had witnessed those events came to believe in Jesus; others reported what had happened to the Pharisees. They became concerned Jesus would attract wide support and the consequence of this would be "The Romans will come and destroy both our holy place and our nation" (11:47-48). Caiaphas, the high priest, says: "it is better for you to have one man die for the people than to have the whole nation destroyed (11:49-50). And "from that day on they planned to put him to death" (11:53). The effect of describing the Council meeting and the decision it reached is that John's gospel places moral responsibility for Jesus's crucifixion on the Jewish leadership. This is an intriguing transfer of responsibility. The simple historical fact is that Pontius Pilate, the Roman governor, was responsible for ordering the crucifixion of Jesus. But the Gospel of Matthew has a further transfer of moral responsibility, from Pilate to Jews more generally. As Jews shouted for Jesus's crucifixion, Pilate "took some water and washed his hands before the crowd, saying, "I am innocent of this man's blood; see to it yourselves" (Matt. 27:24). The people, all Jews, then replied: "His blood be on us and on our children!" (Matt 27:25). In Matthew 27:25 the Jews purportedly accepted responsibility for Jesus's blood for themselves and future generations.

This is the basis for the deicide charge, which has attached to Jews down the centuries. It is important to recall that these words are not a transcript of words actually spoken by historical characters but were put into the mouths of Jews by the gospel writer, writing many years after the events he describes. But the consequences have rippled down the centuries. In the course of writing this book, I interviewed a Jewish student, educated in Ireland during the last decade, who told me she had often been bullied at school because, she was told, she and other Jews had killed Jesus. Happily, the Catholic church effectively repudiated the deicide charge in a papal document, *Nostra aetate*, issued in October 1965. It says: "the Jewish authorities and those who followed their lead pressed for the death of Christ; still, what happened in His passion cannot be charged against all the Jews, without distinction, then alive, nor against the Jews of today".[7]

A number of early church fathers such as Tertullian and Cyprian were very hostile to Jews. They contributed to a body of early church literature known as *Adversos Iudaeos*, "Against the Jews". Among other things, this argued that Jews had always been reprobates, guilty of idolatry, depravity and murdering prophets; that God had rejected the Jews in favour of a new elect drawn from Gentiles; that the Old Testament had foreseen that this would happen; that Jews are blinded from a proper understanding of the Old Testament, and that Jews therefore fail to see that the Mosaic Law has been fulfilled spiritually in Jesus and has therefore been abrogated. Some early church fathers extended this theology to what is perhaps its logical conclusion, namely that Jews should not be tolerated at all. Ambrose, for example, argued for the destruction of a synagogue on the basis that "there [should] be no building in which Christ is denied."

However, and in contrast to Nazi antisemitism, mainstream Christian thinking did not go so far as to suggest that Jewish people and Jewish practice should be eliminated. The teaching of Augustine of Hippo (354-c.430) was decisive in this regard. He saw Jews as a stubborn and accursed people who had murdered the Son of God, but he also saw the continuation of Jewish life and the dispersal of Jews in Christian lands as part of a divine plan to facilitate the ultimate triumph of Christianity. By remaining steadfast to the books and practices of the Old Testament Jews would act as witness to the truth of the New Testament. By surviving in abased conditions, cut off from their homeland and subservient to Christianity, Jews would bear witness to the adverse consequences of not embracing Christianity. In other words, the continued existence of Jews, albeit in a scattered and debased condition, served an important Christian purpose. Jews should therefore be tolerated and allowed to practise their religion, but they were to be subservient. The teaching of St. Augustine perhaps goes a long way towards explaining why Jews survived in the diaspora over so many centuries.

Pope Innocent III (1198-1216) thought very carefully about the role of Jews in the world. He accepted the basic principles of Augustine's teaching but sought to develop and expand upon them. In a letter to a French count of 1208 he likened Jews to Cain, who God protected with his mark: "although they ought not to be killed, lest the Christian people forget the divine law, yet as wanderers ought they to remain upon the earth, until their countenance be filled with shame and they seek the name of the Lord Jesus Christ."[8] At the Fourth Lateran Council of 1215 Pope Innocent gave further substance to the notion that, while Jews should not be eliminated, papal power should enforce their inferior, subjugated and enslaved status.

Accordingly, the Council prevented Jewish moneylenders from extorting "oppressive and excessive interest" from Christian borrowers; it banned Jews from holding public office; it forbade baptised Jews from returning to their previous religious rites; it decreed that Jews must wear distinguishing marks on their clothing and also that they must avoid appearing in public from Holy Thursday until Easter Sunday.[9]

The early teachings of the Christian church, including those of Augustine of Hippo and Pope Innocent III, may seem remote from the mass murder of Jews in Lithuania in the 1940s. But it is important to understand that those teachings turned the Jew into 'the other' across Christian civilization and over a very long period. This Christian theology affected where Jews could live and what occupations they could be engaged in. It meant that Jews were perennially perceived as outsiders and often as scapegoats. Christian antisemitism most certainly does not, of itself, explain the Holocaust but it is difficult to imagine the Holocaust happening without that background.

A new, racially based, form of antisemitism developed in the second half of the nineteenth century. This drew on both old and new forms of science. The old one was animal husbandry, the science of breeding. Its proponents believed that people are like breeds of dogs or horses, each with distinctive qualities that can be enhanced by selective mating. "Thus Germans, like their German shepherds, were good fighters; the French, like their poodles, were showy; and the British, like their bulldogs, were tenacious."[10] The new science was Darwinism. Brilliant, subtle and transformative, Darwin's theory of evolution was also capable of being, and was, widely misunderstood. Social Darwinism developed from it as a kind of mutation. This purported, in an unscientific way, to apply biological concepts of natural selection and survival of the fittest to sociology, economics and politics. Social Darwinism emerged at a time in which various ideas swirled about which today are generally regarded as crackpot and pseudo-scientific, but which led to racism and antisemitism. For example, Arthur de Gobineau wrote a widely-read three-volume *Essay on the Inequality of the Human Races,* which appeared between 1853 and 1855. Gobineau divided humanity into three great racial blocks: the white peoples, supposedly spiritual and creative; the yellow peoples, supposedly materialist and imitative; and the black peoples, supposedly sensual and primitive. Even more absurd and sinister, Gobineau linked the enduring success of a civilization with the purity of its dominant race. He was not alone in thinking there was a connection between external appearances and the innate characteristics of people. Johann Lavater, inventor of physiognomy, thought there was a connection between the shape of faces and some individuals' superior character while Franz Joseph Gall, inventor of phrenology, posited a connection between the shape of peoples' heads and superior character. Other thinkers became interested in the origins and historical relationship of languages, recognising Sanskrit as the root of most Indo-European languages. Unhappily, the German philologist Friedrich Schlegel turned the descriptive classification of languages into a hierarchical one, deciding that the grammar of Sanskrit-based languages is more advanced than that of other language families, particularly Semitic ones, and that this is proof of more sophisticated imagination and intellectual capacity on the part of those who spoke Indo-European languages. This enabled some antisemites to decide that Jews had been moulded over time by their language and their original desert environment in ways which were fundamentally different from most Europeans. Appearance and language were said to set Jews apart from Europeans. Europeans could only thrive by inbreeding and preserving their purity: "Jews were immutably alien, they had to be contained and expelled, not converted or absorbed."[11]

This was a real witches' brew. Careful reading of Darwin does not support it. Indeed, modern science tends to the opposite viewpoint, namely that inbreeding can be harmful and lead to congenital ailments and an increased risk of illness.

Before World War 1 antisemitism in Germany did not appear to present a substantial or immediate threat to Jews. Indeed, there were grounds for modest optimism: the Prussian state had taken firm action against the last outbreaks of ritual murder accusations at Konitz in 1900; the election of 1912 saw a rout of the antisemitic parties and returned 19 deputies of Jewish descent to Parliament. Prominent Jewish industrialists such as Walther Rathenau and Albert Ballin were even becoming part of the Kaiser's entourage.

World War 1 was a shattering trauma for German society.[12] 1.7 million young men died and another 4.3 million were severely wounded. Industrial output fell by 40 per cent. The Second Reich collapsed and the Kaiser was forced to abdicate. A turning point in German attitudes to Jews occurred in 1916 when German generals, anxious to divert public and parliamentary attention from their military failures, authorised the *Judenzählung*, the "Jew Count". The Generals hoped to demonstrate that Jews were avoiding military service and that this largely explained German failures on the battlefield. Actually, the census showed that Jews were modestly overrepresented in the military. 100,000 Jews served in the German army, 80,000 in combat; 35,000 were decorated and 12,000 were killed.[13]

Shamefully, military leaders concealed these results and declined to refute inaccurate figures that were leaked to the antisemitic press. This contributed to an atmosphere in which even many of Germany's leaders were antagonistic to Jews, blaming them for Germany's military misfortunes: by February 1918 Kaiser Wilhelm II had persuaded himself that an international Jewish conspiracy lay behind Germany's military failures and General Ludendorff began contemplating expulsion of two million Jews from the part of Poland he expected Germany to annex on winning the war.

A number of circumstances made Germans more receptive to antisemitism after World War 1. The German military and political leadership were not clear with the German population that the entry of America into the war and the failure of the 1918 spring offensive meant the German armed forces were unable to continue fighting and had to seek an armistice; effectively, they had been defeated but, because this was obfuscated, it was not obvious to much of the population. This created an environment in which people could believe wartime sacrifices had been in vain and that Germany had not really been defeated but had been 'stabbed in the back'. Jews, together with liberals and leftists, were scapegoated for undermining the war effort. A sense of national crisis developed in the early post-war years. It grew from the combined effects of the Versailles Treaty, the huge debts run up during the war and difficulties demobilising the army. By 1923 runaway inflation rendered the currency virtually worthless. Sebastian Haffner was a young German who wrote a brilliant memoir of his life and the political events in Germany from 1914, when he was seven years old, until 1933. He fled his homeland in 1938 and made a new career in England before returning to Germany after World War II. His memoir has been published in English under the title *Defying Hitler*. He described the inflation of 1923:

> Anyone who had savings in a bank, bonds or gilts, saw their value disappear overnight. Soon it did not matter whether it was a penny put away for a rainy day or a vast fortune. Everything was obliterated. Many people quickly moved their investments only to find that it made no difference... The old and unworldly had the worst of it. Many were driven to begging, many to suicide.[14]

Other circumstances made Germans more receptive to antisemitism after World War 1. There was the linking of Jews to the spectre of Communist revolution. It was well-known that Leon Trotsky, one of the most prominent leaders of the Bolshevik revolution, was Jewish and other Jews such as Rosa

Luxemburg, Kurt Eisner and Béla Kun had been at the forefront of attempts at left-wing revolution in Germany and Hungary in 1918-19. Jews were demonised as agents of Communism and therefore of destructive change which threatened economic wellbeing. There was also resurgent interest in the infamous *Protocols of the Elders of Zion*. This document purported to be a collection of transcripts of meetings of Jewish leaders planning a conspiracy to foment discord within nations for the purpose of enhancing Jews' power and wealth. Following the Bolshevik revolution of 1917, fleeing supporters of the defeated Tsarist regime brought this document to western countries, where it was devoured by gullible audiences. The first German edition of 1920 sold 120,000 copies. It seemed to count for little that *The Times* of London conducted a thorough investigation, and conclusively demonstrated that the *Protocols* was a forgery.[15] Above all, antisemitism increased as Germany experienced a catastrophic economic recession in the period 1928-1932: at that time over one-third of the workforce was unemployed; industrial production dropped by 42 per cent, the stock market collapsed by 60 per cent, and there was a reduction of real wages among those still in employment by 15 per cent.[16]

Against this backdrop of political and economic instability Hitler came to power in Germany in January 1933. From then on, antisemitism was official German government policy. But the nature of the antisemitism evolved, changing in character at a number of distinct turning-points and becoming ever more extreme. In the first years of Nazi power, broadly from 1933-1938, the emphasis was on transferring Jewish jobs and property into non-Jewish hands and strongly encouraging Jews to emigrate from Germany. As early as 1933 laws were passed to purge Jews from the German civil service (which included the law courts and hospitals), as well as excluding Jews from cultural institutions such as theatres, orchestras and newspapers, and imposing a *numerus clausus* on Jews who could be admitted to secondary schools and universities. A significant turning point came in 1938. This probably reflected Hitler's conviction that Jews, inherently disloyal, would present a major security risk if, as seemed likely, there was another major European war. In 1938, among many hostile acts, Jewish communities were deprived of their legal status and their right to own property, Jews were required to be instantly recognisable by acquiring uniform middle names – Israel for men and Sarah for women – and by having a large red '*J*' stamped on the front page of their passports. 1938 also saw the unleashing of a wave of destruction and plunder in what became known as *Kristallnacht*, an infamous pogrom in which at least 91 Jews were killed and following which at least 300 Jews committed suicide. A further

36,000 Jewish men were then rounded up. Until early 1939 German antisemitic policy appeared to be aimed at removing Jews from public life, seizing their property and strongly encouraging them to emigrate. From January 1939 Hitler began to use the language of extermination. On twenty-first January 1939 he told the Czech foreign minister, František Chvalkovský, that the Jews of Germany would be annihilated unless other nations cooperated in deporting them and, nine days later, in a speech to the Reichstag, he predicted the annihilation of the Jewish race in Europe in the event of a new world war. With the invasion of Poland in September 1939, German antisemitism evolved into a policy of deportation. Jews were to be transferred to an obscure and relatively empty dumping ground. At first, it was proposed this be an area called Nisko on the San River at the western edge of the Lublin district of the General Government. Later, deportation plans contemplated mass transfer of Jews to the French colony of Madagascar, but these plans came to nought because Germany failed to defeat Britain in summer 1940 and control of the seas remained in British hands. Finally, Germany contemplated deporting Jews to Siberia above the Arctic Circle. This plan obviously depended on defeat of the Soviet Union, which was not achieved.[17]

With the Nazi invasion of the Soviet Union in June 1941 plans for deporting Jews to a dumping ground were put to one side and Nazi antisemitism assumed the character of mass murder. Some of the reasons for this change have been explored in earlier chapters. They include: a sense of jubilation at early Nazi victories and the feeling that the 'Jewish problem' could be dealt with decisively and finally under cover of war; concern that, if they were not killed, Jews would consume food that would otherwise be available for Germans; fear that Jews would spread disease; and fear that Jews would engage in sabotage behind German lines and that any Jewish survivors would be likely to try to exact revenge.

Antisemitism was fundamental to the behaviour of most German perpetrators of the mass murder of Lithuania's Jews. It is impossible to imagine the Holocaust in Lithuania but for the fact that antisemitism had so deeply penetrated and profoundly affected great swathes of German society. But one needs to recognise that there was considerable variation in the outlook of different Germans responsible for perpetrating the Holocaust and one needs to look at different characters and different motivations in some detail to understand what really drove them to behave as they did.

The individual more responsible than anyone else for the Holocaust in Lithuania, and elsewhere, was of course Adolf Hitler. His hatred of Jews was obsessive and pathological. There has been a mountain of historical writing about Hitler's antisemitism, but the fundamental causes of his obsession with this subject remain strangely elusive. It may be that during his time in pre-war Vienna or during his time in the trenches in World War 1 there were traumatic incidents we do not know about: perhaps he was swindled by one of the Jewish dealers who sold his pictures in pre-war Vienna, or perhaps he received an unwelcome homosexual advance from a Jewish man. This is idle speculation, but such speculation arises from the fact that we simply do not really understand what made him quite so obsessed and so fanatical about Jews. Before World War 1 he had famously failed to gain admission to the Vienna Art Academy. He eked out a marginal existence in a house set aside for single men in the twentieth district of Vienna, living on funds left him by his family and on the proceeds of sale of his pictures to art dealers, two of whom were Jewish.[18] There is little evidence that he was antisemitic before or during World War 1. Indeed, Reinhold Hanisch, who knew Hitler well during his Vienna years, emphasised that Hitler had a number of Jewish friends and companions in the men's home in which he lived, some of whom he relied on to sell his pictures. Another anonymous resident of the men's home said in 1912 that "Hitler got on exceptionally well with Jews, and said at one time that they were a clever people who stick together better than the Germans do."[19] Nonetheless, various poisonous antisemitic doctrines swirled around pre-war Vienna and it is likely Hitler absorbed some of this. "Could it have been that this very proximity, the dependence of the great artist on Jews to off-load his little street paintings, at precisely the same time that he was reading and digesting the antisemitic bile poured out by Vienna's gutter press, served only to underline and deepen the bitter enmities taking shape in his mind ?"[20] If Hitler was antisemitic during the years of the First World War he must have been quite discreet about it because in 1918 he was recommended for the Iron Cross First Class by Lieutenant Hugo Gutmann, a Jewish adjutant in the List Regiment.[21] Towards the end of the war, Hitler was gassed and was in hospital in Pasewalk at the time of the Armistice in November 1918. Announcement of the Armistice shook him to his core and induced something approaching a psychological crisis. Hitler later described how shattering he found the experience of listening to the announcement of Germany's defeat: "It became impossible for me to stay on and listen. While all went black again about my eyes, I groped and tumbled my way back to the dormitory, flung myself on my bed, and buried my burning head in the sheets and pillows." Horror turned to anger and hatred. In *Mein Kampf*, he said: "Did all this [i.e. the horror of the war] happen only so that a gang of wretched criminals could lay their hands on the fatherland? In these nights hatred grew in me, hatred for those responsible for this deed."

Hitler remained in the army after discharge from hospital in Pasewalk. His commanding officer received a letter from a soldier asking why Germany had lost the war and instructed Hitler to make the response. His answer of 16 September 1919 is long and contains his first explicit writing about Jews. Among other things, he says that Jews were exploiting nations, undermining their strength, and infecting them with a racial tuberculosis.[22] This fanatical loathing of Jews, in which Jews were regarded by him as Germany's principal adversary, indeed as a dangerous disease infecting the German nation, was to stay with Hitler until the very end of his life. In his political testament dictated to his secretary, Traudl Junge, in his last days in the bunker in Berlin, and dated 29 April 1945, he continued to rage ludicrously against 'international Jewry' blaming it, among other things, for starting World War Two. Undoubtedly, Hitler's thinking was deeply influenced by the long history of antisemitism, and particularly by the racial turn of antisemitism in the late nineteenth century; but, in the end, the depth of his fury seems beyond rational historical analysis. One suspects there was some psychological disturbance, the precise cause of which remains obscure, but which was probably connected to his failure as an artist in pre-World War 1 Vienna, and his trauma at Germany's defeat in November 1918, which for him, as for others, came as an unexpected and terrible shock.

Some of the most senior figures in the Nazi regime became such significant perpetrators of the Holocaust from a desire to please Hitler and to ingratiate themselves with him. They well understood that fanatical antisemitism was fundamentally important to Hitler, but that Hitler rarely gave formal written instructions on any subject, and never about the Holocaust. By trying to anticipate what they thought Hitler wanted and acting with extreme solicitude in fulfilling what they supposed he wanted, they were driven, in competition for his favour, to ever more radical positions. This zealotry was a characteristic, among others, of Heinrich Himmler, head of the SS and, after Hitler, probably more responsible than anyone else for perpetrating the Holocaust in Lithuania and elsewhere. Himmler, born in 1900, had been strongly antisemitic from the early 1920s. We know from his diary entries that by 1922 he had become obsessed with the 'Jewish question'. He held many discussions on this subject with his classmates and his reading was dominated by antisemitic tracts.[23]

Those who met Himmler in later years tended to be struck by his seemingly unprepossessing personality and his ungainly appearance. He was short, near-sighted and poorly coordinated. One Gauleiter remarked: "If I looked like him, I would not speak of race at all". Observers tended to be struck by two particular characteristics: first, that he appeared to exist in a kind of fantasy world. He was interested in astrology and herbalism, took delight in torchlight rituals and was apparently convinced that he was the reincarnation of German Emperor Heinrich I ("the Fowler", who died in 936). But, as well as this, he was very methodical and diligent about attending to bureaucratic details. These characteristics, when mixed with a fanatical desire to do Hitler's bidding, made Himmler so dangerous. We know that Hitler and Himmler spent long periods of time together between 1938-1942 and Himmler's main biographer in the English language, Peter Longerich, believes they used much of this time together to plan the Holocaust.[24] Many historians now think that the nearest we get to a paper trail connecting Hitler directly to the Holocaust is Himmler's appointment books for 1938 and 1942: "They [the appointment books] reveal how closely radicalisations of Nazi policy towards Jews followed meetings between the two men."[25]

Many of the principal Nazi perpetrators were strongly motivated to behave as they did by reasons of ideology. They were truly won over by, indeed inspired by, Nazism's combination of antisemitism, its ideas of Aryan racial superiority, its explanations for Germany's defeat in World War 1 and its enthusiastic embrace of Lebensraum. It is worth identifying three particular characteristics of many senior Nazi perpetrators who were convinced by these ideological arguments.

First, many of them were relatively young. There is an interesting book by Michael Wildt, called *An Uncompromising Generation.*[26] He looked at the life histories of 221 people who held senior positions in the Reich Security Main Office (RHSA), the SS office most responsible for the Holocaust. He found that 60 percent of them were born between 1900 and 1910, and another 17 percent were even younger. Among the senior Nazis most responsible for the Holocaust, Heinrich Himmler was born in 1900, Rudolf Hoess in 1900, Ernest Kaltenbrunner in 1903, Reinhard Heydrich in 1904, Adolf Eichmann in 1906 and Joseph Mengele in 1911. These were ambitious young men, anxious to prove themselves. Significantly, they had not experienced the horrors of the trenches in World War 1 but had grown up against the depressing backdrop of military defeat, post-war political crisis and economic turbulence.

Secondly, many of them were very highly educated. As many as one-third of the 221 RHSA leaders who Michael Wildt researched into held PhDs, many from leading German universities including Heidelberg,

Leipzig and Tubingen. All four of the first *Einsatzgruppen* commanders held a PhD. Franz Walter Stahlecker became commanding officer of *Einsatzgruppe A* on 6 February 1941. In June 1941 Einsatzgruppe A followed Army Group North into Lithuania, Latvia, Estonia and parts of Russia west of Leningrad. Stahlecker, as commanding officer of *Einsatzgruppe A*, was therefore directly responsible for the murder of the Jews of Pikeliai, and the surrounding area. Stahlecker had obtained a doctorate in law from the University of Tubingen in 1927, then, as now, a leading German university. 11 of the 17 officers of Stahlecker's *Einsatzgruppe A* were lawyers and nine of them had doctorates.[27] We also know that of the 15 officials who attended the Wannsee Conference, convened in the Berlin suburb of Wannsee in January 1942 to plan the implementation of the 'Final Solution', no fewer than eight held academic doctorates, many in law.[28]

Having spent nearly forty years of my life practising law there is something especially disconcerting about knowing that some of the people most directly responsible for the mass murder of the community from which my ancestors came held PhDs in law from leading academic institutions.

It is not easy to explain why so many very highly educated Germans should have played such a leading role in Holocaust atrocity. These were clearly able young men and were inspired by a romantic view of war and a hunger for action. Perhaps it was a case of their having very high IQ, but low emotional intelligence. Up to a point, they had been trained to suppress emotional intelligence, indeed to seek to eliminate human empathy. They used the word *Gefühlsduselei,* (which could be translated as 'spraying of feelings') which encapsulates the contempt they felt for emotion, sentiment and human sympathy. Everything was justified if it promoted the interests of the German master race through revenge and racial cleansing.[29] The fact that leading Holocaust perpetrators were so highly educated undoubtedly affected the way the Holocaust unfolded. One gets a sense of this from Stahlecker's report of 15 October 1941. He writes about how he initiated mass murder in the Baltic states. It is full of a certain kind of cleverness: it is both cunning and deceitful, but also reveals considerable organisational ability:

> It was the duty of the Security Police to set in motion these self-cleansing movements [i.e. murder of Jews], and to direct them into the correct channels in order to accomplish the purpose of the cleansing operations as quickly as possible. It was no less important,

> in view of the future, to establish the unshakeable and provable fact that the liberated populations themselves took the most severe measures against the Bolshevist and Jewish enemy quite on their own, so that the direction by German authorities could not be found out...[30]

A third point about the kind of German people particularly attracted to Nazi ideology is that a disproportionate number of them came from the Baltic states. Probably, this was no coincidence. In various essays, the distinguished philosopher Isaiah Berlin draws attention to: "a well-known psychological phenomenon that outsiders tend to idealise the land beyond the frontier on which their gaze is fixed." He goes on to say:

> Hugh Trevor-Roper has justly remarked that the most fanatical nationalism arises in centres where nationalities and cultures mingle, where friction is sharpest, in, for example…the Baltic provinces which formed Herder, the independent Duchy of Savoy, in which de Maistre, the father of French chauvinism, was born and bred, or Lorraine, in the case of Barres or De Gaulle. It is in these outlying provinces that the ideal vision of the people or the nation as it should be, as one sees it with the eyes of faith, whatever the actual facts, is generated and grows fervent.[31]

It is no coincidence that Alfred Rosenberg came from Reval, now Tallinn in Estonia in the Baltic. Rosenberg was the Nazi party's main racial theorist and did more than anyone to develop the idea of *Lebensraum*, the idea that racially inferior people, particularly Jews, should be cleared from the Baltic states and that this area should be colonised by German settlers. This idea grew out of the history of German settlement of this area following the Baltic crusades. A disproportionately high number of Germans, who had backgrounds in the Baltic states, participated in the Holocaust in Lithuania.

Other Germans became Holocaust perpetrators less for reasons of ideological conviction than from a sense that the demands of war meant that tough choices had to be made. Jews were presented as a severe risk to the German war effort and therefore hard decisions about them had to be made. German planners thought there would simply be too many mouths to feed in German-occupied Europe. They thought World War 1 had been lost because of instability on the home front, largely a consequence of hunger, and this must not be repeated. The priorities were regarded as being to avoid unrest on the home front, to feed the German army, to feed the

German civilian population and to feed allies on the home front. Jews were categorised as 'useless eaters' and therefore they needed to be disposed of. There was also a notion that Jews in Eastern Europe lived in squalid, over-crowded conditions where there was a high risk of the spread of infectious diseases. As those diseases might make German soldiers unwell, many Germans thought it understandable that senior officers had decided to dispose of Jews.

Such an outlook overlooked the fact that Jews were heavily over-represented in medical professions and that Jews had a long tradition of valuing cleanliness very highly. For example, Jews routinely washed hands before meals, in contrast to many other eastern Europeans. Moreover, the Nazi policy of forcing Jews into ghettos had deliberately increased Jewish over-crowding and poverty and so the heightened risk of disease was, in most respects, a consequence of this strategy. Germans were also concerned that Jews might become partisans behind their front lines and pose a threat to supply lines and to German soldiers. Actually, the concern about Jewish partisan activity was overstated. So rapid and devastating was the German onslaught against the Jewish civilian population in Lithuania during summer and autumn 1941 that much of Lithuanian Jewry was already destroyed before the remnant had the chance to consider becoming partisans. Even then, practical constraints, such as how to escape from the ghetto, how to acquire arms, and how to face down hostility from non-Jewish partisan groups, meant that Jewish partisan activity was relatively limited.

Many German perpetrators behaved as they did because they felt they had a strong sense of the need to obey orders and to fulfil the oath they had sworn. This was deeply imbued in German culture. Writing in 1939, Sebastian Haffner said:

> As Bismarck once remarked, moral courage is a rare virtue in Germany, but it deserts a German completely the moment he puts on a uniform. As soldier and officer, he is ... courageous on the field of battle…Yet he is timid as a lamb at the thought of opposing authority. It is not death he fears, but this particular death, which scares him out of his wits. That makes any idea of insubordination ... altogether impossible for the German military – whoever happens to be in power.[32]

Haffner goes on to analyse the way that a very strong sense of comradeship influenced many young German men and turned them, if not into Nazis, then "certainly into usable Nazi material."[33] In the early 1930s Haffner was training to be a *Referendar*, a legal student who, in time, could hope to become a judge. In 1933 he, together with other young *Referendars* from across Germany, was sent to Jüterbog, a barracks town in the south of Brandenburg, for basic military training. There were drills, marching, and much singing of military songs. Haffner asks how this group of intelligent young men, who in most cases had not known each other and had not been Nazis before they were sent to Jüterbog, could so quickly develop a sense of comradeship which turned them into "usable Nazi material". He recognises that the explanations are various and complex: at a superficial level, these men wanted to pass their law examinations and it became clear to them that successful completion of their military training was a prerequisite. There were "mysterious hints that the 'camp report' would play a major part in determining the outcome of the examinations". Haffner also thought it was decisive that these young men had been caught completely off guard and had had no idea of what would be done to them or how to resist it. Finally, he recognised that "a typically German aspiration began to influence us strongly… this was the idolisation of proficiency for its own sake, the desire to do whatever you are assigned to do as well as it can possibly be done". "We find a deep, numbing, sinful pleasure in doing anything, be it a decent and important job, a wild adventure or a crime, as well as can be. This feeling robs us of the ability to think about the significance of what we are doing." It is remarkable that, writing some years before the Holocaust, Haffner sensed the real dangers posed by this German sense of comradeship:

> We trusted one another without reserve in all the actions of the day and had boyish battles and fights. We were all the same. We floated in a great comforting stream of mutual reliance and gruff familiarity. Who would deny that that brings happiness?... And yet I know for certain that this very comradeship can become the means for the most terrible dehumanisation – and that it has become just that in the hands of the Nazis.

Haffner became very aware that "comradeship completely destroys the sense of responsibility for oneself, be it in the civilian or worse still, the religious sense". "It was comradeship which in a few weeks in a camp in Jüterbog had moulded us – *Referendars* after all, with an intellectual, academic education, future judges – into an unthinking, indifferent, irresponsible mass."

The need to obey, to honour the oath which had been sworn, and an overpowering sense of loyalty to comrades goes some considerable way to explaining participation in the Holocaust of many Germans, particularly of those in more back-room roles. Famously, Hannah Arendt gave expression to the idea of the faceless bureaucrat, perpetrating evil while assiduously doing a seemingly dull office job. She called this 'the banality of evil'. Arendt developed the idea while witnessing some of the trial of Adolf Eichmann in Jerusalem between April and December 1961, and she set out her thinking in her book *Eichmann in Jerusalem.*[34] The concept of the banality of evil is undoubtedly an important idea, and it does help explain the behaviour of many German bureaucrats who facilitated the Holocaust. However, with the passage of time, it seems clear that Arendt misjudged Eichmann. Her misjudgements arose for a number of reasons: she allowed her ideas about totalitarianism, the subject of one of her previous books, to dominate her analysis of Eichmann, particularly in that she thought the totalitarian nature of the Nazi regime *ipso facto* deprived Eichmann of almost all agency; she failed to appreciate that at his trial Eichmann was deliberately trying to cultivate the idea of himself as an unimportant backroom worker, simply obeying orders; Arendt was absent at critical moments of the trial; and she allowed the prejudices of an acculturated German Jew towards *Ostjuden* to colour her judgements, and was particularly hostile to the prosecutor Gideon Hausner, whose Galician Jewish background she rather disdained. Arendt's view of Eichmann as a banal bureaucrat went against the balance of evidence produced to the court in Jerusalem and against the evidence, not available to her but which subsequently came to light, contained in minutes of Eichmann's conversations with Sassen and other Nazis in Argentina during the post-war years. It is clear from the records of these conversations that Eichmann was, and remained, a fanatical antisemite, had some agency during the war years and did not at all regret his conduct.[35] Indeed, his only regret was that he had not killed more Jews.

Sadism was another motivation for German participation in the Holocaust in Lithuania. There might be any number of ways to illustrate the extreme character of this sadism. A simple way of doing so, chosen fairly randomly, is to look at the powerful memoir of Abraham Sutzkever, which is called 'From the Vilna Ghetto to Nuremberg'.[36] Sutzkever lived in Vilnius. At the beginning of his memoir, he describes three experiences which affected him and his close family and which shed light on German behaviour in Vilnius shortly following the German invasion of June 1941. The first concerned an elderly Rabbi called Dr. Yankev Vigodski. The Rabbi was 85 years old, quite ill and could barely walk. After the Germans began rounding up and killing the male Jewish population of Vilnius, many Jews called on Rabbi Vigodski seeking his advice and assistance. He rose from his bed, dressed in black clothes and went off to find Murer, the Nazi in charge of Jewish affairs: "The old man approached him, introduced himself, and informed the new master of the great injustices being committed against the Jews. Murer did not respond with a single word. He slid a white glove over his hand and tossed Vigodski down the stairs." Badly bloodied, the Rabbi staggered home. Shortly afterwards, Vigodski was forcibly taken from his home to Lukiškės prison where Sutzkever's wife encountered him and was treated to a graphic account of what had occurred. The second experience concerns Abraham Sutzkever's mother. In early August 1941 edicts were posted up in Vilnius. One of them said "Jews are forbidden from walking on the sidewalk. They may walk only in the gutters and only in single file." Sutzkever's mother "momentarily forgot the German regulations and stepped on the sidewalk. A stormtrooper grabbed her by the hair and struck her face with his whip. When she fell to the ground, lying in her own blood in the gutter, he burst out in thunderous laughter and left." The third experience concerns Abraham Sutzkever himself. On 5 August 1941 he was detained by a drunk German stormtrooper. Two other stormtroopers soon appeared. They were driving two Jews, Rabbi Kassel, who was 80 years old, and Moyshke, a young boy. The stormtroopers had unfurled a Torah scroll along the length of the road. The scroll was covered in tyre tracks. A pile of other Torah scrolls lay nearby. The three Jews were made to undress, dance naked around a pyre of burning Torah scrolls, and sing. They were then ordered to tear up the piled Torah scrolls and toss them into the flames. After some time, the Jews were ordered to get dressed: "The stormtroopers left, seemingly very pleased with themselves." It is important to note that no Jew was killed in any of these three incidents. The incidents are not untypical examples of how Germans behaved to Jews in Lithuania. And yet most dispassionate observers would think that, by all normal standards, there is something deeply extraordinary, and sick, about human beings behaving to other human beings in this way. There appears to be a kind of sadism at work; a delight in cruelty and in witnessing the suffering of others.

Jealousy can be closely associated with sadism. Precisely how those two complex psychological phenomena are connected is the subject of arcane debate, and beyond the scope of this book. What is clear is that from the late nineteenth century Jews in German-speaking countries enjoyed remarkable success. In 1800 there were hardly any Jews among college students, lawyers, doctors or business leaders in the main German-speaking countries. In 1900 Jews accounted for about 4 per cent of the Austrian population, but in Vienna 62 per cent of the lawyers, half the doctors and dentists, 45 per cent of the university medical faculty and one-quarter of the total faculty were Jews, as were some 55 percent of the professional journalists, 40 percent of the directors of publicly traded banks and 70 percent of the board members of the Vienna stock exchange. In Hungary, at the same time, Jews accounted for 34 percent of the lawyers and 48 percent of the physicians. In Prussia, Jews constituted less than one percent of the population in 1910-11, but 5.4 percent of the university students and 17 percent of the students in the University of Berlin. In 1912, Jews constituted 0.95 per cent of the population of Germany but made up 31 percent of the wealthiest families.[37] This extraordinary success had been made possible by a more liberal political climate across much of the German-speaking world, but there were also cultural reasons, specific to the Jewish tradition, which help explain this success.

Many Jewish families had traditionally placed great emphasis on their children being involved in religious study, memorising texts and debating their meaning. Such skills were transferable and helped young Jews train for careers in medicine and law. Much Jewish success in the world of business represented an evolution of economic roles previously permitted to Jews. Moneylenders might become bankers; pedlars might evolve to become shopkeepers or even department store owners; cattle traders might become brokers of commodities or stocks. Of course, the great majority of Jews remained poor, especially those in eastern districts, or those who had only recently migrated from the east. But, the striking success of some Jewish people was difficult for ordinary Germans to comprehend, particularly coming as it did after so many centuries in which Jews had appeared to live a marginal and impoverished existence. It was especially difficult for ordinary Germans to understand against a backdrop of repeated Nazi insistence that Germans were the 'master race'.

Unsurprisingly, this was fertile ground for conspiracy theories. Some of these theories were a mutation of medieval traditions, including those, for example, which blamed Jews for plagues and other misfortunes. Other conspiracy theories had a more modern character. Some antisemitism may have been a variation on the Socialist doctrine that there was a conspiracy on the part of capitalists to deprive the proletariat of wealth which was rightfully theirs. Indeed, many on the left saw antisemitism as "the socialism of fools". In any event, the conspicuous success of Jews in German lands, coming after centuries of their abject marginalisation, was little understood by swathes of the German population. Perhaps unsurprisingly, it aroused resentment and, in some quarters, intense jealousy. This became part of the mindset which made the Holocaust possible.

I have tried to show that German perpetrators of the Holocaust had a variety of complicated and overlapping motivations. To a greater or lesser extent, most were motivated by antisemitism, either the long-standing variety rooted in Christian theology, or by more recent and more intense racial antisemitism. Hitler's own intense pathological antisemitism, conceived against the background of his poverty-stricken pre-war Viennese experiences and fuelled by his despair at German defeat in World War 1, was fundamentally important both to the decision to engage in mass murder of the Jews and as to the form the Holocaust took. Senior Nazis around Hitler tried to ingratiate themselves with him by anticipating his wishes that Jews be murdered *en masse*, and then by seeking to follow his wishes with an over-zealous bureaucratic vigour. Some German perpetrators were strongly influenced by ideology, others by more practical arguments that if Jews were permitted to remain alive they would consume too much food, might spread disease and were liable to become partisans. Most Germans in military positions were heavily influenced by the fact they had sworn an oath of loyalty and any sense they might have had of personal moral responsibility for their actions was diluted by intense feelings of comradeship. Other Germans were motivated, among other things, by sadism and intense jealousy of Jewish success. These various motivations were capable of waxing and waning over time within a given individual, and they combined in different ways in different people.

Lithuanian perpetrators of the Holocaust were influenced by some of these same motivations, but the outlook of German and Lithuanian perpetrators was, in some respects, different.

Lithuanian nationalism was different from German nationalism. Lithuania is a small country and ethnic Lithuanians were few in number. Lithuanian nationalism did not have the neo-Darwinian notions of the national community as a master-race, a key feature of Nazism. Lithuanian nationalism has been compared to Slovak, Ukrainian, Irish and Macedonian nationalism in that a rather downtrodden and marginalised community strove for the re-creation of its national identity based on a linguistic community, and realised in a state.[38] Until 1918 Jews were not as much a target of Lithuanian nationalist hostility as were Poles. With the establishment of the Lithuanian state in 1918 things began to change. Jews were increasingly excluded from the concept of Lithuanian nationalism, for two main reasons: the first was linguistic. A small percentage of urban Jews spoke Lithuanian, and some Jewish market traders knew enough words of Lithuanian to broker a deal in the marketplace; but most Lithuanian Jews had Yiddish as their first language, Russian and/or Polish as their second language and so had few bonds connecting them to the linguistic community that defined the Lithuanian nation. Lithuanian Jews also had no particular reason to identify closely with the geographical area that constituted the post-1918 state of Lithuania. They were more likely to identify with "Lite", a swathe of territory that included most of Lithuania but also substantial parts of Latvia, northeast Poland and western Belarus. Many Lithuanian Jews may have found the idea of allegiance to a modern state of Lithuania, based on the Lithuanian language, as strange, even faintly absurd, when contrasted with the more obvious attractions of Zionism and socialism.[39]

Equally, the Lithuanian nationalist movement was never very comfortable about including Jews. One gets a sense of this in the story "Memories of the Old Bridge" by Vincas Kurdika. Kurdika was a Lithuanian poet and physician. He was active in the Lithuanian national rebirth movement. He wrote the music and lyrics of the Lithuanian national anthem. In his story he imagines himself as an old bridge, spanning the Šešupė river. The old bridge is a kind of metaphor for the Lithuanian nation. A good deal of water flows under the bridge into the Baltic. One day a Jew comes along:

> First, he inspected the top of me, poking at me here with his stick and having a kick at me there. Then he surveyed me from below, taking off his boots and wading into the river. He had a squeeze at my piles, then turned back, and so out onto the bank. Then he stopped, counted on his fingers and hurriedly put his boots on again, muttering something the while: "Good; they want their profit, but there will be enough for me..."[40]

As this story illustrates, some shades of opinion within Lithuanian nationalism had for a long time tended to see Jews as alien and exploitative. But Lithuanian nationalism acquired a markedly more radical wing in 1929 with the establishment of a fascist movement called Geležinis Vilkas (Iron wolf). This was set up by Augustinas Voldemaras, after Smetona dismissed him as his deputy. Voldemaras was strongly influenced by Mussolini. Geležinis Vilkas was secretive, had strict monk-like rules and was extremely nationalist. In June 1934 it tried to overthrow the Smetona government. This attempted putsch was led by Petras Kubiliūnas, chief of staff of the

Lithuanian armed forces, but it failed and over 100 Voldemarists were arrested. Nonetheless, Geležinis Vilkas remained active in late 1930s Lithuania, drawing strength from the example of fascist movements elsewhere in Europe, particularly in Germany and Italy, and from a sense that the loss of Vilnius to Poland and of Klaipēda to Germany represented a deep crisis for the Lithuanian nation.

Relatively, there were fewer fascists in Lithuania than in Germany – but there were some and when the Germans invaded in June 1941 some of them were in close contact with elements of the German military. Both the Ypatingasis būrys in the Vilnius area and the Hamann Rollkommando in the Kaunas area were fascist, and were heavily involved in the mass murder of Jews. The motivations of extreme German and Lithuanian nationalists were, however, subtly different. While many German fascists saw themselves as engaged in a holy mission to protect German nationhood from the risk of Jewish contamination, Lithuanian nationalists were more concerned about regaining Lithuanian independence. They thought that by attacking Jews they might ingratiate themselves with the Germans and so make recovery of their independence more likely.

The anti-Jewish fury of many Lithuanians arose from the trauma Lithuania experienced as a result of being occupied by the Soviet Union between June 1940 and June 1941. Many Lithuanians were furious with Jews because they thought Jews had given the Soviets an effusive welcome when they arrived in June 1940. They also thought that Jews had been too active in the Soviet administration of Lithuania. Neither contention contained much truth. A small minority of young Jews welcomed the Soviets in the streets with flowers. However, Christopher Dieckmann estimates that barely 1-2 percent of the Jewish population did this.[41] Soviet Communism was anathema to the overwhelming majority of Lithuanian Jews either because they were property owners, or traditional in their religious observance, or Zionist, or liberal or indeed some combination of these things. Many Jews undoubtedly saw Soviet Communism as preferable to Nazism, but very few saw reasons to embrace the Soviets with enthusiasm. As to Jewish involvement in administering Soviet Lithuania, the best estimate is that about 12-16 per cent of the Communist party in Lithuania were Jews. This was over-representation by reference to the proportion of Jews in the total Lithuanian population, but only very modestly so, and perhaps unsurprising given that Jews were, generally speaking, much better educated than ethnic Lithuanians.

The trauma for Lithuanians derived from the fact that Lithuanians did not put up any resistance to Soviet occupation in June 1940 and, indeed, had welcomed Soviet tanks. Order no. 26 issued by Lithuanian army commander General Vincas Vitkauskas and army chief of staff General Stasys Pundzevičius on 15 June, 1940 ordered the Lithuanian army to stand along the most important roads and welcome the Soviet army in a friendly manner and the acting Lithuanian president, Antanas Merkys, said that Red Army units in Lithuania "have come as a friendly allied army only for the sake of the greater security of Lithuania itself and the Soviet Union..." The question remains as to why, following the Nazi invasion of June 1941, Lithuanians blamed Jews for what many came to regard as the horrors of Soviet occupation. Christopher Dieckmann explains: "People tend to externalise guilt. The general cooperation with the new rulers of the country, the Soviets, was later transferred to the Jews: 'the Jews did this, not us'..."[42]

If Dieckmann's analysis is broadly right it is another, rather depressing, example of Jews being used as a scapegoat. But whatever may or may not have been going on in the collective Lithuanian psyche, the perception, though mistaken, that Jews had welcomed the Soviets and had dutifully served the Soviet regime was a significant part of why many Lithuanians turned on their Jewish neighbours with murderous fury.

One of the principal motivations of the Lithuanian perpetrators of the Holocaust appears to have been theft. Many Lithuanians participated in killing Jews, both directly and indirectly, so as to steal their possessions. There is a remarkable diary by a Polish journalist called Kazimierz Sakowicz. He lived in Ponary, just outside Vilnius, and witnessed, day after day, the murder of the Jews of Vilnius at Ponary. At considerable risk to himself he confided his experiences to his diary. It provides a record of what happened at Ponary between 11 July, 1941 and 25 October, 1943.[43] It is noteworthy that Sakowicz was not Jewish, and at some points in his diary (particularly when describing Jewish involvement in partisan activity) he is quite hostile to Jews. As one reads his diary it becomes clear that Sakowicz thought that the opportunity for stealing Jewish possessions was one of the main reasons for Lithuanian participation in the Holocaust. He says: "For the Germans 300 Jews are 300 enemies of humanity; for the Lithuanians they are 300 pairs of shoes, trousers, and the like."[44]

It seems that theft of Jewish possessions took place all across Lithuania and everything of value owned by Jews was considered to be a legitimate target for plunder.

Testimonies given by survivors to Leyb Koniuchowsky shortly after the war indicate how commonplace theft was in most provincial communities.[4] In Anykščiai, Motl Kuritsky said: "With tears in their eyes, the Jews saw ...

neighbours happily dragging away all their possessions; before the Jews had even left the town, their homes had been stripped bare". In Giedraičiai, Yisrael Katz said: "Jewish possessions were continuously robbed. The partisans used to enter Jewish homes and take whatever they liked..." In Stajėtiškis, Zalman Yoffe said: "Imediately after the Jews were driven out of their homes...peasants from the village and other nearby locations ...broke open the doors and windows and robbed the abandoned farms. Those who succeeded robbed whatever they could get their hands on: furniture, clothing, livestock, and other farm inventory." In Turmantas, Mendel Davidson said: "Using coaches, the partisans took for themselves all the goods and property from the Jewish homes. Others transferred them to the countryside and what was left was robbed by the townlet's residents".[46]

Almost all Jewish-owned property was stolen, both movable and immovable. Property stolen included property that was communally owned, such as synagogues and buildings used for religious and secular education, as well as property owned by Jewish individuals and families such as homes, furniture, cash, jewellery, clothes, cattle and carts. The process of theft was organised, at least to some extent. When Jews were forced into ghettos committees were set up to redistribute Jewish property, in accordance with an order of priority. The German administration and Germans serving in Lithuania were first in line; then came members of the Lithuanian administration; and finally the general Lithuanian population was able to acquire property either by stealing it or at public auction. But in practice the process was far from orderly. There was widespread corruption and squabbling over the distribution of Jewish property.

It seems that people at all levels of Lithuanian society benefitted from the theft of Jews' personal possessions, including those at the top. For example, Jonas Noreika was appointed Governor of the Šiauliai district on 5 August 1941. Once in office, Noreika issued an order that all property, both moveable and immoveable was to be seized from all Jews. Only 200 Reichsmarks was to be left to each Jewish family. Then, on 22 August Noreika ordered that all the Jews of Šiauliai were to be sent to the Žagarė ghetto, within one week. Records in the library of the Lithuanian Academy of Science contain a list of Jewish property that Lithuanian people acquired. It is clear from these records that Jonas Noreika, living at 260 Vilnius Street, Šiauliai, acquired (among other things) one cupboard, one pair of warm boots, a desk, a bookshelf, wooden beds and mattresses, a wardrobe and bedside tables. In other words, Noreika, at the head of Lithuanian administration in Šiauliai, appears to have benefited personally from his own order.[47]

There are three general observations one might make about this widespread plunder of Jewish property and its link to mass murder. First, it seems that many Lithuanians justified theft of Jewish property (to themselves and to others) on the basis that they thought Jews had been exploitative and that their wealth was ill-gotten. Taking property owned by Jews was therefore perceived by them less as theft than as return of property to rightful Lithuanian owners. The argument was manifestly absurd given that most property owned by Jews had been acquired by them in accordance with applicable law and that many Jews were anyway poor or very poor. Nonetheless, the argument that property was being restored to rightful Lithuanian ownership played into an old trope of the Jew as a bloodsucker and it helped assuage Lithuanians' feelings of discomfort that they were contravening the fundamental (Christian and Jewish) principle "Thou shalt not steal".[48] Secondly, the act of theft was capable of making people more, not less, antisemitic because these people needed to justify their actions to themselves. And, thirdly, the fact that the occupying German regime permitted, indeed encouraged, theft by Lithuanians of Jewish property made the Germans more popular in Lithuania. It helped stabilise their regime by giving Lithuanians a vested interest in its continuance. [49]

Once Jewish-owned property found its way into Lithuanian hands most Lithuanians became very determined not to give it back. This was so whether the property was stolen or given to Lithuanians on a temporary basis for safekeeping in the hope that its rightful Jewish owners would recover it after the war. There is a diary by a Lithuanian woman called Ona Šimaitė. During the Nazi occupation she hid a number of Jews and arranged that some of their property be stored for safekeeping with her Lithuanian acquaintances. Ona was very troubled and upset when, after the war, she asked these acquaintances to return property to the Jewish people she had saved, and they refused to do so.[50]

It is possible to read Sakowicz's Ponary Diary as a description of, and a series of reflections about, theft as a motivating factor in Lithuanian murder of Jews. One is struck by the vast quantity of possessions which are stolen and the colossal administrative task of sorting them out: "All the property of the murdered was off-loaded from the wagons and put on the ground. It made an enormous mountain of things - food, pillows, mattresses, baby carriages, baskets, kitchen equipment, sacks with potatoes...clothes - all the stuff mixed together."[51] Some of the theft and murder was carried out, so to speak, to order. For example, Sakowicz describes how a Shaulist finds clothes to fit the wife of a local peasant [Waclaw Tankun]; the Shaulist finds, and then kills, a Jewish woman of Tankun's wife's size in the hope that the Jewish woman's clothes would fit Tankun's wife.[52] Quite often, arrangements were made by Jews with local Lithuanians to protect them in return for payment but such arrangements were often dishonoured by their Lithuanian protectors. Sakowicz describes the behaviour of a Lithuanian called Tretiak: "Tretiak hid rich Jews in the houses of peasants. He simply distributed 2-3 Jews with the villagers and then regularly took money from the Jews... When the money ran out, Tretiak appeared with a rifle and took the Jews, and they were never seen again."[53] Sakowicz comments obliquely, and rather laconically, about the fact that this extraordinary behaviour was carried out by many Lithuanians who professed to be God-fearing Catholics. His diary entry for 1 November 1941 says: "God-fearing representatives of the Catholic Lithuanian nation liquidated four truckloads of Jews…November 1 (Saturday) was All Saints' Day. It did not disturb their executions."[54]

In the end, and in spite of itself, Sakowicz's diary perhaps demonstrates the limitations of theft as an explanation for Lithuanian participation in the mass murder of Jews. For example, his diary contains horrific descriptions of women and young children being bludgeoned to death with rifle butts on the edge of pits. There are also graphic descriptions of German-trained dogs chasing victims to their death as Lithuanians stand by laughing.[55] The desire to steal possessions is too simple, convenient and clinical an explanation for much of the Lithuanians' behaviour towards their Jewish neighbours.

It seems to me that the efforts historians have made to explain Lithuanians' behaviour towards Jews during the period of Nazi occupation still leaves a gap in our understanding. Historians have tried to explain the behaviour of Lithuanian perpetrators of the Holocaust by reference, among other things, to Lithuanian nationalism, long-standing antisemitic sentiments with roots in Christian theology, trauma at being occupied by the Soviet Union and the desire of poor people to steal the possessions of their Jewish neighbours. Perhaps future writers on this subject will look more to psychology for an explanation. Most people in every age and every society have known that, in all ordinary circumstances, one does not kill neighbours. But in Lithuania in 1941 many people became, as it were, inoculated against that normal application of conscience. What particular trauma was it, and what exactly was the psychological impact of the trauma, that caused so many people to set aside those normal ways of thinking about their neighbours? It may be that very vigorous antisemitic ideology was what inoculated many people in Germany against 'normal' attitudes to their neighbours. It may be (although this is rather less obvious) that trauma at the first Soviet invasion was what inoculated many people in Lithuania against 'normal' attitudes to the Jews living there. There is a sense that there is more work to be done in this area and that historians will need to use new techniques, including psychological techniques, to reach a fuller and deeper understanding of what really motivated Lithuanian perpetrators of the holocaust.

Much of the discussion about the attitudes of Jewish victims of the Holocaust in Lithuana, as elsewhere, was for a long time overshadowed by discussion of whether Jews failed to put up enough of a fight and went too meekly to their deaths. Did they go 'like sheep to the slaughter'? This phrase derives from two biblical sources. In Isaiah 53 a virtuous servant is murdered but does not protest: "Like a sheep being led to the slaughter or a lamb that is silent before her shearers, he did not open his mouth" (Isaiah 53:7). His silence is praised because there was no "deceit in his mouth". In Psalm 44 the martyrdom of Jewish people persecuted for their religion is again presented positively: "nay, but for thy sake are we killed all the day; We are accounted as sheep to be slaughtered" (Psalms 44:23). Both biblical references imply there can be something laudable about going like sheep to the slaughter. During the Holocaust in Lithuania the phrase first seems to have been used by Abba Kovner in a pamphlet of 1 January 1942 in which he sought to encourage Jews in the Vilnius ghetto to resist the Germans:

> We will not be led like sheep to slaughter. True we are weak and helpless, but the only response to the murders is revolt. Brethren, it is better to die fighting like free men than to live at the mercy of the murderers. Arise, Arise ...[56]

After the war, in a speech Kovner gave to members of the Palmach, he clarified that his pamphlet of 1 January, 1942 was intended to encourage a fighting spirit but that he did not mean to suggest that Holocaust victims had actually gone like sheep to the slaughter; and he was at pains to emphasise how difficult effective resistance had been, as evidenced by the fact that other victims of the Nazis such as Soviet prisoners of war and Polish officers had also, for the most part, failed to fight back vigorously.[57]

Most serious scholars of the Holocaust in Lithuania do not now believe that Jews went like sheep to the slaughter, but they do accept that this was a widely-held view in the Jewish world (and beyond) for a number of years after 1945. This may have been because the idea of Jewish passivity during the Holocaust conformed with stereotypes about diaspora Jews held by the

Jewish community in Palestine and, after 1948, in Israel.[58] And some Israelis thought Holocaust victims were foolish and the authors of their own misfortunes for not emigrating to Palestine before the war. The idea of Jewish Holocaust victims being passive may also have been reinforced by photographs and film footage of survivors of liberated Nazi concentration camps, which made many Holocaust survivors appear emaciated and pathetic looking.

The trial of Adolf Eichmann in Jerusalem in 1961 marked a decisive turning-point. The prosecutor, Gideon Hausner, repeatedly pressed witnesses on whether Jews had gone 'like sheep to the slaughter'. The trial served (as intended by Israeli prime minister David Ben-Gurion) to educate the Israeli public, and the wider world, about the Holocaust generally, including about the difficulties of Jewish resistance in Nazi-occupied Europe. After the trial, Israeli public opinion shifted decisively against blaming Jewish victims of Nazi persecution for failing to fight back vigorously and instead tended to place blame exclusively on the perpetrators. Revisionist Zionist poet Uri Zvi Greenberg said: "It is a crime to say that in the time of Hitler diaspora Jewry could have gone to their deaths differently". And, from the other side of the political divide, the labour Zionist writer Haim Guri said:

> We should ask forgiveness from countless numbers for having judged them in our hearts...we often generalised categorically and arbitrarily that these poor souls [went to their deaths] 'as sheep to the slaughter'. Now we know better.[59]

Much of the criticism of how Jews in Lithuania behaved during the Holocaust has centered on the activities of the Jewish Councils, known as the 'Judenrate'. Their role was to administer Jewish ghettos and to liaise with the German and Lithuanian authorities. In the eyes of their critics, the Jewish Councils and other prominent Jews who played a leading role in administering ghettos during Nazi occupation, became 'enablers' of the Holocaust.[60]

However, it is important to note that the prominent Jews who served on the Jewish Councils did not seek this role, but agreed to take it on because they thought they had a communal responsibility to do so. There are interesting records of a meeting which established the Kaunas Jewish Council. The meeting took place on 5 August 1941 in Dauksos Street, Kaunas. A decision had to be made as to who would lead the Jewish Council, who would be members of it and what role it should play. About

30 people attended the meeting. Germans wanted the Council to be their instrument. Jews did not want this. Initially, no Jew would accept the role of leading the Council. Eventually, Rabbi Yaakov Moshe Schmuckler begged Doctor Elkhanan Elkes to lead the Kaunas Jewish Council: "In our most tragic hour...when the murderer's sword is suspended over our heads... you shall be with us and we will all be with you, until we arrive at the great day of salvation!" The Rabbi's intervention was greeted with much weeping but a reluctant Dr. Elkes, pale and silent, agreed to take on the role.[61]

It seems that the main strategy of the leaders of the Jewish Councils was to ensure that Jews in the ghettos worked hard, as directed by Germans and Lithuanians, so that the Germans had a vested interest in preserving the lives of many Jews. In other words, the Jews should become an indispensable resource for the German war effort. The Jewish Councils took the view that physical resistance to the Germans was unrealistic because Jews in the ghettos were unarmed and untrained and such resistance ran the serious risk of provoking disproportionate retaliation by the Germans or to their destroying the entire Jewish community in the ghetto. If at least some Jewish lives could be preserved for a period of time then, it was hoped, the war might eventually be won by the allies and some Jews be saved.[62]

The leaders of the Jewish community in Lithuania were strongly criticised for the strategy they pursued, both at the time and subsequently. Jacob Gens in Vilnius attracted particular obloquy. There were two main criticisms. First, that this strategy involved handing over Jews to be murdered, whenever Nazis requested this, as they frequently did. Gens defended his actions on the basis that the ends justified the means; in other words, that some Jewish lives had to be sacrificed so that other Jews could live. Gens and other Jewish leaders in the Vilnius ghetto agonised because Jewish religious teaching seemed to point in opposite directions: seven centuries earlier Maimonides had written: "If the pagans ask you [Jews] to deliver up one of your number so that he might be killed, you must remain steadfast and not deliver up a single Jewish soul". On the other hand, and seemingly in total contradiction of Maimonides, the chief Rabbi of Kaunas, influenced by an obscure passage in one of the commentaries, took the view that: "If an evil decree threatens disaster for the entire community, Jewish leaders must summon the courage to save a remnant of the people."[63] Faced with the terrible dilemma of how best to proceed, the Jewish Council in Kaunas took the course of action favoured by the Chief Rabbi of Kaunas.

The second strong criticism of the Jewish Councils was that they suppressed information they acquired about what was really happening to

Jews at local killing sites. For example, in October 1941 two Jewish youngsters escaped from the Ninth Fort on the edge of Kaunas. They returned to the ghetto and gave a report to the Jewish Council of Kaunas of what they had witnessed. They said that Jews were separated into groups of 100, ordered to undress and were then shot by Lithuanian units under the supervision of a handful of German soldiers. The killings lasted for a day and a night. The victims' clothes were collected for repair, cleaning and despatch to Germany. The Lithuanian shooters divided the valuables of the murdered Jews among themselves.[64]

The Jewish Council of Kaunas was reluctant to pass this information to the wider Jewish community in Kaunas. There were questions about whether the reports were entirely credible. There was concern that, if made known, the reports would cause panic and alarm; that they would hugely depress the community; and that it would undermine the strategy of some cooperation with the German and Lithuanian authorities which was being pursued by the Jewish Council. The information was therefore suppressed. A similar approach was taken by the Jewish Council in Vilnius when, in late September 1941, it became aware of massacres at Ponary. When information about what was really happening at Ponary and the Ninth Fort eventually reached the wider Jewish community in Vilnius and in Kaunas, the Jewish Councils were condemned for suppressing information, and the integrity of members of those Councils was called into question.

This criticism was unfair. The leaders of the Jewish Councils were in a position where they and their community faced what have been called "choiceless choices".[65] For a short period, when the German army invaded in June 1941, there was a chance for Jews to run away to the Soviet Union, or to hide. After that, there was really no strategy. Whether Jews took up armed resistance or whether they tried to cooperate with the Nazis and the Lithuanian authorities, in the end the overwhelming likelihood was that they would be killed. The tiny minority who survived did so mainly because they were very lucky. As Christoph Dieckmann has said: "Various Jewish Councils in Lithuania…behaved differently to some extent, but the result was the same, the extermination of the Jewish population in all urban ghettos."[66] It is therefore unreasonable to blame leaders of Jewish Councils for participating in the killing of Jews. There were no choices they could make which would safeguard their community for long. This position contrasts with that of Lithuanian policemen, and members of Lithuanian battalions, many of whom did have a choice, and who chose to participate in the murder of Jews and cannot therefore be regarded otherwise than as perpetrators. The one thing which, in Dieckmann's view, might have made a difference to the fate of Jews in ghettos would have been substantial help from non-Jews. He points out that 15,000-20,000 Jews lived in the Vilnius ghetto for about two and a half years at a time when 150,000 non-Jews, both Poles and Lithuanians, lived in the same city. More Jews might have survived had they received substantial help from those non-Jews. Sadly, this was not forthcoming.

There were two other particular reasons why Jews collectively did not respond with greater physical force to the way they were treated. The first reason is that, as one of their earliest priorities, the Nazis targeted, and removed, natural leaders of the Jewish community. As intended, this left the Jewish community disorientated. What happened in Kaunas serves as a good example. The first order to the 'Judische Ältestenrat' was issued on 18 August 1941. It was to organise a contingent of 500 volunteers associated with the community intelligentsia – physicians, lawyers, architects, teachers and other university graduates – allegedly for labour in municipal archives. When the the number of volunteers fell short of what was required, Lithuanian partisans went into the ghetto and recruited by force. These 500 highly educated Jews were marched out of the ghetto, and were never seen or heard from again. It later transpired they had been shot by the Lithuanian Third Operational Group (a militia) in the Fourth Fort at Panemunė. A second reason Jews did not react with greater physical force was the difficulty they had in comprehending the true nature and extent of what they were up against. Many older Jews had good memories of Germans from the First World War and had grown up thinking of Germany as a civilized country. The Nazi occupiers tried to obscure what they were doing to the Jewish population of Lithuania. Even when Jews became aware of what was actually happening to their community they found it difficult to process such information and organise a response involving physical force. They were also constrained by fear of savage reprisals for any action they took. Writing after the war, Abba Kovner said: "As the Jews of Vilnius had no paradigm of such dreadful slaughter, and as they had heard of the Warsaw ghetto with its half-million Jews who had remained there for three years…they believed that while they would face a life studded with vicissitude, the slaughter of millions was outside the realm of possibility."[67]

Jews in Nazi-occupied Lithuania found ways to resist which did not involve use of physical force. There was a kind of spiritual resistance. In earlier centuries Jewish spiritual leaders customarily argued that, in the face of extreme danger, Jews should rely on *Kiddush haShem*, the sanctification of the holy name. It was essential to live life to please God and, in the face of an existential crisis, a good Jew should sacrifice his or her own life so as to be able to die as a Jew. In wartime Lithuania many Jewish religious authorities thought the principle of *Kiddush haShem* should be subordinated to the principle of *Kiddush haChaim*, the sanctification of Jewish life. In other words, detailed observance of Jewish laws, including dietary laws and laws about Sabbath observance, were in the prevailing circumstances to be regarded as less important than doing anything which preserved Jewish life. Jewish religious leaders also placed emphasis on the importance of *Amidah*, which might loosely be described as perseverance. Jews were, above all, to carry on living and to do so in accordance with the highest ideals possible in the circumstances. They must educate their children about Jewish history, establish Jewish theatres and play Jewish music. A surprisingly lively Jewish cultural scene developed in Vilnius. There was a ghetto theatre and there were concerts. In behaving in this way some felt that Jews were, at a spiritual and cultural level, resisting their oppressors. Yehuda Bauer, great early historian of the Holocaust, has written extensively about *Amidah* as a form of resistance. It begs intriguing questions about whether some activities which might be thought self-serving and unworthy, such as smuggling, should actually be regarded as a form of religiously sanctioned resistance. If smuggling food into a ghetto enables Jewish people who would otherwise starve to remain alive, contrary to what their enemies intend, then arguably that becomes an act of resistance.[68]

Another interesting example of cultural resistance was smuggling Jewish books into the Vilnius ghetto so as to ty to save them from destruction. The background to this was that a German called Dr. Johannes Pohl was director of a Nazi organisation based in Frankfurt called "The Institute for the Study of the Jewish Question". In January 1942 Pohl was sent by the *Einsatzstab des Reichsleiter Alfred Rosenberg*, or Rosenberg Squad, to hunt for Jewish treasures in Vilnius. Pohl and his staff were instructed to seize Vilnius's great collection of Jewish books. The most valuable books would be sent to Pohl's institute in Frankfurt for a Nazi-infused "study of the Jewish question" and the rest would be burned. The Nazis used 40 ghetto inmates as slave-labourers to sort, select, pack and transport the materials either to Frankfurt or to nearby paper mills. This group was nicknamed "the Paper Brigade" and was informally led by poet Shmerke Kaczerginski. He and his group smuggled thousands of books and manuscripts past German guards into the ghetto where they were stored in an underground book-bunker 60 feet beneath the Vilnius ghetto, which Abraham Sutzkever had helped build. Work came to an abrupt end on 23 September 1943 when German forces and Estonian auxiliaries liquidated the ghetto.

Most members of the Paper Brigade were murdered but Kaczerginski and Sutzkever survived by fleeing to forests outside Vilnius, where they tried to join Soviet partisans. Unhappily, antisemitism was widespread among partisan groups and they received a cold welcome. In the post-war period Kaczerginski and Sutzkever returned to Vilnius, uncovered the cultural treasures the Paper Brigade had hidden, and attempted to create a Jewish Museum. They found the Soviet authorities unsympathetic. Both men fled to the United States, where they worked closely with Max Weinreich, head of YIVO in New York. Together, they sought to transfer as many rescued books as they could to the United States, out of the reach of Soviet officials, who had already allowed some of the surviving material to be destroyed. Eventually, in 1995-6, some of the hidden materials arrived at YIVO in New York. It seems reasonable to regard the work of the book smugglers as an act of moral and cultural defiance in the face of genocide. Zelig Kalmanovitch, one of the book smugglers, said in his diary that he viewed their activities as an "existential statement...that literature and culture were ultimate values" worth preserving and an "expression of faith that there would be a Jewish people after the war, which would need to repossess its cultural treasures". David Fishman, a leading historian on the activities of the book smugglers, makes a powerful case that it is right to think of the Paper Brigade's work as a form of meaningful resistance to genocide.[69]

I have suggested a number of reasons why, early in the period of Nazi occupation of Lithuania, Jews rarely resisted with physical force. Many of the natural leaders of the Jewish community had been murdered; Jews were unarmed, untrained and unsupported by external powers; there were fears of overwhelming retaliation; the not unreasonable calculation was made that if Jews worked hard, and made themselves indispensable to the German war effort, then some at least might be spared until the Allies were able to rescue those who survived; Jews in the modern world did not have a military tradition but instead tended to see the world in a pacific way: "It will not save your soul if you kill a German in revenge. It will save your soul if you read a psalm…[and]... if you observe all the commandments..."[70] Above all, perhaps, many Jews found it very difficult really to process, and to credit, the enormity of the assault launched against them and their civilization, even if, at one level, they knew what was going on.

However, Jewish attitudes about the use of force did gradually change.

There was more physical resistance in Vilnius than in Kaunas. This was partly because the area around Vilnius was more forested than the area around Kaunas, so escape to forests was logistically more straightforward, and also because about 15,000 Polish Jews had fled to Vilnius in 1940-1941, without their families. Many of these were young men, who were not constrained by fear that their acts of resistance would be met with retaliation against their family.

The first partisan organisation of the Vilnius ghetto was founded on 21 January, 1942, and was known in Yiddish as *Fareynikte Partizaner Organizatsye* or FPO. Its leaders came from very different backgrounds: there were Zionists, Communists and Bundists. Most members of the FPO were aged between 17 and 24. Two battalions were organised in the ghetto, about 240 people altogether. They conducted military training and smuggled weapons and other useful materials into the ghetto. These included Russian-language handbooks from the Russo-Finish war with instructions about manufacturing bombs and grenades. The existence of these battalions was mainly kept secret from inhabitants of the ghetto until April 1943. Strategy then changed: on 4 April, 1943 about 4,000 Jews from the small ghettos in the Vilnius region were taken to Ponary and murdered; at about the same time news arrived of the Warsaw ghetto uprising; and in July 1943 Yitzhak Wittenberg, leader of the FPO, surrendered and was then murdered. A few of the Jewish partisans left the ghetto and went to the nearby Naroch forest. The two FPO battalions felt the time for resistance had arrived. They took up arms when the Germans attempted final liquidation of the ghetto. But the FPO was utterly overwhelmed, its defence efforts largely ineffective. This plainly illustrates the quandary Jews were in. The Jewish councils had long tried to have dealings with the German (and Lithuanian) authorities but were unable to prevent liquidation of the ghetto; the Jewish combatants tried armed defence but were no match for hugely better armed German forces. This was 'the choiceless choice'. In the absence of substantial outside assistance, it seems there was no strategy Jews could have adopted which would have kept most Lithuanian Jews alive. By autumn 1943 there were, at best, only two kinds of forceful, physical resistance still open to the very few Lithuanian Jews who remained alive.

The first was to flee the ghettos, go to nearby forests and become involved in partisan activity. This was far from easy: living in forests was uncomfortable and dangerous and Jewish partisans faced hostility from much of the local population as well from some of the Russian and Lithuanian partisans. Approximately 850 Jews fled to the forests from Vilnius, 600 from Kaunas, 50 from Šiauliai and 50 from Švenčionys. The main centres of partisan activity were in the Rūdninkai and the Naroch forests. As it turned out, flight to the forests was quite an effective survival strategy. It is thought that of the 1,800 Jews who fled to the forests about

1,500 survived. This was mainly because the Jewish partisans hid from their enemies and tended to avoid direct military encounters. Instead, Jewish partisans attacked German transport units, seeking to disrupt German army supply lines. They also attacked transports carrying forced labourers, with the aim of setting them free.

The second method of resistance was to contemplate physical acts of revenge. It is an intriguing counterfactual question as to why there were relatively few physical acts of revenge by Jews against Germans in the post-war period, and what might have happened if there had been more. Most Holocaust survivors found that their willingness to participate in physical acts of revenge against their persecutors abated very quickly. In his seminal book *Night,* Elie Wiesel describes this phenomenon. He says that during his time in concentration camps he often thought about the revenge he would take on Germans. But this feeling evaporated almost as soon as he was liberated:

> Our first act as free men was to throw ourselves on the provisions. We thought of that. Not of revenge…And even when we were no longer hungry there was still no one who thought of revenge. On the following day some of the young men went to...get some potatoes and clothes...but of revenge not a sign…[71]

It is striking that after the war there were comparatively few Jewish acts of physical revenge against Germans, given that in the war many Jews in hiding seem to have kept themselves going by longing for revenge, and that there was an expectation among much of the German population that Nazi defeat would lead to fearsome revenge being exacted. Some might think that taking physical revenge would have been a 'natural' reaction, even if they do not go as far as Nietzsche in thinking that one of the main reasons for the construction of memory is in order *to make revenge possible.*[72]

Explanations as to why this desire for physical revenge evaporated quickly are, perhaps, to be found more in the realms of psychology than history. There was a desire to 'move on' and to put the horrors of the past behind them. This combined with a strong sense, rooted in Jewish humanitarian values, that the most effective revenge was to have families, to live among Jews in the land of Israel, and to perpetuate the memory of the Holocaust.[73] Many Jews thought 'justice' a more appropriate and authentically Jewish response than acts of physical 'revenge'. There seems to have been a sense that Jewish desire for revenge should be channelled down non-violent paths: many refused to buy German goods, travel to Germany, listen to Wagner's music or accept reparations from Germany; they followed efforts of the 'Nazi-hunters' with keen interest. These non-physical acts of revenge seemed safer, in that they carried little risk of retaliation, and were more aligned with Jewish values.

However, before all Jewish people could 'move on' some violent acts of revenge were contemplated. Shortly after the war ended, Abba Kovner and a handful of other survivors went to see the killing pits at Ponary just outside Vilnius and then visited the forced labour camp and death camp in Majdanek. They were appalled. Kovner recruited about 50 Holocaust survivors, mainly Jewish partisans, to an organisation called Nakam ('Revenge'). He formulated detailed principles that Nakam would be based on: he thought that Jews were not safe from another Holocaust-level genocide; that many different countries had participated in murdering six million Jews, and that the idea that so much Jewish blood could be shed without reprisal must be erased from the memory of mankind. He thought laws of the time were inadequate to punish such an extreme event as the Holocaust and he planned a huge act of revenge. In Nakam's view, the Holocaust had been made possible by the collaboration of the German people as a whole and so vengeance should also be collective.[74] The first plan, known as Plan A, was to poison the water supply in four German cities, Hamburg, Frankfurt, Munich and Nuremberg. The first three were chosen because they were large German cities and the last because it had been a Nazi party stronghold. The objective appears to have been to kill six million German civilians in revenge for the Holocaust.

Some significant steps were taken towards implementation of this plan. A member of the group, Willek Schwerzreich, an engineer from Cracow who spoke fluent German, acquired a position with the municipal water company in Nuremberg. He obtained the plan of the city's water system and control of the main water valve, and he worked out where poison should be introduced to have maximum impact. Kovner travelled to Mandatory Palestine to try to obtain the poison, disguising himself as a Jewish Brigade soldier on leave. Precisely who he met and what he did there remains obscure. Dinah Porat, a historian who has written one of the main books on this subject, says that two unequivocal conclusions can be drawn from the series of meetings Kovner held in Mandatory Palestine. "First, some of the leaders of the Yishuv and the upper echelons of the Haganah knew about Plan A. Second, none of the Yishuv leaders agreed with Kovner at any time in any way regarding Plan A. Quite the opposite was true; they did not speak about Plan A or do anything to implement it."[75] Kovner was introduced to Ephraim and Aharon Katzir, chemists at the Hebrew University of Jerusalem who persuaded the head of the chemical storage facility at the Hebrew University to eqip Kovner with poison, although it seems they did so thinking Kovner would use it to implement Plan B (discussed below), and not Plan A.[76] In December 1945, carrying his cans of poison in a duffel bag, Kovner travelled by ship to Alexandria, with false papers identifying him as a Jewish Brigade soldier returning from leave. From Alexandria, Kovner took ship for Toulon. However, he aroused suspicion and was arrested by the British authorities. Before his arrest, he threw most of his poison overboard. Other Nakam members claimed he had been betrayed by the Haganah but it is more likely he was arrested as a suspected senior member of Aliyah Bet (an organisation which arranged illegal immigration of Jews to Mandatory Palestine). He was not interrogated about Nakam and, after two months in jails in Egypt and in Palestine, he was released.

The significance of Nakam's Plan A is that substantial steps were taken towards implementing it. Had things turned out slightly differently and, in particular, had Kovner not been arrested, then it is conceivable that the plan might have succeeded. The consequences of that are a matter for speculation. Perhaps the post-war world would have been more wary of engaging in anti-Israeli and antisemitic activity; perhaps it would have acted as a deterrent for those considering other genocides; but perhaps, on the other hand, it would have re-doubled German fury against Jews and incited antisemites everywhere. What is clear is that leaders of the Jewish community in Mandatory Palestine, and elsewhere, were almost universally opposed to plans for massive acts of physical revenge such as Nakam's Plan A. Most historians have characterised Kovner's obsession for revenge as evidence of psychological trauma and as conduct which "raised doubts about the moral character of a man who held himself and others to high moral standards".[77] Kovner did not return to Plan A, or to any other plan of comparable scale, and after about two months in jails in Egypt and in Palestine his involvement in Nakam came to an end.[78]

Nakam also had a Plan B. This was to poison 12,000-15,000 prisoners, mainly former SS officers and prominent Nazis, imprisoned by the United States at the Langwasser Internment camp near Nuremberg. Bread for the camp came from a single bakery in Nuremberg, the *Konsum-Genossenschaftsbackerei*. Six members of Nakam managed to obtain employment there. They smuggled arsenic into the bakery and, on the evening of Saturday 13 April, 1946, painted arsenic onto the under-side of some 3,000 loaves of black bread. Black bread was chosen because Nakam was anxious not to poison any of the American guards who they knew only ate specially issued white bread; black bread was just eaten by the German prisoners. On 23 April, 1946 *The New York Times* reported that 2,283 German prisoners of war had fallen ill from poisoning, 207 of whom had been hospitalised and were seriously ill. None of these are thought to have died, but the reasons they did not do so remain unclear. It seems there was sufficient arsenic in the bakery to kill 60,000 people. It may be that members of Nakam spread the arsenic poison too thinly on the loaves or, alternatively, that the prisoners became suspicious their bread had been poisoned and therefore ate very little of it. In any event, nobody died and Nakam considered Plan B a failure. In effect, this marked the end of their efforts to exact physical revenge on Germans and, as has been said, other acts of physical revenge after that time were very few and far between.[79]

One is left with the overwhelming impression that there was little that most Lithuanian Jews could have done to avoid the almost total destruction of them and their world. Both the Jewish communal leadership and individual Jews faced 'choiceless choices'. The handful of Jews who survived did so more by luck than anything else. For a variety of reasons, physical resistance was almost impossible. But there was a quiet dignity about the inner spiritual and cultural resistance in which many engaged and which was firmly rooted in Jewish religious values and history.

When one considers the role of 'bystanders' in the Holocaust in Lithuania, some of the fundamental questions are: which states, organisations and individuals might have come to the aid of the Jews in their hour of need but declined to do so, or failed to do so effectively, and what were the reasons for this failure? Those who might have helped include: the Allied powers (the United States, Great Britain and the Soviet Union); the neutral powers (Portugal, Spain, Turkey, Sweden and Switzerland); Church authorities, including the Vatican; and individuals in close proximity to Jews in need of help, but who failed to provide it.

The kind of assistance which the United States and Great Britain might have provided changed over time. From January 1933, when the Nazis came to power, until September 1939, when Germany invaded Poland, the most effective help might have been to permit Lithuanian Jews to migrate to their countries. But the doors for would-be migrants were rather firmly closed. Before 1905 Britain had very few restrictions on immigration. Controls introduced in 1793, at the time of the Napoleonic wars, had been repealed in 1836. Between then and 1905 there was no immigration control apart from a loosely policed system of registration on entry. The Aliens Act 1905, while not explicitly a measure to control immigration of eastern European

Jews, was in effect designed to do just that. Many such would-be immigrants were categorised as 'undesirable'.

There was further substantial tightening of controls during the First World War. By 1933, immigration to Britain was very difficult. Government policy was framed against a background of severe economic depression and mass unemployment along with a fear that immigration would exacerbate racial tensions. Jews in German controlled lands were desperate to leave. In the mid 1930s the British government was prepared to admit nurses and domestic servants, a policy which led to about 20,000 young middle-class Jewish women from Nazi occupied lands re-characterising themselves as maids. After Kristallnacht the British government was also prepared to admit a relatively small number of Jewish children from Germany, but without their parents. In all, about 70,000 Jews were admitted to Britain during the 1930s, overwhelmingly from German, Austrian and Czech lands.

Immigration to the United States was also difficult. It had an elaborate system for the admission of immigrants, based on quotas by country of birth. Additionally, regulations adopted by President Hoover during the economic depression provided that visas were only to be given to those not likely to become a charge on public funds. In most cases, this meant the would-be immigrant needed to obtain an affidavit from a family member willing to promise to provide financial support, should this be necessary. In short, then, it was very difficult for Lithuanian Jews to migrate to Great Britain or to the United States between January 1933 and September 1939 because, against a backdrop of economic hardship, immigration controls were very tight. Jews fleeing German controlled territory were marginally more likely to be admitted, both because they tended to be better off and better educated and also because they were thought more in need of rescue. In the 1930s few appreciated that Nazi Germany posed an existential threat to Lithuanian Jewry.

After the outbreak of war in September 1939 it became even more difficult for would-be Jewish emigrants to reach Britain or the United States. The logistics of getting to Britain or the United States were almost insuperable. Moreover, British and American official attitudes towards Jewish refugees became still harder. There was fear that spies might enter Britain and America, disguised as refugees, a fear which led Britain to intern many pre-war Jewish refugees on the Isle of Man. There was also fear that if Britain or America expressed willingness to accept some Jews then larger numbers of Jews would be 'dumped' on their shores. There was also concern that overt acts of support for the Jewish community in Europe would play into the Nazi narrative that the western allies were controlled by Jews and doing the bidding of a secret and sinister Jewish cabal.[80]

Once war broke out, other countries might have assisted Jews by issuing them with visas. The conduct of Chiune Sugihara shows what might have been done more widely. Sugihara was the vice-consul of the Japanese Consulate in Kaunas. His duties were to report on Soviet and German troop movements and to try to ascertain whether Germany planned to attack the Soviet Union. When the Soviet Union occupied Lithuania in summer 1940 Lithuanian Jews became Soviet citizens. This made it all but impossible for them to leave for anywhere other than for other parts of the Soviet Union. However, Polish Jews who had fled to Lithuania after the Nazi invasion of Poland in September 1939 did not automatically become Soviet citizens. Soviet authorities gave them the right to apply for Soviet citizenship. Most did so, but about 4,000-5,000 declined to apply to become Soviet citizens, for a variety of reasons, but mainly because they were religiously devout or because they were strongly Zionist. The only way for such people to escape this trap was to obtain permission to leave the Soviet Union in transit to somewhere else. The Dutch consul in Kaunas, Jan Zwartendijk, agreed that these Polish Jews living in Lithuania could say that Curacao and Surinam, Dutch colonies in the Caribbean, was their final destination. Sugihara decided to issue Japanese transit visas to enable these Jews to leave. He did this on his own initiative, and without the authority of the Japanese government. With the Dutch confirmation of the final destination, the Japanese transit visa and payment in US Dollars to Intourist (the Soviet travel agency), Soviet transit visas could also be obtained. By issuing Japanese transit visas, Sugihara helped over 2,000 Polish Jewish refugees leave Soviet-occupied Lithuania. Indeed, we know that 2,180 Jews left Lithuania in the summer of 1940, reaching the Japanese city of Kobe.[81] Most, but not all, of these Jews would have travelled on Japanese transit visas issued by Sugihara.

There are a number of important points to make about the way Sugihara behaved: first, it is important to acknowledge that at the time he issued the transit visas he had no means of knowing that Lithuania would be invaded by Nazi Germany and that most of its Jewish population would be murdered. But, he was alive to the desperate plight of Polish Jews who had fled to Lithuania, who were clearly deeply fearful of Nazi Germany, having already fled the Nazi invasion of Poland. Secondly, while the issue of about 2,000 transit visas may appear relatively modest it has been estimated by the Simon Wiesenthal Centre that about 40,000 people alive today would not be alive but for the issue of those visas. Thirdly, Sugihara's own account, as well as the observations of those who knew him, suggest his primary motivations were human sympathy and compassion. In 1985 Sugihara explained:

> People in Tokyo were not united. I felt it silly to deal with them. So, I made up my mind not to wait for their reply. I knew that somebody would surely complain about me in the future. But I myself thought this would be the right thing to do. There is nothing wrong in saving many people's lives…The spirit of humanity, philanthropy…neighbourly friendship…with this spirit I ventured to do what I did…[82]

Sugihara's conduct is striking because it stands in stark contrast to the general reluctance of most governments and members of the diplomatic community to assist Jews in Lithuania, as elsewhere in Nazi-occupied Europe, in the period between September 1939 and June 1941.

The scope for governments and for the diplomatic community to assist Jews in Lithuania was curtailed yet further following the German invasion of the Soviet Union in June 1941. Reports of what the Nazis and their collaborators were doing to Jews in the east did reach western governments, albeit piecemeal and slowly, during the remainder of the war. There were a number of notable occasions when graphic details were communicated to western governments. On 12 September, 1941 British intelligence informed Winston Churchill that "the [German] Police are killing all Jews that fall into their hands." In August 1942 Gerhart Riegner, who worked for the World Jewish Congress in Geneva, informed the US State Department and the British Foreign Office that he had information that Nazi Germany was planning to murder millions of European Jews. In October 1942, Jan Karski, a Pole, was taken to the Warsaw ghetto. There, he saw what he described as "a people expiring, breathing its last before my eyes".[83] He became a kind of courier between the Polish underground and the Polish government in exile. He arrived in Britain in November 1942 before travelling on to the United States, where he remained. He met President Roosevelt, to whom he communicated a graphic account of the annihilation of Jews in eastern Europe. On 10 April, 1944 two Slovak Jews, Rudolf Vrba and Alfred Wetzler, escaped from Auschwitz and prepared a detailed report about what was happening there. This report was circulated to allied governments and to a number of prominent figures.[84]

From these and other sources, allied governments were well aware of the campaign of mass murder being conducted by Nazi Germany and its collaborators against Jews in eastern Europe. At different times, Jewish organisations suggested various steps that allied governments might have taken: they could have bombed German cities, accompanying the bombing campaign with a leaflet drop making very clear to the German population what their government was doing to Jews in eastern Europe and explaining that allied action was in direct retaliation for it; they could have taken Germans in western countries hostage, demanding that the campaign of mass murder cease and that, if it did not, retaliation would be taken against the hostages; they could have tried to make sure that Jews in eastern Europe were fully informed of what the Nazis and their collaborators were doing to other Jews in eastern Europe so that Jews did not go ignorantly to their deaths or unwittingly facilitate their own destruction; and they could have bombed centres of mass murder, including Auschwitz, and the railway tracks leading to them.[85]

The reasons why Allied governments did not do more to try to help the persecuted Jews of eastern Europe are complicated: undoubtedly, there were considerable practical obstacles to providing substantial help. There were difficulties in understanding what was really happening to the Jews of eastern Europe; difficulties in putting special operations forces into relevant areas; and difficulties in accurately bombing sites far removed from allied airforces' home bases, without killing large numbers of innocents. But there was also, within the British Foreign Office and within the U.S. State Department, a culture which was often distinctly cool towards the notion of assisting Jews. There were various reasons for this: policy considerations involving Palestine and the Arabs; a legalistic concern about the status of Jewish refugees as enemy aliens; obsessive concern about the possibility of planted German spies among the refugees; and a desire to concentrate on the single objective of winning the war. But, it is difficult to avoid the conclusion that there was also some antisemitism at work. In September 1944, for example, and in response to a rather desperate plea by a Jewish leader, a Foreign Office official noted: "In my opinion, a disproportionate amount of the time of this office is wasted on dealing with these wailing Jews." What makes this comment especially deplorable is that it was made at a time when the full facts of what was happening at Auschwitz were well known to the Foreign Office.[86]

A final but important reason for the Allies' failure to provide meaningful support to the Jews of eastern Europe was the all too human difficulty which these governments faced in truly absorbing the scale of what was taking place. They may have understood at one level what was going on, but could not really process the magnitude of it. The point is well made by William J. Casey, a U.S. naval lieutenant in the Office of Strategic Services, who was stationed in London from 1943:

> We knew in a general way that Jews were being persecuted, that they were brought to camps, and that brutality and murder took place at these camps. But few if any comprehended the appalling magnitude of it. It wasn't sufficiently real to stand out from the general brutality and slaughter which is war…such reports as we did receive were shunted aside because of the official policy in Washington and London to concentrate exclusively on the defeat of the enemy.[87]

It is arguable that Christian religious authorities, particularly in the Catholic church, were another kind of 'bystander'. Catholic church authorities might have spoken up more forcefully to protest against the persecution and murder of Jews. Controversy centres on the relative silence of Pope Pius X11 during the Holocaust. Calm discussion of this subject was made difficult by the fact that, for a long time, much relevant evidence was unavailable. Vatican archives were sealed on the death of Pope Pius X11 in 1958 and only made accessible to researchers in March 2020. Scholars have now trawled through those archives. The results are revealing.[88]

The first question is whether the Pope actually knew what was happening to Jews during the war. It is true that the murder of many Lithuanian Jews took place so quickly after the German invasion of June 1941 that details about the mass murder arrived in the West only after many Lithuanian Jews had already been killed. However, it is now very clear that, in addition to information about the Holocaust which was in the public domain, the Pope also received a series of detailed confidential briefings about the mass murder of Jews in Nazi occupied eastern Europe. For example, in October 1941 the Nuncio in Bratislava passed on a report from the Bishop in charge of Slovakia's military chaplains. The Bishop reported: "The Jews are simply being shot…systematically murdered, without distinction of sex or age."[89] In November 1941 Pope Pius X11 met Father Pirro Scavizzi, an Italian military chaplain, who gave him a detailed eye-witness account of the mass murder of Jews on the Eastern Front. In January 1942 Pius X11 met Father Scavizzi again, following another visit he made to the Eastern Front. The Father gave Pius X11 a further full and hair-raising account of what he had seen. He said: "It is clear that it is the government of occupation's intention to eliminate as many Jews as possible".[90]

A number of other detailed, confidential accounts about the Holocaust were communicated personally to the Pope. These included a report from the Archbishop of the Ukrainian Greek Catholic Church in August 1942; a report from President Roosevelt's envoy, Myron Taylor, in September 1942, and a report from Italian businessman Signor Malvezzi in September 1942.

And in December 1942 the British envoy to the Vatican, Francis D'Arcy Osborne, sent the Pope a detailed memorandum about the Holocaust which, among other things, declared "One out of three million Jews in Poland have already been murdered… the Archbishop of York declares that 'We are witnessing the deliberate massacre of a nation'".[91] There can be no serious doubt but that from autumn 1941 Pope Pius X11 was very fully informed about the Holocaust, indeed one might suspect he was better informed about it than almost anyone else.

As the Holocaust unfolded there were many pleas from Allied leaders, from Catholics and Jews, for Pope Pius X11 to speak up and unequivocally denounce what was happening. For example, on 12 September 1942 the Belgian and Polish ambassadors went to the Apostolic Palace to issue a joint appeal to the Pope to speak up. Representatives of other German-occupied lands, including the Netherlands, Norway, Czechoslovakia and Yugoslavia supported this message. Osborne, the British envoy, told the Pope: "A policy of silence in regard to such offences against the conscience of the world must necessarily involve a renunciation of moral leadership and a consequent atrophy of the influence and authority of the Vatican". The American envoy, Harold Tittman, sent a similar appeal on behalf of the American government. These appeals came from so many different parts of the world that Monsignor Tardini, who served in the Vatican Secretariat and worked closely with Pope Pius X11, was moved to append a rather disconsolate handwritten marginal note in the files at the end of September 1942: "Even Peru!" [92]

Despite these many appeals, Pope Pius X11 never referred specifically in public to the persecution or mass murder of the Jews during the war years. The nearest he came to it was in his Christmas radio broadcast in December 1942. In a rather well-buried passage on the twenty-fourth page of his text the Pope lamented the "hundreds of thousands of people who, through no fault of their own, and solely because of their nation or race have been condemned to death or progressive extinction." The Pope did not specifically refer to Jews as victims.

In order to understand the very limited nature of what the Pope said about the Holocaust, as it was unfolding, it is important to consider some of the steps which, at least in theory, he might have taken, but decided not to take. He could have excommunicated Hitler and other leaders of the Nazi regime. This course of action was urged upon him. In May 1940, a group of women styling themselves "The Catholic women of Italy" wrote to him to say: "In past ages, the Holy Pontiffs excommunicated monarchs and potentates many times solely for having rebelled gainst the sacred laws of the church. Today…then, excommunicate these monsters or it will be too late."[93] It was also open to the Pope to excommunicate other leaders. For example, he could have excommunicated Joseph Tiso, a Catholic priest who, from 1939, was president of the Slovak Republic. In March 1942 the Papal Nuncio in Bratislava reported to the Pope that Tiso planned the "imminent mass deportation of all the Slovakian Jews in Galicia and the Lublin region regardless of age, sex and religion." Tiso ordered this deportation on his own initiative, not at the direct command of the Nazis. The Papal Nuncio in Bratislava reported to the Pope that when he (the Nuncio) protested to Tiso, Tiso "dared to say (he who makes such a show of his Catholicism) that he does not see in it anything inhumane or anti-Christian".[94] The Pope could also have excommunicated Catholics he knew to have committed acts of atrocity. Indeed, the Pope briefly contemplated this course of action during and after his conversations with Scavizzi, but decided against it because, so he said, it would not stop the slaughter and might spur even greater anger against Jews.[95] A further course of action the Pope could have taken would have been to issue a papal encyclical. Indeed, his predecessor, Pope Pius X1, was preparing an encyclical before his death in February 1939. Shortly after Hitler's visit to Rome in spring 1938 Pope Pius X1 decided there should be an encyclical denouncing Nazi racism and antisemitism. He asked John LaFarge, an American Jesuit, to draft it. But the Jesuit superior general, Wlodimir Ledóchowski, thought by many to be a strident antisemite, did all he could to sabotage it. The encyclical only arrived in draft on the Pope's desk in January 1939. It was accompanied by a cover note from the Jesuit superior general, urging the Pope not to issue it.[96] Pope Pius X1 died the following month, before the draft encyclical was in final form. Nonetheless, this episode suggests that the issue of a papal encyclical condemning antisemitism was a course of action open to Pope Pius X11. It was a policy pursued, but not concluded, by his immediate predecessor. Pope Pius X11 could also have spoken firmly against antisemitism, perhaps to a substantial audience of bishops gathered in St. Peter's Basilica. If wartime travel difficulties made such a gathering impractical, the Vatican printing office could have printed and arranged circulation of copies of what the Pope would have said. Again, the conduct of Pius X11's predecessor offers an intriguing precedent. Pope Pius X1 invited three hundred bishops to Rome to celebrate the tenth anniversary of the Lateran Accords on 11 February 1939. Pius X1 intended to use that occasion to make a forceful denunciation of Fascism. However, on 6 February 1939 Pope Pius X1 became ill and was confined to bed. He then proposed that a printed version of what he would have said in the basilica should be circulated. On 10 February 1939 Pope Pius X1 died. His intended denunciation of Fascism did not see the light of day.

One can only speculate about what might have happened if Pope Pius X11 had forcefully denounced the persecution and mass murder of Jews, using a combination of the tools at his command: excommunication, papal encyclicals and public statements. This is the realm of counterfactual history, which the wise enter with caution. Sometimes, however, one can only appreciate the full significance of not doing something (in this case, the Pope unequivocally denouncing the mass murder of Europe's Jews) by contemplating what might have happened if that thing had been done. It is very possible that, if the Pope had clearly denounced the Holocaust as it was taking place, some Catholics, and some others, would have been deterred from participating, directly or indirectly, in murdering Jews and that many Jews would have been more alerted to the nature and scale of the mass murder being perpetrated upon them and would not unwittingly have done things which made it easier for their murderers to kill them. In this context, it is powerfully suggestive that Rudolf Vrba and Fred Wetzler, the first Jews to escape from Auschwitz and provide a full report about what was happening there, were strongly motivated by the belief that if international figures of moral authority, such as the Pope, publicised and condemned what was happening in Auschwitz then, while Jews would still find active resistance difficult, they would at least be fully alerted. They might well panic, but they would not innocently and meekly board trains "for the east", and this would make their mass murder in Auschwitz more difficult.[97]

The fundamental question is why the Pope chose not to denounce the Holocaust as it was taking place. The first part of the answer is to do with the character of the man. Many observers thought he lacked a strong personality. Even before Eugenio Pacelli became Pope Pius X11 the Spanish ambassador to the Vatican remarked "he is completely devoid of will and character". Following the Nazi invasion of Poland the Polish ambassador to the Holy See thought "he carried caution and impartiality to a point approaching pusillanimity and condonation". Moreover, the Pope liked Germany. He had spent a number of years there in the inter-war years. He spoke German fluently and had deeply imbibed its culture. He often told visitors how much he had enjoyed his time living in Germany. For example, the Pope met German foreign minister, Joachim von Ribbentrop, in his private library in the Vatican in March 1940. After Ribbentrop conveyed personal greetings from Hitler, the Pope spoke expansively about his many years in Germany, describing them as perhaps the happiest in his life. The

Pope had a tendency to speak in a florid style, always trying to find balance, avoiding clear and direct speech. What he said often went over the heads of his audience. He sought to disguise his personal political views, but those who knew him well thought him politically on the right. Wladmir d'Ormesson, French emissary to the Papacy until October 1940, wrote a report on his departure from office in which he said "The Pope seems to me above all to be a conservative of a monarchical stamp."[98]

Another suggested explanation for the Pope's reluctance to speak out against the Holocaust is that his advisers were fearful that some of the reports he received had not been verified and might be exaggerated. For example, in October 1942 Monsignor Angelo Dell'Acqua, who the Pope treated as his expert on Jewish questions, counselled the Pope against making a response to U.S. envoy Myron Taylor's request for a papal condemnation of atrocities against Jews. He said: "It is necessary to be certain that [the news contained in Ambassador Taylor's letter] corresponds to the truth, because exaggeration comes easily for the Jews." When, in December 1942, D'Arcy Osborne asked Monsignor Tardini to try to persuade the Pope to denounce the Holocaust he was met by the argument that the Pope should remain silent because papal authorities had not been able to verify the alleged atrocities. [99] Such justifications for the Pope's reluctance to speak out are rather unconvincing. The Pope had received so many accounts of mass murder of Jews, many of them from reputable sources, that even if some details were unverified or exaggerated, the basic facts of what was happening were not in serious doubt.

A part of the problem was that the culture among many senior figures in the Vatican was unsympathetic to Jews. One small example among many: in March 1943 Angelo Roncalli (who later became Pope John XX111) was papal delegate to Istanbul. He sent a telegram to the Vatican indicating that the 20,000 Jews still alive in Slovakia risked deportation to Poland at the end of the month. Could the Pope please intervene with the head of the Slovakian government (the Roman Catholic priest, Jozef Tiso) requesting that 1,000 Jewish children be permitted to migrate to Palestine? They would do this with authorisation from the British, and with permision to transit through Turkey. When Roncalli's request reached the Vatican it was passed to Monsignor Di Meglio to evaluate. His lengthy report, which was sent to the Pope, considers why, until recently, Jews had been disinclined to settle in Palestine:

> It is known that most Jews are mainly dedicated to industry and… commerce. This commerce remains quite profitable for them when

> they find themselves living among Christians. If, on the contrary... the Jews come together, one has an enormous gathering in of ... swindlers, while lacking those to be swindled. Therefore, most Jews had no desire to migrate to Palestine.[100]

Such was the character and quality of some of the advice received by the Pope.

The Vatican may have been nervous about criticising Fascist mistreatment of Jews because it was sensitive to accusations of hypocrisy stemming from the Vatican's historic treatment of Rome's Jews. Jews had lived in Rome for 2,000 years, but their living conditions had taken a serious turn for the worse in the mid-sixteenth century. In 1555, Pope Paul 1V issued the papal bull *Cum nimis absurdum*. This mandated that Jews live in a walled ghetto (the construction of which they had to pay for), and into which they were locked at night. They were subject to laws designed to limit contact with Christian neighbours. They had to wear a distinguishing yellow hat and badge and were forbidden to trade in anything other than food and second-hand clothes. They were required to attend conversionary sermons at a nearby Catholic church. If Jewish children were seized and baptised they could then not be raised as Jews and were taken from their families.[101] These draconian anti-Jewish laws only came to an end with the conquest of the Papal States by Italian military forces in 1870. This history made some papal advisers think it would be hypocritical for the Papacy to denounce Fascist mistreatment of Jews and this was a sensitivity which some leading Fascists exploited aggressively. For example, in July 1942, Roberto Farinacci, a long-standing member of the Grand Council of Fascism, had his newspaper *Il Regime Fascista* pronounce that: "We, Fascist Catholics, are anti-Jewish because we have learned to combat these enemies of Christian civilization from the Doctors and Saints of the Church..."[102]

Opinions about the wartime conduct of Pope Pius X11 are sharply divided. His defenders argue that he found himself in a very delicate diplomatic position. They emphasise that he had a great responsibility to protect the interests of the Papacy and the Catholic church and that he did this with considerable skill. This line of argument suggests the Pope's reluctance to speak out against the Holocaust was a consequence of this prudence and diplomatic skill. He was careful to say that it was not the role of the Papacy to involve itself in temporal affairs. During the first part of the war, when German victory seemed probable, it was sensible for him to take care not to fall out with the likely victors. It was right that he was mindful of the responsibility he bore towards the many Catholics in

German-speaking lands, whose way of life he thought threatened by anti-Catholic tendencies in parts of the Nazi hierarchy. As the war progressed, the Pope became increasingly concerned that German armies might invade the Vatican, depose him, and replace him by someone more pliant. During the later stages of the war, when Allied victory seemed likely, the Pope's overriding concern was that Soviet Communism should not take over western Europe and pursue vigorously anti-Catholic policies. By being scrupulously careful not to fall out with the Fascist regimes, the Pope may also have hoped to place himself in the role of possible peacemaker. In other words, the Pope's many defenders emphasise that he trod a very careful diplomatic path, ever mindful of the interests of the Catholic church, and that he played a difficult hand with considerable skill. Pope Pius X11 is now on the path to sainthood. He was declared a 'Servant of God' in 1990 and 'Venerable' in 2009. He will be beatified when the Vatican is able to attribute one scientifically inexplicable miracle to Pius X11's intercession. A second miracle will result in canonisation (sainthood).

Those who criticise Pope Pius X11's failure to speak against the Holocaust acknowledge the sensitivities of his diplomatic position, but think he showed a serious failure of leadership. It might be said that, as head of a great world religion, his paramount task in dark times was to provide clear moral guidance. Many contemporaries were exasperated by his failure to do this. When D'Arcy Osborne, Britain's envoy to the Vatican, submitted a report to London in July 1942, a Foreign office official appended a handwritten note to the report, which reads: "Papal timidity becomes ever more blatantly despicable."[103] Many felt the Pope was insufficiently understanding that Jews faced an existential crisis, and suspected a lack of sympathy towards Jews, rooted in ancient religious antagonisms. Many things fed into this sense that there was a coldness, even hostility, towards them. There was the contrast between his silence about the Holocaust and his willingness to speak up about other moral questions. He was especially vexed by womens' and girls' immodest dress. In May 1941 he made a speech to members of the Girls Catholic Association in which he told them it was crucial for them to "combat the dangers of immorality in the areas of women's fashion, sport, hygiene, social relations and entertainment".[104] There was the fact that the Pope continued to refrain from public condemnation of the Holocaust even when atrocities towards Jews were taking place right in front of him. In October 1943, some 1,259 Jews of Rome were rounded up and sent to the military college compound, which was located just outside the walls of the Vatican. This was no more than a few hundred metres from where the Pope resided. Many were also unimpressed that such private interventions as the Pope made were invariably directed towards trying to protect Jews who had been baptised as Christians, but not towards protecting Jews. As a result of Papal interventions with the Nazi authorities, a small number of Rome's baptised Jews (and an even smaller number of Jews married to Christians) were released. But, on 18 October, 1943, 1,007 Jews of Rome were transported by trucks from the military college compound through the streets of Rome to Tiburtina train station, and thence to Auschwitz.

A feeling that there was coolness, even hostility, from the Vatican towards Jews persisted into the post-war world. A month after Rome's liberation, Palestine's two chief Rabbis sought an urgent audience with Pope Pius X11 to discuss the desperate plight of Europe's remaining Jews. They were to be disappointed. A note on the Vatican file reads: "As for the audience requested by Chief Rabbi Herzog of Jerusalem, the decision of the Holy Father is this: 'He believes it well not to respond.' "[105] Post-war, many observers were concerned by the fact that senior bishops of the Catholic church, particularly Alois Hudal, were involved in 'the Ratline', a secret network which helped prominent Nazis escape Europe for Latin America.[106] It is thought that the escapes of Josef Mengele, Alois Brunner and Adolf Eichmann were all facilitated by the Ratline. Whether Pope Pius X11 was involved, albeit indirectly, with Hudal's Ratline activity is not clear, but some researchers suspect he may have been.[107] It does seem clear that the Papacy was involved with questions about whether Jewish children given to Catholics for safekeeping during the war years, and baptised by them, should be returned to Jewish families post-war. There was a cause célèbre concerning two French Jewish boys, Robert and Gerald Finaly. David Kertzer, who has read widely in the recently opened Vatican archives says:

> the documents show occasional allusions by the Pope to the suffering recently experienced by the Jewish people… [but] ...what comes through is that the prerogatives of the Catholic church mattered above all else: that, according to church doctrine, baptism, even against the family's wishes, gave the church the right to claim the children. This was what motivated the monks and nuns who moved the boys around, under fictitious names, from one hiding place to another...[108]

With some justification, many feel that, both during and after the war, the Pope failed firmly and unequivocally to condemn the persecution and mass murder of Europe's Jews. His diplomacy may have helped the papacy navigate through difficult times but many regard his reluctance to speak up as a serious failure of moral leadership.

The Pope's silence almost certainly influenced the conduct of Catholic clergy in Lithuania. Post-war, some Lithuanian priests sought to explain and excuse their conduct on the basis that the Vatican had not provided clear instructions as to what to do. One might find such excuses unconvincing. They may be a way of externalising guilt, of distancing themselves from accepting responsibility. One would like to think a priest should not need to be told that one does not kill innocent people and steal their property because they have different beliefs. Nonetheless, strong papal leadership might have stiffened the resolve of Lithuanian clergy. Again this is counterfactual, but if the Pope had categorically denounced the atrocities against Jews it is probable that Lithuanian priests would more firmly have told Lithuanians they must behave respectfully towards their Jewish neighbours; they might have hidden more Jews, and encouraged other locals to hide more Jews, and they might have sought to protect more Jews by helping them pretend they were Christians, either by providing Jewish children with counterfeit birth certificates or by 'converting' them.

Some Lithuanian priests, such as Jonas Gilys of Varėna, were outspoken in supporting Jews. On 9 September 1941 Gilys went to the Lithuanian police precinct in Varėna and asked to speak with Jews who had been arrested. Permission was denied, but he went anyway. Gilys offered to convert arrested Jews to Christianity. Some agreed, and were saved. On 14 September, 1941 Gilys preached in his church. Unknown to him, Lithuanian police were listening. The local police report provides a record of what he said:

> Human beings are being beaten by uniformed Lithuanians. Old people, pregnant women are pushed around and the forests of Varėna are soaked in the blood of innocent people. They suffered horribly. Even before their blood had dried, their property was plundered.[109]

However, the most senior churchmen in Lithuania were not helpful to Jews. The highest representative of the church in Lithuania was Archbishop Juozapas Skvireckas. His deputy was Bishop Vincentas Brizgys. In late June 1941 they, and other prominent Lithuanian church leaders, sent Hitler a congratulatory telegram. Shortly afterwards former Prime Minister Ambrazevičius came to see Skvireckas and asked him to make a public statement regarding the persecution of the Jews but Skvireckas and Brizgys declined to intervene. A little later, a Jewish delegation met Skvireckas and asked him to urge Catholics to desist from participating in the murder of Jews. The archbishop responded that he could only weep and pray, but the Church could not help.[110] Skvireckas's diary entry for 30 June, 1941 provides an insight into his thinking:

> The thoughts of *Mein Kampf* concerning the poisonous Bolshevist influence exercised by Jews on the nations of the world are worthy of note. The ideas are interesting indeed. They...present an insight into reality…this testifies to the correctness of his [Hitler's] views.[111]

A report by Karl Jäger suggests that the Bishop of Kaunas, Brizgys, forbade all clergymen to help Jews in any way at all. And Brizgys is thought to have collaborated with the Holocaust in Lithuania in a number of other ways, including by writing antisemitic tracts and by authorising priests to continue performing sacramental rites for members of Lithuanian partisan units.

It seems that attitudes of senior Catholic clergy towards Jews became somewhat more sympathetic from 1943 onwards. The change probably reflects growing disillusion with the reality of German occupation of Lithuania, together with a growing understanding that Germany might lose the war. From this time, Bishop Brizgys began to support very discreet efforts to conceal Jewish children.

In the absence of clear moral leadership from the Archbishop and the Bishop, the reactions of local parish priests to massacres of Jews were varied and complex. We know a little about what happened in the Telšiai district, the administrative district in which Pikeliai is located. Some priests, including one Valentinas Jadversis, seem to have instigated pillaging, humiliation and killing. Others tried to keep out of the way, claiming they were ill or that their rescue efforts were too late. There were a small number of righteous priests who, at considerable personal cost, tried to resist the murderous policies. For example, a priest called Dambrauskas tried to prevent the killing of Jews in Alsėdžiai. Lithuanian nationalists retaliated by killing 30 Jewish women and children outside his home and burying them on his property. Other priests seemed positively to delight in Jewish suffering. Chana Golenbo describes what happened in Nevarėnai:

> As the Jews were taken away from the townlet, the priest stood laughing near the partisans. Brencys [a farmer in Nevarėnai] assured the priest that he was cleaning the townlet's streets of the Jewish garbage. The priest was greatly pleased with the expression and burst out laughing.[112]

In recent years, the Lithuanian Catholic church has come to recognise that there were serious shortcomings in its wartime conduct. On 14 April, 2000, on the occasion of a day of repentance and apology, Archbishop Sladkevičius wrote a letter in which he said: "During the war years some of the Church's children failed to show enough love to persecuted Jews or take all possible measures to protect them...The Church's memories are burdened with all representations of anti-Semitism."[113]

The term 'bystander' also includes individual Lithuanians who found themselves in close proximity to Jews who were being persecuted. These individuals might have intervened to help the Jewish person, or persons, being victimised, but for various reasons chose not to do so. As Mary Fulbrook says, "the implication is that the bystander has a moral duty to act in some way on behalf of the victim".[114] Often the role of being a bystander was fleeting: the opportunity for intervention arose quickly, and then disappeared. Sometimes there was an important difference between the outward demeanour of the bystander, which might have given the impression that the bystander was distanced and callous, and the true inner feelings of the bystander, which may have contained elements, perhaps substantial elements, of sympathy for the victim.

There was a complex variety of reasons why individual Lithuanians did not intervene to help their Jewish neighbours in their hour of need: they may have been antisemitic; they may have been blinded by ideology, or simply regarded Jews as 'the other'; they may have thought Jews were collectively responsible for the hardships of the period of Soviet occupation and taken pleasure in the misfortune of Jews; they may have been attracted by the opportunity to steal Jewish possessions, occupy Jewish homes and rape Jewish women; they may have thought it politic to ingratiate themselves with the Germans; they may have been drunk or just very simple people who could not easily distinguish right from wrong; they may have been terrified of the risk of reprisals against them or calculated that other people near them would have been likely to react adversely had they come to the support of Jews. In other words, to the extent that they thought about this at all, the bystander found there was a reason of some kind which overrode any moral imperative they might have felt to come to the aid of those in need.[115]

This is not to deny or belittle the assistance that some individual Lithuanians did provide to Jews. The Israeli Holocaust Museum, Yad Vashem, has recognised more than 720 Lithuanian gentiles as 'Righteous among the Nations' for their help in sheltering Jews during the war-time years. This number almost certainly understates the extent of help actually provided by Lithuanians to Jews because many cases were not reported. A disproportionate amount of the help provided was to Jewish children. Precise numbers do not exist, but it is estimated that between 180 and 400 Kaunas Ghetto children were successfully hidden with the help of local Lithuanians, and survived the Holocaust.[116] Other Lithuanians who helped Jews survive include Bronius Gotautas, a monk, and Jouzas Striapis of Sarneliai who was instrumental, with family and friends, in concealing and caring for almost 40 Jews, including women and children, and most of whom survived. Onna Shumaite, librarian at the University of Vilnius, was also involved in clandestine activity to assist Jews.[117]

The motivations of those Lithuanians who did assist Jews were very varied. Some were motivated by a strong sense of religious obligation. Others were simply people of very kindly disposition. Some, including the librarian of Vilnius University, felt that it was incumbent on educated people to be respectful of those who came from a background different from their own. Some Lithuanians helped particular Jews because they had been on close terms with them pre-war, either because they had business connections with them or because they were neighbours and felt a sense of obligation to them. And some motivations contained a substantial element of self-interest. There were Lithuanans who assisted Jews in return for payment and who stopped their support when Jews became unable to continue payment. Other Lithuanians were willing to shelter young Jewish children, but not Jewish adults, because they thought it safer to shelter children, or that they might perform a good deed by having the children baptised, or because they were unable to have children of their own and saw an opportunity to acquire young children and bring them up in their own way. Some who helped Jews derived a certain pleasure from the sense of control they acquired over the lives of others, whether protecting or betraying them, and particularly if those Jews, or others like them, had exercised a degree of authority over them in the pre-war period.

Given the circumstances in which Jews found themselves in war-time Lithuania it is arguable that what might have made a difference, and enabled more Jews to survive, would have been substantial assistance from non-Jews. Such help might have come from foreign governments, religious authorities, the local non-Jewish population or some combination of these. In the event, relatively little help was forthcoming. This general reluctance of the bystander to intervene goes a considerable way towards explaining how the Holocaust happened in Lithuania.

Notes

1 Raul Hilberg, *Perpetrators, Victims, Bystanders: The Jewish Catastrophe, 1933-1945* (Aaron Asher Books, 1992).
2 Christina Morina and Krijn Thijs, *Probing the Limits of Categorization: The Bystander in Holocaust History* (Berghahn Books, 2018) Chapter 1: *Bystanders: Catchall Concept, Alluring Alibi, or Crucial Clue?* By Mary Fulbrook.
3 Hayes, pp. 4–5.
4 Steven Katz, *The Cambridge Companion to Antisemitism* (Cambridge University Press, 2022), p. 42.
5 Steven Katz, p. 48.
6 Steven Katz, pp. 49–50.
7 Steven Katz, pp. 52–53.
8 Solomon Grayzel, *The Church and the Jews in the XIIIth Century: A Study of Their Relations During the Years 1198-1254, Based on the Papal Letters and the Conciliar Decrees of the Period* (Hermon Press, 1966), p. 127.
9 Grayzel, pp. 308–13.
10 Hayes, p. 15.
11 Hayes, p. 18.
12 Dieckmann and Vanagaitė, pp. 13–21.
13 Hayes, p. 53.
14 Sebastian Haffner, *Defying Hitler: A Memoir* (Hachette UK, 2012), pp. 46–47.
15 The *Protocols* appear to be a rather crude amalgamation of two works of fiction from the 1860s: Hermann Goedsche's German novel *Biarritz* and Maurice Joly's satire *Dialogue between Machiavelli and Montesquieu in Hell.*
16 Hayes, p. 67.
17 Hayes, pp. 72–113.
18 J. Sydney Jones, *Hitler in Vienna, 1907-1913: Clues to the Future* (Cooper Square Press, 2002).
19 Ian Kershaw, *Hitler, 1889-1936: Hubris* (Penguin, 1999), p. 64.
20 Kershaw, p. 66.
21 Kershaw, p. 96.
22 Hilberg, p. 5.
23 Adrian Weale, *The SS: A New History* (Hachette UK, 2010), p. 42.
24 Peter Longerich, *Heinrich Himmler: A Life* (OUP Oxford, 2012).
25 Hayes, p. 149.
26 Michael Wildt, *An Uncompromising Generation: The Nazi Leadership of the Reich Security Main Office* (University of Wisconsin Press, 2009).
27 Prit Buttar, *Centuries Will Not Suffice: A History of the Lithuanian Holocaust* (Amberley Publishing, 2023), p. 32.

28 Laurence Rees, *The Holocaust: A New History* (Penguin UK, 2017), pp. 252–53.
29 Hayes, pp. 147–48.
30 Saul Friedlander, *The Years of Extermination: Nazi Germany and the Jews, 1939-1945* (HarperCollins e-books, 2009), p. 223.
31 Isaiah Berlin, *Against the Current: Essays in the History of Ideas* (Pimlico, 1997), pp. 258–59.
32 Haffner, p. 33.
33 Haffner, p. 221.
34 Hannah Arendt, *Eichmann in Jerusalem* (Penguin UK, 2006).
35 Bettina Stangneth, *Eichmann Before Jerusalem: The Unexamined Life of a Mass Murderer* (Random House, 2016).
36 Abraham Sutzkever, *From the Vilna Ghetto to Nuremberg: Memoir and Testimony* (McGill-Queen's Press - MQUP, 2021).
37 Hayes, pp. 28–29.
38 Michael MacQueen, 'The Context of Mass Destruction: Agents and Prerequisites of the Holocaust in Lithuania', *Holocaust and Genocide Studies*, 12.1 (1998), 27–48 (p. 27).
39 MacQueen, p. 29.
40 N. B. Jopson, 'Memories of the Old Bridge', *The Slavonic Review*, 4.10 (1925), 142–46.
41 Dieckmann and Vanagaitė, p. 26.
42 Dieckmann and Vanagaitė, p. 26.
43 Kazimierz Sakowicz, *Ponary Diary, 1941-1943: A Bystander's Account of a Mass Murder* (Yale University Press, 2005).
44 Sakowicz, p. 16.
45 Koniuchowsky.
46 David Bankier, *Expulsion and Extermination: Holocaust Testimonials from Provincial Lithuania* (Yad Vashem, the International Institute for Holocaust Research, 2011), pp. 72–81.
47 Dieckmann and Vanagaitė, pp. 143–44.
48 Jan Tomasz Gross and Irena Grudzinska Gross, *Golden Harvest: Events at the Periphery of the Holocaust* (Oxford University Press, 2016), p. 11.
49 Dieckmann and Vanagaitė, p. 146.
50 Julija Sukys, *'And I Burned with Shame': The Testimony of Ona Šimaitė, Righteous Among the Nations: A Letter to Isaac Nachman Steinberg* (Wallstein Verlag, 2008).
51 Sakowicz, p.74.
52 Sakowicz, p. 39.
53 Sakowicz, p. 114.
54 Sakowicz, p. 38.

55 Sakowicz, p. 99.
56 Patrick Henry, *Jewish Resistance Against the Nazis* (CUA Press, 2014). See article by Richard Middleton-Kaplan, *The Myth of Jewish Passivity*.
57 Yael S. Feldman, '"Not as Sheep Led to Slaughter"? On Trauma, Selective Memory, and the Making of Historical Consciousness', *Jewish Social Studies*, 19.3 (2013), 139–69 (pp. 145–46)
58 Tom Lawson, *Debates on the Holocaust* (Manchester University Press, 2010), p. 236.
59 Hanna Yablonka and Moshe Tlamim, 'The Development of Holocaust Consciousness in Israel: The Nuremberg, Kapos, Kastner, and Eichmann Trials', *Israel Studies*, 8.3 (2003), 1–24 (pp. 17–18).
60 Arendt.
61 Dieckmann and Vanagaitė, p. 206.
62 Sutton, pp. 169–84.
63 Sol Littman, *War Criminal on Trial: The Rauca Case* (Lester & Orpen Dennys, 1983), p. 76.
64 Greenbaum, p. 325.
65 Dieckmann and Vanagaitė, pp. 233–38.
66 Dieckmann and Vanagaitė, pp. 234–35.
67 Sutton, pp. 170–71.
68 Yehuda Bauer, *The Death of the Shtetl* (Yale University Press, 2009).
69 David E. Fishman, *The Book Smugglers: Partisans, Poets, and the Race to Save Jewish Treasures from the Nazis* (University Press of New England, 2017).
70 Dieckmann and Vanagaitė, p. 292.
71 Elie Wiesel, *Night* (Hill and Wang, a division of Farrar, Straus and Giroux, 2006).
72 Berel Lang, 'Holocaust Memory and Revenge: The Presence of the Past', *Jewish Social Studies*, 2.2 (1996), 1–20 (p. 16).
73 Dina Porat, *The Fall of a Sparrow: The Life and Times of Abba Kovner* (Stanford University Press, 2009), p. 210.
74 Lang, p. 5.
75 Porat, p. 226.
76 Porat, pp. 224–26.
77 Erich Haberer, 'Kovner, Abba: The Fall of a Sparrow: The Life and Times of Abba Kovner', *Biography*, 35.2 (2012), 425–26.
78 Porat, pp. 230–32.
79 Stephen G. Fritz, *Endkampf: Soldiers, Civilians, and the Death of the Third Reich* (University Press of Kentucky, 2004), pp. 264–65.
80 Louise London, *Whitehall and the Jews, 1933-1948: British Immigration Policy, Jewish Refugees and the Holocaust* (Cambridge University Press, 2003).

81 Dieckmann and Vanagaitė, pp. 343–45.
82 Hillel Levine, *In Search of Sugihara: The Elusive Japanese Diplomat Who Risked His Life to Rescue 10,000 Jews from the Holocaust* (Free Press, 1996), p. 259.
83 Jan Karski, *Story of a Secret State* (Houghton Mifflin, 1943), p. 323.
84 Jonathan Freedland, *The Escape Artist: The Man Who Broke Out of Auschwitz to Warn the World* (Hachette UK, 2022).
85 Martin Gilbert, *Auschwitz and the Allies: A Devastating Account of How the Allies Responded to the News of Hitler's Mass Murder* (Rosetta Books, 2015).
86 Gilbert, Chapter 32
87 William Casey, *The Secret War Against Hitler* (Berkley Books, 1989).
88 David I. Kertzer, *The Pope at War: The Secret History of Pius XII, Mussolini, and Hitler* (Oxford University Press, 2022).
89 Kertzer, pp. 214–15.
90 Kertzer, p. 225.
91 Kertzer, pp. 236–56.
92 Kertzer, p. 238.
93 Kertzer, p. 137.
94 Kertzer, pp. 225–26.
95 Kertzer, p. 225.
96 Kertzer, p. 14.
97 Freedland.
98 Kertzer, p. 178.
99 Kertzer, pp. 242 and 257.
100 Kertzer, p. 275.
101 Frank J. Coppa, *The Papacy, the Jews, and the Holocaust* (CUA Press, 2006), p. 29.
102 Kertzer, p. 230.
103 Kertzer, p. 231.
104 Kertzer, p. 201.
105 Kertzer, p. 440.
106 Philippe Sands, *The Ratline: The Exalted Life and Mysterious Death of a Nazi Fugitive* (Alfred A. Knopf, 2021).
107 Michael Phayer, *Pius XII, the Holocaust, and the Cold War* (Indiana University Press, 2008).
108 David Kertzer, *The Atlantic*, (August 2020)
109 Christoph Dieckmann, *Deutsche Besatzungspolitik in Litauen 1941-1944* (Wallstein Verlag, 2016), Vol 2: p. 906.
110 Lazar Goldstein-Golden, *From Ghetto Kovno to Dachau* (E. Goldshṭeyn, 1985), p. 66.

111 Sutton, p. 128.
112 Bankier, p. 174.
113 Dieckmann and Vanagaitė, p. 358.
114 Morina and Thijs, p. 16.
115 The relative lack of support received by Jews in Lithuania is in contrast to the support Jews received in Warsaw. Gunnar S. Paulson has estimated that 7-9% of the population of Warsaw was involved in helping Jews: Gunnar S. Paulsson: *Secret City* (Yale University Press) p.248.
116 Solomon Abramovich and Yakov Zilberg, *Smuggled in Potato Sacks: Fifty Stories of the Hidden Children of the Kaunas Ghetto* (Vallentine Mitchell, 2011), p. 27.
117 Greenbaum, p. 378.

10

The End of the War

By summer 1944 Soviet forces had advanced westwards across a wide front and were pressing into the Baltic states. By then, the great majority of Lithuania's pre-war Jewish population was dead. Of the handful who remained alive, some were in hiding and others had been sent by the Germans to concentration camps further west.

My grandfather and his London-based family did not know what had become of their relations in Lithuania and had no way of finding out. They feared the worst.

One can view the last year of the war, and the immediate post-war period, through the lens of two individuals, one German and one Jewish. Both were what one might describe as relatively 'ordinary' people and both had a connection, but not a close connection, with Pikeliai.

The German is a man called Gottlob Herbert Bidermann. Bidermann was a front-line infantryman. He belonged to the German Wehrmacht's 132nd Infantry Division, formed in September 1940. This Division saw action in the brief Balkan campaign of April-May 1941, but was then a part of Operation Barbarossa in June 1941. The Division was not an elite unit and Bidermann did not win remarkable decorations. His two Iron Crosses, Crimea Shield and Close Combat Badge were quite standard awards for an infantry veteran who served on the Russian front, and survived. After the war, Bidermann wrote a memoir, *In Deadly Combat,* which describes his wartime experiences.[1]

In October 1944, as Soviet forces pressed westwards into the Baltic states, Bidermann, then serving with The Second Company of Regiment 437, found himself billeted in Pikeliai. It is striking that Bidermann's extensive and well-written memoir says nothing about the fact that Pikeliai's Jewish population had vanished. Their absence must have been obvious to him because Pikeliai was a tiny shtetl where Jews had constituted two-thirds of the population at the end of the nineteenth century.[2] Before June 1941, the synagogue had been one of the main buildings, the Jewish cemetery one of the most prominent landmarks, and Jewish-owned homes, distinctive in their construction, were located everywhere in the shtetl.

Perhaps Bidermann, like many other Germans, was determined not to see. Instead, there is a sense that Bidermann regards himself as engaged in an epic and heroic struggle on behalf of German, Christian civilization against advancing Soviet armies, which he perceives as a kind of terrible, barbarian horde.

Bidermann describes the refugees, many of them ethnic Germans, fleeing westward before the advancing Soviet armies: "Ahead of our withdrawing forces, the roads remained packed with refugees fleeing from the red menace that followed at our heels, the ox carts and farm wagons, the women, children, and elderly marching through the sodden roads in files of misery and sorrow".[3] Bidermann clearly derived comfort from the sense that there was German cultural influence in Pikeliai, and that the clergy had been the conduit for this: "in the rough-hewn building [where he was billeted] I discovered spiritual books [in German] from the seventeenth and eighteenth centuries as well as a lengthy manuscript describing the art of chemistry as being 'the source of all knowledge' by Dr. Johann Caspar Ellenrieder, printed in Hamburg in 1723…I spent nights reading [it] by candelight".[4] Bidermann saw himself as engaged in fighting for Christianity, and was comforted that he enjoyed the protection of the Madonna. He describes how Pikeliai came under intense Soviet artillery fire which set his building ablaze. He pulled a bullet-ridden painting from the wall, and removed it from its frame. It was the Madonna. Bidermann found it miraculous that "not a single bullet had struck the face or body of the Holy Virgin" and kept the painting constantly at his side until his last leave in Germany. As Bidermann's regiment prepared to withdraw from Pikeliai, he saw the inhabitants seeking refuge in the surrounding forests in anticipation of the Soviets' arrival. "The priest left us to accompany them to their haven of relative safety, but not before giving us his blessing…we were grateful for his words of comfort."[5]

It is very clear from Bidermann's account that he, and those around him, were absolutely determined to carry on fighting, and not to surrender. When he goes home on leave in January 1945 he is appalled by the devastation he sees in Germany: "we observed first hand the destroyed cities and factories; we experienced the hopelessness of the people, the innocents who suffered for the folly of others, the pain of the women and children who we were supposed to be protecting"; but Bidemann has no qualms about returning to the Courland pocket to continue the fight.[6] German determination to keep battling was sustained by rumours that, if they won, the Bolsheviks would reduce German living standards to below those of Russians, and also by entirely misplaced hopes that the western allies might intervene to rescue Germans at the last moment, or join with them in the struggle against Bolshevism.

On 9 May 1945 Germany surrendered, and German troops in the Courland pocket were taken prisoner. They were force-marched into the Soviet Union, terrified by the fear of "not knowing what was to become of us and, more important, of our families in Germany"[7]. They were compelled to endure an "endless march along roads through swamps and forests...The column moved painfully between heavily armed guards lining the road sides...to an unknown destiny..."[8] Soviet soldiers looted German prisoners of their personal possessions. Many from the officer class were summarily shot. Bidermann was imprisoned in a succession of camps in the Soviet Union, including Borovitschi and camp "Gagri". Eventually, after 1,080 days in captivity, but in very poor health, Bidermann was released and permitted to return to Germany. He was more fortunate than many German soldiers he fought alongside in the Courland pocket, and who surrendered to the Soviets in May 1945. Many of them did not see their homes again.

A Jewish perspective on the end of the war, and on the immediate post-war period, is provided by the experiences of one of my grandfather's cousins, a woman called Rosa, a relation on his mother's side of the family. Rosa did not write a memoir. What I know about her experience was related to me by my father.

Rosa grew up in Liepāja, in Latvia. Most of her immediate family were murdered by the Nazis in 1941-2. She was compelled to work as a slave labourer in different parts of the Baltic until autumn 1944. Then, as Soviet armed troops moved west into the Baltic area, she was deported to Stutthof, a concentration camp near Danzig on the Baltic. Conditions were atrocious. In January 1945, as Soviet armies drew near, she was sent on what were to become known as the 'Death Marches'. She survived, liberated by the Allies. At the end of the war, Rosa had no family still alive in the Baltic states, and little inclination to return to Liepāja. Somehow, probably through the International Tracing Service, she made contact with my Grandfather, JD, then living in Blackheath in south London. JD was prepared to have her come and live with him and his family, but on one condition: she was not to talk about her wartime experiences to his children, for fear that doing so would traumatise them. Rosa lived with JD and family in Blackheath between 1945 and 1948 and then emigrated to Israel. The 'lesson' she said she had learned from her wartime experiences was that it was unsafe for Jewish people to rely on non-Jews for their security and wellbeing. Instead, they should take their protection into their own hands.

Rosa's experience represents in microcosm many of the wider themes of the Jewish experience in the Baltic states at the end of the war and during the immediate post-war period.

The advance of the Red Army through the Baltic states in July 1944 led to inmates of the concentration camps being evacuated to Stutthof, near Danzig. This evacuation took place pursuant to a general directive that Himmler issued in June 1944. For various reasons, Himmler, who had probably discussed this matter with Hitler, did not want concentration camps and their inmates to fall into the hands of the advancing Red Army. He was concerned to try to conceal from the outside world how the Nazis had treated the Jews and others. He was also concerned that a breakdown in order at those camps would threaten the security of SS and other German military personnel. Above all, perhaps, in summer 1944 Himmler did not want to forfeit control of the many prisoners in the camps who at that time played a vital role in the German war production system and were an important source of income for the SS. Himmler's directive was badly drafted and confused those to whom it was addressed. Nonetheless, from July 1944 about 25,000 Jews from the Baltic states (mainly from Kaunas, Vilnius and Riga) were sent to Stutthof, so as to be out of the line of the advancing Soviet forces.[9] These 25,000 Jews constituted most of what then remained of the Baltic Jewish community. A substantial majority were women. At about this time, about 16,000 Hungarian Jews were also sent to Stutthof, as were many Polish Jews from the Łódź and Bialystock ghettos and thousands of Polish citizens who had survived the crushing of the 1944 Warsaw Uprising. [10]

Stutthof is in an attractive location, 34 kilometres east of Danzig, and three kilometres from the base of the Vistula sandbank on the Baltic coast. Before the war, the village of Stutthof had been a fishing village, surrounded by beautiful forests of fir and pine trees, among which were interspersed occasional silverbirch and oak trees. The character of the Stutthof camp changed over time. From September 1939 until 1940 it was used as the main point for collection and imprisonment of Poles and Jews forcibly removed from the Polish corridor and from the former Free City of Danzig. It was then used as a work education camp to 'correct the attitudes' of Forced Labourers, mainly Poles and Soviet citizens, who were not working in the way the Germans required. From January 1942 Stutthof was incorporated into the so-called WHVA and became a part of the concentration camp system. Finally, from summer 1944 onwards, Stutthof became a kind of great overflow camp of Eastern Europe into which the remnant of Baltic Jewry was deposited, along with Jews from other parts of Europe. There was a main camp and many satellite camps. Jews who were thought unfit for work were to be killed straightaway and the others were to be worked to death. It also became a camp where deliberate mass murder was practised.[11]

Conditions in Stutthof were atrocious. A powerful memoir by Helen Lewis, deported to Stutthof in August 1944, well describes the combination of circustances which made life there so appalling: [12] first, there was the anxiety of not knowing what was going to happen: "We sat and lay around all day, waiting, not knowing for what, becoming more and more depressed..." Then, there was the terrible winter weather: "When the weather changed, with winds howling and rain turning into snow, our frozen and starving bodies silenced even the bravest spirits and clearest minds". "The bits of clothing we had been given offered no protection against the winter climate". There was a desperate shortage of food: "the meal was soup and your luck with it depended as much on the angle of the ladle in the barrel as on the goodwill of the kitchen workers. If the ladle was lying fairly flat on the surface you got a bowl of warm water with a faint aroma of what might have been". Illness was a constant worry, with typhoid and dysentery almost ubiquitous. The inmates were menaced by constant roll-calls, beginning at a ludicrously early hour. Most of the SS guards, many of whom were women, behaved with scarcely imaginable savagery: "At the first roll-call the *Oberaufseherin*, the SS commandant, Emma, wanted us to know that she personally had been instrumental in the extermination of the Jewish children from the Riga ghetto. The SS chief commandant was just the same, she promised, and we would get to know the others in time." Above all, the inmates of Stutthof and its sub-camps well understood that if they slackened at their work they would be murdered: "Being too weak to fulfil the required work-load meant a ride on the lorry…and the gas chambers".[13]

Stutthof and its many sub-camps became vitally important to the German war economy. 105 Stutthof sub-camps were eventually established throughout northern and central German-occupied Poland, with 23 new sub-camps opened in the second half of 1944. A total of 26,251 Jews were sent to the new sub-camps in 1944. If one includes non-Jewish prisoners, there were about 33,000 prisoners at all the sub-camps in 1944. Some workers were forced to work in SS-owned businesses such as the German Equipment Works (DAW), providing for the needs of the German army. They were put to work manufacturing and repairing weaponry, repairing tracks and military airfields, building fortifications and clearing bombs. Others laboured in local brickyards, in private industrial enterprises, in agriculture or in the camp's own workshops. A Focke-Wulf airplane factory was constructed at Stutthof. Many private German industrial concerns became critically dependent on Jewish slave labour. These Jewish people were literally worked to death. [14] Post-war Polish records suggest that of the approximately 110,000 registered prisoners who passed through Stutthof, approximately 80,000 died. The most common cause of death was *Vernichtung durch Arbeit*, annihilation by work, a shorthand for murder by a combination of physical exhaustion, disease, malnutrition, exposure to a harsh climate and abuse. The rest were deliberately murdered either by what was called *Genickschussanlage*, in which a prisoner was shot in the back of the neck with a special device, or by lethal phenol injection. Later on, Jewish prisoners were also murdered by gas. At first, murder by gas was committed in the car of a narrow gauge railway and, after September 1943, in a small gas chamber at Stutthof.[15]

In January 1945 it was decided that the remaining inmates of Stutthof and its sub-camps should be removed from the path of advancing Allied armies. Some were sent across the Baltic by boat while others were marched away from the camp. These so-called 'death marches' were chaotic, with former camp inmates often going on long, seemingly purposeless, marches and sometimes just going round in circles. The best estimate is that of the approximately 750,000 prisoners in the whole concentration camp system at the beginning of 1945 approximately 250,000, which is to say almost 35 per cent, died on these death marches. On some death marches the proportion of prisoners who died was as high as 80 per cent, while on others it was 20 per cent or less. It is thought that at least one quarter of the victims of the concentration camp system died in the last five months of its existence.[16]

Helen Lewis describes the sense of purposelessness on these death marches: "After a few days of wandering on icy roads through hostile villages, we began to realise that we were, in fact, going nowhere; we just kept walking in ever decreasing circles." The Jewish prisoners were "escorted by the fiercest and most dreaded SS guards, who shouted their '*Schneller, Schneller!*' as if they wanted to hear the sound of their own voices". At night, the Jewish prisoners slept in empty churches or barns, or just on the side of a road. Initially, they had some bread to eat but "when the bread was finished we had to rely on the goodwill of the villagers for a drop of soup or milk. Some gave, others didn't". "The liquid diet, combined with the grim unhygienic living conditions took its toll: the majority of us became very ill with a form of dysentery". Those unable to keep up or who crossed the guards in some way were summarily shot. Helen Lewis describes how "with increasing exhaustion and hunger, we lost our grip on reality and our minds began to wander. Many of us had hallucinations, in which we saw mirages in the snowstorm. In the end, it was more than most people could tolerate". "One morning I took my blanket and without a word went to lie down among the dying. I pulled the blanket over my face and gave up." [17]

Many Jews who survived the death marches described their frustration at not understanding what the Germans thought such marches were supposed to achieve. Some light on this subject is shed by testimony given at the trial of Paul-Werner Hoppe, the second commandant of Stutthof, who was tried and convicted as an accessory to murder in 1955. Hoppe testified that, as the Soviets advanced westwards in September 1944, the Gauleiter of Danzig, Albert Forster, decided to evacuate Stutthof. Inmates were to be moved as far as possible from the advancing armies. The formal evacuation order, "Einsatzbefehl No 3", was signed by Hoppe on 25 January, 1945. However, there were conflicting opinions about how to implement the order. One plan was to transfer the inmates of Stutthof to a sub-camp of Stutthof near Lauenberg in Pomerania about 87 miles west-southwest of Stutthof; a second plan was to send the inmates by ship from Danzig and Gotenhafen to Germany, either to Lübeck or to the camp at Neuengamme. In his trial testimony Hoppe said that when he issued his evacuation order in January 1945 agreement had not been reached as to which of these different evacuation plans should be implemented. Unsurprisingly, confusion ensued.[18]

The salient fact about the death marches is that centrally directed Nazi German policy had broken down. It was no longer possible either to work Jews to death or systematically to murder those whose labour was not considered useful. Instead, Jews were moved away from advancing Allied armies for a number of reasons: so that their labour might be used elsewhere at some future time; so that they should not fall alive into the hands of Allied armies and be in a position to testify to German atrocities; and, so it was thought, to protect Germans, including German civilians, from the risk of Jewish revenge attacks in the post-war world. The guards were especially brutal because they were anxious about what would happen to them at the end of the war.[19]

The consequence of the breakdown in central Nazi German policy was that decision-taking about the mass murder of Jews was, in effect, decentralised. "The guards walking alongside the prisoners were the ones who had the power to decide who should live or die, and their decision was not a spontaneous act but calculated from several factors, including utility and local conditions."[20] A number of local circumstances combined to make evacuation of Stutthof especially horrific: there was the terrible Baltic weather, the fact that some evacuations were by inadequate barges across the Baltic Sea to Hamburg, Flensburg and Neustadt, that huge numbers were being evacuated and that Jewish evacuees sent on marches were sharing the roads with thousands of German refugees fleeing oncoming Russian armies, and that German refugees took priority if there was competition for basic necessities.

Many memoirs describe how prisoners unable to keep up with the march were killed. Helen Lewis recalls that suddenly, in the middle of one night, the guards decided to move on. Those unable to march were left behind in the barn in which they had been sleeping. Later, she learned that some girls who were relatively strong were promised food from the SS if they did a certain job: "They were bundled into a sleigh and driven back to the barn. There they found the whole row of women, murdered, bayonetted to death. Among them were a few who had been in reasonably good health but had refused to leave behind sisters, cousins, dearest friends. The job was to bury the bodies so that the Red Army would not find them. The barn was then burned down."[21]

Memoirs by Jewish survivors of death marches describe the attitude of local people who were now seeing inmates of concentration camps passing through towns and walking along streets and paths, where previously they had been hidden from view behind camp walls. There was a certain numbness and shock, a desire not to become involved, but also a deliberate looking away from what was in front of them. Joseph Katz arrived in Stutthof from Riga in October 1944 and was evacuated in January 1945. He describes being marched through the streets of Danzig :

> Our route takes us by old patrician houses and stately churches to the Danzig railway station. People look at us in astonishment, some even with sympathy…I have the sense that people became very serious when they saw us, that they stopped for a moment in their tracks, shook their heads and walked on, recognising that nothing good was going on.[22]

Another theme of many memoirs is reflection about why some of those on death marches survived, while others did not. Luck played a major part, particularly as to whether or not the prisoners had sufficient food and whether they stayed healthy enough to keep up. The attitude of the guards immediately around the captives was crucial. So too was having an intimate supportive group of fellow prisoners, be they people from one's home town, relatives or friends acquired in the camp. Some of those who survived did so by seizing an opportunity to escape from the column of marchers. Usually, the decision to escape was taken without prior planning. It might be when there was an aerial bombardment or when the prisoners sensed that guards had momentarily become lax. Escape did not guarantee survival. Guards sometimes shot prisoners in the act of attempted escape or conducted a hunt for escaped prisoners. The routes of the death marches were often crowded with retreating army units, police and SS forces and Volkssturm companies. Some of these people regarded escaped Jewish prisoners as a danger to be eradicated mercilessly, if encountered. Helen Lewis describes the moment of her escape:

> The road was congested and the column had to stop for a moment. On my left I saw a ditch, filled high with snow, and beyond it a house, a faint light shining through its blinds…I knew I had only one choice; I took one leap towards the ditch and allowed myself to fall into the soft snow. Our chief commandant came out [of the house]. *'Los,los!'* he shouted. They [the column of marchers] started to move and minutes later I was on my own for the first time in almost three years.[23]

Jews who survived death marches did so either because they escaped or because they were eventually liberated by the Allies. The main camp at Stutthof was liberated by the Soviets on 8 May, 1945. In the less than four-month period between the order for Stutthof to be evacuated on 25 January and its liberation by the Soviets on 8 May some 25,000 prisoners died, some in the camp and others in the process of evacuation. In other words, 30 per cent of the camp's victims died in the last months of the war.

A major evacuation of Stutthof took place by sea on 25 April, 1945. After that, only about 100-150 prisoners remained in the main camp. SS guards set fire to the Jewish barracks, burning alive the sick prisoners still lodged inside. By the time soldiers of the 48th Army of the 3rd Belorussian Front arrived on 8 May, there were no Jewish prisoners left in the main camp in Stutthof. Many of those who survived the evacuation made their way, one way or another, to what became known as Displaced Persons' Camps, or DP Camps.

At war's end, a few Jewish survivors emerged from hiding in Lithuania. Others had been liberated by Allied armies. Most found they were unwelcome in their former homes, to which they were anyway reluctant to return.

Those who did return found the silence, desolation and loss overwhelming. They tended to want to leave quickly. Chaim Grade describes returning to Vilnius:

> All that is left is walls, roofs, pillars, cornices, tottering beams. All that is left is broken bedsteads, the rusty entrails of Primus stoves, twisted forks, knives, spoons – without the mouths. And I am left with eyes without tears…I cannot squeeze even a single tear from my eyes. An entire row of shops shuttered and bolted.
>
> 'Open up, you brigand, open up.'
>
> No one laughs, no one coughs, no one answers.[24]

Generally, Jews who had survived moved westwards to be under the care of occupation authorities in the western zones of Germany, in assembly centres or DP camps established by the United Nations Relief and Rehabilitation Administration (UNRRA). In summer 1945 there were about 53,000 Jewish DPs, but this grew to about 250,000 at the start of 1947. The increase was mainly the consequence of Jews returning from the Soviet Union. DP camps were of different sizes and character. The biggest were at Hohne (formerly Belsen), Feldafing, Föhrenwald, Zeilsheim and Landsberg. These were mainly repurposed army barracks. Other DP camps were small, and consisted of requisitioned apartment blocks, schools, hotels and garages. The number of Jews in DP camps fell rapidly after the establishment of the State of Israel in May 1948, which led to mass migration. Just before May 1948 there were 165,000 Jewish DPs still in Germany. By September that year the number had fallen to 30,000, but a 'hard core' of DP inmates remained, and the last DP camp only closed in February 1957.

A number of survivors, and of those who cared for them, have described the experiences and sentiments of Jews in the DP camps. Initially, there was elation at having survived although, given their weakness, such elation could be dangerous. Evelyn Le Chêne, working with the American military, suggests that: "Many died from sheer joy. They had lived on hope, on fear and on their nerves for so long that the sudden relaxation of tension, when it came, was too much for them".[25] Most suffered from an acute sense of isolation and loneliness. This is well described by Jane Leverson, a member of the Quaker Relief team who arrived in Belsen six days after its liberation. She says: "I was with an Austrian and a Yugoslav, Jewish doctors, on the evening of the 4th May, when a Polish nurse burst into our room, sobbing bitterly, that the war had ended, and she had no home, no family, no friends, where should she go ?"[26] At first, infectious disease was very common in the Camps and a number of rescued Jewish prisoners died from eating food that was too heavy for them.

Once their health improved, many Jews began to occupy themselves with cultural and religious activities. Jewish newspapers appeared, usually in Yiddish. There was *Undzer Vort* in Bamberg, *Dos Fraye Vort* in Feldafing and *Undzer Shtime* in Belsen. Historians and scholars among the survivors established historical commissions to document the mass murder of their communities, a task undertaken as much as a holy duty as a dispassionate act of scholarship.[27] There was theatre, although the fact that many of the plays re-enacted aspects of ghetto life and the camps suggests many performances were more a way of confronting a traumatic past than entertainment.

Above all, Jewish survivors seemed to be concerned by three main things. The first was to find any surviving member of their family. One aid worker was very struck by this. Koppel Pinson, a professor of German history who worked in DP camps in Germany for a year from October 1945, noted in an article published in 1947 that Jewish survivors threw themselves into "an almost mad hunt for family and friends".[28] Other aid workers were impressed, if bemused, by the persistence and resourcefulness with which many Jewish survivors in DP camps moved about in search of family:

> How these people manage to move about at all in this heavily guarded country is indeed difficult to understand...They go forward and backward...from camp to camp wherever they believe they may find some member of their family, and we here are not even able to go from one camp to another without travelling papers, and without being checked time and again.[29]

Jewish survivors searching for relatives were considerably helped by UNRRA's Central Tracing Bureau and by the tracing facility operated by the Red Cross. Jewish DPs listened to public radio broadcasts which read out names of Jewish surviors and they scoured newspapers which contained lists of survivors. For many, the search for surviving family was to prove fruitless and the best plan was to start a new family. There was a widespread feeling that the best revenge on a world which had attempted to obliterate Jews was to reproduce as quickly as possible. The Jewish DP camps in

Germany are thought to have had the highest birth rate in post-war Europe. At Belsen, in the two years after liberation, 1,438 Jewish marriages took place and some 500 circumcision ceremonies were performed.[30] But there was an underlying sadness: "Weddings were performed, children were born, and anniversaries were celebrated, but not with a normal happiness; more like a forced smile."[31]

A second concern of Jewish DPs was that, initially, they had to live alongside non-Jewish DPs in the DP camps. This happened because the western Allies housed DPs according to nationality, without regard to the fact that many DPs were Jewish. Non-Jewish DPs had become DPs for a variety of reasons. Some had been forced labourers, and some had volunteered for work in Nazi Germany. But others had been Nazi collaborators, including camp guards. Jewish DPs found it unbearable to live alongside their persecutors, especially when violence erupted, as happened periodically. There was, for example, a serious incident when Polish DP police burnt down a synagogue during Hannukah in December 1945. The mistake of housing Jews alongside antisemitic non-Jews was, arguably, one that should not have been made given that there had been recurrent criticism of the British government on this subject in the context of the 'enemy aliens' (many of them Jewish) interned on the Isle of Man during the early years of the war.[32] As time passed, the Americans, and later the British, came to see that the policy of housing Jews and non-Jews side by side in DP camps was unsustainable. The catalyst for change was the Harrison Report. In June 1945 President Truman commissioned Earl G. Harrison, the Dean of the University of Pennsylvania Law school, to visit DP camps and produce a report about conditions there. His report was highly critical (if a little overblown):

> As matters now stand, we appear to be treating the Jews as the Nazis treated them except that we do not exterminate them. They are in concentration camps in large numbers under our military guard instead of SS troops.[33]

As a result of the Harrision Report the Americans, and later the British, moved to a policy of accommodating Jewish DPs separately from non-Jewish DPs. This brought comfort and relief to many Jewish DPs.

A third major concern of Jewish DPs was how and where to rebuild their lives. In Rosa's case, this meant trying to rejoin distant family members still alive, and the only ones she knew of lived in England. But British immigration law meant that joining them was far from straightforward.

The post-war British government actively sought immigrants, but it did not seek Jewish immigrants. This was partly because there was a feeling that further Jewish immigration would stir up antisemitism and partly because conflict over the future of Palestine hardened attitudes towards the plight of homeless Jews. There were just three immigration schemes, all involving relatively small numbers. The first was a scheme to admit up to 1,000 children who had been in concentration camps. Orphans up to the age of 16 were eligible. They were to stay in hostels, and their admission was to be on a temporary basis. The foreign secretary, Ernest Bevin, wanted to avoid concentrating young Jewish people in big towns and suggested, perhaps implausibly, steering them towards agricultural or nursing employment in the countryside. Altogether, about 730 child survivors under 16, mainly of Polish nationality, who had been found in Germany at the end of the war, arrived in Britain on this scheme. A second scheme was a 'distressed persons' scheme, and was announced on 13 November, 1945. This authorised the admission of certain categories of distressed person with relatives in Britain and was aimed at survivors of concentration camps in Germany and Austria. Such people were subject to an employment restriction. The applicants needed to have a relative in the United Kingdom willing to guarantee accommodation and maintenance. It particularly targeted elderly people who had a special 'need of filial care' and young people who had a special need for a guardian's care. Rosa was fortunate to be able to take advantage of the third of the six categories: "Females under twenty-one...who have no relatives to look after them abroad, but have a relative in the United Kingdom able and willing to take them into his household".[34] The scheme was modest: after six months of operation only 220 people were admitted under it. The third scheme, announced in Novemeber 1946, was the revival of the labour permit scheme to recruit female domestic workers from Europe.

The reluctance of the British government to admit Jewish refugees was in striking contrast to the enthusiastic welcome extended to non-Jewish refugees under the European Volunteer Worker (EVW) schemes. From late 1946 some 100,000 EVWs were recruited from DP camps. These immigrants were invited to fill staffing gaps in Britain's hospitals and industries. The guidelines for selecting EVW candidates explicitly favoured nationals from Latvia, Lithuania and Estonia. Equally explicitly, Jews, ex-enemy nationals and *Volksdeutsche* were excluded. Checks on immigrants admitted from the Baltic countries were perfunctory, with the consequence that some EVWs who came to Britian had a distinctly murky wartime past which led, some four decades later, to a number of investigations for suspected war crimes. The EVWs were welcomed in such numbers because there were serious staff shortages in post-war Britain and, perhaps, because their admission enabled Britian to dispose of politically problematic DPs in occupied Europe. Reasons for Britain's reluctance to take Jewish survivors were rarely articulated in public but the likeliest explanation seems to be a general sense that the admission of Jews risked stirring up antisemitism.[35]

Many Jewish survivors in DP camps passionately wanted to go to Palestine. Hanna Yablonka calls this: "an instinctive 'gut' Zionism rooted in a loss of faith in the European emancipation and the profound sense of humiliation that [Jews] felt during the years of destruction."[36] Jewish determination to go to Palestine may have been stiffened by what Jewish DPs perceived as insensitivity on the part of the British government, still seeking to limit Jewish migration to Palestine for fear of straining relations with the Arab world. The British limited Jewish migration to Palestine to 1,500 per month. In consequence, many Jews tried to reach Palestine by an underground channel known as *brichah*. Many travelled on repurposed merchant ships, but were intercepted by the British navy and incarcerated in refugee camps on Cyprus, either at Caraolos or at Xylotymbou, tantalisingly close to Palestine. British policy on Palestine became increasingly difficult to sustain. Britain was faced with Jewish survivors who felt that Zionism was, to quote Samuel Gringauz, "a historical mission, a debt to the dead, a retribution towards the enemy and a duty to the living." Gringauz also articulated the view, common among Jewish DPs, that "the continuation of the Jewish national abnormality [dispersal in the diaspora] means the danger of a repetition of the catastrophe."[37] In the face of such adamantine determination, as well as fierce Arab resolve to prevent Jewish settlement in Palestine, Britain had little alternative but to surrender its mandate and allow the United Nations to determine the future of Palestine. The Soviets, keen to take advantage of an opportunity to reduce British influence in the Middle East, supported partition. The State of Israel was declared on 14 May, 1948. About 135,000 Jewish DPs moved from DP camps in Germany to the new State of Israel between May and September 1948. Other Jews who had found temporary refuge in other countries also moved to Israel. Rosa was among this group. Some Jewish DPs sought new lives in other parts of the world, particularly in the United States. This became more straightforward when the United States eased immigration restrictions in the Displaced Persons Act of 1950. By 1952, over 80,000 Jewish DPs had emigrated to the United States.

With Jewish DPs moving to other parts of the world, particularly to Israel and America, the last DP Camp in continental Europe, at Föhrenwald in Germany, closed in February 1957. The inhabitants who remained were rehoused in nearby apartment blocks.

Notes

1 Gottlob Herbert Bidermann, *In Deadly Combat: A German Soldier's Memoir of the Eastern Front* (University Press of Kansas, 2000).
2 Schoenburg and Schoenburg. The census of 1897 shows there were then 1206 Jewish people on Pikeliai, constituting 68% of its population.
3 Bidermann, p. 248.
4 Bidermann, p. 251.
5 Bidermann, p. 252.
6 The Courland Pocket was an area of the Courland Peninsula where Army Group North and the Reichskkommissariat Ostland were cut off and surrounded by the Red Army for almost a year, between July 1944 and 10 May 1945
7 Bidermann, p. 287.
8 Bidermann, p. 293.
9 Ruth Schwertfeger, *A Nazi Camp Near Danzig: Perspectives on Shame and on the Holocaust from Stutthof* (Bloomsbury Publishing, 2022), p. 111.
10 Daniel Blatman, *The Death Marches: The Final Phase of Nazi Genocide* (Harvard University Press, 2011), pp. 51–64.
11 Geoffrey P. Megargee, *The United States Holocaust Memorial Museum Encyclopedia of Camps and Ghettos, 1933–1945: Volume I: Early Camps, Youth Camps, and Concentration Camps and Subcamps under the SS-Business Administration Main Office (WVHA)* (Indiana University Press, 2009) Stutthof Main Camp.
12 Helen Lewis, *A Time to Speak* (Blackstaff, 2010).
13 Lewis, pp. 65–84.
14 Megargee: Stutthof Subcamp System.
15 Schwertfeger, pp. 118–19.
16 Blatman, p. 12.
17 Lewis, pp. 87–95.
18 Schwertfeger, p. 143.
19 Dan Stone, *The Holocaust: An Unfinished History* (Penguin UK, 2023), p. 227.
20 Blatman, p. 157.
21 Lewis, p. 91.
22 Schwertfeger, p. 133.
23 Lewis, pp. 92–93.

24 Chaim Grade, *My Mother's Sabbath Days: A Memoir* (Rowman & Littlefield, 1997), p. 336.
25 Evelyn Le Chêne, *Mauthausen: The History of a Death Camp* (Methuen, 1971), p. 169.
26 Dan Stone, *The Liberation of the Camps: The End of the Holocaust and Its Aftermath* (Yale University Press, 2023), p. 111. Jane Leverson was my wife's great-aunt.
27 "A Folk Monument for our Destruction and Heroism': Jewish Historical Commissions in Dispacled Persons Camps in Germany, Austria, and Italy,"in: Avinoam Patt and Michael Berkowitz (Eds.) "We are Here": New Approaches to Jewish Displaced Persons in Postwar Germany (Detroit 2010).
28 Koppel S. Pinson, 'Jewish Life in Liberated Germany: A Study of the Jewish DPs', *Jewish Social Studies*, 9.2 (1947), 101–26.
29 Stone, *The Holocaust*, p.247 citing Miriam Warburg: 'Conditions of Jewish children in a Bavarian Rehabilitation Camp'.
30 Stone, *The Liberation of the Camps*, p. 167.
31 Jacob Biber, *Risen from the Ashes* (Star Publishers, 2005), p. 54.
32 Simon Parkin, *The Island of Extraordinary Captives: A True Story of an Artist, a Spy and a Wartime Scandal* (Hachette UK, 2022), pp. 228 & 313.
33 Leonard Dinnerstein, *America and the Survivors of the Holocaust* (Columbia University Press, 1982), pp. 291–305.
34 Hansard: 13 November 1945, volume 137. cc 839-42
35 London, pp. 252–71.
36 Stone, *The Liberation of the Camps*, p. 172.
37 Samuel Gringauz, 'Jewish Destiny as the DPs See It: The Ideology of the Surviving Remnant', *The Posen Library of Jewish Culture and Civilization ; Volume 9: Catastrophe and Rebirth*, 1947, 420.

11

Post war

Very few Lithuanian Jews survived the Second World War. Of the approximately 220,000 Jews living in Lithuania in June 1941 only about 3.6 percent, or 8,000, remained alive in May 1945. This was one of the lowest survival rates in Nazi occupied Europe. The process of how to remember and come to terms with the mass murder of Lithuanian Jewry has been complex, both for ethnic Lithuanians and for Lithuanian Jewish survivors and their descendants; and it has been substantially influenced by post-war geopolitics.

In May 1945 the Soviet Union was in occupation of the Baltic states. For some time, the British and Americans had recognised they had no alternative but to accept that, in the post-war world, the Baltics were in the Soviet sphere of influence. In March 1942 Churchill wrote to Roosevelt to say: "the Atlantic Charter ought not to be construed so as to deny Russia the frontiers she occupied when Germany attacked her" and in September 1943 Roosevelt told his confidante Archbishop Spellman: "The European people [in the Baltics] will simply have to endure Russian domination."[1] The fate of the Baltics was sealed on 9 October, 1944 when Churchill met Stalin in Moscow and sketched out a post-war partition of Europe, which accepted that the Baltics fell within the Soviet sphere of influence. This private understanding was rather obscured at the Yalta conference in February 1945, which invoked the Atlantic Charter and the right of all peoples to choose the form of government under which they live, but made no specific reference to the future of the Baltics. In effect, the Western Allies recognised the absorption of Lithuania into the Soviet empire, but did so in a quiet way which allowed misunderstandings to develop.

Some Lithuanians thought that if they rose up against Soviet rule then the Western Allies would intervene and help them push back the Soviets. Jonas Noreika (who bore the *nom de guerre* 'General Storm') returned to Vilnius in November 1945 and quickly set about creating a 'National Council of Lithuania', designed to coordinate anti-Soviet partisan forces. Noreika and other leaders of the the Council were arrested in March 1946 and Noreika was executed in February 1947. Noreika's granddaughter, Silvia

Foti, has described how, in the Lithuanian district of Chicago in which she grew up, her grandfather was widely regarded as a national hero for his efforts to lead a rebellion against Soviet control. But the hard reality was that such an uprising could only have succeeded with substantial Western support, and it was wholly unrealistic to think such support would be forthcoming. Foti concludes that her grandfather's "purported rebellion was little more than a quixotic suicide mission; it was never a serious challenge to the Soviets' grip on Lithuania."[2]

Nonetheless, a sporadic partisan war against the Soviets continued until about 1953. The Soviet authorities sought to impose Soviet communism on Lithuania and ruthlessly to suppress dissent. They deported many Lithuanians to Siberia. The precise numbers are uncertain, but the best estimate is that between about 120,000 and 150,000 Lithuanians were deported to Siberia and to the gulags. Of these, perhaps 12,500 were deported expressly for supporting partisans. Many of the later deportees were farmers who the Soviets regarded as excessively well-off.[3]

This immediate post-war history of Lithuania shaped how the Holocaust was perceived and remembered there. Because there were very few Jews left and the handful who emerged from hiding or trickled back tended to be traumatised and marginal, they were in no position to shape discourse about the Holocaust. Most of the immediate post-war Jewish community in Lithuania were Russian Jews who were settled in Lithuania by the Soviet regime and they generally had no real understanding of or connection to pre-war Lithuanan Jewish life. Many of the Lithuanians who had been directly involved in killing Jews had fled west. The Lithuanian population in general was disinclined to talk about the Holocaust because they found the subject uncomfortable and they did not know who they could trust. Many had benefited from the Jews' disappearance, and now lived in their former Jewish neighbours' homes and used their clothes and other posessions. Silence seemed prudent. Furthermore, many Lithuanians became consumed by their own anxieties and trauma at living under Soviet occupation. In their eyes, this was of far greater and more immediate concern than the wartime suffering of the Jews. The Soviet government tended not to acknowledge the uniqueness of the tragedy of European Jewy, and obscured the fact that Jews had been killed because they were Jews. To have acknowledged this would have contradicted the Soviet notion of "the Great Patriotic War" as an epic struggle beteen Nazism and Communism. The Soviet regime described Jewish victims simply as "soviet people", and the killers were not characterised as Lithuanians but as products of socio-economic classes that were enemies of the proletariat.[4] For all these reasons, the Holocaust was not a part of public discourse in Lithuania in the early post-war years.

Nonetheless, reasonably full information about what had happened to the Jews of Lithuania was available to those who sought it. One way of doing this was by consulting testimonies collected by Leyb Koniuchowsky. Koniuchowsky was born in Lithuania in November 1910. During the German occupation he lived in the Kaunas ghetto, but he escaped and found shelter in a bunker at a farmer's home where he remained until liberation. From 1944-1946 he travelled around war-battered Lithuanian towns collecting testimonies from the handful of Jewish survivors. Later, he took testimonies from Jews in DP camps in Germany. He was thorough in taking evidence, even requiring witnesses to sign their testimonies.[5] Another source of information about the Holocaust in Lithuania was the *Einsatzgruppen* trial, one of the "Subsequent Nuremberg trials", which took place between September 1947 and April 1948. This trial covered events which took place both within Lithuania and beyond it. However, the outline of the Holocaust in Lithuania was fully and horifically described.[6] At a less formal level, basic information about the Holocaust in Lithuania was available to those who could travel there by asking older Lithuanians what had happened. Travellers and memoirists report their experience of locating mass execution sites in Lithuania by going to a provincial community, engaging an elderly local in conversation, and asking them to direct the visitor to where Jews had been killed. Invariably, the local was able to help.[7]

A gap in understanding opened up between academics, on one hand, and the government and swathes of the Lithuanian population, on the other hand. Broadly speaking, Lithuanian academics (and academics based in Western countries) who were engaged in studying the history of the Holocaust in Lithuania well understood the bare facts of what happened, although inevitably there were differences of emphasis between them. However, its critics argue that the Lithuanian government has often been less than candid about this past and it seems that much of the Lithuanian population, particularly the younger generation, is not well-informed about the details of what happened to Jews in Lithuania during the Holocaust.

Lithuania became independent on 11 March 1990. The question of how to deal with the Holocaust quickly became relevant in the context of seeking admission to the European Union and to NATO. Admission to both was regarded as important in ensuring the continuing security and wellbeing of the newly independent state. A number of matters relating to the Holocaust needed to be addressed:

Acknowledgement of guilt for Holocaust crimes and the issue of an apology;
Commemoration of the victims;
Prosecution of heretofore unprosecuted local perpetrators;
Documentation (recording of an accurate historical narrative);
Education (introducing Holocaust education and rewriting local textbooks); and
Restitution.[8]

Lithuania joined NATO and the EU in 2004. However, the question of whether the Lithuanian government and people have adequately tried to come to terms with the Holocaust in Lithuania remains controversial. The principal areas of contention are the extent of Lithuanians' collaboration in the Holocaust and whether Lithuanians' mistreatment at the hands of the Soviet regime can be regarded as comparable to mistreatment of Jews at the hands of the Nazis and their collaborators.

These fundamental areas of controversy have led to disagreement about a host of other matters. Many Jews, and others, are concerned that many of the memorials put up in the Soviet era, some of which remain in place, do not refer to the fact that the victims were Jewish or that their killers were Lithuanian. Some of the anger this causes can be sensed in Efraim Zuroff's description of visiting the Lietūkis Garage monument in July 2015:

> We are standing in front of the Lietūkis garage monument which says that several dozen Jews were killed here, but does not say by whom. Maybe it was a volcano, maybe a tsunami, maybe an earthquake. What we do know is that just a few days after [the] German invasion, on June 27, 1941 several dozen Jews were beaten to death with crowbars by Lithuanians at the Lietūkis Garage.[9]

There is anger that statues and plaques commemorating Lithuanians who were responsible for Holocaust atrocities remain in place, although it should be said that the thinking behind erecting these memorials was to celebrate Lithuanians' efforts to resist the Soviets, and not their activities against Jews. There is also anguish about the contrast between the dignified memorials to Lithuanians and the inadequate character of memorials to Jews. Silvia Foti describes visiting Telšiai with her Jewish guide Simon Dovidavicius :

> The harsh contrast between the two memorials – the dignified Chapel of Torment honouring seventy-four Lithuanian men and the

> simple stone marking the burial site of 7,500 Jews from the same area – could not have been more telling…Simon wondered aloud, 'why does our government spend so much money for seventy-four Lithuanians and so little for 7,500 Jews?'... And the answer was self-evident: Lithuanians refused to recognise their role in the deaths of Jews, and they refused to accord Jews - in death as in life – the same honour and dignity shown to their "own" dead. The Jews, despite having been Lithuanian, were eternally "the other". The lack of will to acknowledge this obdurate antisemitism meant that there was no guilt or shame, either - without which there could be no self-knowledge, no remorse, and no atonement.[10]

There is indignation at the neglect of the mass graves of the Jewish victims. In summer 2015 Efraim Zuroff (a Jewish man who worked for the Simon Wiesenthal Centre) and Rūta Vanagaietė (a well-known Lithuanian writer) travelled together around Lithuania, visiting many mass execution sites. They found that "many of [the mass execution sites] were utterly neglected, while numerous others were hard to find, and there were several which were not identified in any way". It seems it was this sense of "neglect and indifference to the victims" that made them so determined to "inform Lithuanian society about the scope and nature of this terrible tragedy".

Another concern was that the smaller regional museums across Lithuania have little material about the Jews who lived in those communities, notwithstanding that for many centuries Jews had constituted a substantial proportion, often a majority, of those communities. In August 2015 Zuroff and Vanagaitė visited the Tauragė Regional History Museum and asked a friendly museum worker if his museum displayed any infomation about the 4,000 Jews of Tauragė who were murdered. The response was : "No, we don't have anything about the four thousand Jews who were murdered, but we are very proud of other parts of our exhibition, like the collection of pennies from the United States."[11]

Some Jewish survivors and their descendants remain angry at the extraordinary wholesale theft of Jewish possessions. Hardly any possessions were returned and no reparation was made. About 50,000 Jewish families in Lithuania perished. They left behind homes, land, livestock, furniture, jewellery and money. There were Jewish owned businesses and communal institutions including factories, shops, pharmacies, hospitals, taverns, restaurants, schools, synagogues and libraries. They were stolen. Much of the looting was brazen and shameless. Gold teeth in the corpses of Jewish victims were especially prized. Bodies were dug up and the gold teeth taken.

Individuals tended to justify these thefts on the basis that Jews were the 'other' and by reference to old tropes. In April 1988 Saulius Beržinis interviewed a simple Lithuanian woman called Regina Prudnilova. She had worked as a servant for Jewish people. She said:

> They said Jews can't live without the blood of Christians; when they have their holidays, they need to taste at least a drop of blood. When the Germans invaded, the Jews didn't have the right to anything. The Lithuanians looted the shops and carried everything off...They took a bit of everything, and I took [stuff] home too.

An insight into the position taken by the Catholic church on theft and receipt of stolen property is revealed by reports read at a 1942 conference of Bishops. Valentinas Brandisauskas has written about this:

> The predominant attitude in the reports is that if the property was stolen by a poor parishioner, and only for his most urgent individual needs, then that property could remain at his disposal. But if a person had taken more than he was able to use, then that person had to return it, and optimally to the church, although he was allowed to give it to the poor as alms or to charitable organisations. An exception was made for the immoderate looters of Jewish property who were former partisans and who became partisans for noble reasons. Restitution was not required of them because they had risked their very lives at the beginning of the war.

It is striking that these reports suggest Bishops were less concerned by breach of the seventh commandment - "Thou shalt not steal" - and breach of the fundamental biblical injunction to behave respectfully towards neighbours than by pragmatic concerns about equitable distribution of stolen goods.[12]

Controversy also surrounds what are perceived to be the limited steps taken by the Lithuanian authorities to apologise properly for the Holocaust and bring to justice those Lithuanians who perpetrated it. There have been some efforts at apology: in 1995 the then President of Lithuania, Algirdas Brazauskas, addressed the Knesset (the Israeli parliament) and offered a public apology to the Jewish people for Lithuanians' participation in the Holocaust and gave assurance that Lithuanian war criminals would be prosecuted "publicly, consistently and conscientiously"; and in an event marking the 60th anniversary of the Holocaust in Lithuania, held in

September 2001, the Seimas (the Lithuanian parliament) was addressed by Alfonsas Eidintas, a historian named as Lithuania's next ambassador to Israel, who sought to describe and explain the Holocaust in Lithuania. However, efforts to bring perpetrators to justice have been very limited, and have met with almost no success. More than a dozen alleged Lithuanian perpetrators living in the United States were denaturalised and deported to Lithuania for concealing their participation in death squads and local security police units, but they were not punished. Under American pressure, two senior security police commanders, Aleksandras Lileikas and Kazys Gimžauskas, were put on trial in Vilnius but the process became so drawn-out that they became medically unfit to stand trial and so could not be punished. The identity of many of the Lithuanians strongly suspected of being perpetrators is known. In 1999 Lithuanian Jews living in Israel came up with a list of suspected Lithuanian perpetrators. This is known as the "Melamed List", named after Yosef Melamed, Chairman of the Association of Israeli Litvaks. The list appeared in a publication called *Lithuania: Crime and Punishment*. The Lithuanian government gave this list to the Genocide and Resistance Research Centre of Lithuania, which, following review, decided that 1,050 had participated in the mass murder of Jews between 1941 and 1945 and indeed that others had done so. In 2012 the Centre presented a list of 2,055 names to the Lithuanian government. However, no action has been taken in relation to that list. The list briefly appeared on the Centre's website but was then taken down and has not been seen since. It has not been published and there have been no prosecutions.

No real explanation has been offered as to why people on this list have not been prosecuted. One can only speculate as to the reasons: it may be that the Lithuanian government was concerned that, had there been prosecutions, it would have drawn attention to the fact that Stalin sent some Lithuanian murderers of Jews to the camps and this would have played into Putin's narrative of Lithuanians as Nazis. It may be there was concern that the lapse of time since the war meant there were real difficulties about ensuring a fair judicial process; and it may simply have been there was a feeling that prosecution of some Lithuanian perpetrators would have traumatised Lithuanian society for benefits that were unclear. Rūta Vanagaitė describes talking to the deputy councillor of the Lithuanian government about the list. She asked questions:

> 'Why are you hiding it? Why is nobody investigating it any further? Why are Lithuanian historians not being asked to go on with their research?'

The answer?

> 'Whatever we Lithuanians do, it will not be enough. Jews will never forgive us, so what's the point of further research?'[13]

The role of the Genocide and Resistance Research Centre has itself become the subject of controversy, with some Jews and others concerned that it has tried to whitewash the record of Lithuanian heroes who committed Holocaust crimes. The Centre drew particular criticism for a statement about Grant Gochin's lawsuit seeking the removal of a plaque honouring Jonas Noreika, a Lithuanian hero, on account of his role in leading the rebellion against Soviet rule, but strongly suspected of having previously overseen the mass murder of Jews in northern Lithuania.The Centre's statement suggested Noreika was not complicit in the Holocaust, and also gave the impression that Lithuanians were not responsible for killing Lithuanian Jews. The role of the Centre in overseeing the content of the Museum of Genocide Victims has also been controversial. The Museum emphasises the crimes committed by the Soviets against the Lithuanians, and de-emphasises mass murder of the Jews of Lithuania.

Lithuania is far from unique in finding it difficult to face, and to grapple with, a troubling past. In one form or another, many nations have aspects of their past they find difficult to deal with. America has its past treatment of native Americans and black slaves; Britain has its involvement with slavery and its colonial legacy. There are some recurring patterns about things which are controversial: the role of apology; whether recompense and compensation are appropriate; and the role of statues and other memorials.

Lithuania was not unusual in finding that parts of its population willingly collaborated with the Nazis. In almost all countries the Nazis occupied they found willing collaborators (although there were one or two honourable exceptions, including Denmark).[14] The Nazis even found collaborators in the Channel Islands where the local police and government authorities cooperated with German police to identify the Islands' Jews, a small number of whom were subsequently deported to Auschwitz and Belsen.[15]

It is tempting to think that forgetting a difficult past, whether deliberately or otherwise, is quite 'normal', both at a national and at a personal psychological level. In 1882 the Frenchman Ernest Renan gave a lecture at the University of the Sorbonne in which he argued that nations are based as much on what people jointly forget as on what they remember. He did not consider that race was the basis for the unification of people, arguing that the French nation was ethnically diverse. Nor were language or religion the basis for solidarity because language "invites people to unite, but does not force them to do so" and "religion has become an individual matter". Instead, Renan thought a nation was the result of a contractual understanding between citizens, a 'daily plebiscite', and that nations are based as much on what people forget as on what they remember. He thought "Forgetfulness, and [even] historical error are essential in the creation of a nation", and that historical research, by revealing unwanted truths, can even endanger nationhood". He thought all nations are founded on acts of violence which are then forgotten:

> The essence of a nation is that all individuals have many things in common, and also that they have forgotten many things. No French citizen knows whether he is a Burgundian, an Alan, a Taifale, or a Visigoth, yet every French citizen has to have forgotten the massacre of Saint Bartholomew, or the massacre that took place in the south in the thirteenth century.

Most modern readers find Renan's ideas anachronistic and some of them distinctly unattractive; but, he was perceptive in understanding that myth-making has been important in constructing the idea of 'a nation' and that this has often involved deliberately forgetting uncomfortable and violent pasts.

The psychology of individuals who forget difficult past events was famously explored by Sigmund Freud. He wrote extensively about what he termed '*Verleugnung*', which might be translated as 'denial'. He discussed the phenomenon of a person faced with a fact that is too uncomfortable to accept. The person rejects it, insisting that it is untrue despite what might be overwhelming evidence to the contrary. The denial can take different forms: 'simple denial', in which the reality of the unpleasant fact is entirely denied; 'minimisation' in which the fact is admitted but its seriousness is denied; and 'projection', in which both the fact and its seriousness are admitted but responsibility is denied by blaming somebody or something else. These days many psychoanalysts apparently regard denial as the first stage of a coping cycle.[16] It may be that this Freudian analysis helps explain the wilful forgetting of many Lithuaninas about their, or their compatriots', involvement in the Holocaust in Lithuania.

The way that modern Lithuania has tried to deal with its wartime past perhaps raises two particular questions.

The first is why it has proved so difficult for Lithuanians and Lithuanian Jews to address this past. A part of the answer, connected to trauma, has to do with Lithuania's post-war misfortunes. Many Lithuanians found the experience of Soviet occupation terrifying. Friends and colleagues were deported to Siberia and elsewhere deep inside Russia. If spared this fate, their lives were usually characterised by poverty, apprehension about some of their neighbours and concern about falling out with the Soviet regime. Many Lithuanians found Soviet occupation so overwhelming that it gave no space for contemplation of the fate of Jews. Moreover, it became difficult for Lithuanians, particularly in younger age groups, to understand the Holocaust in Lithuania because the Soviets did not permit candid public discussion of it. Some were silent from a sense of shame at how their Jewish neighbours had been treated. Others were silent out of fear that their theft of Jewish owned possessions would be exposed. Others again were reluctant to speak because they did not know who they could trust, and they were conscious that many people still held distinctly hostile opinions about Jews. The tiny handful of Jews who remained in Lithuania were traumatised by the destruction of their families and communities and worried for their own safety. They feared violence from those who had stolen their possessions. They were overcome by the apparently senseless and inexplicable mass murder of their community and understandably angry about it. It may be that in recent years the character of this anger has changed. Since Lithuanian independence in 1990 some foreign-born descendants of Lithuanian Jews appear to have developed an anger about what they perceive to be the unwillingness of the Lithuanian government, and substantial sections of the Lithuanian population, to make it their business to understand the involvement of some Lithuanians in the Holocaust and to demonstrate appropriate remorse. There is suspicion that this denial comes, at best, from a continuing lack of interest in a Jewish community who were their near neighbours for the best part of 600 years and, at worst, from a continuing dislike of Jews. Rightly or wrongly, this seems in certain quarters to be perceived as a continuing slight, as a mark of disrespect.

A second question is whether any useful purpose is really served by trying to persuade the Lithuanian government and its people to become better informed about Lithuania's Holocaust history, and to evidence more remorse. Advocates of such an approach tend to say that doing so would help ease trauma, both Lithuanian and Jewish, and also that education about the Holocaust would make it less likely that a comparable event could ever be repeated. Clearly, there are fine intentions and a good deal of idealism behind such thinking, but whether it is right is unknowable.

There have been two notable recent efforts to facilitate a wider understanding of the Holocaust in Lithuania. The first is a book called *Our*

People. It was jointly written by Rūta Vanagaitė and Efraim Zuroff in autumn 2015 and published in Lithuania in January 2016. Vanagaitė is a well-known Lithuanian writer. She believes members of her family played a role in the mass murder of Jews in Lithuiania. Zuroff is an American born Israeli historian and Nazi hunter, a director of the Simon Wiesenthal Center. He has Jewish family roots in Lithuania. They decided that together they would tour sites in Lithuania where Lithuanians had engaged in mass murder of Jews. They approached this task with apprehension:

> Would we be able to travel together in the same station wagon from one killing site to another for what ultimately lasted forty days? Would we be able to interact respectfully with each other with the shadow of the decimation of Lithuanian Jewry hanging over us? And most important of all, would this trip yield an experience that could create a basis for a book that would be read widely in Lithuania and reveal the true scope of Lithuanian complicity in the Shoah and the intentional cover-up of that unpleasant truth ever since the country regained its independence in 1990?

They got on well. Their book became an immediate bestseller, with the initial printing of 2,000 copies selling out within 48 hours. Four further larger print runs sold out within months. But then the Lithuanian government and Vanagaitė's publisher became anxious. In October 2017 the publisher announced it was severing relations with her and destroying all 27,000 copies of her six books (only one of which concerned the Holocaust). After Vytautas Landsbergis, a senior Lithuanian politician, suggested she "should do her countrymen a favour and commit suicide", Vanagaitė felt unsafe remaining in Lithuania. She moved to Jerusalem to be near Zuroff.[17]

However, there was considerable public discussion of the book in Lithuania. It was as though a genie had been let out of the bottle: "The discussion spills over into readers' lives – at work, around the dinner table, even becoming the topic of conversation at funerals."[18] A great deal of hostility was directed towards Vanagaitė. At the annual Lithuanian book fair in February 2016 (before leaving for Jerusalem) "there [was] so much hate, antisemitism and threats" towards her that Vangaitė needed a security guard at her side for the whole duration of the fair. Opinion was very divided. Many ordinary people told Vanagaitė that Jews got what they deserved and "that the book serves Putin's propaganda purposes, and that maybe it's inspired and/or financed by the Kremlin." On the other hand, a meeting of the country's leading psychotherapists "admitted that while they personally had been aware of the basic facts of the Holocaust, until reading the book, they had never fully internalised the scope of the tragedy...because for Lithuanians, the Jews were always "them"... You cannot mourn if you do not know what you have lost". For them, the book was revelatory.

Publication of the book caused Vanagaitė personal anguish and hardship. But she is consoled: "It doesn't matter that *Our People*, like all my other books, has been removed from the bookstores in Lithuania, and that no bookstore dares to sell it anymore. The learning process has already begun – an important part of healing for Lithuanian society."[19]

Another book by a Lithuanian which caused a stir in the publishing world and prompted wide public discussion in Lithuania about the war years, is *The Nazi's Granddaughter* by Silvia Foti.[20] Foti grew up in the Marquette Park district of Chicago, an area "composed chiefly of exiled Lithuanians and their children, all still grieving over the loss of their country and intent upon reclaiming it."[21] Foti's grandfather was Jonas Noreika, widely revered in Marquette Park for his role in leading a post-war Lithuanian rebellion against Soviet rule. Foti basked in reflected glory: "The aura of heroism seemed to have been transferred magically to me, to inform my very essence. A diamond tiara couldn't have made me feel more special".[22] Foti's mother had spent many years claiming she was writing a book about Jonas Noreika, but she had not done so. On her deathbed, her mother made Silvia promise that she would complete this task. Foti travelled to Lithuania to inter her mother's and her grandmother's ashes. "It seemed that everywhere we looked in Lithuania, there were indications of how much Jonas Noreika was revered". But then she visited a school which had been named in honour of Jonas Noreika. The school director told Foti he had "got a lot of grief at first, when we picked the name" and went on to tell Foti, in a whisper, "he [Noreika] was accused of being a Jew-killer". Foti describes her reaction to hearing this news:

> My mother and grandmother had never mentioned any such accusation. Nor had anyone else I knew. My legendary grandfather was part of my identity, my DNA. I felt such shame at hearing him accused of being a Jew-killer, shame I didn't want to face. *My grandfather was a hero. He was.*[23]

Foti felt obliged to honour her mother's deathbed wish that she write a book about Noreika. Gradually, she came to suspect that her mother must have deliberately put off writing the book because she had uncovered Noreika's involvement in wartime atrocities. Among the papers which her mother had assembled to help write her book Foti discovered various antisemitic tirades by the young Noreika. As her research deepened, she was driven to the inescapable conclusion that Noreika "had served as chief of Šiauliai District under the command of Gebietskommisar Hans Gewecke for nineteen months. During that time, he signed documents sending thousands of Jews to be sequestered in a ghetto from which they were despatched to their deaths."[24] Foti felt that her grandfather could have declined to serve the Nazi regime, as other Lithuanians did, and that his later act of resistance to the Nazis, declining to raise a Lithuanian SS regiment, 'paled in comparison'. In a way which bears some similarities with the Vanagaite/Zuroff relationship, Foti became friendly with a Jewish man called Simon Dovidicius and together they travelled around Lithuania, visiting sites where Jews had been killed. They "forged an unusual bond". There was no suspicion of or resentment toward each other.[25] It became ever more clear to Foti that in the early period after the German invasion of June 1941 her grandfather "had been at the very center of the repugnant events", with his first base in Plungė and then in Telšiai.

Foti's reaction is interesting.

> I was incensed at the magnitude of the cover-up, the lies I had been told by my own family...As my old naivete and denial were replaced by dread certainty and a devastating awareness of betrayal, I began to vibrate with anger. A peculiar icicle formed in my throat and extended into my belly. All of my uncertainty about writing this book vanished, and I vowed to finish it if it was the last thing I did.[26]

A number of different things seem to have fed Foti's anger: that substantial numbers of Lithuanians, including her own grandfather, had been involved in murdering Jews; that the character and extent of this collaboration with the Nazis had been hidden during the post-war period by many of her own family and friends as well by other Lithuanians – in other words, that she had been lied to by people she thought she could trust; that she felt much of Lithuania's past continues to be mythologised, with a narrative which often appeared officially sanctioned, which downplays Lithuanian involvement in the murder of the Jews, and seeks equivalence between Lithuanian hardships under the Soviets and the treatment of Jews during the period of the Nazi occupation. Foti was also appalled that people in her wider family continued to believe the blood libel that Jews abduct and kill Christian children at Passover. Foti feels:

> Denial and obfuscation worked during the Soviet occupation when Lithuanians were not allowed to analyse their history, when it was forbidden to discuss anything except what they were told to evaluate.
>
> But now the country has been free for nearly 30 years, Lithuania has the freedom – and responsibility – to look at its actions during the Holocaust squarely in the eye.
>
> We must face our grandparents' misdeeds. It is time.

Vanagaitė and Foti are exceptionally brave. They have made valiant efforts to understand Lithuania's difficult past and make it easier for others to do so. In the deepest sense they have done what historians are supposed to do. It has been traumatic. It is clearly their hope that facing up to a difficult past will facilitate healing and reconciliation for much of Lithuanian society, but it is too soon to know if this will happen. Much may depend on whether future Lithuanian governments support this endeavour. Absent such support it could be that such painfully honest investigation of the past will mainly be the preserve of a narrow group of intellectuals in Lithuania and a wider community of international scholars who are interested in the Second World War and the Holocaust.[27]

Notes

1 Robert Ignatius Gannon, *The Cardinal Spellman Story* (Doubleday, 1962), pp. 222–23.

2 Silvia Foti, *The Nazi's Granddaughter: How I Discovered My Grandfather Was a War Criminal* (Simon and Schuster, 2021), pp. 85–86.

3 Foti, p. 349.

4 Rūta Vanagaitė and Efraim Zuroff, *Our People: Discovering Lithuania's Hidden Holocaust* (Rowman & Littlefield, 2020), p. 2.

5 Leyb Koniuchowsky, *The Lithuanian Slaughter of its Jews* (Amazon, 2020).

6 Benjamin Ferencz, *Make It Count: An Extraordinary 100-Year-Old Man's 9 Lessons for Living a Life to Be Proud Of* (Little, Brown Book Group Limited, 2023).

7 Father Patrick Desbois, *The Holocaust by Bullets: A Priest's Journey to Uncover the Truth Behind the Murder of 1.5 Million Jews* (St. Martin's Publishing Group, 2008).

8 Vanagaitė and Zuroff, p. 3. This list is set out in the Introduction to 'Our People'.

9 Vanagaitė and Zuroff, p. 59.
10 Foti, pp. 310–11.
11 Vanagaitė and Zuroff, p. 132.
12 Vanagaitė and Zuroff, pp. 205–7.
13 Vanagaitė and Zuroff, p. 50.
14 Leo Goldberger, *The Rescue of the Danish Jews: Moral Courage Under Stress* (NYU Press, 1987).
15 Madeleine Bunting, *The Model Occupation: The Channel Islands Under German Rule, 1940-1945* (Random House, 2014). The experience of Jews in the Channel islands prompts one to speculate about what might have happened to Britain's Jews, had it been occupied.
16 Sofía K. Ogden and Ashley D. Biebers, *Psychology of Denial* (Nova Science Publishers, Incorporated, 2010).
17 Vanagaitė and Zuroff, pp. ix–xi.
18 Vanagaitė and Zuroff, p. 215.
19 Vanagaitė and Zuroff, p. 220.
20 Foti.
21 Foti, p. 37.
22 Foti, p. 22.
23 Foti, p. 63.
24 Foti, p. 250.
25 Foti, p. 273.
26 Foti, p. 305.
27 The task of historians in Lithuania has not been straightforward. In writing about the historians Evaldas Balčiūnas and Dovid Katz, Foti says: "Balčiūnas and Katz had both endured harrassment by the Lithuanian government, lost their jobs, and been followed and interrogated by the police. Eventually, they were declared 'enemies of the state'. These men are true heroes of Lithuania who took enormous risks to publicize the story in spite of the nation's determination to maintain its tale of innocence at all costs".

Conclusion

I wrote this book between 2021 and 2024, about 140 years after my great-grandfather left the Baltic. For most of the last 140 years it would have been difficult for a descendant of an emigrant to write a history of the Jews in Lithuania. Jews who left in the late nineteenth century tended to turn their back on the old country, regarding it as benighted, a place of poverty and persecution. Their energies were directed to remaking their lives in a new world and they did not want to think about the past. In any event, most late nineteenth century Jewish emigrants lacked the secular education necessary for writing history. Then there was the dislocation wrought by the First World War and the horror of the Holocaust. Most Jewish family and friends who had stayed in the Baltic were killed in the Holocaust; and the remnant who survived did not want to remain there after 1945. Descendants of Lithuanian Jewish emigrants in the West were traumatised by the Holocaust. They did not want to discuss it. Then there was the long period of Soviet occupation, a time of oppressive Communist control, when access to information was strictly controlled and travel to the region was all but impossible for most people based in the West. It took a number of years for the clouds of this oppressive state control to begin to lift. Only after Lithuania joined the EU and NATO have some of the values of liberal democracy begun to be implanted and become embedded. This feels a good time to write about the modern history of the Jews in Lithuania.

I am the third generation descendant of a Jewish emigrant. The third generation is an interesting moment in which to write history. Some who write about Herodotus (c.484-420 B.C.E), widely regarded as the first historian, comment on his 'third generation reachback'. Herodotus gathered information by talking to people. He was able to talk to people who had talked to people who had been eye-witnesses to significant historical events. This is what is meant by 'third generation reachback'. I was able to talk to my father who had talked to his grandfather about what now seems the remote world of late nineteenth century Jewish Lithuania. I have not relied on those conversations in writing this book. But such conversations add a dimension, and they give colour. It is a link which is not usually available to the fourth and later generations.

As one looks back at the history of the Jews in Lithuania over the last 140 years it is difficult to avoid the conclusion that the 'big picture' is almost unutterably bleak. Two great world powers, Tsarist Russia and Nazi Germany, were very hostile to Jews. During Tsarist times Jews were constrained as to where they could live and as to how they could earn a living. They were afflicted by a mass of deliberately discriminatory laws which made their lives uncomfortable, and sometimes unbearable. They lived in fear of violence. Some emigrated and others would have done so, had that been practicable. In the period of Nazi occupation, Jews were subjected to ruthless mass murder. About 96 per cent of Lithuania's pre-war Jewish community was killed, a higher proportion of the population than in any other Nazi occupied country. To all intents and purposes Jewish life in Lithuania was wiped out.

The pretexts for hostility and violence towards Jews, and then the murder of Lithuania's Jewish community, were many and varied: at different times, Jews were accused, among other things, of being communists and of being rapacious capitalists. They were accused of making Lithuanians drunk, of not doing any 'proper work', of being 'useless eaters'. Extraordinarily, they were accused of abducting Christian children to use their blood in Passover celebrations. Nazi antisemitism was more racial in character than Tsarist-era antisemitism, but what all manifestations of antisemitism had in common was that Jews were perceived as 'the other'. In the end, it is difficult to avoid the conclusion that this 'othering' came from the deep-seated Christian notion of Jews being responsible, in perpetuity, for the death of Jesus and that it was therefore necessary to keep them apart. This idea was given added force by the canons of the Fourth Lateran Council of 1215 which provided for Jews to be labelled as Jews, confined to ghettos, and restricted to particular business activities Christians did not wish to engage in. The idea of Jews as wicked and dangerous and therefore to be kept apart was to become deeply embedded in Christian Europe. It was in vain to point out that Jesus was Jewish. His family, friends, associates and the apostles were also Jewish. And moreover, the fundamental 'golden rule' of Christianity (found in Matthew 7:12 and in Luke 6:31) is that others, including Jews, should be treated as you would want to be treated yourself.

Over time, and perhaps as a reaction to how they were being treated, devout Jews developed beliefs and practices which kept Jews apart from non-Jewish neighbours and made them seem very different. For centuries in Eastern Europe, Jews lived in separate communities, observing their own rules and practices and engaging in negligible social interaction with non-Jewish neighbours. In the modern world this separateness made Jews vulnerable. If one does not know a neighbour one is precluded from those minor judicious interventions which can forestall and defuse local tension. Rabbi Hugo Gryn grew up in Berehovo in Carpathian Ruthenia, formerly Czechoslovakia and now Ukraine. Its Jewish community was destroyed, but he survived Auschwitz, came to Britain and went on to serve as senior rabbi of West London Synagogue for 32 years. He told me that he thought the 'apartness' he witnessed and experienced in Berehovo had been a source of trouble, allowing all manner of minor jealousies and misunderstandings to fester and grow, and he determined to do his best to prevent continuation of such problems by throwing himself into inter-faith dialogue. Making an effort to get on with one's neighbours offers no panacea, as the experience of the highly emancipated Jewish community of pre-war Germany attests. Nonetheless, in a modest way and at the margins, making an effort to know and get on with neighbours can, in some circumstances, help to reduce tension.

Salo Baron was one of the great twentieth century writers about Jewish history. Writing about medieval Jewish history, Baron cautioned against "the lachrymose conception of Jewish history", by which he meant writing about Jewish history in a way which emphasises tragedy. He said: "suffering is part of the destiny [of the Jews], but so is repeated joy as well as ultimate redemption."[1] However, one would need to be an extravagant optimist to see the recent history of Jews in Lithuania as anything other than lachrymose. But do any rays of light shine through a story which I have described as "almost unutterably bleak"?

One ray of light is to emphasise that, for many years, Lithuania was a good place for Jews to live. In the early modern period, Jews were expelled from many Western European countries. Some of the more notable expulsions include those from England in 1290; from France in 1306; from Hungary in 1360; from Austria in 1420-21; from Spain in 1492; and from Portugal in 1496; at different times Jews were expelled from many of the German states. Jews found refuge in the Polish-Lithuanian commonwealth. For some centuries Jews enjoyed considerable autonomy in Lithuania. It became a great centre for Jewish culture and learning. Napoleon described Vilnius as the 'Jerusalem of the north' when his armies passed through in 1812. And the Vilna Gaon had a lasting influence on Jewish religious thought and practice. At the end of the nineteenth century Vilnius was heavily Jewish. The census of 1897 showed that Jews constituted 40 per cent of the population of Vilnius, Poles were 31 per cent, Russians were 20 per cent and Lithuanians a mere 2 per cent. In other words, parts of Lithuania had large Jewish communities and (albeit with increasing difficulty after 1795), their way of life flourished.

Another ray of light is that some of the thinking which most sustained hostility to Jews before the Holocaust has changed. It is highly significant that in *Nostra Aetate,* issued by Pope Paul V1 in 1965, the Catholic Church formally absolved Jews from continuing responsibility for the death of Jesus. It says, "what happened in His passion cannot be charged against all the Jews, without distinction, then alive, nor against the Jews of today". On antisemitism, *Nostra Aetate* says that the Church "decries hatred, persecutions, displays of antisemitism, directed against Jews at any time and by anyone." There were difficult debates within the Catholic Church to enable it to get to the point where *Nostra Aetate* could be agreed, and many Jews (and others) were disappointed that the language used was not stronger. It proved impossible, for example, to persuade the Catholic Church to attach the word 'condemn' to its criticism of antisemitism. However, *Nostra Aetate* represents a significant change in Catholic theology and thinking. It may take many years for this new thinking to percolate down and affect most members of the Catholic laity, but it is a promising development. It is also positive that, since 1945, eugenics, which was a powerful ideological prop to much Nazi racial thinking, has been widely discredited and is no longer taken seriously in most educated circles.

Perhaps a final 'ray of light' is to reflect on the lives of some of the Jews who left Lithuania to make lives elsewhere. They carried with them the traditions and approaches to life and learning acquired either by them or their forebears in Lithuania. They achieved success in various walks of life, including as politicians, writers, musicians and scientists. They moved to many different countries in the West, including the United States, South Africa and England. Some, including members of my family, even moved to Ireland, and flourished there. But the story of Lithuanian Jews in Ireland, remarkable if relatively little known, must be the subject of my next volume.

Notes

1 Robert Liberles, *Salo Wittmayer Baron: Architect of Jewish History* (NYU Press, 1995), pp. 117–18.

Bibliography

Abramovich, Solomon, and Yakov Zilberg, *Smuggled in Potato Sacks: Fifty Stories of the Hidden Children of the Kaunas Ghetto* (Vallentine Mitchell, 2011)

Alroey, Gur, *Bread to Eat and Clothes to Wear: Letters from Jewish Migrants in the Early Twentieth Century* (Wayne State University Press, 2011)

Alroey, Gur, 'Information, Decision, and Migration: Jewish Emigration from Eastern Europe in the Early Twentieth Century', *Immigrants & Minorities*, 29.01 (2011), 33–63

American Jewish Committee, *The Jews in the Eastern War Zone* (American Jewish committee, 1916)

Antin, Mary, *The Promised Land* (West Margin Press, 2020)

Arad, Yitzhak, *Ghetto In Flames* (KTAV Publishing House, Inc.)

Arendt, Hannah, *Eichmann in Jerusalem* (Penguin UK, 2006)

Babel, Isaac, *1920 Diary* (Yale University Press, 2002)

Babel, Isaac, *The Complete Works of Isaac Babel* (W. W. Norton, 2005)

Bankier, David, *Expulsion and Extermination: Holocaust Testimonials from Provincial Lithuania* (Yad Vashem, the International Institute for Holocaust Research, 2011)

Baron, Salo W., *Ghetto and Emancipation*, (Menorah Journal 1928)

Bartal, Israel, *The Jews of Eastern Europe, 1772-1881* (University of Pennsylvania Press, 2011)

Bauer, Yehuda, *The Death of the Shtetl* (Yale University Press, 2009)

Berlin, Isaiah, *Against the Current: Essays in the History of Ideas* (Pimlico, 1997)

Berman, Hannah, and Melisande Zlotover, *Zlotover Story: A Dublin Story with a Difference* (Hely Thom Limited, 1966)

Biber, Jacob, *Risen from the Ashes* (Star Publishers, 2005)

Bidermann, Gottlob Herbert, *In Deadly Combat: A German Soldier's Memoir of the Eastern Front* (University Press of Kansas, 2000)

Blatman, Daniel, *The Death Marches: The Final Phase of Nazi Genocide* (Harvard University Press, 2011)

Bloom, Cecil, 'The Politics of Immigration, 1881-1905', *Jewish Historical Studies*, 33 (1992), 187–214

Bloxham, Donald, *The Final Solution: A Genocide* (OUP Oxford, 2009)

Blum, Alain, Thomas Chopard and Emiolia Koustova 'Survivors, Collaborators and Partisans?: Bringing Jewish Ghetto Policemen before Soviet Justice in Lithuania', *Jahrbücher Für Geschichte Osteuropas*, 68.2 (2020), 222–55

Bon, Gustave Le, *The Crowd: A Study of the Popular Mind* (T.F. Unwin, 1926)

Briedis, Laimonas, *Vilnius, City of Strangers* (Baltos Lankos 2021)

Browning, Christopher R., *Ordinary Men* (HarperCollins 2017)

Buloff, Joseph, *From the Old Marketplace* (Harvard University Press, 1992)

Bunting, Madeleine, *The Model Occupation: The Channel Islands Under German Rule, 1940-1945* (Random House, 2014)

Buttar, Prit, *Centuries Will Not Suffice: A History of the Lithuanian Holocaust* (Amberley Publishing, 2023)

Carlebach, Elisheva, and Deborah Dash Moore, *The Posen Library of Jewish Culture and Civilization, Volume 6* (Yale University Press, 2019)

Casey, William, *The Secret War Against Hitler* (Berkley Books, 1989)

Cesarani, David, *Port Jews: Jewish Communities in Cosmopolitan Maritime Trading Centres, 1550-1950* (Routledge, 2014)

Cesarani, David, *The Final Solution: Origins and Implementation* (Routledge, 2002)

Commons, Great Britain Parliament House of, *Royal Commission on Alien Immigration. Minutes of Evidence Taken Before the Royal Commission on Alien Immigration. Vol. II.* (House of Commons, 2007)

Coppa, Frank J., *The Papacy, the Jews, and the Holocaust* (CUA Press, 2006)

Coxe, William, *Travels Into Poland, Russia, Sweden, and Denmark: Interspersed with Historical Relations and Political Inquiries* (S. Price, 1784)

Dawidowicz, Lucy S., *The Golden Tradition: Jewish Life and Thought in Eastern Europe* (J. Aronson, 1989)

Desbois, Father Patrick, *The Holocaust by Bullets: A Priest's Journey to Uncover the Truth Behind the Murder of 1.5 Million Jews* (St. Martin's Publishing Group, 2008)

Deutscher, Isaac, *The Non-Jewish Jew: And Other Essays* (Verso Books, 2017)

Dieckmann, Christoph, *Deutsche Besatzungspolitik in Litauen 1941-1944* (Wallstein Verlag, 2016)

Dieckmann, Christoph, and Rūta Vanagaitė, *How Did It Happen?: Understanding the Holocaust* (Rowman & Littlefield, 2021)

Diner, Hasia R., *The Jews of the United States, 1654 to 2000* (University of California Press, 2006)

Dinnerstein, Leonard, *America and the Survivors of the Holocaust* (Columbia University Press, 1982)

Dubnov, Semen M., *History of the Jews in Russia and Poland: From the Earliest Times Until the Present Day* (Jewish Publ. Soc. of America, 2017)

Elon, Amos, *The Pity of It All: A Portrait of Jews in Germany 1743-1933* (Penguin UK, 2004)

Endelman, Todd M., *The Jews of Britain, 1656 to 2000* (University of California Press, 2002)

Erickson, Charlotte, 'Jewish People in the Atlantic Migration, 1850-1914', *In Patterns of Migration*, 1914 (1850), 1–18

Evans, Nicholas J., 'The Port Jews of Libau, 1880–1914', *Jewish Culture and History*, 7.1–2 (2004), 197–214

Evans-Gordon, William Eden (Sir), *The Alien Immigrant* (BiblioBazaar, 2016)

Feldman, David, *Englishmen and Jews: Social Relations and Political Culture, 1840-1914* (Yale University Press, 1994)

Feldman, Yael S., '"Not as Sheep Led to Slaughter"? On Trauma, Selective Memory, and the Making of Historical Consciousness', *Jewish Social Studies*, 19.3 (2013), 139–69

Ferencz, Benjamin, *Make It Count: An Extraordinary 100-Year-Old Man's 9 Lessons for Living a Life to Be Proud Of* (Little, Brown Book Group Limited, 2023)

Fishman, David E., *The Book Smugglers: Partisans, Poets, and the Race to Save Jewish Treasures from the Nazis* (University Press of New England, 2017)

Foti, Silvia, *The Nazi's Granddaughter: How I Discovered My Grandfather Was a War Criminal* (Simon and Schuster, 2021)

Frederic, Harold, *The New Exodus: A Study of Israel in Russia* (W. Heinemann, 1892)

Freedland, Jonathan, *The Escape Artist: The Man Who Broke Out of Auschwitz to Warn the World* (Hachette UK, 2022)

Friedlander, Saul, *The Years of Extermination: Nazi Germany and the Jews, 1939-1945* (HarperCollins e-books, 2009)

Fritz, Stephen G., *Endkampf: Soldiers, Civilians, and the Death of the Third Reich* (University Press of Kentucky, 2004)

Gannon, Robert Ignatius, *The Cardinal Spellman Story* (Doubleday, 1962)

Gartner, Lloyd P., 'Notes on the Statistics of Jewish Immigration to England 1870-1914', *Jewish Social Studies*, 1960, 97–102

Gartner, Lloyd P., 'The Great Jewish Migration 1881-1914: Myths and Realities', *Shofar*, 4.2 (1986), 12–21

Gilbert, Martin, *Auschwitz and the Allies: A Devastating Account of How the Allies Responded to the News of Hitler's Mass Murder* (Rosetta Books, 2015)

Goldberger, Leo, *The Rescue of the Danish Jews: Moral Courage Under Stress* (NYU Press, 1987)

Goldstein-Golden, Lazar, *From Ghetto Kovno to Dachau* (E. Goldshṭeyn, 1985)

Gráda, Cormac Ó, *Jewish Ireland in the Age of Joyce: A Socioeconomic History* (Princeton University Press, 2016)

Grade, Chaim, *My Mother's Sabbath Days: A Memoir* (Rowman & Littlefield, 1997)

Grayzel, Solomon, *The Church and the Jews in the XIIIth Century: A Study of Their Relations During the Years 1198-1254, Based on the Papal Letters and the Conciliar Decrees of the Period* (Hermon Press, 1966)

Greenbaum, Masha, *The Jews of Lithuania: A History of a Remarkable Community, 1316-1945* (Gefen, 1995)

Gringauz, Samuel 1900-1975, 'Jewish Destiny as the DPs See It: The Ideology of the Surviving Remnant', *The Posen Library of Jewish Culture and Civilization; Volume 9: Catastrophe and Rebirth*, 1947, 420

Gross, Jan Tomasz, and Irena Grudzinska Gross, *Golden Harvest: Events at the Periphery of the Holocaust* (Oxford University Press, 2016)

Haberer, Erich, 'Kovner, Abba: The Fall of a Sparrow: The Life and Times of Abba Kovner', *Biography*, 35.2 (2012), 425–26

Haffner, Sebastian, *Defying Hitler: A Memoir* (Hachette UK, 2012)

Hatton, Timothy J., and Jeffrey G. Williamson, 'After the Famine: Emigration from Ireland, 1850–1913', *The Journal of Economic History*, 53.3 (1993), 575–600

Hayes, Peter, *Why?: Explaining the Holocaust* (W. W. Norton & Company, 2017)

Henry, Patrick, *Jewish Resistance Against the Nazis* (CUA Press, 2014)

Hertzberg, Arthur, *The Zionist Idea: A Historical Analysis and Reader* (Jewish Publication Society, 1997)

Herzl, Theodor, *The Diaries of Theodor Herzl* (Victor Gollancz, 1958)

Hilberg, Raul, *Perpetrators, Victims, Bystanders: The Jewish Catastrophe, 1933-1945* (Aaron Asher Books, 1992)

Hinkkanen-Lievonen, Merja-Liisa, *British Trade and Enterprise in the Baltic States, 1919-1925* (SHS, 1984)

Howard, Michael, *The First World War* (Oxford University Press, 2003)

Howe, Irving, *World of Our Fathers: The Journey of the East European Jews to America and the Life They Found and Made There* (Phoenix, 2000)

Hundert, Gershon David, *Jews in Poland-Lithuania in the Eighteenth Century: A Genealogy of Modernity* (University of California Press, 2004)

James, John Thomas, *Journal of a Tour in Germany, Sweden, Russia, Poland, During the Years 1813 and 1814* (J. Murray, 1816)

Johnson, Eric M., 'Demographics, Inequality and Entitlements in the Russian Famine of 1891', *Slavonic & East European Review*, 93.1 (2015), 96–119

Jones, J. Sydney, *Hitler in Vienna, 1907-1913: Clues to the Future* (Cooper Square Press, 2002)

Jopson, N. B., 'Memories of the Old Bridge', *The Slavonic Review*, 4.10 (1925), 142–46

Kalme, Albert, *Total Terror. An Exposé of Genocide in the Baltics* (Appleton-Century-Crofts, 1948)

Karski, Jan, *Story of a Secret State* (Houghton Mifflin, 1943)

Katz, Dovid, *Words on Fire: The Unfinished Story of Yiddish* (Basic Books, 2004)

Katz, Steven, *The Cambridge Companion to Antisemitism* (Cambridge University Press, 2022)

Katz, Steven T., *The Shtetl: New Evaluations* (NYU Press, 2009)

Kershaw, Ian, *Hitler, 1889-1936: Hubris* (Penguin, 1999)

Kertzer, David I., *The Pope at War: The Secret History of Pius XII, Mussolini, and Hitler* (Oxford University Press, 2022)

Koniuchowsky, Leyb, *The Lithuanian Slaughter of Its Jews: The Testimonies of 121 Jewish Survivors of the Holocaust in Lithuanian, Recorded by Leyb Koniuchowsky, in Displaced Persons' Camps (1946-48)*, 2020

Koss, Andrew N., 'War within, War without: Russian Refugee Rabbis during World War I', *AJS Review*, 34.2 (2010), 231–63

Kuznets, Simon, *Immigration of Russian Jews to the United States: Background and Structure* (Routledge, 2017)

Lang, Berel, 'Holocaust Memory and Revenge: The Presence of the Past', *Jewish Social Studies*, 2.2 (1996), 1–20

Lawson, Tom, *Debates on the Holocaust* (Manchester University Press, 2010)

LeChêne, Evelyn, and Evelyn Le Chêne, *Mauthausen: The History of a Death Camp* (Methuen, 1971)

Levene, Mark, 'The Balfour Declaration: A Case of Mistaken Identity', *The English Historical Review*, 107.422 (1992), 54–77

Levin, Dov, *The Litvaks: A Short History of the Jews in Lithuania* (Berghahn Books, 2000)

Levine, Hillel, *In Search of Sugihara: The Elusive Japanese Diplomat Who Risked His Life to Rescue 10,000 Jews from the Holocaust* (Free Press, 1996)

Levitats, Isaac, *The Jewish Community in Russia, 1772-1844* (Columbia University Press, 1943)

Lewis, Helen, *A Time to Speak* (Blackstaff, 2010)

Liberles, Robert, *Salo Wittmayer Baron: Architect of Jewish History* (NYU Press, 1995)

Liekis, Šarūnas, ChaeRan Y. Freeze, and Antony Polonsky, *Jews in the Former Grand Duchy of Lithuania Since 1772* (Littman Library of Jewish Civilization, 2013)

Littman, Sol, *War Criminal on Trial: The Rauca Case* (Lester & Orpen Dennys, 1983)

Lohr, Eric, 'The Russian Army and the Jews: Mass Deportation, Hostages, and Violence during World War I', *The Russian Review*, 60.3 (2001), 404–19

London, Louise, *Whitehall and the Jews, 1933-1948: British Immigration Policy, Jewish Refugees and the Holocaust* (Cambridge University Press, 2003)

Longerich, Peter, *Heinrich Himmler: A Life* (OUP Oxford, 2012)

Lozansky, Riva, *If I Forget Thee—: The Destruction of the Shtetl Butrimantz* (Remembrance Books, 1998)

Lozansky-Bogomolnaya, Rivka, *Wartime Experiences in Lithuania* (Vallentine Mitchell, 2000)

MacQueen, Michael, 'The Context of Mass Destruction: Agents and Prerequisites of the Holocaust in Lithuania', *Holocaust and Genocide Studies*, 12.1 (1998), 27–48

Maimon, Solomon, *The Autobiography of Solomon Maimon: The Complete Translation* (Princeton University Press, 2020)

Malkin, Carole, *The Journeys of David Toback: As Retold by His Granddaughter* (Schocken Books, 1981)

Marrus, Michael R., 'The Theory and Practice of Anti-Semitism', in *The Origins of the Holocaust* (KG Saur, 2011), pp. 172–84

Matthäus, Jürgen, 'German Judenpolitik in Lithuania during the First World War', *The Leo Baeck Institute Yearbook*, 43.1 (1998), 155–74

Megargee, Geoffrey P., *The United States Holocaust Memorial Museum Encyclopedia of Camps and Ghettos, 1933–1945: Volume I: Early Camps, Youth Camps, and Concentration Camps and Subcamps under the SS-Business Administration Main Office (WVHA)* (Indiana University Press, 2009)

Mendelsohn, Ezra, *Jews of East Central Europe Between the World Wars* (Indiana University Press 1983)

Mendes-Flohr, Paul R., and Jehuda Reinharz, *The Jew in the Modern World: A Documentary History* (Oxford University Press, 2011)

Miron, Dan, *The Image of the Shtetl and Other Studies of Modern Jewish Literary Imagination* (Syracuse University Press, 2000)

Mishell, William W., *Kaddish for Kovno: Life and Death in a Lithuanian Ghetto, 1941-1945* (Chicago Review Press, 1999)

Misiunas, Romuald J., 'Fascist Tendencies in Lithuania', *The Slavonic and East European Review*, 48.110 (1970), 88–109

Montefiore, Sir Moses, *Diaries of Sir Moses and Lady Montefiore: Comprising Their Life and Work as Recorded in Their Diaries from 1812-1883 ...* (Belford-Clarke Company, 1890)

Morina, Christina, and Krijn Thijs, *Probing the Limits of Categorization: The Bystander in Holocaust History* (Berghahn Books, 2018)

Nathans, Benjamin, *Beyond the Pale: The Jewish Encounter with Late Imperial Russia* (University of California Press, 2002)

Newman, Aubrey, 'The Poor Jews' Temporary Shelter: An Episode in Migration Studies', *Jewish Historical Studies*, 40 (2005), 141–55

Ofek, Adina, 'Cantonists: Jewish Children as Soldiers in Tsar Nicholas's Army', *Modern Judaism*, 1993, 277–308

Ogden, Sofía K., and Ashley D. Biebers, *Psychology of Denial* (Nova Science Publishers, Incorporated, 2010)

Oshry, Ephraim, and Efroim Oshry, *The Annihilation of Lithuanian Jewry* (Judaica Press, 1995)

Parkin, Simon, *The Island of Extraordinary Captives: A True Story of an Artist, a Spy and a Wartime Scandal* (Hachette UK, 2022)

Paulsson, Gunnar S, *Secret City: The Hidden Jews of Warsaw 1940-1945* (Yale University Press 2002)

Petrovsky-Shtern, Yohanan, *Jews in the Russian Army, 1827-1917: Drafted Into Modernity* (Cambridge University Press, 2009)

Petrovsky-Shtern, Yohanan, *The Golden Age Shtetl: A New History of Jewish Life in East Europe* (Princeton University Press, 2015)

Phayer, Michael, *Pius XII, the Holocaust, and the Cold War* (Indiana University Press, 2008)

Pinson, Koppel S., 'Jewish Life in Liberated Germany: A Study of the Jewish DPs', *Jewish Social Studies*, 9.2 (1947), 101–26

Polonsky, Antony, *The Jews in Poland and Russia: 1914-2008* (Littman Library of Jewish Civilization, 2010)

Polonsky, Anthony, *The Jews in Poland and Russia: Volume II: 1881 To 1914* (Littman Library of Jewish Civilization, 2019)

Porat, Dina, *The Fall of a Sparrow: The Life and Times of Abba Kovner* (Stanford University Press, 2009)

Rees, Laurence, *The Holocaust: A New History* (Penguin UK, 2017)

Richmond, Theo, *Konin, A Quest* (Vintage 1996)

Rybak, Jan, *Everyday Zionism in East-Central Europe: Nation-Building in War and Revolution, 1914-1920*, 1st edn (Oxford University Press, 2021)

Sakowicz, Kazimierz, *Ponary Diary, 1941-1943: A Bystander's Account of a Mass Murder* (Yale University Press, 2005)

Samet, Moshe, 'The Beginnings of Orthodoxy', *Modern Judaism*, 8.3 (1988), 249–69

Sands, Philippe, *The Ratline: The Exalted Life and Mysterious Death of a Nazi Fugitive* (Alfred A. Knopf, 2021)

Schapiro, Leonard, 'The Rôle of the Jews in the Russian Revolutionary Movement', *The Slavonic and East European Review*, 40.94 (1961), 148–67

Schoenburg, Nancy, and Stuart Schoenburg, *Lithuanian Jewish Communities* (Rowman & Littlefield, 1996)

Schwertfeger, Ruth, *A Nazi Camp Near Danzig: Perspectives on Shame and on the Holocaust from Stutthof* (Bloomsbury Publishing, 2022)

Seton-Watson, Hugh, *The Russian Empire 1801-1917* (Clarendon Press, 1967)

Shneidman, N. N., *Jerusalem of Lithuania: The Rise and Fall of Jewish Vilnius : A Personal Perspective* (Mosaic Press, 1998)

Sirutavicius, Vladas, and Darius Staliunas, *A Pragmatic Alliance: Jewish-Lithuanian Political Cooperation at the Beginning of the 20th Century* (Central European University Press, 2011)

Sklarew, Myra, *A Survivor Named Trauma: Holocaust Memory in Lithuania* (SUNY Press, 2020)

Spetter, Allan, 'The United States, the Russian Jews and the Russian Famine of 1891–1892', *American Jewish Historical Quarterly*, 64.3 (1975), 236–44

Staliunas, Darius, *Enemies for a Day: Antisemitism and Anti-Jewish Violence in Lithuania under the Tsars* (Central European University Press, 2015)

Stangneth, Bettina, *Eichmann Before Jerusalem: The Unexamined Life of a Mass Murderer* (Random House, 2016)

Stanislawski, Michael, *Tsar Nicholas I and the Jews: The Transformation of Jewish Society in Russia, 1825-1855* (Jewish Publication Society of America, 1983)

Stein, Louis, 'The Exile of the Lithuanian Jews in the Conflagration of the First World War (1914-1918)'

Stone, Dan, *The Holocaust: An Unfinished History* (Penguin UK, 2023)

Stone, Dan, *The Liberation of the Camps: The End of the Holocaust and Its Aftermath* (Yale University Press, 2023)

Sukys, Julija, *'And I Burned with Shame': The Testimony of Ona Šimaitė, Righteous Among the Nations: A Letter to Isaac Nachman Steinberg* (Wallstein Verlag, 2008)

Sundbäck, Esa, 'The Baltic States, Finland, and British Economic Expectations in the Early 1920s', *Journal of Baltic Studies*, 33.3 (2002), 307–21

Sutton, Karen, *The Massacre of the Jews of Lithuania: Lithuanian Collaboration in the Final Solution, 1941-1944* (Gefen Pub., 2008)

Sutzkever, Abraham, *From the Vilna Ghetto to Nuremberg: Memoir and Testimony* (McGill-Queen's Press - MQUP, 2021)

The Vanished World of Lithuanian Jews ed. by A. Nikžentaitis, D. Staliūnas and S. Schreiner (Rodopi, 2004)

Ury, Scott, 'Migration as Redemption: The Myth and Memory of Jewish Migration from Eastern Europe to the New World', *Jewish Culture and History*, 20.1 (2019), 3–22

Vanagaitė, Rūta, and Efraim Zuroff, *Our People: Discovering Lithuania's Hidden Holocaust* (Rowman & Littlefield, 2020)

Veidlinger, Jeffrey, *In the Midst of Civilized Europe: The Pogroms of 1918-1921 and the Onset of the Holocaust* (Pan Macmillan, 2021)

Vital, David, *A People Apart: A Political History of the Jews in Europe 1789-1939* (OUP Oxford, 2001)

Voren, Robert van, *Undigested Past: The Holocaust in Lithuania* (Rodopi, 2011)

Weale, Adrian, *The SS: A New History* (Hachette UK, 2010)

Weizmann, Chaim, *Trial and Error: The Autobiography of Chaim Weizmann* (Harper, 1949)

Wex, Michael, *Just Say Nu: Yiddish for Every Occasion (When English Just Won't Do)* (HarperCollins, 2008)

Wiesel, Elie, *Night* (Hill and Wang, a division of Farrar, Straus and Giroux, 2006)

Wildt, Michael, *An Uncompromising Generation: The Nazi Leadership of the Reich Security Main Office* (University of Wisconsin Press, 2009)

Wischnitzer, Mark, *To Dwell in Safety: The Story of Jewish Migration Since 1800* (Jewish Publication Society of America, 1949)

Wynn, Natalie, 'The History and Internal Politics of Ireland's Jewish Community in Their International Jewish Context (1881-1914)' (unpublished PhD Thesis, Trinity College Dublin, 2015)

Yablonka, Hanna, and Moshe Tlamim, 'The Development of Holocaust Consciousness in Israel: The Nuremberg, Kapos, Kastner, and Eichmann Trials', *Israel Studies*, 8.3 (2003), 1–24

Yerushalmi, Yosef Hayim, *Zakhor: Jewish History and Jewish Memory* (University of Washington Press, 2011)

Index

Note: Page numbers in italics are illustrations. References to notes are indicated by 'n' after the page number (250n13).

1920 Diary (Babel) 119

Abramovitsh, Sholem Y. 20, 21, 22, 23, 25, 31
Abramowicz, Berent 7
acculturation 36, 131–33
Adler, Chief Rabbi Nathan 81
Adler, E.N. 81
Adversos Iudaeos 199
Aesti 4–5
Afanassiev, Alexander 42
Africa, South 73–74
Agnon, Shmuel Yosef 25, 28
agriculture 10, 42, 93
agunah/agunot viii, 29, 53
Akmenė 82, 83, 152, 154
Aksakov, Ivan 30
Aleichem, Sholem 20–21, 22
Alexander II, Tsar 15–16, 38, 54, 58, 63
Alexander III, Tsar 54, 60, 64, 68
Alexei, Tsar 7
Aliens Act 1793 (UK) 70
Aliens Act 1905 (UK) 70, 98, 233–34
Aliens Registration Act 1914 (UK) 70
Aliens Restrictions Act 1919 (UK) 70
Alliance Israelite Universelle 82
allied governments, aware of mass murder being conducted by Nazi Germany 236–38
amber 4–5
America *see* United States
American Jewish Committee 92, 104–5
American Jewish Joint Distribution Committee ("the Joint") 111, 115
American Joint Reconstruction Foundation ('the Foundation') 115
Amidah viii, 227
Angel, Moses 81
Antanas, Kerys 154
anti-Judaism 196, 197–98
Antin, Mary 57, 66, 69, 72, 76
antisemitism 196, 200, 214, 215, 220, 287
- in late nineteenth century Lithuania 56, 57–58
- and Plehve's policies 91
- German 112, 201–4
- and crowd behaviour 120
- in inter-war Lithuania 129, 130
- and annexation of Klaipėda (Memel) 137–39
- and Lithuanian Activist Front

(LAF) 144–45, 146
and Hitler 205, 206
shown by British Foreign Office 237
and *Nostra Aetate* 289
apology to the Jewish people for Lithuanians' participation in the Holocaust 276
Arad, Yitzhak 158–59, 165
Arendt, Hannah 212
assimilation 13–14, 15, 36, 41
Augustine of Hippo 199
Auschwitz 236, 237, 241
Austria-Hungary, declared war on Serbia 102
"Auto-Emancipation" (Pinsker) 77

Babel, Isaac 119
"the Back'sche plan" 158
Baltics
showing present day borders (map) *xiii*
attracted by Nazi ideology 208–9
in the Soviet sphere of influence 271–72
Baron, Salo 50, 288
Baskin, Joel 44
Bauer, Yehuda 227
Belsen 266
Ber, R. Dov 10
Bergelson, Dovid 20
Berlin, Isaiah 209
Berlin Haskalah 36–37, 38, 40
Berman, Lieb 69
Berzinis, Saulis 276
Bevin, Ernest 266–67
Bialik, Hayim 22
Bidermann, Gottlob Herbert 255–57
Bielskis, Julius 114–15
Black Hundreds 91–92
Blaine, James G. 68
blood libels 7, 56–57, 94, 96, 283, 287
Bloxham, Donald 159
Bolsheviks 100–101, 117–19, 124, 126
Bolshevism 142, 155
'Book For Adults' (Valancius) 57
Booth, Charles 81
Brandisauskas, Valentinas 276
Brazauskas, Algirdas 276
brichah 268
The Brief Travels of Benjamin the Third (Abramovitsh) 22, 25
Britain
policy of dispersal 82
immigration controls 233–35, 266–68
British Jews 79–81
Brizgys, Bishop Vincentas 246, 247
Browning, Christopher 112
Brutzkus, Julius 92
Bubnys, Arunas 157, 159
Buloff, Joseph 110
Bulota, Andrius 56
the Bund 98, 100–101
Butrimonys 179–81, 182, 183–84, 187–88, 192
ghetto 185
mass graves 189–90
bystander 195, 196, 233, 238, 248, 249

Cantonists 13, 62–63
Casey, William J. 237–38
Catherine the Great 23–24
Catholic Church 238–48, 276, 289
Catholics, Lithuanian 94–95, 246–48

cemetery
old, site of in Pikeliai Plate 12
and the shtetl 31
Central Office of Migration Affairs 75
chain migration 82–83
chazan, definition viii
children, Jewish
helped by Lithuanians 249
survivors sent to Britain on immigration scheme 267
Chmielnicki, Bogdan 7
Christianity 56–57, 94–95, 196–200
Churchill, Winston, on Soviet sphere of influence 271
Communism, associated with Jews 127, 140–43, 146, 202–3, 217
Communist party of Lithuania (the "CPL") 139, 142
comradeship, sense of, as usable Nazi material 210–12, 215
concentration camps 171–73, 236, 237, 241, 258–60, 266
On the concept of a Science of Judaism (Wolf) 19
conscription 13, 61–65, 85
conspiracy theories, about Jews 214
conversion to Christianity 13, 14, 38, 63, 132, 243
Cork, Mayor 85
Cork Jewish community 91
Cornelius Tacitus 4–5
Cossack and peasant rebellion 7
Council of Lithuania 9
Courland 43, 83
expulsion of Jews from 105–6, 114
Coxe, William 11
cultural resistance 227–28, 233
Currie, Donald 73, 74
Darwinism 200
Daugirdas, Tadas 115
Davidson, Mendel 219
In Deadly Combat (Bidermann) 255
death marches 260–63
'decapitation plan' 158
Defying Hitler (Haffner) 202
deicide charge 197–98
'Delegates Trip to Lithuania' (Bielskis) 114–15
Dell'Acqua, Monsignor Angelo 242
'*De Non Tolerandis Judaeis*' 7
deportation of Jews, policy of Germany 204
Depression, Great 130
Deutscher, Isaac 99
Deutsche Verwaltung für Litauen 110
Deutschlander, Leo 109
Dieckmann, Christoph 158, 168–69, 217, 218, 225–26
"*Di nisrofim*" (Abramovitsh) 21
"The Dispersed of Israel" (Poupko) 77
Displaced Persons (DPs) 267, 268
Displaced Persons' Camps (DP Camps) 263, 264–66, 268–69
'distressed persons' scheme 267
divorce 29, 30, 53
Dolgorukov, Count Ivan 24
domestic violence 30
d'Ormesson, Wladmir 242
Dovidicius, Simon 283
Dubnow, Simon 8, 9, 58–59, 62, 98, 104

eastern front, First World War 102–4
Eastern Yiddish 25
Eichmann, Adolf 223
Eidintas, Alfonsas 277

Eidukas, Juozapas 94
Einsatzgruppen 151–52, 208
trial 273
Elkes, Doctor Elkhanan 170, 224
Elyan, Larry 84
Elyan, Reverend Meyer 84
emotional intelligence, suppressed by leading Nazis 208
employment, Jewish 42, 66–67, 69, 81, 129
the enlightenment 37
Epelboim, Avrum 28
Eretz Yisrael viii, 39
Essay on the Inequality of the Human Races (Gobineau) 200
Estonia, Lithuanian Jews moved to 172, 173
European Volunteer Worker (EVW) schemes 267–68
Evans-Gordon, Major William 55, 69, 76, 80–81, 80n60
on Liepāja 44, 73
on poverty of the Jews 65
evil, banality of 212
execution sites in Lithuania, map *xx*

Falkenhayn, Erich von 102
family unit, Jewish 29–30
famine of 1891 67–68
Fareynikte Partizaner Organizatsie (FPO) 229
First World War 101–14, 201–2
Fishman, David 228
Folkist parties 127
Foti, Silvia 271–72, 274–75, 282–84
Fourth Lateran Council of 1215 57
France, Germany declared war on 102
Frankel, Chaim 162–63
Franz Ferdinand, Archduke 101–2
Franz-Joseph, Emperor 102
Frederic, Harold 14, 16
Freud, Sigmund 120, 279
Fuchs, Tanya 141
Fulbrook, Mary 195, 196, 248

Galen, Clemens Graf von 160
Gall, Franz Joseph 201
Gediminas, Grand Duke 5
Geležinis Vilkas 130, 216–17
General Jewish Workers' Alliance 98, 100–101
Genocide and Resistance Research Centre 277, 278
Gens, Jacob 224
German Jews 109
German military administration 109–11, 112
Germany
declared war on Russia on 1 August 1914 102
and Klaipėda 125–26
ethnic Germans, and ethnic Lithuanians fled to after Soviet occupation of Lithuania 144
and Lithuanian Activist Front (LAF) 145–46
and Operation Barbarossa/invasion of Soviet Union, June 1941 149–50, 204
invasion of Lithuania, 21 June 1941 164–65, 180
in and after World War 1 201–2
surrendered on 9 May 1945 257
get viii, 53
Gewecke, Hans 164
ghettos 149, 155, 172, 185, 186
Vilnius 165, 169, 172, 174, 224, 227–28

Kaunas 166–67, 173, 174, 249
and Jewish Councils 167–71
Šiauliai 172–73, 174
no help given to Jews from non-Jews 226
Warsaw 236
Gilys, Jonas 246
Gobineau, Arthur de 200
Goebbels, Joseph 150
Goldberg, Lea 133
Goldbergas, Jokubas 131
Goldhagen, Daniel 112
Goldsmid, Colonel A.E. W. 81
Golenbo, Chana 247
Gordon, Judah Leib 41
Gospel of Matthew 198
Gospel of St. John 197, 198
Grade, Chaim 264
graves, mass 189–90, 275
site of in Mažeikiai where most of the murdered Jews of Pikeliai are buried 155–56, Plate 17
Great Britain *see* Britain
Great Famine of 1891 67–68
Greenbaum, Masha 142–43, 152, 175n6
Greenberg, Uri Zvi 223
Gringauz, Samuel 268
Grodzienski, Hayim Ozer 115
Grunwald (Tannenberg), Battle of 5
Gryn, Rabbi Hugo 288
Guri, Haim 223
gymnazya viii

Haffner, Sebastian 202, 210–11
Haganah viii, ix
Haidamack 12
halacha viii
Hamann, Joachim 161–62, 164
Hamann Rollkommando 161, 162, 217
Hame'asef (periodical) 40
Hanisch, Reinhold 205
Hanukkah, definition viii
Haredi viii, 35
Harrison Report 266
Haskalah viii, 36–41
Hausner, Gideon 223
Hayes, Peter 201, 250n13
Hayyim, R. of Volozhin 33
Ha-zeman (periodical) 71
heder viii, 33
Heingartner, Robert Wayne 133–35
herem viii, 9
Hersch, Liebmann 52
Herzen, Alexander 62
Herzl, Theodor 77, 99
Heydrich, Reinhard 151
Hibat Tsiyon 39
Hilberg, Raul 195
Hilfsverein der deutschen Juden 111
Himmler, Heinrich 161, 171, 206–7, 258
Hitler, Adolf 159–60, 203, 204–6, 207, 215
Hitler's Willing Executioners (Goldhagen) 112
Hollweg, Theobald Bethmann 102
Holocaust
about 225,000 Jews in Lithuania before Nazi invasion of June 1941 148–49
German invasion on 22 June 1941 until December 1941 149–54, 157, 159, 160–62, 165–67, 182, 183–84, 186–88
18,000 Jews, mostly men, murdered before the end of July 1941 151

by December 1941 only about twenty per cent of the pre-war Lithuanian Jewish population remained alive 157
January 1942 until March 1943 149, 172
April 1943 until July 1944 149, 172–73, 174
estimated about 96 per cent of pre-war Jewish population of Lithuania murdered 148
need to dispose of Jews to ensure sufficient food during the war 158, 161, 209–10, 215
stealing Jews' possessions, motivation for Lithuanians 180, 185, 186, 189, 218–21, 225
responsibility for 204–5
and concern that German soldiers might catch infectious diseases from Jews 210
sadism, motivation for German participation in 212–13, 215
antisemitism, motivation for participation in 215
Lithuanians blamed Jews for Soviet occupation 218
Pope Pius X11 very fully informed about 239
acknowledgement of guilt to gain admission to the European Union and to NATO 273–74
Einsatzgruppen trial 273
apology to the Jewish people for Lithuanians' participation in the Holocaust 276
efforts to bring perpetrators to justice very limited 276
how modern Lithuania has tried to deal with its wartime past 279–82
wilful forgetting of many Lithuanians about their, or their compatriots', involvement in 279
Holy Land, longing to return to 32
Hoppe, Paul-Werner 261
hostage-taking, of Lithuanian Jews 108
Hovevey Tsiyon 39
Howard, Sir Michael 102
Howe, Irving 47, 50
Hundert, Gershon David 12, 17n19
Hungarian Jews 258
'hunger plan' 158

ICA (Jewish Colonization Association) 71
Ignatiev, Nikolai 54–55
immigration controls 233–35, 266–67, 268
industrialisation 41–42, 95
Industrial Removal Office (IRO) 74, 81–82
Innocent III, Pope 199–200
intermarriage 132
Ireland
Jewish population 50–51
why chosen as place of emigration 78–79, 83–86
and policy of dispersal 81–82
Isaiah 53 222
Ish-Shalom , Rosa 257–58, 266, 267, 268
Israel, State of, declared on 14 May, 1948 268
Ivinskis, Zenonas 141, 143

Jäger, Karl 162, 167
James, John Thomas 11
jealousy, of Jews' success by Germans 213–15
Jerusalem of Lithuania (Shneidman) 165
Jesus 197–98
Jewish autonomy, In Lithuania 125, 127, 128
Jewish Board of Guardians 81
Jewish children, helped by Lithuanians 249
Jewish Colonization Association (ICA) 74
Jewish Congregational Union's Dispersal Committee 82
Jewish Councils xi–xii, 170, 223–25
Jewish Lads Brigade 81
Jewish partisans 175, 210, 229–30, 231
Jewish police units 170–71
Jewish refugees 267, 268–69
Jewish survivors 264–67, 268–69, 271, 273
Jewish Territorial Organization (ITO) 74
"Jews: An Economic and Social Glance" (Maliauskas) 57
Jews' Free School 81
"The Jews in the Eastern War Zone" (American Jewish Committee) 92
the Joint (American Jewish Joint Distribution Committee) 111, 115
Journal of a Tour in Germany, Sweden, Russia, and Poland, during 1813 and 1814 (James) 11
Der Judenstaat (Herzl) 77
Kaczerginski, Shmerke 227, 228
kahal ix, 8–9, 13, 30
Kalmanovitch, Zelig 228
Kalme, Albert 144
Karaites 5–6
Karakazov, D. 15–16, 54
Karski, Jan 236
Katz, Joseph 262
Katz, Steven 18
Katz, Yisrael 219
Katzenelenbogen, Uriah 131
Kaunas 133–35, 168–69, 173–74, 226
  Governor 97
  expulsion, May 1915 105–6
  massacre of Jews in Lieutūkis Garage in June 1941 150–51, 166, Plate 13
  Jewish Council 223–24, 225
  Rabbi 224
  ghetto 249
  Lietukis Garage monument 274
kehillot 9, 14
Kerensky commission 105
Kertzer, David 245
kest ix, 29
khappers ix, 62
Kiddush haChaim ix, 227
Kiddush haShem ix, 226–27
Kinderaktion 172–73
Kissileff, Count 14–15
Klaipėda (Memel) 125–26, 138–39
Klykoliai, Jews of 83
Knights, Teutonic 5
Königsberg/Kaliningrad 40
Koniuchowsky, Leyb 218, 273
Kovner, Abba 222, 226, 231–32
  pictured among other members of the United Partisan Organisation during the

Vilnius ghetto uprising of 1943 Plate 14
Kozyr-Zirka, Oleksii 117–18
Kristallnacht 203–4
Kubiliūnas, General Petras 137, 216–17
Kurdika, Vincas 216
Kuritsky, Motl 218–19
Kuzhi incident, 1915 105

labour permit scheme 267
Landa, Rabbi Ya'akov 115–16
landsman ix, 82
Lannoy, Guillebert de 6
Lantin, Barbara 49
Lavater, Johann Caspar 37, 200–201
Lebensraum 160, 209
Le Bon, Gustave 120
Le Chêne, Evelyn 264
Lefin, Mendel 36
Leizeris, Naika 132
Lenin, Vladimir Ilich 100
Lestchinsky, Jacob 75
Leverson, Jane 264–65
Lewis, Helen 259, 260–61, 262
Liepāja 43–44, 73
 the Great Synagogue, St. Joseph Cathedral and the Market in 1912 Plate 5
 port Plate 6
Lietūkis Garage
 massacre of Jews in June 1941 Plate 13, 150–51, 166
 monument 274
Lietuvos aidas 131–32
Lilienblum, Moses Leib 39
Lilienthal, Max 38
Linetski, Yitschok Yoel 20
Lipsett, E.R. 82
liquor trade 11, 28–29
'Lite' xi–xii, 216
 map *xv*
Lithuania
 Jewish population 108, 114, 126, 132, 139, 148–49
 independence after First World War 113–16, 124–26
 Soviet occupation 124, 140–44, 146, 217–18, 235
 German invasion of, 21 June 1941 148, 180
 estimated about 96 per cent of pre-war Jewish population of Lithuania murdered 148
Lithuanian Activist Front (LAF) 144–46, 156–57, 182
Lithuanian Jewish Council xi–xii
Lithuanian language 5
Lithuanian National Council (Lietuvos Taryba) 124
Lithuanian priests 246–48
Lithuanians, who did assist Jews 248–49
Lithuanians Businessmen's Union 129
Lithuanian Seimas, meeting room Plate 10
Lithuanian soldier guarding a group of Lithuanian Jews in Vilnius in July 1941 Plate 15
Lithuanian Soviet Socialist Republic (the LSSR) 142–43
Litvaks ix, 69, 70, 74, 82
 and peddling 79
 and acculturation 132–33
Longerich, Peter 207
Lozansky Bogomolnaya, Rivka 178–94
Ludendorff, General 109
Lukys, Pranas 146

Mackeviciene, Judita 169
Madagascar, plans to deport Jews to 204
Mahshoves, Ba'al 66
Maimon, Solomon 25–26, 29, 33
Maimonides, Moses 26, 224
Majdanek camp 231
Maliauskas, Antanas 57
malines 173–74, 175
Marcus, David 48
marriage rate 67
Marrus, Michael R. 56
Maskilim ix, 24–25, 36, 38, 39, 40–41
massacres
  by Ukrainian Cossacks 7
  by *Haidamack* 12
  of Jews in Lietūkis Garage in Kaunas in June 1941 Plate 13, 150–51, 166
  pogrom of 25-27 June 1941 166
  at Ponary 225, 229
  see also murder, mass; pogroms
Matthew, Gospel 198
matzo ix, 56, 94
May Laws 54–55, 68, 85
Mažeikiai
  killings in August 1941 152, 154
  site of mass grave where most of the murdered Jews of Pikeliai are buried 155–56, Plate 17
Megilat ha-esh (Bialik) 22
Mein Kampf (Hitler) 205–6
Meitess, Arieh Leib 10
"Melamed List" 277–78
memorials to the Holocaust 274–75
"Memories of the Old Bridge" (Kurdika) 216
memory, collective 18–20
Mendelssohn, Moses 37
Mensheviks 100–101
mentally ill, murder of 159–60
Merkys, Antanas 218
migration, chain 82–83
mikveh ix, 31
the military, and Jews 61–65, 85, 201–2
Milyukov, professor 107
minyan ix, 31
Miron, Dan 20, 22–23, 31
Mishell, William 166–67
mitzvah ix, 192
Molotov-Ribbentrop Pact 139, 140
Montefiore, Lady 14
Montefiore, Sir Moses 14–15
Motylewicz, Jerzy 27
murder, mass 149, 156, 204, 221, 238, 242, 287
  of Pikeliai Jews 27
  Nazis tried to hide evidence of 156
  by December 1941 only about twenty per cent of the pre-war Jewish population alive 157
  in Vilnius 165
  in Kaunas 166
  in Butrimonys 187
  and Stahlecker 208–9
  and Hitler 215
  at Stutthof 258
  and Genocide and Resistance Research Centre 277
Museum of Genocide Victims 278
Mutual Assistance Agreement 139

Nakam 231, 232–33
nationalism, Lithuanian 95, 215–16
Nazi Germany
  seized power in 1933 137
  policy of killing the entire Jewish population in Lithuania 148

and Operation Barbarossa 149–50, 158, 204
see also Germany
The Nazi's Granddaughter (Foti) 282
The New Exodus (Frederic) 16
New Testament 196–97
Nicholas 1, Tsar 13–15, 61–62, 63
Nicholas II, Tsar 91, 92
Night (Wiesel) 230
Nikolaevich, Grand Duke Nikolai 104
Ninth of Av ix, 114
Niselevich, Frida 173
Der Nister 20
Noreika, Jonas 219, 271–72, 278, 282–83
Nostra Aetate 289
'Novy Voshkod' 103–4
The Noyek Story (Marcus) 48
Nuremberg Laws 156

Ober Ost 109–11, 112
obey, Germans need to, and participation in the Holocaust 210, 215
Operation Barbarossa 149, 158, 204
Orthodoxy, Jewish 116
Osborne, Francis D'Arcy 239, 242, 244
Oshry, Rabbi Ephraim 166
Ossovsky, Zalma, Rabbi of Slobodka 151
Ostjuden ix, 212
Our People (Vanagaitė and Zuroff) 280–82
Ovruch 117–18

Pale of Settlement ix, 4, 35–36, 38, 48
map *xiv*
poverty 65–66, 92–93
de facto end of 107
Palestine 77, 268
Palmach, definition ix
Paneriai Forest 165, 172
Panevėžys 93–97
Paper Brigade 227–28
partisans, Jewish 175, 210, 229–30, 231
Partyka, Joanna 11
Passover ix, 19, 49
and blood libels 56, 57, 94, 96, 283, 287
Passports, 1890 Regulations 43, 44
Pašvitinys pogrom 93–97
Paul 1V, Pope 243
peddling, in Ireland 79, 83, 85
Peretz, Y.L. 20
perpetrators 195, 196, 225, 277
Perpetrators Victims Bystanders (Hilberg) 195
Petrovsky-Shtern, Yohanan 36
Phalen Commission 55, 60, 92
Pikeliai (Pikeln) 4, 18, 27, 35, 39, 42–43
old buildings where Jews probably lived and worked Plate 7, Plate 8
site of the old synagogue Plate 11
site of the old cemetery Plate 12
site of the mass grave in Mažeikiai where most of the murdered Jews of Pikeliai are buried Plate 17, 155–56
population, 1897 108
Jews murdered in August 1941 152
Stahlecker responsible for the murder of the Jews 208
and Bidermann 255–56

pilpul 33
pinkas 9
Pinsker, Leon 77
Pinson, Koppel 265
Pius X1, Pope 240–41
Pius X11, Pope 238–40, 241–46
Plehve, Vyacheslav Konstantinovich von 91
Pobedonostsev, Konstantin 54
Pocius, Jonas 94
Pocius, Julius 94
pogroms 35–36, 47, 48, 58–60, 61
  Panevėžys and Šiauliai, 1900 93–97
  between 1918 and 1921 117–20
  1941 151, 166
  Kristallnacht 203–4
Pohl, Dr. Johannes 227
Poland
  Third Partition of 8, 12
  annexation of Vilnius 114, 124, 125, 126, 127, 138
police units, Jewish 170–71
Polish Jews 228–29, 235, 258
Ponary
massacre 225, 229
pit 231, Plate 16
Pontius Pilate 198
Porat, Dinah 231–32
Poupko, Rabbi Israel Mayer Kagan 77
poverty, in the Pale of Settlement 65–66, 92–93
Prapuolenis, Leonas 146
Prienai pogrom 61
Princip, Gavrilo 101–2
prisoners of war, Soviet 158
privilegium 8
property, Jewish, stolen *see* theft of Jewish possessions
Protocols of the Elders of Zion 203
Prudnilova, Regina 276
Psalm 44 222
Purim x, 32

Rabinovitsh, Volf 21
Radziwill, Countess 30
Radziwill, Prince 26
railway routes for emigration 72–73
Rasputin, Grigory 91
Rastikis, General 156
Ratline 245
Reb Treytl (Spektor) 21
Red Army 124, 139, 146
refugees 267–69
Reif, Khonon 152–55
religious holidays 32
Renan, Ernest 278–79
Renteln, Theodor 157
resistance
  spiritual 226–27, 233
  physical force 226, 228–30, 233
  cultural 227–28, 233
Revelation, Book of 197
revenge, physical acts of 230–31
Riegner, Gerhart 236
Rivkes, Moises 7
Rome's Jews 243, 244, 245
Roncalli, Angelo 242
Roosevelt, President Franklin, on Soviet sphere of influence 271
Rosenberg, Alfred 145, 157, 209
Rosenberg Files 157
Russia 8, 12–15, 30–31
  and Liepāja 43
  Jewish emigration from 98
  in the First World War 102–8
  expelled Jews from Lithuania 105–8, 113–14
  two revolutions 112–13

Red Army invaded Lithuania 124
and the Bolsheviks 126
About 12,000 Lithuanian Jews escaped to after the German invasion, June 1941 150
see also Soviet Union
Russian Jews
fought in First World War for Russia 103
accused of being German spies in First World War 104–5, 107
settled in Lithuania by the Soviet regime 272

Sabbath, in the shtetl 31–32
sadism 212–13, 215
Sakowicz, Kazimierz 218–19, 220–21
Samogitians 4–5
Satan, and Jews 197
Sayers, Joseph (JD) 1, 257
pictured on his wedding day, in 1932 Plate 3
Sayers, Michael 1, Plate 4
Scher, Aaron 98
Scher, Hiya Henna 98
Scher, Jacob 98
Scher, Myer (later Sayers) 1, 4, 18, 42–43, 54, Plate 2
pictured celebrating his golden wedding, in 1948 Plate 1
working in Vainode 44
migrated to Ireland 47, 50
possible fear of conscription 64
why he emigrated 85–86
in Cork 91
became a naturalised British subject in 1901 97–98
in 1921 120–21
traded with the Baltic states 124
worried about his family in Lithuania 135–36
anxiety about Germany's invasion of Lithuania 148
Scher, Philip 98
Scher, Zisse 97–98
Schiff, Jacob 81–82
Schlegel, Friedrich 201
Schlieffen Plan 102
Schmuckler, Rabbi Yaakov Moshe 224
Schwerzreich, Willek 231
Sedak, Baruch 174
Sephardi x
Serbia, Austria-Hungary declared war on 102
Sery, Aron 118
shammes x, 32
shipping routes for emigration 72–74
Shloyme Reb Khayims (Abramovitsh) 23
Shneidman, Noah 165
shohet x, 6
Shokhet, Leizer 94
shootings, mass 148, 151, 162, 165, 186
shtadlan x, 9–10
shtetl 19–25, 26–30, 31–34, 35–36, 41, 44
defining characteristics x, 18
Shumaite, Onna 249
Šiauliai 83, 93–97, 162–63, 172–73, 174, 219
Siberia, plans to deport Jews to 204
Šimaitė, Ona 220
Singer, Isaac Bashevis 20, 28
Škirpa , Kazys 144, 145–46
Skvireckas, Archbishop Juozapas 150, 246–47
Sladkevicius, Archbishop 248
Sleževičius, Mykolas 113

Slobodka murders 151
Smetona, Antanas 127, 128, 140
smuggling
  across Russian border 71
  food, into ghettos 169
  Jewish books into the Vilnius ghetto 227–28
Sobibor, and murder of Vilnius's Jews 172
Sobotin, A. 66
Social Darwinism 200
Socialism 98–100
Sonderaktion 1005 156
Sorge, Richard 150
South Africa 73–74
Soviet Union
  occupied Lithuania between June 1940 and June 1941 139–44, 146, 217–18, 235
  and Operation Barbarossa, Nazi invasion of 149–50, 158, 204
  Lithuanian Jews escaped to 174, 225
  took German troops in Lithuania prisoner 257
  Baltics, Soviet sphere of influence 271–72
Spektor, Mordkhe 21
spiritual resistance 226–27, 233
S.S. Kursk, carried Jewish emigrants from Liepâja to London 73
Stahlecker, Franz Walter 208–9
Stalin, Joseph 150
Stankus, Antanas 163
St. John, Gospel 197, 198
Streckenbach, Bruno 151
Striapis, Jouzas 249
Struck, Herman 109
Stutthof concentration camp 258–60, 261–62, 263
Sugihara, Chiune 235–36
Sukkot x, 32, 34
supersessionism 197
survivors, from the Holocaust 174–75, 264–67, 268, 271, 273
Sutzkever, Abraham 212–13, 228
synagogue
  old, site of in Pikeliai Plate 11
  and the shtetl 31
Synod of the Four Lands 9

T4 action 159–60
Talmud x, 23, 32, 33
Tannenberg, Battle of 102
Taryba 111, 113
taverns 28–29
Temporary Jews Shelter, London 74
Teutonic Knights 5
theft of Jewish possessions 180, 185, 186, 189, 218–21, 225
  hardly any returned and no reparations paid 275–76
Third Partition of Poland 8, 12
Tiso, Joseph 240
Torah x, 37, 197, 213
Totleben, Governor-General of Vilnius 59
trade 30–31, 42, 129, 130
traders, Jewish, in Vilnius Plate 9
Travels into Poland, Russia, Sweden and Denmark (Coxe) 11
trefah x, 64
Trotsky, Leon 202
Turchinowitz, Father 12

Ūkininkas 95–96
Ukraine
  Cossack and peasant rebellion 7
  pogroms between 1918 and 1921 117–19, 120

ultra-Orthodoxy 127
An Uncompromising Generation (Wildt) 207
United States
attraction of emigrating to 76
immigration controls 234–35, 268
Uvarov, Serge 38

Valancius, Bishop 57
Vanagaitė, Rûta 275, 277–78, 281, 282, 284
Vehu Haor (Goldberg) 133
Viekšniai 83, 152–53
Vigodski, Dr. Yankev 212–13
Vileisis, Jonas 96
Vilna Gaon 38, 288
'From the Vilna Ghetto to Nuremberg' (Sutzkever) 212–13
Vilnius
Lithuanian soldier guarding a group of Lithuanian Jews in July 1941 Plate 15
seized by Poland, October 1920 114, 124, 125, 126, 127, 128, 138
fell to the Bolsheviks, 1918 124
returned to Lithuania, 1939 139
German invasion of, June 1941 164–65
ghetto 165, 169, 172, 174, 224, 227–28
Jewish Council 225
and physical resistance 227–28
census of 1897 showed that Jews constituted 40 per cent of the population 288–89
violence 30
see also murder, mass; shootings, mass
Vitkind, Avrom-Moyshe 179
Voldemaras, Augustinas 216
Vrba, Rudolf 236, 241
Vytautas 5, 6

Warsaw ghetto 236
Warsaw ghetto uprising 171
Wartime Experiences in Lithuania (Lozansky Bogomolnaya) 179–80
Weizmann, Chaim 65
Wengeroff, Pauline 32
Wessely, Naftali Hirz 37
Western Yiddish 34–35
Wetzler, Alfred 236
Wetzler, Fred 241
Wiesel, Elie 31–33, 230
Wigoder, Geoffrey 49
Wigoder, Myer Joel 49, 69
Wildt, Michael 207
Wilhelm, Kaiser 102
Witte, Count 91–92, 99
Wittenberg, Yitzhak 229
Wolf, Immanuel 19
'Words of Peace and Truth '(Wessely) 36–37
World History of the Jewish People (Dubnow) 58–59
The World of the Shtetl (Wiesel) 32
World War 1 101–14, 201–2
Eastern Front, map *xix*

Yablonka, Hanna 268
Yanushkevich, General Nikolai 104, 107–8
Yeirushavitshius, Yanas 193–94
Yekopo 106, 115
Yerushalmi, Eliezer 163, 172–73
Yerushalmi, Yosef Hayim 19
yeshiva x, 27, 33, 127

Yiddish x, 18, 24–25, 33–34, 40, 104
Yishuv x, 231
YIVO x, 143, 228
Yizkor, definition x
Yizkor books 26–27
Yoffe, Zalman 219
Yoke of Inheritance 5
Young Bosnia Movement 101
Ypatingasis būrys 161, 165, 217
Zakhor (Yerushalmi) 19
Zeitung der 10. Armee 110
Zemaiciu prietelius 132
'From Zhogger to Cork' (Elyan) 84
Židikai 83, 152
Zilazne, Mashe 53
Zionism 76–77, 116–17, 127, 268
Zuroff, Efraim 274, 275
Zwartendijk, Jan 235